The Jewish Encounter with Hinduism

Interreligious Studies in Theory and Practice

Series Editors: Aimee Light, Jennifer Peace, Or Rose,
Madhuri Yadlapati, and Homayra Ziad

Palgrave's new series, *Interreligious Studies in Theory and Practice*, seeks to capture the best of the diverse contributions to the rapidly expanding field of interreligious and interfaith studies. While the series includes a diverse set of titles, they are all united by a common vision: Each volume advocates—explicitly or implicitly—for interreligious engagement, even if this involves a critique of the limits of this work as it is currently defined or embodied. Each volume provides models and resources—textual, theological, pedagogic, or practical—for interreligious dialogue, study, or action. The series models a commitment to religious pluralism by including books that begin from diverse religious perspectives. This does not preclude the publication of books dedicated to a specific religion, but the overall series reflects a balance of various faiths and perspectives.

Dialogue for Interreligious Understanding: Strategies for the Transformation of Culture-Shaping Institutions
Leonard Swidler

The Jewish Encounter with Hinduism: Wisdom, Spirituality, Identity
Alon Goshen-Gottstein

Same God, Other god: Judaism, Hinduism, and the Problem of Idolatry
Alon Goshen-Gottstein

The Jewish Encounter with Hinduism

Wisdom, Spirituality, Identity

Alon Goshen-Gottstein

First published 2016 by
PALGRAVE MACMILLAN

The author has asserted their right to be identified as the author of this work in accordance with the Copyright, Designs and Patents Act 1988.

Palgrave Macmillan in the UK is an imprint of Macmillan Publishers Limited, registered in England, company number 785998, of Houndmills, Basingstoke, Hampshire, RG21 6XS.

Palgrave Macmillan in the US is a division of Nature America, Inc., One New York Plaza, Suite 4500, New York, NY 10004-1562.

Palgrave Macmillan is the global academic imprint of the above companies and has companies and representatives throughout the world.

ISBN 978-1-349-57610-4
E-PDF ISBN: 978–1–137–45529–1
DOI: 10.1007/978-1-137-45529-1

Distribution in the UK, Europe and the rest of the world is by Palgrave Macmillan®, a division of Macmillan Publishers Limited, registered in England, company number 785998, of Houndmills, Basingstoke, Hampshire RG21 6XS.

Library of Congress Cataloging-in-Publication Data is available from the Library of Congress.

A catalogue record for the book is available from the British Library.

To teachers in the line of the Divine Light

Who have been gateways and sources of inspiration

Swami Sivananda

Swami Chidananda

Sri Yogeshwar

Cover image: Prince Dara Shikoh visits a sage (possibly the Jewish Sarmad, see Chapter 4), in a prefiguration of the present Jewish-Hindu encounter. By Hunhar II, mid-18th century.

Contents

Preface

In many ways, the present project is a summary of a lifelong journey, both spiritual and academic. The number of individuals who have contributed to it is therefore as extensive as the number of individuals who have helped form me in these dimensions, a list too long to enumerate, though never too long to recall in my heart with gratitude.

The inspiration of some salient individuals is already expressed in the book's dedication. Others are appreciated in the dedication to the complement volume, *Same God, Other god.*

In terms of the more narrowly focused academic project, gratitude is due to friends who have been pointers along the way. Both books are the serendipitous outcome of another project, much more humble in its origins. Without Eugene Korn's insistence that *Jewish Theology and World Religions*, which we jointly edited, be published, the present project would have never come under consideration. I benefited from the wisdom and ongoing work of several colleagues who read my work and shared their own with me. These include Alan Brill, Daniel Sperber, Richard Marks, and Paul Fenton. My work is all the richer for their contributions. I shared the manuscript with several Hindu friends. I am grateful in particular for the detailed responses of Swami Agamananda (Martha Doherty), who engaged my argument in a considered and detailed way.

I am very proud of this work launching a new series of publications in interreligious studies at Palgrave Macmillan. Starting with Or Rose, the series editors showed faith and enthusiasm for the project from the start and their appreciation has sustained me through multiple revisions. I believe this work, with its particular balance of perspectives—descriptive, analytical, sympathetic, and engaged—is the kind of work for which they have launched this series and I am grateful to them for that. I am particularly grateful to Madhuri Yadlapati. Her keen mind, broad understanding, and deft editorial skills have made working with her a true pleasure.

Two editors at Palgrave Macmillan have made the otherwise gruesome task of turning a manuscript into a book so much more pleasant. Jenn McCall made sure the book found a secure home and Phil Getz ensured it was a comfortable home, bringing to it his wonderful and gentle human skills, along with his professional dedication.

On a more personal note, because this book reflects so much personal engagement, its creation is also something of a family affair. My sons, Elisha and Neriya, have journeyed to India and engaged the subject matter of the book both first-hand and in continuing dialogue with me. Neriya's continuing interest in the subject matter and the unfolding of the book have helped sharpen the argument at many points.

Therese, my wife, has been my partner on the journey, engaging me along the way in all matters of substance and supporting me in all matters of procedure. The journey to India was undertaken with her. She is very present in the white spaces between the black letters.

Introduction

Jews and Hindus are closer to each other now than ever before, and their relationship is worthy not only of description but also of reflection. This may be the most succinct summary of the present work. It describes a relationship that many are not aware of and in so doing seeks to state what is at stake in that relationship. I argue that this is a relationship that is not only interesting but also one that has great vitality and the potential for transformation of both communities, though the present work is written from a Jewish perspective.

To describe we must have some distance. To reflect we must be engaged. While I seek to be both descriptive and reflective, I do recognize that this work is ultimately written from an engaged perspective and not from any neutral vantage point. It grows out of a personal journey, described in the first chapter, and the personal dimension is close to the surface throughout. But even more significantly, in discussing the Hindu-Jewish encounter I approach its various dimensions from a position of deep engagement with and care for the Jewish tradition (balanced by profound appreciation for the spiritual life as lived beyond Judaism, and in particular through Hinduism). Therefore, description leads to engagement, which involves thinking with the eyes and concerns of my tradition. This includes asking what the encounter means for it and taking a stand on the encounter, and more broadly on the Hinduism I have come to appreciate. While descriptive at its foundations, the present work brings much of myself to it, including my theological self. As my theological concerns are deeply intertwined with engagement of other religious traditions—in this case, Hinduism—my thinking moves between articulating a Jewish theology of religions/Hinduism and spiritual, educational, pastoral, and theological reflections that relate to Judaism, its long-term needs, and the spiritual growth and processes that presently affect it. Thus, the present project that has description at its foundations is really an expression of a personal spiritual process as well as of theological reflections that simultaneously, and in mutually enriching and interrelated ways, addresses both the outside (a view of Hinduism) and the inside (a view of Judaism).

My orientation is theological and interreligious, but the discussion does not follow a program of predefined theological or philosophical categories. Rather, I attempt to describe a reality as I see it, from my admittedly engaged perspective. The categories and subject headings represent my perception of what matters most, what are the issues, and what is at stake in the relationship. And as the discussion unfolds, I reflect on the meaning of various processes, movements, and ideas, seeking to integrate them into my own view of Judaism and its relationship to other religions. Being engaged means taking a stand and making the argument for it. This I seek to do by bringing to the discussion the riches of my learning, the tools of reasoning of traditional and academic learning, and a positive and open approach to Hindu spiritual life, based on decades of study, relationships, and various degrees of immersion and personal experience.

Approaching the Hindu-Jewish encounter from a purely descriptive perspective would lead to a description of historical and present-day points of contact and would also include constructive reflections on the future of the relationship.[1] Approaching the encounter from the perspective of internal Jewish concerns involves doing all that, but it also involves taking stock of what the Jewish tradition itself is concerned about, what are its needs, and what are its breaking points or points of crisis, as these play out within a given relationship. The encounter does not require us to enter into the halachic, Jewish-legal, status of Hinduism as idolatry. An internal Jewish engagement of the subject cannot overlook it. Similarly, the problem of religious identity and how it is impacted by the Jewish-Hindu encounter may be of certain descriptive interest, but it takes on a different urgency when it is explored in the context of the concerns of the Jewish community and how the encounter might impact them. Or to take another example: a purely descriptive perspective might make do with the statement that many Israeli travelers to India are seeking spirituality. An engaged perspective must examine what this reality means to present-day Judaism, what does it say about its spiritual resources, and what position should it take with regard to Jews approaching Hindu traditions as spiritual resources. What I have done in these and other matters, then, is to try to be as fair and balanced in my description as I could while at the same time thinking through, critically and constructively, from within, what the encounter means to the Jewish tradition, its present-day reality, and its contemporary theological and spiritual challenges. This project is therefore as much about my own reading of Jewish spiritual reality as it is about Hinduism and the encounter between the two realities. If I have been successful, the two perspectives should be mutually illuminating.

This is perhaps the moment to share something about the final form the project has taken, as it has matured for publication and to share not only what this volume will do but also what it will not do. If we bring internal Jewish concerns to bear upon a view of Hinduism and the meaning of engaging it for the Jewish community, one issue will emerge as the primary concern, certainly for Orthodox Judaism—the concern about Hinduism's worship of images and idols and relatedly its belief in a multitude of deities. The problem of idolatry, known in Hebrew as *Avoda Zara*, foreign worship, indicating wrong worship, be it with reference to the object of worship or the means of worship, is one of the foundational issues that Judaism tackles in relation to any religion. The status of another religion as Avoda Zara is of foremost concern in terms of legitimating that religion, enabling various kinds of interaction with its practitioners, and obviously also for the possibility of drawing spiritual enrichment and inspiration from it. My own thinking through the issue of Avoda Zara has been so extensive as to take me beyond any description, including description of existing attitudes to Hinduism as Avoda Zara, to a total revisioning and rethinking of what the category itself might mean, a revisioning that is very much informed by the unique challenges of the spiritual and religious self-understanding of Hinduism. As it turns out, the chapter on Hinduism as Avoda Zara, originally titled: "Confronting the Worship of Images," ended up being of equal length to the entire present manuscript. In consultation with editors at Palgrave Macmillan, it was decided to extract this chapter from the book and turn it into a self-standing monograph, now titled *Same God, Other god: Judaism, Hinduism, and the Problem of Idolatry*. The original title of the present volume, *Beyond Idolatry*, which sought to suggest there was something to the Jewish-Hindu encounter beyond the problem of idolatry, still describes well the intention behind the present volume, suggesting that what will be dealt with here is all that is beyond the subject matter of idolatry, namely the Hindu-Jewish encounter itself. As to a discussion of idolatry, that is the subject of the complementary volume.

There are several good reasons for dividing our discussion into two, beyond the commercial sense of marketing needs. What started out as a discussion of Jewish views of Hindu image worship ended up being a thorough study and reflection of what the very category of Avoda Zara means, with Hinduism serving as a prime example, but not the only one. The book engages Christianity no less seriously and on the whole is as interested in rethinking the category of Avoda Zara as it is in taking a stand vis-à-vis Hinduism. Not only its length, but also its shift in perspective to a Jewish theory of Avoda Zara justified taking this discussion out of the original manuscript. Moreover, the discussion was thicker and more elaborate, often appealing to halachic sources, and therefore requiring a different kind of reading that would interrupt the argument of the present book.

From another perspective, there is a fundamental difference in emphasis between the discussion of the encounter and a discussion of Hinduism as Avoda Zara. Let us capture this in terms of "us" and "them." The engaged presentation of the encounter places a focus on what concerns us—the impact on Jewish individuals, on seekers, of adopting Hindu thoughts and practices. The discussion of Avoda Zara, by contrast, focuses more on "them": what is *their* status, can we affirm *their* faith as legitimate, and what is the halachic status of *their* rituals when practiced by them. Of course, any discussion of "them" also has implications for "us," but the difference in emphasis does seem to be real, further justifying breaking the discussion into two volumes. Thus, the original project was broken into two, with some correspondence to the different frames of reference—external-descriptive as the grounds for the present work and internal- reflective-analytical for the volume on Avoda Zara.

Breaking the original manuscript into two does leave a lacuna in the present work. The most obvious solution to this lacuna is to suggest to the reader that her reading is incomplete until both volumes have been read. It has been impossible to totally cleanse traces of one volume from the other, and some passing references to subject matter, understandable in their own right, but lacking full documentation, remain in this book. Without seeking in any way to do the subject justice, I do wish to also briefly spell out some moments of encounter that are related to the problem of Hindu worship. These are real historical moments where the problem of Hindu worship has figured in contemporary Jewish views of and relations with Hinduism. As concerns opinions of sages who sought to pronounce on the status of Hinduism, these are brought out in *Same God, Other god.*

There is one particular moment in the early twenty-first century that expresses an important dimension of the encounter and that centers on the problem of Hinduism as Avoda Zara. This defining moment illustrates just how much present-day engagement with Hinduism is a contemporary reality that cannot be sidestepped. It also illustrates the problematics associated with learning about another religion and how to, or how not to, go about doing so.

Orthodox Jewish women cover their hair after marriage. Some do so by wearing a kerchief or a hat. Others by wearing a wig, known as a *sheitel* in Yiddish. Now, sheitels can be made of synthetic material or human hair. Clearly the latter is aesthetically preferable, but it requires a steady source of human hair to keep up the industry. While there are different sources for natural human hair, apparently the most convenient and largest source are Hindu temples. In South Indian temples, there is a custom among devotees, both men and women, of shaving their heads as an offering to the deity. This is undertaken as a vow, either in order to fulfill a particular request or as an act of pure devotion. South Indian temples are thus a major source of human hair for the international wig industry. Particularly prominent is the temple of Venkateshwara, Balaji, in Tirupati. Thousands of men and women offer their hair at this temple, and the trustees of the temple gather it, sort it according to grade, treat it, package it, and then sell it on the international market. This is one of the sources of Tirupati's great wealth. Now, Jews are not allowed to derive any benefit or pleasure from Avoda Zara. This fact comes into potential conflict with the use of hair offered to the deity in Hindu temples. That wigs of ultra-Orthodox Jewish women had their provenance in Hindu temples would therefore constitute a problem. The question came up in 2004. Was the offering of hair by Hindu devotees an offering of Avoda Zara that should be forbidden to Jewish women? The natural thing would be to study the matter firsthand. And so, a prominent London rabbi was sent as an emissary of Rabbi Yosef Shalom Elyashiv, at the time the leading figure of ultra-Orthodox Jewry and its halachic figurehead, to Tirupati to study the matter personally. Rabbi Aharon Dunner made his way to Tirupati, and was able to return home after 48 hours with mission accomplished. He was able to provide the needed information based upon which Rabbi Elyashiv would rule that wigs that originated in Hindu temples could not be worn by Jewish Orthodox women. Following this visit, Rabbi Elyashiv issued a ruling that wigs should be burned. Idolatrous offerings may not be used in any shape and the only way to dispose of them is by burning. This reflects the Torah's strong concern with idolatry and how it seeks to avoid it at any cost. This cardinal value found one of its most recent expressions in relation to the worship of devoted Hindu girls, with whom the prospective Jewish wig bearers would never have any contact. The wigs were to be burned. This made headline news, as Jews in Israel and New York were pictured burning wigs on street corners.[2] It also deeply offended the Hindu community in ways that the Rabbis never imagined, and perhaps to date have not realized. It also reflected badly on hassidic and ultra-Orthodox Jews in general.

A detailed discussion of the reasoning that informed both sides of the sheitel crisis is undertaken in *Same God, Other god*. What matters for present purposes is the recognition that Avoda Zara is a vital concern for the Jewish community and one that informs its views of other religions. Therefore, from the internal Jewish perspective, reaching a stand on the status of Hinduism as Avoda Zara is inseparable from its ability to engage Hinduism in a meaningful and positive way. Differently put, a Jewish theology of religions cannot be divorced from concerns of interfaith dialogue or even of comparative theology, both of which are in some way addressed in the present volume. The complement volume does the work of a Jewish theology of religions with regard to its most formative category, that of Avoda Zara.

Avoda Zara has not been completely expunged from the present volume. It appears as a subject of great concern in at least one additional significant context: the summits of Hindu and Jewish leadership that took place three to four years following the wig-burning incidents. The summits are discussed in detail in the present volume and I have kept discussions of Avoda Zara as they have emerged as part of these concrete moments of encounter.[3]

The book's original unfolding took into account the centrality of Avoda Zara as the formative category by means of which Jews regard Hinduism. Accordingly, it sought to make the point that Avoda Zara is only one of various lenses through which Judaism could look at Hinduism, and that this lens is itself conditioned by concerns of certain Judaisms and what they prioritize. Some of that argument is now lost, with Avoda Zara having become the focus of a self-standing volume. Nevertheless, it is still worth considering the different chapters of the present book as suggestive of the multiple dimensions of the Jewish-Hindu encounter. As stated, the categories chosen reflect my own assessment of what is central either to the experience of the encounter or to the concerns of Jewish thinking and reality, as considered from within. Because I am of the opinion that there is more to Jewish-Hindu relations than the problem of Avoda Zara, and because I am indeed concerned that exclusive focus on this problem obscures the vision of so much that is vital and meaningful in that relationship, I have identified various loci—in the literature and in reality—that allow Jews to think of Hinduism in terms other than those of Avoda Zara. These loci include the following:

A. *Wisdom and the view of India as a land of sages*. This view persists over thousands of years and is one of the most important lenses through which Judaism and Hinduism can engage. Related to this are the challenges that Hindu metaphysics and philosophy pose to Jewish religious thought and the exploration of where Jewish theology, itself at an impasse, might advance if a more serious dialogue with Hinduism was undertaken. These discussions lead to a focus on specific philosophical and theological questions. In framing these I shall be aided both by insights from comparative religious studies and by my own accumulated experience, growing out of hundreds of hours of engaging leading Hindu swamis, leaders, and thinkers in a Jewish-Hindu philosophical conversation.

B. *Spirituality as a source of contemporary draw to Hinduism.* The suggestion that spirituality is a field in its own right is itself the source of present-day attraction of Jews, especially many Israeli youth, to Hinduism. This project involves describing the dialogue and encounter of travelers, that is, much of the present-day encounter, and suggesting what it is that young Jewish seekers turn to Hinduism for. Along with this is offered an evaluation of Jewish spirituality and its discontents, in an honest and self-critical look that is necessary if we are to make sense and to formulate educational recommendations that grow out of the realities described.

C. *The encounter with saints.* Much of the encounter takes place in relation to religious teachers and ideal role models, whom we shall refer to simply as saints. In this sense, it is a very high-end elitist encounter, exposing Jews to some of the finest spiritual expressions of Hinduism, often far removed from popular day-to-day Hinduism, practiced by millions of Hindus. The reflective complement to this descriptive work could take various expressions. I have sought to identify what a Jewish view of Hinduism might find challenging in the approach to Hindu teachers and saints. I note having just slipped back to "a Jewish view of," religion, in other words to the domain of theology of religions, which touches on concerns of the complement volume. The reason is precisely that that approach to saints and teachers does cross over into the realm of Avoda Zara, thereby raising some fundamental halachic and spiritual questions, with reference to these individuals. But it also raises questions of a more philosophical and theological nature, especially related to the status of the unique holy person, and these too will be examined.

D. *The concern for identity is not strictly speaking a site for encounter.* Rather, it is an outcome or a by-product of the encounter. As the encounter advances, individuals find themselves assimilating various habits, practices, and beliefs, all of which impact their identity. How have Jewish and Hindu identities come together in the lives of individuals who have been deeply impacted by Hinduism? There is more than one model to appeal to and the discussion will seek to identify, analyze, and evaluate various models. As stated already, the decision to address identity as a rubric under which the Hindu-Jewish encounter is studied betrays not only my Jewish perspective but also the agenda that comes with it. While the decision is informed by ideological concerns, it is also a useful rubric under which to share stories of some prominent individuals who have made Hinduism their home and how they continue to relate to their Jewish identity. The study of lives, and especially of their literary testimony, as sites for the encounter is a fruitful arena for appreciating how individuals have reconciled or relate to the two religions and how the encounter embodied in one particular life can teach us lessons that are of significance for the encounter as such.

The dual perspective of this work—descriptive and reflective—means the emphasis shifts from one perspective to the other both in the framing of chapters and in the book's discourse. Some chapters, like discussion of the Jews of India and the recent summits of religious leaders, start off from descriptive foundations, even as they continue to pose theoretical questions that are relevant to the internal theological and identitarian concerns of a Jewish perspective. Other chapters frame the discussion from the more theoretical and engaged angle, even as they provide various material and anecdotal information that grounds and provides context for the more theoretical conversation. As a book about encounter, I believe it requires this kind of complex and rich discourse, moving from one dimension to the other. In sharing in this way I draw on my own experience and journey, which was itself characterized by the dual perspective of learning about Hinduism and exploring how as an Orthodox Jew I might appreciate it. I believe this kind of multidimensional approach is very suitable to the task at hand, providing information even as it draws the reader into the insider's perspective of what is at stake. In other words, I hope through this method to not only provide the reader with information that is of interest but to actually draw her into the heart of the encounter, sharing its import for me and what I consider its import to be for others. At the end of the day the reader will have to judge whether the fusion of horizons—descriptive and reflective, personal and collective—is helpful to her understanding of the Jewish-Hindu encounter and how much insight she has gained by following this particular path. I personally express the hope that reading this book will not only be a moment of reading *about* an encounter, but in some small way will actually itself *be* an encounter.

1

Situating the Project: Personal and Collective Dimensions

A student of Hindu-Christian relations will find enough books dedicated to the subject to fill a library shelf, perhaps even several shelves. Specific themes, the history of relations, comparative presentations of the two religions, and a dialogue between the two theologies are taken up by both Hindu and Christian scholars. By contrast, very little has been written about Hindu-Jewish relations. Not a single monograph is dedicated to an overview of the relations and to exploring their theological significance for either side. No extensive, let alone comprehensive, effort has been undertaken to describe and to reflect upon a range of historical, theoretical, and practical issues that are pertinent to the relations between these two major faith traditions. The little that has been written will obviously be highlighted in the present work and to a large extent provides its background.

The discrepancy between the fairly extensive treatment that Hindu-Christian relations have received and the sparse attention paid to issues relevant to Judaism's encounter with Hinduism need not really surprise us. Christians have been engaged with Hinduism for centuries, on some level even for millennia. While an ancient Jewish community in India also claims such hoary roots,[1] and while some vague knowledge of India was available to Jews during all periods of history,[2] it is only during the course of the twentieth century, especially in the latter decades, that extensive contact with and exposure to Hinduism began to leave their mark in the Jewish community and in Jewish writings. Thus, a broad and full encounter between Judaism and Hinduism is only several decades old. It therefore stands to reason that an examination of what is at stake in both theological and practical terms has not yet been undertaken.

The task of surveying the Jewish-Hindu encounter is intimidating. I am forced to share the question that I have asked myself time and again since I undertook this project: Am I the appropriate person to undertake a presentation of the Jewish encounter with Hinduism? It might therefore be helpful to recall how this project came to be. My own work in interreligious relations has been carried out mainly through the instrument of the Elijah Interfaith Institute, which I founded in 1996. Work on the interreligious front has led to work in the field of theology of religions. It has become obvious to me that serious engagement with other religions must involve a reexamination of one's own views of those religions. Furthermore, in my understanding, a contemporary view of other religions is an important component of any present-day theology. Accordingly, in the context of Elijah's work, I have initiated several research and reflection projects, specific to individual religious traditions, that bring together experts of those traditions to reflect upon the theology of religions, particular to that tradition. Following a conference of Jewish theologians and thinkers, held at the University of Scranton in 2005, Eugene Korn and myself undertook to edit a volume of essays on Judaism and World Religions.[3] It would have been easy enough to be content with contributions concerning Judaism's views of Christianity and Islam, or with contributions on religious pluralism in general. However, I felt it was imperative to also include "Eastern" religions, particularly Hinduism and Buddhism, in the purview of our discussions. Part of the contemporary challenge of Judaism, in relation to world religions, comes precisely from the new opportunities provided by the various encounters with these religions and by how these encounters redefine Judaism's challenges in relation to world religions.[4] Eugene and I thus hunted around for someone who could write an essay on Jewish-Hindu relations, from the angle of a contemporary Jewish theology of world religions. The number of scholars who could undertake such a task is extremely limited. A couple of people we approached turned us down. We may have overlooked some, one, probably no more than someone. We could not find an author to write the essay. I was not willing to give up on including Hinduism in our volume and had little choice but to volunteer myself for the task. As is the case with all too many of my projects, the essay outgrew its original scope. Thankfully, I was able to see this project through. Given how little has been written on the subject and how complex it really is, I had little difficulty in accepting the shift from article to monograph. The shift does, however, underscore still further the question of my own credentials in writing this work. I shall offer my apology for meeting this challenge in biographical terms.

Let me begin with my late uncle David. Some years ago he informed me of the great concern he felt when I was still pre–Bar Mitzvah that I might end up converting to Hinduism, and of his subsequent relief that I had eventually remained a faithful Jew. Facts aren't exactly as my uncle David recalled them, but, as in many rabbinic legends, we are able to locate their "historical kernel." My exposure to Hinduism does indeed predate my Bar Mitzvah. I was only 11 years old when my parents took me on a visit to India, as part of a visit to several countries of the orient, en route from Israel to the United States, where my father was to spend two sabbatical years. Clearly, that visit left its imprint on me, or, as my aunt Rita (uncle David's wife) would put it: something got into me. I have no explanation for why India remained a source of fascination, interest, and attraction for nearly 50 years since, while Thailand, Cambodia, Japan, and other eastern lands left no deep impression on my young soul.

I was probably 15 years of age when I started visiting Hindu temples in London (that is where Uncle David lived). While I was never tempted to join such a community, nor to engage in Hindu worship, I was fascinated by the religious life of communities like ISKCON (popularly known as Hare Krishna) and spent many hours discussing theological fine points with its members. Interest in things Indian prompted me to practice Transcendental Meditation in my late teens and to delve into the philosophical tenets of the system, expounded by Maharishi Mahesh Yogi. This form of practice was complemented by academic studies. Beginning in the mid-70s, and over several years, I took quite a number of courses in Hinduism with David Shulman. I was among his first students and a close friend for many years. I even made some efforts to study Tamil, though I never attempted Sanskrit and except for two words and two grammatical terms, little has remained of my efforts at Tamil. My own personal spiritual quest continued with many years of training with a teacher, who was herself ordained by a great Indian sage, Swami Sivananda. Understanding Hinduism remained a staple of my spiritual and intellectual diet.

Interest in and engagement with Hinduism entered a new phase with the foundation of the Elijah Interfaith Institute in 1996 in Jerusalem as the Elijah School for the Study of Wisdom in World Religions. The original name of the school provides the rationale for including Hinduism in interreligious dialogue in Jerusalem, despite the fact that there is no significant Hindu community in Israel. The vision sought to make the wisdom of all religious traditions the subject of academic study as well as of interfaith dialogue, in Jerusalem. Our annual summer school gathered a community of scholar-practitioners from different faith traditions. Scholars of Hinduism were regularly invited to Jerusalem as part of the Elijah summer school program. This provided me with the opportunity to learn from, and to have a dialogue with, some of the leading Hindu figures in the field of religious studies in the United States. The annual meetings of the American Academy of Religion and of the Society for Hindu-Christian Studies also provided more than a decade's worth of contact and engagement with a broad range of scholars working on theological issues from within Hinduism, or in dialogue with it.

As Elijah grew, so did my relationship with Hinduism deepen. In 2002, following the *Intifada*, the organization changed course. Working in Jerusalem and bringing to it scholars and students from all over the world was no longer feasible. Elijah went international. Instead of working with students, it concentrated its efforts on working with world religious leaders. These are served by interreligious think tanks. Thus, contact with Hindu scholars continued through the medium of collaborative think tanks that I organized. But now a new level of contact with Hindu reality presented itself through relationships formed with Hindu religious leaders. Work with the Elijah Board of World Religious Leaders provided me with the opportunity to cultivate personal relations, leading to further theological engagement, with major Hindu religious figures, representing a cross-section of the complex religious reality known as Hinduism.

It was Sri Sri Ravi Shankar who was responsible for breaking down the interior wall that had previously kept me away from India, mostly for reasons of feeling inadequate to explore India's spiritual significance. While I may not be more spiritually fit for the task now than I was a decade ago, my work has taken me that way, and I have attempted to meet the challenge. Sri Sri's invitation to visit

India, in 2003, paved the way to a series of extended visits to India, on an annual basis, since then. These visits focused on religious communities and centers of learning and worship. They provided me with the opportunity to think through the issues of this book through ongoing dialogue with some outstanding personalities, as well as through a process of continuing observation, listening, and reflection. I have spent months in some of the leading ashrams. I should mention in particular the Sivananda Ashram in Rishikesh, and the Sadhana Kendra Ashram near Dehradun. Both ashrams have become home, in different ways. In both I received immensely from the wisdom and spiritual perspective of resident sages. Swami Yogaswaroopananda, of the former ashram, has spent dozens, well over a hundred I imagine, of hours with me, discussing issues that are seminal to a Jewish understanding of Hinduism, particularly issues related to the worship of idols and how these are viewed in Hinduism. Chandra Swami, of the latter, has shared his wisdom on a large range of issues relevant to this project. Personal friendships and relationships have played an important role in allowing me to enter the mind space, understanding, and feeling of Hindus, how they live their spiritual life, and how they approach God. Of the many important friendships with which I was blessed over the years of my travels to India, the one that was formed with Swami Atmapriyananda is particularly significant in the context of the present work. This senior monk of the Ramakrishna Order, who became an active partner in the work of the Elijah Institute, opened for me the gates of understanding through a unique combination of mind, heart, and spirit that provides continuing inspiration to me as a person, as well as to the present project. Through him, I have come to appreciate the Ramakrishna Order, its vision, and above all the spiritual testimony of its founder.

Many other sages, ashrams, and temples, in different parts of India, North and South, form part of the story, and it is a story that is far from having reached its final chapter. I consider all issues that will be raised in the present book to be a work in progress, items requiring further thought and deliberation. In fact, one of my main contentions is that it is too early for us to conclude with any finality anything with regard to Hinduism. Its reality is simply too complex and our knowledge of it too recent to be able to resolve the complicated issues involved in the Jewish encounter with Hinduism. It has taken Christianity hundreds of years to advance in its relationship with Hinduism and even then the process is ongoing and incomplete, subject to change and continuing growth in mutual understanding. Mutual understanding between cultures as complex as Judaism and Hinduism cannot be reached within the scope of a high-level meeting or two, the reading of a handful of books, or even the studied reflection of one or more specialist devoting time to exploring these issues. The questions raised by the encounter require time, process, and a degree of comfort and familiarity that we may not be able to attain even within the scope of a generation.

Still, we must begin somewhere. And we are certainly at a point in time when it has become imperative to address the issues of the Jewish-Hindu encounter. But before describing the broader context, I should conclude the personal narrative by suggesting where I think I have arrived in my own personal journey. I do not consider myself an expert on Hinduism, certainly not in the sense of possessing the expertise that would allow me to teach it academically. My own expertise is in the field of Jewish thought and theology, and it is from that perspective that I approach the Jewish encounter with Hinduism. But I do bring to the encounter a unique personal story of continuing interest, exploration, study, engagement, and dialogue with Hinduism. I am not familiar with any other author who possesses the Jewish halachic and philosophical tools to engage in this study, or who has enjoyed the kind of extensive engagement with Hinduism that I have. Clearly, this does not ensure that these realities have come together in my mind in a way that is satisfactory to myself or to others. It only suggests that enough of a foundation has been laid to invite me to meet the challenge.

I might not have considered filling the vacancy in the table of contents for the volume on Jewish Theology and World Religions even a few years ago. I think what has changed within is probably my degree of comfort and feeling at home in the Indian religious reality. This is more a matter of psychology than of philosophy, but I consider it significant for purposes of the present undertaking. In many ways, I no longer feel that sense of strangeness toward Hindu religious reality that the outsider does. Clearly, I remain an outsider, continually learning and repeatedly surprised by the wealth of Indian religious life. Every trip provides additional opportunities for further nuances, more detailed understanding, and indeed additional surprises, concerning how Hindus live their religious life. But all these now take place in the context of a basic comfort with Hindu religious reality. It is different, but it is no longer strange. I consider the breaking down of such psychological barriers an essential aspect of deep interreligious engagement. It is as true of Hindu-Jewish relations as it is of any relationship between different religions and their practitioners. As long as we are governed by our sense of strangeness and otherness, especially as this sense of strangeness feeds the sense of distance and even revulsion that has characterized the history of our tradition in relation to another, we have not yet reached the level playing ground from which our engagement with another religion should take place. If we seek to genuinely understand and to work our way through the core issues that are typical of the relations between two religions, we must first come to that psychological or mental space of comfort and of acceptance of the other's religious reality as something "normal," at least not shocking, bizarre, or offputting. How can we seriously study another religion if our sense of its strangeness and our feeling of being put off by it dictate what we see and how we interpret it?

I noted during my visit in 2009, while I was already thinking through the issues of this article-turned-book, that I had reached the point of psychological comfort, perhaps maturity, that would allow me to publicly reflect on Hinduism and my own experience of it. I no longer felt surprised, outraged, or shocked. I could move into a certain kind of mentality that characterized those Hindus with whom I was spending time (obviously, there are many other Hindus, with other states of mind, that would no doubt continue to surprise me or to make me feel like the extreme stranger, unable to build bridges of understanding). I could see it their way, rather than just being told this is how they saw it. Which does not mean this became my viewpoint. It only means that I could anticipate and predict from within, so to speak, how my Hindu friends would respond and react, how they would see religious reality, and how this could make sense, given their premises and particular vantage point. This, I submit, is an appropriate point from which to conduct the kind of reflection that this book undertakes.

In a more personal vein, I would say that the point at which my engagement with Hinduism reached a maturity that would allow me to integrate my process and share it with others is when the voices of Hindu thought and experience became personal. Let me explain. For a long time I had encountered Hindu thoughts through books and through official teachings, delivered by individuals who had been trained to instruct or teach in accordance with an official teaching. Many of the religious leaders and representatives I encountered were but carriers of a message of the tradition, for which they were but a mouthpiece. As I know from myself and from relationships formed in other contexts, the teachings of the tradition from which one speaks must be integrated with the person, her experience, particularity, and uniqueness. The spiritual life becomes real when one encounters not simply a living voice that recounts age-old teachings, but a rich meeting point of the teachings of a tradition and the riches and complexities of a person who makes that tradition come alive and in some small but significant way redefines or restates it, through the reality of her person and its testimony. This is also the point where the frailty of the individual comes through and, even more importantly, the struggles and imperfections that are a major part of the spiritual life. Early encounters with Hinduism led me to encounter the official, idealized face of the tradition, divorced from its human reality, and therefore challenging, maybe even threatening, in its rarefied but unreal idealism. Relations make the spiritual real, and relationships with individual teachers made their spiritual life real, in its humanity, in its struggles, in its complexities. It took years and various experiences to attain that point. But I would say that in parallel with growing familiarity and loss of the sense of strangeness grew the ability to view my Hindu friends and interlocutors as fully human and consequently fully real. Their spiritual life was thus something that came through their real life. At that point it became sufficiently real and credible for me, allowing me to integrate the lessons learned through those encounters into my own process and to share it with others.

The strongly personal context within which the present project is couched makes it necessary to be clear about what can be expected from the present exercise. As already intimated, I do not seek final answers to complex questions. At this point, I believe we should focus on getting a clearer sense of the questions themselves. If I am an authority on anything it is on my own process, my own story. And this story consists of thousands of small questions, asked over decades, that amount to larger questions, through which I seek to get a grasp over complex religious realities and their possible relations. If I have what to contribute to others, be they spiritual seekers, halachically minded authorities, or theologians seeking to reflect upon another religion, it lies in formulating the questions, conceptualizing the issues, and only tentatively offering my own responses, based on my personal experiences and understanding.

There are very few fields in which one enjoys the privilege of not worrying about finality, or even novelty, in one's writing for the very reason that one is laying the foundations for a future discussion. This book is about beginning a process, rather than concluding it. If I am able to convey some of the complexity of my own process, the kinds of issues I have had to struggle with, and the multi-dimensionality of the issues involved, I will consider this a major contribution to a discussion that might otherwise fall into easy stereotypes that can only lead to exclusion, rejection, and contempt.

Because this book grows so much out of my own personal intellectual and spiritual journey, I have decided to not mask these components, but rather to expose them. I know what I think I know because of experiences, encounters, dialogues, and a process that has been personal, even while based upon academic foundations. There is no point converting the discussion to a completely academic, philosophical, or halachic mode of discourse. It seems to me much truer to the process and to its potential import for future readers to maintain the first-person voice and the impact of personal experience and reflection and to incorporate these into the more neutral and objective discourse one might expect of such a work. I have therefore chosen to engage the subject matter of the Jewish encounter with Hinduism from the dual perspectives of general and theoretical considerations as these are complemented by personal stories, impressions, conversations, and anecdotes. Fidelity to my own personal process may be the best way to stimulate genuine and open reflection in the future reader.

This particular vantage point also dictates the specific emphasis of this book. A completely neutral description would seek to engage both sides of the relationship. A focus on Hindu-Jewish relations would accordingly consider the implications of this relationship for both sides. While some observations may be made along the way, it is clear that this book is written from a specifically Jewish perspective. Hence, questions like what Judaism might have to offer Hinduism are not the focus of this work. Nor does it seek to do justice to Hindu attempts at understanding Judaism. In fact, a consideration of typical Hindu views of Judaism is important for an appreciation of a significant asymmetry in the relationship, as well as for understanding the primary concerns of the present volume.[5]

When Jews encountered Hinduism, over the ages and especially during the past century, they have met Hinduism on its own terms. Hinduism was not seen through the lens of another religion. Jews approaching the Hindu-Jewish encounter thus came "clean" to the encounter. The same may not be said of Hindus. The Jewish community in India has been numerically very insignificant. Hence, Judaism never became part of the Indian consciousness of religious minorities. More significantly, until very recently, when Hindu thinkers confronted Judaism, they did so in the context of their confrontation with Christianity. For many Hindus, Judaism is still indistinguishable from Christianity, as I have discovered repeatedly during my visits to India. India's great thinkers seem to have never had the opportunity to consider Judaism on its own terms. Swami Vivekananda is paradigmatic.[6] An examination of his references to Judaism reveals that he only knows Judaism as the forerunner of Christianity. Vivekananda's contribution to Hindu thought, taken in historical context, is to affirm Hindu identity and the message of Hinduism, in the face of prevailing Christian norms and ideals, reinforced by the colonial context. Vivekananda is thus in a situation of confrontation. Judaism is viewed through this confrontation, in a manner indistinguishable from Christianity. The only Judaism known to Vivekananda is that of the Old Testament. While he does possess some sense of the personality of the modern Jew, he seems to know nothing of postbiblical Judaism. In any event, Judaism is only of interest to him in the context of his own comparison and confrontation with Christianity.[7]

The same is true of another important Hindu figure, Swami Dayananda,[8] except for the fact that his views are even more polarized than those of Vivekananda, and hence his critique of Judaism more uncompromising.[9] Hindu authors end up, unwittingly, perpetuating Christian stereotypes of Judaism, in the context of their ideological struggle against Christianity. Things only begin to change as Jews and Judaism are gradually encountered on their own terms.[10] Gandhi had significant contact with Jews.[11] However, it seems that the contact was primarily with Jews,[12] rather than with Judaism.[13] It is only with the advent of interreligious dialogue in recent decades that Judaism is beginning to be appreciated by Hindu thinkers and leaders on its own terms. I believe the situation is gradually changing. Political relations, Indian interest in the State of Israel, as expressed in the media and elsewhere, and the flood of Israeli tourists to India all contribute to rectifying this problem.[14]

But even if Judaism is acknowledged as a religion on its own terms, there remains something asymmetrical in the present encounter. The encounter seems to be much more significant for the Jewish side than it is for the Hindu side. Its impact is felt much more deeply within the Jewish community. Accordingly, it makes sense to examine the meaning of the encounter primarily from a Jewish perspective. I therefore see nothing wrong with a discussion that examines this relationship primarily from a Jewish viewpoint, bringing to it the concerns, questions, and modes of thinking typical of the Jewish side. Appreciating this particularity will hopefully be beneficial to mutual understanding.

A presentation of the Jewish encounter with Hinduism, especially one that is so deeply grounded in a long-standing personal quest, must be descriptive, but it must also go beyond the descriptive dimension. We must begin with a description of the facts, be they the religions, their similarities, contemporary processes, or an understanding of what is at stake. What there is to describe, be it in the realm of history of religions or in the realm of contemporary sociological and political movements, provides the basis for reflection and assessment. These go beyond mere description; they call for an evaluation. In Jewish terms, such an evaluation has both halachic and philosophical dimensions. Ultimately, such an evaluation touches on our very understanding of what it means to be Jewish in today's world and on our deepest self-understanding. Hence, as is the case in any genuine process of dialogue and mutual understanding, full appreciation of Judaism's encounter and relations with Hinduism is closely related to fundamental issues of Jewish identity and self-understanding. The encounter and the relationship, as well as issues of self-understanding, draw from timeless truths as well as from the attempt to state the implications of such timeless truths in terms of the here and now of today. One cannot, therefore, simply describe the reality. Description is also interpretation and evaluation.

It would, however, be a mistake to assume that one can simply move from the descriptive to the prescriptive. Not only does such a move assume a position of authority that I, perhaps anyone else as well, lack, but it also assumes an ease of transition from one dimension to the other that does not really exist. The issues at hand are complex to such a degree that, at least in my own view, we cannot simply move from a description of a reality to passing "judgment" or issuing halachic *pesak* in relation to it. In stating this much, I have in mind the concerns of both volumes, including references to Avoda Zara. It would be much truer to the complexity of the issues at hand, and for that matter to my own personal process, to therefore highlight the process, the questions, and the ongoing quest. The same spirit that leads me to consider this the beginning of a long-term conversation, rather than a final or even intermediary station along the way, leads me to conceptualize this work in terms of learning how to state the issues and how to frame the questions. Thus, the move from the descriptive to the prescriptive perforce takes us through that middle ground of learning how to think from within, how to frame the categories and concepts, and how to work our way through method and meaning. My goal in writing this work is therefore to advance a conversation. I seek to move the conversation from the starting point of strangeness to an engagement that grows out of greater familiarity and from the descriptive level to the space where we can learn how to formulate our thoughts, how to grapple with the issues, and how to frame what we need to struggle with. If I am successful, future conversations will be enriched by the present work and consequently more clearly focused. Normative and halachic conclusions may have to wait until we have reached such a point.

2

The Hindu-Jewish Encounter: The Present Context

Jews and Hindus had no significant contact for millennia. With the exception of a tiny Jewish community in India and the occasional contact made possible through travel and commerce, India was a distant memory. It left an impression on Jewish literature, but never made it to the status of a significant other.[1] I am not aware of Judaism making any impression on Hindu religious, legal, or philosophical literature, until the twentieth century.[2] It is only during the twentieth century that the relationship between Judaism and Hinduism started to come into its own and indeed, this relationship may still be a thing of the future.

There are three contexts in which this relationship has developed. The first two are relatively uncharged, while the third is complex and fraught with spiritual and pastoral challenges and will occupy most of our attention. The first context is that of mass emigration of Hindus to the West, creating what is referred to as the Hindu diaspora. The Hindu diaspora is actually an important component in the continually changing face and self-identity of Hinduism, as I suggest in what follows. The fact that Jews and Hindus meet in diaspora is thus significant both in terms of the context of the encounter and in terms of the types of Hinduism that Jews encounter in the diaspora. What is most important in relation to this aspect of the encounter is that it is fundamentally an encounter between equals.[3] Unlike the Hindu-Christian encounter, there is no history of power relations and attendant asymmetries to complicate Jewish-Hindu relations. Jews and Hindus increasingly find themselves as neighbors in various metropolitan centers in the United States and Europe. I have noted with interest how, over the years, Hendon, a township in North London where many Jews (including, my uncle David) reside, has absorbed a significant Hindu community. Jews and Hindus encounter each other on a daily basis in the streets, in shops, etc. While the contact may be superficial, neighborly relations by definition provide unexpected opportunities for engagement that can neither be programmed nor controlled. Hendon is one of hundreds of townships in the West where this phenomenon takes place. The common concerns of Jews and Hindus in societies in which they are minorities lead to the formation of alliances in addressing common issues of social concern and daily communal life.

Common living also leads to some level of interfaith engagement. Interfaith councils now exist in most towns in the United States and in many places across Europe. As "Interfaith" has become a movement within society, some form of it has reached the local community level. While this form may not be sophisticated nor need it represent the kind of challenges mentioned in the following part of the text, it does provide an opportunity for some Jews and some Hindus to come together, recognizing and accepting their religious differences, within a communal framework. If in mid-twentieth-century contact and dialogue between different religions within a community was almost exclusively a matter for Jews and Christians, by early twenty-first century, all religions were represented within local interreligious councils.

The context of interreligious dialogue is thus the second context in which the Jewish-Hindu encounter takes place. Such dialogue is not limited to the local community level. It takes place on the international level as well. Several organizations, including Elijah's Board of World Religious Leaders, bring together leaders of all faith traditions and provide a framework for Jewish and Hindu leaders to come together. In such contexts, leaders of Judaism and Hinduism, along with leaders of other religions, tackle common theological and spiritual challenges, especially as they affect society at large. The Hindu-Jewish encounter is not at the forefront. However, as both religions draw from their respective resources in an attempt to address common concerns, Jewish and Hindu leaders gain a better understanding of each other and come to know some of each other's faith tenets and practices. The context of interreligious leadership summits is also the one in which the first and second Jewish-Hindu leaders' summits, discussed in detail later in this book, have taken place.[4] The two contexts for interfaith encounters mentioned so far are relatively safe, as far as their implications for Jewish identity and practice are concerned. Jews and Hindus come together primarily in the framework of some broader social context to which they both belong and which they jointly address. There is little, in these contexts, that is specific to these two traditions, and the dynamics are the same as with other partners in similar situations of common living and representation, be they Muslim, Buddhist, or members of any other religious community.

The third context in which Jews encounter Hinduism is far more charged and consequently constitutes a much greater challenge from the philosophical, pedagogic, pastoral, and even halachic perspectives. Over the course of the past 40 to 50 years, we have witnessed a continuing exposure of Jews to Hinduism in ways that have significantly altered their religious identity and practice and that have constituted novel challenges to religious thought and to Jewish leadership. Individual thinkers were drawn to Hindu thought already during the first part of the twentieth century.[5] Individual Jewish travelers were attracted to the spiritual life, as they encountered it in India, and made it their own.[6] But these never amounted to a movement. One can only speak of Jewish exposure to Hinduism as a movement beginning in the late 60s and early 70s, with the wave of Indian *gurus* and spiritual teachers coming to the West. Jews were arguably the most receptive to the teachings of the East. Whatever religious group or particular religious teaching came from the East, Jewish followers featured heavily among the new faithful.[7] Jewish representation in groups such as ISKCON, Transcendental Meditation, Self Realization Fellowship, Ramakrishna Mission, Siddha Yoga, Divine Light Mission, and many others far outnumbered their proportional representation within society. A telling illustration: about half of the successors in the leadership of ISKCON, following the death of the founder, were Jewish. Disproportionate representation applies as much to high governmental positions and Nobel prizes as it does to Jewish membership in various religious groups and cults. In many instances, the involvement of Jewish disciples has been long lasting, and various religious groups and organizations that have developed through the coming of Indian teachers to the West now feature Jewish people in leadership positions. Several examples will be mentioned at a later point, when discussing issues of Jewish identity and how it is impacted by exposure to Hinduism. The context of Jewish conversion to Hinduism or the adoption of Hindu practices and identity was obviously not conducive to broader theoretical reflection on the Hindu-Jewish encounter. It was on the whole either a problem that had to be managed and controlled, even by means as extreme as de-programming, or, as was more often the case, considered a matter to be ignored and avoided. A noteworthy exception are those groups active in the *ba'alei teshuva* movement, that is, the movement of bringing Jews who had not been practicing Judaism back to a life of religious observance and affiliation. These groups did tackle the problem, but primarily in relation to those who had found their way from Indian gurus to the Yeshiva hall. The Lubavitcher Rebbe encouraged the development of Jewish meditation; others highlighted spiritual teachings that could appeal to graduates of Indian religious groups.

The first wave of exposure to India happened primarily in English and was mainly an American phenomenon, with significantly weaker European repercussions. It could therefore be conveniently brushed aside or dealt with as a diaspora phenomenon, a part of the broader crisis or instability of Jewish identity in US Jewry, or from an Israeli perspective—in the Jewish diaspora. Some of the movements did reach Israel, Transcendental Meditation being a notable example, but it reached Israel stripped of specifically Hindu trappings, and it, like other movements, was dealt with on an *ad hoc* basis. The implications of these specific movements as expressive of a broader encounter between Judaism and Hinduism were not yet apparent in the 70s and 80s.

All this changed in the 90s. India became an issue, a challenge, and a spiritual opportunity for Israelis. This occurred through extensive Israeli travel to India, a phenomenon that continues to this very day. The change was largely dependent on the establishment of diplomatic relations between Israel and India and by the ease of travel between the two countries. India became a major destination for travel. We might note, already at this point, that the kind of encounter enabled through travel has been completely asymmetrical. Israelis travel to India in masses; Indians do not travel to Israel, except for those traveling in work-related contexts or in the self-contained contexts of (Christian or Muslim) pilgrimage.

Travel to India was never simply travel (if travel is ever that). It was part holiday and part escape, but also part spiritual quest. The proportions of the different elements motivating travel to India vary according to the age group involved. Sociologist Daria Maoz has conducted extensive studies of the motivation and practices of different travelers to India and notes that motivation, and consequently how time is spent in India itself, varies according to the age groups. The older the traveler, the more his or her travel is informed by a spiritual quest, often finding expression in long-term commitment to spiritual practices learned in India.[8] What is noteworthy, however, is that in all age groups we find some aspect and some degree of spiritual pursuit.

Maoz goes further. She suggests that in many ways the travel to India constitutes a kind of rite of passage, coming as it does at crucial points in the life of the individual. Accordingly, she sees the visit to India as fulfilling a particular psychological and spiritual function in the personal life of the traveler and points to a correspondence between the different stations of life and the respective rites of passage undertaken by traveling to India.

Hundreds of thousands of travelers from Israel to India end up creating a cultural and spiritual climate that cannot be ignored. Israeli exposure to India is slowly becoming a fact of Israeli society. Maoz notes that 20 percent of Israeli travelers to India are religious, that is, they come from the *dati* sector within Israeli society, having imbibed the knowledge of Torah and practical Judaism and they continue to observe the *mitzvot* as part of their ongoing practice. This was certainly not the case several decades earlier, when American Jews joined the ranks of Hindu-inspired religious groups. Of course, the individual observant Jew may have been motivated to take up a specific practice of meditation or even to affiliate himself or herself with a specific religious group. But the high percentage of religious representation in the continuing Israeli passage to India, actually corresponding to their representation within broader society, is a definite novum. In fact, the breadth of the phenomenon is such that it is no longer limited to religious youth, chilling out following their stressful army service. Rabbis have started traveling to India as well. I personally know of several rabbis, who have teaching positions in various Yeshivot, affiliated with the *Dati-Leumi*, religious Zionist, movement, who have gone on their own spiritual journeys to India. Some have done so in order to better understand what their students are undergoing. But quite a number of rabbis of the younger generation have traveled to India as part of their own personal quest and out of their own personal curiosity and intrigue with all that concerns the Jewish encounter with Hindu spirituality and civilization. Having advised such travelers personally, I can testify to their interests. They are serious spiritual seekers, in search of deeper meaning within their own tradition, in search of spirituality, and in pursuit of spiritual bridges of understanding between Jewish religiosity and Hindu wisdom and spirituality. This too is, I submit, a complete novum and a sign of the times.

This movement of Israeli, particularly religious, travelers to India has already yielded one collection of essays.[9] What is interesting about these essays is how many of them, though certainly not all, are written from the perspective of practicing Orthodox Jews. One of the rabbis who, following his students, went on a journey to India also offers his reflections on India, spirituality, and his own educational concerns.[10] Almost all authors are deeply steeped in Jewish sources and their visit to India is assessed in terms of its contribution to their own understanding of Judaism and the enhancement of their own spiritual life. The lead essay, by the volume's editor, Elhanan Nir, is particularly interesting in this context. Nir, who is a teacher of Kabbalah and Hassidut, offers a series of reflections born of various encounters he had in India and seeks to fathom their meaning for his own spiritual understanding of Judaism. I note his essay, in particular, because of the implied challenge of the essay and the inherent difficulties it points to. Nir resorts to what may be termed "snapshot theology." Rather than a detailed exposition of ideas, he shares with us snapshots that reflect his personal experiences and we follow him as he attempts to ground them within a Jewish experiential framework. What is noteworthy is both how relevant his experiences are to his Judaism and, at the same time, how difficult the Indian experience is to categorize neatly, from within conventional Jewish categories. Everything is relevant, yet something eludes the writer and the reader as they try to make sense of the whole. Something about India, and by extension about Hinduism, remains beyond definition, beyond grasp, and beyond easy containment within traditional Jewish categories. It is all urgent, all relevant, and still all different in ways that make a conclusive assessment of it nearly impossible. We watch Nir and his fellow writers struggle to formulate what the encounter with India means to them as practicing Jews. In so doing, they demonstrate the breadth and the complexity of the encounter. Their experience suggests that the encounter is indeed far more complex and elusive than what one might think, based on facile application of Jewish laws of idolatry to the religious reality of India.

Nir's volume makes us aware of one additional factor that is essential to understanding this form of Jewish engagement with Hinduism. The encounter with Hinduism is undertaken by travelers. This is actually a unique, perhaps unprecedented, context for an extensive encounter with another religion. Judaism's relations with other religions have typically taken place in the context of common living, most usually when Jews have been a minority in a host culture, practicing another religion. The Bible is concerned with idolatry, primarily as it relates to the encounter of Jews and Canaanites in the Holy Land, either prior to or following Israel's settlement in the Holy Land. Most Jewish attitudes to other religions, developed during the Middle Ages, were articulated under the framework of common living, and often under the pressures—financial and otherwise—that such common living brings with it.[11] Several individual Jews, who have visited India through the ages, offered us their testimonies and reflections on the religious life they saw.[12] But, never before has there been a situation of mass encounter of Jews with another religious tradition, undertaken primarily in the context of travel.

There are various implications to the context in which this new encounter is taking place. The encounter does not threaten home and the stability of its institutions, at least not immediately and visibly. It occurs in a distant place, which affords it a kind of neutrality and safety. Its detachment from ongoing daily life means that Israelis are not really subjected to the fullness of Hindu or Indian life and are free to, consciously or not, pick and choose those aspects of the Hindu tradition that appeal to them and with which they seek to interact. Consequently, disturbing commonalities between Jewish and Hindu cultures can be ignored in favor of highlighting more attractive—if we will, more spiritual—aspects of Hindu culture.[13] Furthermore, this form of encounter facilitates the transport of ideas and practices back home. Rather than two full religious systems encountering one another, we often find processes of selection that lead to highlighting aspects of India that in turn function as cultural and spiritual metonyms for India. These metonymical expressions of India are then exported and in some way integrated back home when the travel ends and the traveler returns home. The uniqueness of this type of encounter is thus not limited to its context and circumstances. It applies equally to the possibility of integrating its fruits within Judaism, once the traveler returns home. A traveler may be able to import more easily practices and ideas as inspiration and enrichment to his or her spiritual life, than a neighbor may. A dialogue or encounter of travelers is thus a very particular form of encounter and it is one of the characteristics of Judaism's present encounter with Hinduism. It makes the encounter in many ways easier to conduct. It also makes its impact more long lasting, inasmuch as its fruits can be more readily assimilated. Finally, the fact that the encounter takes place through the medium of travel could account for the striking silence of rabbinic authorities and educators regarding the encounter, inasmuch as it often involves crossing halachic boundaries, especially in relation to Avoda Zara, the fundamental prohibition of worshipping other gods, which one would never consider possible in one's homeland.

To the three contexts in which the Jewish-Hindu encounter takes place, we might add a fourth, the academic encounter.[14] Here too, the situation is asymmetrical. Jews seem to take a great interest in the academic study of things Hindu and Indian. By contrast, I am not aware of a single Hindu expert of Judaism.[15] Several factors may account for this discrepancy. India, for historical reasons, does not cultivate religious studies as part of its academic enterprise. Given that Judaism, if it exists at all in public consciousness, is barely distinguishable from Christianity, there would be little impetus to undertake serious study of Judaism. Jews by contrast, have been interested in things Indian for quite some time.[16] As Arun Singh, Indian ambassador to Israel, notes in his introduction to a collection of studies on India based on contemporary Israeli research, Israel is the only country in the world where over 90 percent of the students attending introductory classes on Hinduism and India have actually visited India.[17] And classes on things Indian are some of the best attended classes in the humanities in Israel. Academic studies are often the "next step," following in-person exposure to Indian reality. That a volume of Israeli studies on India can be published is a token to the centrality of India in the Israeli Academy, itself an expression of the prominence of India in contemporary Israeli psyche and experience.[18] Tiny Israel has far more to say, academically, regarding India than the entire subcontinent does concerning Israel and Judaism.

The encounter of Jews with Hinduism over the past 40 years or so constitutes a unique pastoral, spiritual, and theological challenge. It comes at a point in time in which Jewish identity is undergoing intense change and when the quest for religious meaning and spirituality is intensive. The educational challenge is greater when Hinduism becomes a source of inspiration, as well as a form of practice, even for people who profess Judaism as their spiritual path. The nuanced challenges posed by this situation require more than the kind of blanket condemnation and rejection that some circles would provide as a default response. The complexity of Jewish life, existence, and identity encounters the complexity of Hindu spiritual life and evolving self-definition. The coming together of these complexities in individual lives and in broader movements calls for analysis and perspective that are equally complex and able to chart a path through these rich and complicated realities. As already intimated, we may not yet be at the point of providing answers, while the facile answers that some offer may not be adequate to the task at hand. The process may take time. A first step is to comprehend the situation in its complexity and to frame the relevant questions accordingly. It is my hope that the present work will make a meaningful contribution to this end.

The passage to India functions for many Israeli travelers as a kind of rite of passage into the particular stage of life towards which the travel leads. Perhaps this is true not only of the travel of individuals but of the entire encounter between Judaism and Hinduism. It is a tantalizing thought to consider the present Jewish engagement with India, in its entirety, as a kind of rite of passage, not only for the travelers to India, but also for Judaism itself, as it reaffirms its identity, self-understanding, and spirituality and as these take on new iterations, generation after generation, in relation to prevailing circumstances. Perhaps a generation or more of travelers will bring into Judaism the accumulated experiences, reflections, aspirations, and maybe even practices that will allow Judaism itself to grow, through this encounter, in accordance with its own mission and purpose. The sum total of individual passages to India may amount to a greater rite of passage, that of Judaism itself, as it grows through its encounter with Hinduism.

3

The Jews of India: What Can We Learn from Them?

I have already noted Nathan Katz's description of the Hindu-Jewish encounter as "an ancient encounter that dates back more than two millennia." Speaking historically, this may be the case.[1] Speaking theologically, and hence in terms of the relevance of that encounter to Judaism's present encounter with Hinduism, the ancient encounter may be of little significance. The question, in my opinion, is not whether Judaism and Hinduism encountered each other, but rather what were the parameters of that encounter and what can it teach us today. It seems to me that that particular encounter contributes little to contemporary concerns, though it may bear indirect testimony to positions that may be helpful to the present encounter.

Several Jewish communities existed in India for periods of hundreds, some say thousands, of years. In one specific respect, India certainly provides important testimony to relations between Jews and non-Jews: we do not know of any religious persecution of Jews or of any anti-Semitism, suffered at the hands of Hindus. Contemporary Hindus take great pride in this fact. A climate of acceptance might also account for what seems to be a lack of confrontation with Hindu religion, on the side of the Jewish community. The type of tension, competition, coercion, and violence that are so typical of Judaism's relationships with Christianity and Islam seems to be completely absent from the experience of Jews in India. This might suggest that ideological tension and religious competition are a function of context. In a context that is tolerant and accommodating, religious competition and ideological tensions may be significantly lower than in religious contexts that are less tolerant. Thus, the toleration enjoyed by the Jews might be mirrored in their own attitudes to the Hindu community.

This is certainly an important insight and it offers a welcome contrast to the history of Jews in relation to other religious communities. However, some additional facts need to be considered before we can make such a statement, and they may well detract from our ability to draw such an unequivocal conclusion from the experience of Indian Jewry. Thriving Jewish communities are also centers of learning. How a Jewish community handles its spiritual challenges and crises will be reflected in the literature produced by a particular community. The literature typically varies. It includes halachic writings, commentaries, responsa, biblical and rabbinic commentaries, and more. Through these various genres contemporary challenges are tackled. The Jewish community in India has produced none of these literatures. Its written artifacts seem to belong to the realm of liturgy and worship, not to the realms of thought and halacha.[2] This is a sign of a small and weak Jewish community. Indeed, for its halachic rulings it would depend on other centers of learning, such as the Jewish center in Iraq. Jews in India do not seem to have made contributions to those genres and forms of thought and creativity that shape our attitudes and that can convey positions, from one generation to another and from one cultural context to another. We therefore do not know how they handled some of the core questions relating to the Jewish-Hindu encounter. How did they understand the religion of their Hindu neighbors? How did they tackle the challenge of idolatry? How did they understand Judaism's role in the big scheme of things? As far as I have been able to discern, we do not have any complete account of these issues.[3] It could mean that the issues were not as important as we might think. If so, the lack suggests that one need not insist on certain issues in Judaism's relations with other religions. As I am about to propose, other factors provided identity markers for Indian Jewry that may have made insistence on theological particularity superfluous. But it might also simply be a sign of a very weak Jewish community that does not share some of the broader foci of Jewish concern and creativity. If so, its testimony is of little relevance to those Jews formed under the canons of thought and practice of the broader Jewish world, who tackle the challenge of encountering another religion through a specific set of questions that must be adequately addressed.

In order to understand the unique features of Indian Jewry, we must revisit the question of Hindu or Indian integration of other religions. For many societies, religion and the boundaries it offers provide the frontiers along which groups define themselves. India seems to have another way of achieving social definition and stability. The caste system functions as a way of establishing identity and regulating relations between different groups. The various dos and don'ts associated with the caste system provide a parallel system to that by means of which religion establishes identity. The relative stability of the caste system is the social background, against which ideological and religious tolerance have flourished in India. Jews and Christians have in various ways also become part of the Indian caste system. The most striking thing about Indian Jewry is how deeply it is impacted by the caste system. Jews are separated from non-Jews through the caste system. One of the striking features of Cochin Jewry was the internal caste-like division between different parts of the community. The practices of Indian Jewry suggest a high degree of acculturation, particularly as related to understanding their own worship and religious life in terms of caste.[4] Thus identity, relationship within, and relationship without are all channeled through categories that are particular to the Indian experience and that are significantly different from what Jewry elsewhere employed for purposes of identity construction.[5]

Against this background of strong definition provided by social institutions we may better appreciate the little that I have been able to find in the literature concerning how Indian Jews perceived their Hindu neighbors. The prevailing attitude was one of recognition of multiple spiritual paths and their validity.[6] Contemporary Jews of Indian origin offer similar answers, even though their own replies reflect a secularized cosmopolitan understanding that already bears the spiritual imprint of such Indian spiritual giants as Ramana Maharshi and others.[7] Still, the impression is consistent. Rather than highlighting the idolatry, strangeness, and otherness of their Hindu neighbors, Indian Jews seem to have reciprocated the acceptance and tolerance they enjoyed through an attitude of respect. If correct, this is itself a significant finding.[8] It suggests that different cultures and different historical contexts will tend to highlight different aspects in the relationships between religions. What seems to us to be of vital concern in the encounter with another religion, in this case with Hinduism, may be itself only one of several options of how that relationship can be constructed and as such both culturally and historically contingent. This relativizing perspective also emerges, as I shall suggest in a later chapter, from an examination of medieval perceptions of India.

Some of the earliest records of Indian Jewry come from the Cairo Genizah, where we find notes of Jewish merchants who write from India, or who have visited India. Goitein, who published these records, comments on the silence of these sources regarding the religion of the people of India:

> The same Geniza letters reveal an astonishing degree of inter-denominational cooperation, matched by almost complete absence of animosity against other communities. Partnerships and other close business relationships between Jews and Muslims, or Hindus, or Christians were commonplace and the members of other religious communities are referred to with the same honorable and amicable epithets as the writers' own brethren. The great dangers shared in common, the feeling that every one's lot was in the hand of the same God, certainly contributed much to that spirit of all-embracing brotherhood, which pervades the India papers of the Cairo Geniza.[9]

Surely the Jews must have realized how different the religious landscape of the Hindus is. How come, then, that this difference is not expressed in their writings? One answer might be that we simply do not have all relevant materials in our possession, either in terms of what made it to the Genizah, or in terms of what has been published from the Genizah. But there might be another answer. The lack of interest of these Jewish merchants may reflect the lack of interest of the Indian Jewish community in these issues. It may, in theory, also reflect their successful resolution. If Jews came to view Hindus as monotheists, who worship different representations of One God, as Hindus could understand themselves, the level of tension in relation to Hindus would obviously be lower than if they showed concern about forbidden idolatrous worship.

It is noteworthy that other travelers, even while they report on Hindu practices that constitute idolatry from the Jewish perspective, are silent on the attitudes of the local Jewish community. The tone is descriptive and we do not hear of a criticism or rejection of Hindu practices, as part of the prevailing attitude of the Jewish community. Thus, Benjamin of Tudela, who describes forms of what he perceives as idolatry, in terms of biblical idolatry attributed to the canaanites, says nothing of contemporary Jewish attitudes.[10] Later travelers, such as Yakov Sapir and David DeBeth Hillel, report on the idolatry of the Hindus, without reporting on rejectionary attitudes of the Jewish community.[11]

4

Sarmad the Jew: A Precursor of the Encounter

While the Jews of India do not teach us much concerning the actual Jewish-Hindu encounter, there is one Jewish personality of the seventeenth century who may be relevant to today's discussions, growing out of contemporary religious encounters. This is Sarmad.[1]

While Sarmad is most often viewed in a Sufi context, in fact, his religious practices incorporated Judaism, Islam, and Hinduism, making him a very interesting precursor for our discussions of both Jewish identity and spirituality, in the framework of the Jewish-Hindu encounter. Significantly, and much like contemporary seekers, Sarmad was not a native-born Indian Jew. Rather, he came to India from the outside, explored India's spiritual riches, and also contributed to them.

Sai'd Sarmad was born a Jew, in Persia, perhaps in Armenia, around 1590. He is buried at Jamia Masjid, in Delhi, and has a following as a great Sufi saint. Little is known of his life, and the literary corpus he has left behind is fairly small—just over 300 pieces of Persian poetry, each poem consisting of four lines, Rubayats or quatrains in English.[2] And yet, in his own day he was a figure of great note, a great mystic who played a role at the Mughal court, with his fate tied to that of his disciple Dara Shikoh, the emperor's son, who was killed by his brother, Aurangzeb. Following Dara, Sarmad too was executed by Aurangzeb, with support of religious clerics, probably in 1651.

The fact that Sarmad made a contribution on Judaism to an early work of comparative religion has drawn attention to him repeatedly over the past century. It is interesting to note that the Jewish authors who wrote on Sarmad spoke of him approvingly, owning and embracing him, or at the very least appreciating his positive contribution from a Jewish perspective. They have acknowledged and accepted "Sarmad the Jew" in a manner that is not usually shown to Jewish apostates and converts to another religion. It would seem a combination of factors has enabled this Jewish embrace of Sarmad:

A. The fact that so little is known of his life allows anyone studying Sarmad to construct him to some extent in his own image. This is as true of traditional Muslim hagiography as it is of recent Jewish scholarship.

B. Sarmad made a contribution to the comparative study of religion, as this applied to his mid-seventeenth-century context. He provided the information for the chapter on Judaism in the *Dabistan* (*Dabistan e-Mazaheb*), a Persian record of the various religious groups and beliefs that were known in seventeenth-century India.[3] This work reflects the spirit of interreligious openness, study, dialogue, and even syncretism that was characteristic of Akbar, the great Mughal emperor, and his great-grandson, Dara Shikoh, mentioned above.[4] The primary source from which we know of Sarmad is the *Dabistan*, and we therefore know of him in a context that is inherently positive as far as Sarmad's relationship with Judaism is concerned. Not only is he the author's informant, he also provides, or collaborates on, an early translation of several chapters of Genesis, incorporated in the *Dabistan*'s presentation on Judaism. Accordingly, he is recognized as making a positive contribution to a view of Judaism and to the propagation of Jewish ideas.

C. Whatever Sarmad's identity, he does not seek to force it upon fellow Jews. In the absence of a Jewish community this is not a significant statement. Still, it is obvious from the structure of Sarmad's thinking that he does not propagate a particular religion, but something beyond religions. Unlike Jewish converts to other religions, Sarmad has not aligned himself with the other religion, in opposition to Judaism.

D. The fact that Sarmad operates in India somehow creates a different dynamic than the more common approach to converted Jews in Europe or under Muslim rule in other territories. The kind of tolerance typical of the court of Akbar is intuitively associated with India, making the case of Sarmad in India somehow different, emotionally, than attitudes to other converts.

E. Inseparable from the previous point is the view of Sarmad as a mystic and the related understanding of mysticism as somehow transcending religious identity. While mystics of Jewish descent are known also in a Christian context, one cannot separate the mysticism of such figures as John of the Cross or Theresa of Avila, if they are indeed of Jewish descent, from its Christian context. Sarmad, by contrast, does allow us to consider him as a generic mystic.

F. Finally, the view of Sarmad as a mystic is closely related to doubts concerning Sarmad's own self-identity.[5] If Sarmad did not consider himself to be a member of another religion, then, in some sense, he never ceased to be Jewish.

Some combination of the above-mentioned points has informed the positive view of Sarmad that we find in the works of authors who have related to him as "Sarmad the Jew."

Interest in Sarmad takes on particular relevance in the framework of Jewish interest in spirituality and in particular in the associations of India and spirituality over the past decades. Interest in both comes with a more open attitude to issues of Jewish identity in particular and to the possibilities of multiple religious identities. To some extent, those who recall Sarmad's person and spiritual message already affirm a mentality that is different from the one that has prevailed for centuries in relation to Christianity, Islam, and Jews who crossed the lines. Let us, then, consider some of the discussions concerning Sarmad the Jew.

Several encyclopedia articles of the first part of the twentieth century refer to Sarmad. Louis Ginzberg, writing in the Jewish Encyclopedia, in 1905, has a brief article on Sarmad. It is worth noting his speaking of Sarmad as "converting" his disciple Abhai Chand to a mixture of Judaism and Islam. The reference is noteworthy both for the recognition of the issue of complex, or multiple, religious identity and for application of the category of conversion to describe religious identities, as these appear in Sarmad's story. One of the issues raised by Sarmad, both by his life story and in his poetry, is the nature of religious identity and the meaning of shifts in religious identity and how they come about. To speak of conversion may in some sense already pronounce judgment on a matter that ought to be a subject of discussion. One of the strategies for owning Sarmad as a Jew is to minimize his conversion to Islam. Certainly, there is a basis for this in Sarmad's own writings. While Muslim descriptions take it for granted that he converted, the sources allow us to query this strong approach to religious boundaries and identities.[6]

Ginzberg offers snippets of Sarmad's views of Judaism as captured in the *Dabistan*. Ginzberg cites one teaching that he considers to show Hindu influence, and a second that shows the impress of Islamist teachings. Very much in the spirit of the day, Ginzberg's analysis of the *Dabistan* focuses on historical influences and portrays Sarmad as a Jewish author who incorporates Hindu and Muslim ideas. Portraying Sarmad thus accords with the view of the Jewish Sarmad, who, like many authors throughout history, absorbs ideas from his surrounding culture.

Walter Fischel, writing in the late 40s and early 50s, is at the forefront of recovering the Jewish Sarmad. In The Bible in Persian Translation,[7] he devotes three pages to Sarmad's Genesis translation, which he describes as "astonishing." Rather than a critical review of Sarmad's views, Fischel prefers to focus on the positive aspects of Sarmad's contributions. The first is that the text is not missionary or in other ways corrupted by the views of another religion. The second is that Sarmad serves as a channel for cultural transmission of Jewish views. This seems to have positive valuation, regardless of the correctness of these views. Finally, Fischel downplays Sarmad's conversion and refers to him as being only superficially Islamized. This obviously helps Fischel to own Sarmad more readily as a Jew.

In 1966, an Indian Jew by the name of I. A. Ezekiel published a work titled *Sarmad (Jewish Saint of India)*.[8] The book was published by Radhasoami Press, belonging to a neo-Sikh group, combining Sikh mystical teachings with some Hindu tenets, especially highlighting the role of the master and viewing contemporary masters as incarnations of God. Radhasoamis have published several works that seek to read world religions or to view classical figures in religious history in light of their own spiritual path. The effort is a two-edged sword. On the one hand, they bring to the table a well-constructed worldview that could provide a hermeneutical key to understanding the spiritual lives of great mystics. On the other, having such a well-constructed view can easily degenerate into forcing one's own religious system upon another.

For purposes of the present discussion, Ezekiel puts forth two theses. The first is an affirmation of Sarmad's Jewishness. Ezekiel significantly downplays Sarmad's Muslim identity.[9] He downplays his Muslim name and other identity markers, so as to feature him more clearly as a Jew. The second, and primary, thesis of the book is that Sarmad was a great Saint or Perfect Master (capitalization consistent in the original, suggesting a technical term within the Radhasoami movement). Ezekiel offers us a reading of Sarmad from the perspective of the Rubayats. The conceptual framework of Radhasoami allows Ezekiel to recognize mystical union, spiritual processes, location of mystical experiences in the body, and various other dimensions of the spiritual life as aspects of Sarmad's experience. Accordingly, Sarmad is portrayed as a mystic, a Perfected Master, on essentially phenomenological grounds, based on a reading of his own works.

Concerning Ezekiel's first thesis, why is it important for him to affirm Sarmad's Jewishness? If Sarmad is beyond religion, then there is little meaning to his being a Jew? Why insist on his Jewishness? Is there anything to Sarmad's Judaism except for his ethnic identity? I can see two reasons. The first might stem from the fact that Ezekiel is himself a Jew. Perhaps had another author written the work, he would not have insisted on Sarmad's Jewishness in the same way. It was somehow important for Ezekiel to affirm that "one of us" is also a great saint. In other words, there may be nothing in this affirmation beyond the comfort of knowledge that even we, Jews, have been able to produce great Indian spiritual luminaries, hence the subtitle of the book—*Jewish Saint of India*.

There may be a second reason. The logic of this publication, as of others produced by the Radhasoami movement, is that all great religions should be read in light of their teachings. Ezekiel's book follows such a pattern. Ezekiel first presents a teaching found in Sarmad's poems, and that is known from Radhasoami theology, and then sets forth to find parallels in the works of other great spiritual masters and of other religions. To find a Jewish saint who so readily offers teachings that are "Radhasoami-like" is thus an affirmation of the validity of these teachings and in its own way a missionary move.[10]

In 1990 the Dalai Lama invited a group of Jewish religious leaders to a dialogue in Dharamsala. This dialogue was captured in Roger Kamenetz's bestseller, *The Jew in the Lotus*.[11] Toward the end of the book,[12] Kamentez describes the travels of the participants in Delhi, following their Dharamsala dialogue, on their way home. A stop at Sarmad's tomb was included in their Delhi visit. Kamenetz's Sarmad picks up where Fischel's left off. Kamenetz quotes Fischel that though nominally a convert to Islam, there's evidence he remained a Jew.[13] He then goes on to tell us of Sarmad's intellectual contribution to the *Dabistan*, and quotes Fischel's approval of it as a means of disseminating Jewish ideas.

Kamenetz relies exclusively on Fischel and this allows him to take the next step. If Sarmad remains Jewish and Sarmad contributes to the *Dabistan*, let us revisit the *Dabistan* in the context of the present Jewish-Buddhist dialogue. Significantly, the chapter on Tibetans and Yahuds are adjacent to one another in the *Dabistan*. And we know that Dara Shikoh, Sarmad's disciple, staged inter-religious debates. It therefore seems very possible, argues Kamenetz, that Sarmad had preceded "us" in Tibetan-Jewish dialogue 300 years ago. There is only one problem with Kamenetz's argument (beyond the lack of any evidence): he has stretched the meaning of "Jewish." From Jewish ethnicity, or even self-identification, he has moved to representation. Sarmad the Jew now becomes the Jewish voice in an interreligious dialogue. That his entire religious tenor is violently opposed to any identification with a particular form of religion and that the last thing he would consider is to debate on behalf of any religion, let alone Judaism, is unknown to Kamenetz. The "myth" of Sarmad the Jew seems to have a life of its own, allowing this kind of present-day identification with Sarmad.

Kamenetz draws a comparison between Sarmad and a contemporary figure—the Jewish-Hindu teacher Ram Das:

> They had much in common: wandering Jews, spiritual seekers in India, an ever-lasting type of syncretic Jew, the polar opposite of the particularist—the spark that flies off the wheel.[14]

This is a very interesting observation. It draws out a parallel between Sarmad and contemporary reality, suggesting that Sarmad may be, in some way, a prototype (in Kamenetz's language—an anagram) for something in contemporary reality. Jews find themselves in India, drawn by its spiritual reality. In the process, they seek spirituality and construct their identity in novel and individual ways. In one way they remain Jewish; in another they have moved away from the fold and created new religious realities. This is a very potent observation. Kamenetz seems unaware of the fact that the parallel with Ram Das is even stronger, given that Sarmad also followed Hindu gods. Sarmad writes:

> What shortcoming didst thou find in the Prophet and in God,
> That thou turned thy face away from God and the Prophet
> And became a disciple of Ram and Lakshman.[15]

Sarmad is indeed a model for present-day-Jewish seekers in India. Like them, he comes from the outside and is not a part of Indian Jewry. He seeks spirituality, in all its forms. And in some way he maintains his Jewish association, even though he has adopted a form of spiritual life that is radically different from that of conventional Judaism. If there is something that distinguishes Sarmad from today's seekers it would be his own ability to contribute back to Judaism or to the dissemination of Jewish knowledge.

Kamenetz concludes by describing a recitation of Kaddish on Sarmad's tomb, a recognition of his being the group's predecessor in dialogue, a culmination of the image of Sarmad the Jew, independently of the Muslim context within which it is offered. One of the members of the Dharamsala dialogue who offered Kaddish for Sarmad was Nathan Katz. Several years later, in 2000, he published an article examining Sarmad's religious identity.[16] Katz's novel contribution is reading Sarmad's Rubayats seeking clues to his religious identity. Katz notes that Sarmad rejects different religions. In fact, the sources brought by Katz all emphasize Sarmad's rejection of religious practice and piety, in favor of a higher spiritual principle.

Sarmad's own self-identity incorporated Judaism, Hinduism, and Islam. His close disciple Abhai Chand composed the following distych, which is considered expressive of Sarmad's own identity:

> I am at once a follower of the Quran, a priest,
> A monk, a Jewish rabbi, an infidel and a Muslim.[17]

This is a fundamental text. It presents a notion of multiple religious identities. Abhai Chand, and, by extension, Sarmad, is affirming his simultaneous identity as a Jew, a Hindu, and a Muslim.

This kind of multireligious identity comes through in relation to another disciple of Sarmad's, the prince Dara Shiko. Dara was a prince with Sufi inclinations, who sought to reconcile Hindu and Islamic traditions. He delighted in religious discussion and was in contact with religious leaders of different groups. He undertook translations of different scriptures, including the Old and New Testament. Dara held a close relationship with Sarmad and even considered him his teacher. Dara addresses Sarmad as "My master and preceptor."[18] If indeed Dara was a disciple of Sarmad's, we may be able to learn something of Sarmad's views of religions from the following description of Dara:[19]

> Dara held no religion. When with Mohammedans he praised the tenets of Mohammed; when with Jews, the Jewish religion; in the same way, when with Hindus he praised Hinduism…he had great delight in talking to the Jesuit fathers on religion, and making them dispute with his learned Mohammedans, or with a Hebrew called Sarmad, an atheist much liked by the prince.

Two disciples can provide complementary testimonies to the one master, thereby allowing us to get a glimpse of his person. What is told of both disciples is striking in its similarity. Both affirm multiple religious identities. Both are spoken of in a threefold manner—Jew, Muslim, and Hindu. Given the absence of Jews in the surrounding, the only reason for affirming Jewish identity would be Sarmad himself. In some way, both disciples identify with Judaism, because they identify with Sarmad.

Complementing these quotes is another quote, pertaining to Dara and his heresy:

> It became manifest that if Dara Shukoh obtained the throne and established his power, the foundations of the faith would be in danger and the precepts of Islam would be changed for the rant of infidelity and Judaism.[20]

It is particularly interesting to consider the final sentence in light of the passage within which it appears. Dara's heresy is described with reference to recognizing the validity of Hinduism and considering Hinduism and Islam equally valid religions. Dara is described as spending time with Brahmins, Yogis, and sannyasis. There is nothing in the description of Dara that would be relevant to Judaism, yet the passage concludes with "the rant of infidelity"—referring to Hinduism—and Judaism. The only way of making sense of this reference is to see it as a reflection of how Sarmad was viewed. Not only is Sarmad considered Jewish, but his teachings are considered as Judaism.[21]

Sarmad seems to provide an option for multiple religious belonging.[22] What is unique in Sarmad's case, as distinct from other contemporary figures, is that Judaism is part of his, and consequently his disciples', religious identity. Niccolao Mannuci speaks of Dara as holding no religion. To an extent this too reflects on Sarmad; what it means is that Sarmad did not consider himself limited within the bounds of one set of practices, one piety. On spiritual and mystical grounds, he was able to establish a relationship with God that allowed him to take distance vis-à-vis all forms of organized religion. This is well documented in his Rubayats.[23] For Sarmad, one can find oneself in any religion, one can speak to any religion, one can speak through any religion, without fully taking on all its practices, let alone identifying with it sociologically. In theory there is no limit to the religions one can work through. But in reality there are limits placed by circumstances of life and learning. Sarmad seems to have been familiar with three religious "languages": Judaism, Islam, and Hinduism. His move away from Judaism does not amount to renouncing Judaism. Rather, it is a quest for deeper experience, which in turn would allow him to affirm his Judaism (though non-exclusively) in new ways. How much he could affirm is, of course, a function of his knowledge. The core attitude is not one of converting from one religion to another, leaving the former behind. For this reason, one should not speak of Sarmad in terms of "conversion" to another religion. Sarmad's path seems to have been one of deepening spirituality and love for God, based upon which he could return and own multiple religious identities, training others to follow such an interreligious spiritual path.

Nathan Katz has listed for us various ways of considering Sarmad's identity—Jewish, Muslim, Mystic, atheist, and Hindu. We are now in a position to offer another formulation—Sarmad held a multireligious identity. This identity was indeed mystically grounded and was based on a recognition of a spiritual reality that both transcends and contains particular religious identities. Within this matrix, Sarmad may be said to have maintained his Jewish identity as well. This is a novel way of affirming Sarmad's Jewishness. Sarmad's Jewish identity is affirmed, without it coming into conflict with other religious identities, which are simultaneously maintained. Sarmad could not, as Kamenetz might fantasize, take the voice of a Jew in the framework of a Jewish debate with the member of another religion. But he could provide a conceptual matrix, born of an existential perspective and an experiential foundation, that allowed him to speak in multiple religious languages. From this perspective, he could also own, affirm, and creatively apply his own maternal identity as Sarmad the Jew.

Sarmad is the most noteworthy Jewish figure on the religious landscape of India, prior to the twentieth century. None of the community leaders or rabbis over the course of thousands of years have left any meaningful legacy in terms of spirituality or deepening religious reflection. In its own way this is symbolic of what India has come to mean to spiritual seekers. Sarmad offers one model for reconciling multiple religious identities, certainly not the only one nor one that ought to be recommended. This is certainly relevant for present-day spiritual seekers, as Kamenetz suggests and as a later chapter of this work will argue at length. But even more than that he is a symbol for the Jewish encounter with India and for how it reshapes and redefines the spiritual life.[24] The Jew from the outside arrives in India, which functions for him as a crucible for spiritual, as well as identitarian, transformation. Sarmad is but one model of how such transformation shapes the religious life of the individual. Farther along we shall encounter others. But Sarmad, much more than the Jews of India, places us before the challenges, opportunities, as well as risks of the passage to India and its implications for the spiritual life of the Jew.

5

Judaism(s) and Hinduism(s)

No religion is a monolith, but some more so than others. This is probably a fair way to sum up the following discussion. It touches on the fundamental assumptions of the present work. When we speak of Judaism's encounter with Hinduism, we implicitly assume a meeting between two entities, which should be described and related to in roughly the same terms and categories. In all probability, such a reference is envisioned along the lines of a meeting between two individuals. The reality, however, is that religions are far more complex. They are constituted by various specific religious, ideological, and practical ways of expressing a broad tradition. Under certain circumstances the different expressions of a religion may recognize one another and be recognized as belonging to the same religion; at other times, even this may be questioned. This issue is relevant for both Judaism and Hinduism, but particularly for the latter. In the case of Judaism, the complexity of definition of what Judaism is and how to recognize its different manifestations as expressions of a single religious system have led Jacob Neusner, and other scholars who follow his lead, to speak of Judaisms, in the plural, rather than in the singular. Thus, Neusner represents each of the different groups operating in late Second Temple and rabbinic times as "a Judaism." Each Judaism has specific practices, a worldview, a social structure, and so on, that make it distinct from another Judaism. The rabbis are "a Judaism," members of the Qumran sect are "a Judaism," hellenistic Judaism is "a Judaism," and so on.[1] This logic applies also to the varieties of Judaism found in later periods, including our own.[2] According to this logic, Orthodox, Conservative, Reform, Reconstructionist, and Renewal Judaisms should each be considered "a Judaism." Such a perspective has merit, inasmuch as it recognizes diversity for what it is, and avoids the essentialist reference to "Judaism" as a monolith, whose essence, ideas, and practices can be stated in abstraction from specific manifestations of particular Judaisms.

Neusner's view is that of the historian. As the historian encounters various related manifestations of a religious tradition, he must make room for all these traditions. History relativizes. From the purely descriptive perspective, one cannot say that one form of Judaism is truer, superior, or otherwise preferable to another. Given the multiplicity of historical expressions of a religious tradition and the need to describe them in an even-handed way, we are led to talk of "Judaisms," rather than of "Judaism."

But the historian's perspective is not the only one. The philosopher approaches religion with a sense of true and false, valid and invalid, legitimate and illegitimate. These too may be measured in relation to historical precedent, but to a large extent these are measured in relation to some understanding of the tradition in an ideal sense. That this ideal sense may itself be a specific historic iteration of the tradition does not detract from its power and legitimacy to provide a canon for measuring the philosophical, spiritual, and ideal values of the tradition and to serve as a yardstick for assessing the different historical expressions of a tradition. Thus, we may speak of a tradition in both descriptive and normative terms.

The tension between the descriptive and the normative applies, in the case of Judaism, not only to the tension between history and philosophy but also, perhaps even more powerfully so, to the tension between history and halacha. Halacha provides an important yardstick for normativity, allowing us to recognize the legitimacy of various expressions of historical Judaism. Thus, history, ideological perspective, and halachic normativity come together in complex ways. Their permutations allow us to suggest a hard core of what would constitute Judaism and what is the theological platform from which it can be described. But this hard core is matched by some soft periphery. Should Sabbateanism and Frankism be described as Judaism? And what of early Israelite religion? And what of the Karaites and Samaritans, etc. etc.? Probably the most challenging issues arise when we explore Christianity, primarily early Christianity, in those terms. The case of early Christianity actually introduces one further criterion into our discussion, that of self-understanding. In addition to the "objective" criteria of history and halacha and the more ambiguous criterion of religious ideology, we have the purely subjective criterion of self-understanding. Self-understanding constitutes identity, and it plays an important role in the definition of religions, religious communities, and their boundaries. Contemporary Judaism presents some unresolved challenges revolving around the application of these complicated and, at times, conflicting criteria. The continuing struggles around the issue of "who is a Jew," as it applies to the Law of Return in Israel, indicate that definition of a religion and of religious identity are never fully resolved and remain open to continuing debate.

We must therefore position ourselves within one particular tradition and speak of Judaism from its viewpoint. Orthodoxy is one such position. It offers a broad spectrum of ideological perspectives, complemented by mostly clear legal guidelines and boundaries that allow us to identify what Judaism is and to speak of it as a whole. My own training and orientation is that of an Orthodox Jew, hence the present work and the assumptions that inform it will be inevitably marked by implicit Orthodox convictions. Given that Orthodox Judaism was the reigning paradigm for most of the past two millennia, one has little difficulty in talking of "Judaism," while envisioning it in terms close to those of Jewish Orthodoxy.[3]

Identifying a normative viewpoint seems to be the safest way to speak meaningfully of a tradition. At the same time, we must also be aware of the limitations of such a perspective. At the very least, we must remain aware of the problematics of definition and of the fact that historically there is always something contingent about the particular viewpoint that has been adopted and the recognition of a particular Judaism as "Judaism." Such awareness might allow us to recall other forms of Judaism as we speak of "Judaism" in the abstract. These may function as checks and controls on our statements, they may provide unanticipated views and possibilities not usually considered within a given normative perspective, and they may invite us to rethink our presentations. In the context of an imagined conversation between two different religious traditions, such as "Hinduism" and "Judaism," it is important to be mindful of historical precedents, configurations of the tradition, and ways of understanding the spiritual life that are broader than conventional normative views. These may highlight our differences or help us bridge them. Regardless, they could make our exchanges richer and possibly more precise. Thus, it seems that adopting a normative perspective, while keeping our horizons open to the testimony of other historical Judaisms, provides the most balanced perspective in how we conceptualize the "Judaism" that we bring into conversation with another tradition.[4]

One final word about the "ism" of "Judaism." Attempts to treat Judaism as a whole, an entity, possessing its own boundaries and distinct identity, have been made for thousands of years. At least since the Hellenistic and Roman periods, we find encounters between the prevailing cultures that seek to identify the ethnos and the religious community of Judaism as a whole, as distinct and identifiable, in relation to other religious communities. The various criteria—ethnic, legal, philosophical, territorial, and religious—have all been put together in varying permutations for thousands of years, in continuing attempts to identify and define the particularity of the religious community currently referred to as "Judaism." Therefore, even if historical precision may drive us to consider referring to Judaism in the plural, as "Judaisms," there is also a long-standing historical tradition in light of which we may legitimately continue to refer to "Judaism," as a whole. At the end of the day, both historical and normative perspectives allow us to address the religious life of the Jews as "Judaism," even if we wish our usage of the term to be more critically informed and more nuanced than its conventional uncritical usage.

I would have never entered the afore-mentioned discussion had it not been necessary to devote equal and even more attention to the problematic term "Hinduism." This term is problematic in ways that are far more complex than the problems associated with "Judaism." The problems associated with "Hinduism" are not merely the problems of the historian of antiquity, who seeks to present her data in an orderly fashion. The problems involved in speaking of "Hinduism" touch upon the very identity and religious life of the Hindu community.[5] They have concrete political ramifications, particularly in today's India. They touch the deepest problems of self-identity and hence impact seriously on the question of Judaism's encounter with Hinduism. If we are somehow able to resolve the question of what we mean by "Judaism" in the framework of this encounter, it is far harder and more complex to provide a parallel answer in the case of "Hinduism." Indeed, the scholarly norm of speaking of the religious traditions in the plural extends to Hinduism as well, leading comparative scholars to talk of "Hinduisms," rather than of "Hinduism."[6] The relations between the descriptive and the normative are far more complex with reference to Hinduism, and the definition of Hinduism itself, including the very use of the term, is therefore much more problematic than in the case of Judaism. Clearly, if we are to speak of Judaism's engagement with Hinduism, we must know what this "Hinduism" is, who speaks for it, and who represents it. These are hot issues within the scholarly and religious communities of Hinduism and remain ongoing subjects for debate. The difficulties in providing unequivocal answers to these questions touch the very heart of the concerns of the present work, making all of its conclusions and suggestions in some way tentative, dependent on the resolution of the question of what "Hinduism" is, and how are we to represent and portray it. That question will not be resolved with any finality in the short term; nor will the problems associated with Judaism's encounter with Hinduism. This does not make our efforts futile. It only places them in the proper context and points to a long process of clarification and thinking that must accompany the present endeavor.

There are several difficulties related to the challenge of constructing a definition of "Hinduism." We lack a historical tradition that conceptualized the religion or religions of India in these terms. It is mostly with the advent of modern studies of religion that "Hinduism" was born as a category.[7] While the category did draw on earlier forms of constructing the identity of a religious community, specifically in contrast with the religious identity of another community, the Muslim community,[8] we do not have any classical Hindu category that would correspond, from within, to the Western religious "ism" of "Hinduism". Indeed, this has been the subject of much contemporary apologetics, debate, and reflection, a significant part of which has taken the line that "Hinduism is not a religion, but…" By "religion," in such a phrase, one usually assumes a set of normative beliefs, common binding practices, and the unified self-identity of a religious community. None of these are universally available for "Hinduism."

Properly speaking, Hinduism could be described as a loose federation of religious traditions. These religious traditions can be quite disparate, or share common features, making them recognizable to each other as species of the same genus. Whatever the case, the relationship between these traditions is not always evident, necessary, and certainly not formal. Hence the immense variety within the beliefs and practices of the diverse religious groups that are lumped together by the external, and increasingly internal, viewer as "Hinduism." The variety pertains not only to the deities worshipped, an obvious consequence of polytheistic practice (as distinguished from belief), but also to the philosophical understanding of the religion, the chain of tradition and authority, the form of ritual practice and observance, the understanding of the goals and purposes of the religion, and more. Both theologically and ritually, the range of legitimate divergence is great. In terms of practice it certainly exceeds the range of legitimate divergence of practice within Judaism, probably even if heterodox groups and sects are included. Philosophically and theologically, the divergence is at least as large as that characterizing the differences between Jewish Philosophy and Kabbalah, probably even greater. Thus, historically, for thousands of years, complementary and partially overlapping religious traditions have been living alongside one another in a basic mode of mutual tolerance and acceptance, notwithstanding obvious intergroup tensions that might erupt from time to time.[9] As already mentioned, social stability and unity were provided by the social structure, rather than by the religious system, thereby allowing great leeway for acceptable differences between different religious traditions.

Attempts at identifying the core or common ground of Hinduism would depend on whether we adopt a descriptive or a normative perspective. From the descriptive angle, it is common to define Hinduism in relation to the acceptance and recognition of the Vedas as the fundamental scripture.[10] The Vedas provide the most universally agreed upon definition for Hinduism. However, not only does this definition not necessarily define the form or actual content of Hinduism, as practiced or believed, it also still leaves broad margins that are not covered. Different groups can be variously considered Hindu or non-Hindu, despite their lack of acceptance of the Veda's authority. Depending on perspectives prevalent at the time, Jainism and Sikhism may be considered as part of Hinduism or as autonomous religious traditions. Modern religious groups, such as the Brahma Kumaris, are in a similar situation. In some ways they are considered by others, as well as by themselves, as coming under the broad umbrella of Hinduism. In other ways, they insist on their autonomous status, outside the Hindu umbrella.[11] While all religions may have margins of ambiguity in terms of definition of membership within the religious group, it appears that "Hinduism" enjoys particularly broad margins, thereby complicating greatly any attempt at definition.

Religious traditions in India have been morphing for millennia. Complicated dynamics have been, and continue to be, at play. There are complex relations between North and South, between the great textual traditions and local practice,[12] between a pan-Indian religious norm and the specific religious practices and beliefs of a given locality. Obviously, it is easier to identify the common core that defines Hinduism when this is approached from the angle of a defined Scriptural tradition, a given set of practices, or a particular philosophical worldview. Thus, identifying "Hinduism" is itself part of the complex interplay of smaller and larger religious currents within the subcontinent. This interplay brings us back to the descriptive and normative perspectives. Adopting the descriptive perspective could mean that everything is Hinduism and heighten the sense of complexity, as well as strangeness, of that tradition. But the descriptive dimension itself cannot overlook the historical dynamics that point to the emergence of an increasingly unified Hindu tradition.

Hinduism, as all religions, has been changing for centuries, in response to the encounter with forces outside it. Under colonial rule, many changes took place in Indian religious life, either through legislation or through the challenges and opportunities presented by encounter with British culture and Christian religion. Internal reform has led to the formation of various religious movements and to new forms of Hindu identity. This is true not only for some of the explicitly reform movements, but also for the birth of new religious communities, some of which enjoy growing popularity. Thus, the Swaminarayan form of Hinduism, which has been described as the fastest growing form of Hinduism, is related to reform, to encounter with the British, and to new ways of recognizing and expressing the religious life of Hinduism.[13] A broad range of religious teachers over the past 150 years have helped shape the religious imagination of what Hinduism is, both in India itself and in the West, creating greater and greater convergence between different understandings of Hinduism. Other external forces have also greatly influenced a growing sense of a unified religious identity. Communications and media have played a great role in spreading religious knowledge and creating a common sense of ownership of many Hindu riches and practices. For example, the great popularity of the TV version of the great epic the Mahabharata is part of the broader movement of developing a common religious heritage, culture, and ultimately identity.

This movement is also greatly aided by demographic and sociological realities associated with migration and the emergence of a powerful Hindu diaspora.[14] Increasingly, when we think Hinduism, we no longer think exclusively within the Indian subcontinent, but within the global context, impacted by the presence of Hindus in most parts of the world. The Hindu diaspora plays an important role in the shaping of Hindu identity and will probably continue to do so in years ahead. Hindus from different localities, practicing different forms of Hinduism, believing in different deities, following different customs, and having diverse understandings of Hinduism itself are forced to share one common temple, one community, limited resources, and common challenges in a new environment.[15] Diaspora Hinduism is not a simple replica of Hinduism as practiced in the sub-continent. Rather, it functions as a means of synthesizing multiple traditions, preferring some over others, and of constructing some sense of a common Hindu identity. This new identity is then projected back to the homeland, through an ongoing two-way communication of ideas and practices. Diaspora Hinduism, one of the loci for Judaism's encounter with Hinduism, is thus itself a force in the shaping of Hindu identity and the concomitant understanding of what Hinduism is, how it functions, and the challenges it presents to Judaism. To take one note-worthy example, Vasudha Narayanan points to the fact that, in Diaspora, Hindus are challenged to explain what the idols they worship are and how they are to be understood. She notes that temple literature in the United States presents Hindu deities in ways that conflict with traditional practice, but make Hinduism more palatable to the Western audience. Idols are, accordingly, merely symbolic.[16] The issue is not whether temple pamphlets in North American temples are getting it theologically or ritually right or not. From the perspective of the present study, we are facing new articulations of core issues that have profound bearing on Judaism's encounter with Hinduism. It is not enough to dismiss certain voices as apologetic. Today's apologetics are tomorrow's faith, especially when it comes to a religious tradition that is as pliable and morphs as easily as Hinduism does. Diaspora thus presents us with new possibilities and opportunities for under-standing Hinduism, even as it continues to serve a unifying function with regard to Hinduism's own self-understanding.

But descriptive and normative cannot be separated, especially when we take into account the increasingly unified presentations of Hinduism, both in India and in the Diaspora. One of the realities associated with the increasing emergence of a unified Hindu self-understanding is the rise in the view of Hinduism from the perspective of a particular philosophical vantage point. Hindu teachers have been coming to the West, specifically to America, since the late nineteenth century, with the visit of Swami Vivekananda. This is considered by many to be a turning point in Hindu self-understanding and its view by and relations with other religions. His visit was followed by wave after wave of Hindu religious teachers who have propounded a particular image of Hinduism. This has done much to shape what "Hinduism" is for both Hindus and non-Hindus.

The voice of this movement is the voice of one of the schools of Indian philosophy, the voice of Vedanta, usually in its nondualistic form known as *Advaita Vedanta*. Followers of this philosophical school see theirs as the ultimate form of Hindu philosophy, incorporating all others within it. It is a monistic worldview that recognizes the unity of all being and sees all diversity, in life as well as in the Divine and its worship, as secondary phenomena, removed in some way from the ultimate reality, and accounted for by various philosophical explanations (illusion, divine play, and more). The figurehead of this line of teaching is the eighth-century teacher Sankara, who for many now functions as the authoritative and ultimate voice of what Hinduism is. It seems fair to suggest that the present-day representativity of Sankara's philosophy and how it has come to speak for increasingly larger portions of Hinduism, if not for all of it, is a phenomenon that is new and that the observer would not have witnessed several hundred years ago. Nevertheless, it is an important part of what Hinduism has become, how it is being represented, and in significant ways also of the course of its own internal evolution. The historical trajectory of Vedanta increasingly standing for Hinduism itself in a public way corresponds to Vedanta's own claims to be the fulfillment of religion and to offer the ultimate framework from within which to view religion. While vedantins are ready to apply this framework not only to Hinduism, but to all religions,[17] this perspective is primarily identified with the spiritual teaching of Hinduism and is thus increasingly viewed as the proper understanding of Hinduism.

Vedantins are in a doubly advantageous position. Their worldview is all inclusive, attempting to account for all forms of religious practice, including the lower, less philosophically informed practice of Hinduism, such as its various smaller, local manifestations.[18] Vedanta need not consider Hinduism as we see it as the final or perfect form of Hinduism. It considers Hinduism in the ideal, accommodates lower and imperfect forms of its religious life as stages along the way, and offers a narrative to bridge the two—the continuing chain of teachers who seek to offer the correct teaching and to elevate humanity to greater spiritual heights. It is thus a total worldview that integrates various expressions of Hinduism as it reflects upon their complex expressions and manifestations. Vedantins enjoy the additional advantage of having a voice, representation and recognition. Most of the major religious teachers of India are indebted to a vedantic understanding and appeal to it, even if they are not philosophically inclined themselves.[19] Thus, Advaita Vedanta has more of a voice in contemporary Hinduism than any other stream. For many, it has therefore come to represent Hinduism and to speak for it.

In the context of the contemporary Hindu encounter with Judaism, Vedanta has played a particularly important role. Not only is the form of Hinduism that many Israelis and Jews encounter that of Advaita Vedanta, but Vedanta's own semi-representative status also informs the diplomatic and more formal dialogue of Hinduism and Judaism. One of India's leading vedantic teachers, Swami Dayananda, has played an important role in gathering religious leaders of the different streams and schools under one organizational umbrella, the Hindu Dharma Acharya Sabha. Such an organizational umbrella serves the purposes of forging a common Hindu identity and making a constructive contribution to the understanding of what Hinduism is. The organizational umbrella is itself a novum, and this new body is itself one expression of the ongoing movement toward solidifying Hindu identity. This new body, under the leadership of Swami Dayananda, is also responsible for the recent formal dialogue of Hindu leaders with the Chief Rabbinate of Israel. In other words, the official voice of Hinduism, that which rabbinical leaders have been asked to relate to and to consider for purposes of dialogue, collaboration, and mutual recognition, is heavily marked by vedantic heritage. Thus, on a formal level, one important aspect of Judaism's encounter with Hinduism is heavily indebted to vedantic teaching and understanding. In one way, this is limiting of the broader Hindu experience. In another, this greatly aids the encounter, by providing an address, a worldview, and the kind of clearly marked identity and self-understanding that allows the dialogue to move forward. Representing Vedanta as Hinduism tilts the scales heavily in the direction of the normative, as opposed to the greater diversity, hence confusion, that arises from the purely descriptive presentation of Hinduism.

The tensions between the descriptive and normative perspectives have been the focus of much thought in the Academy and among those concerned with Hinduism's relations with world religions. The question has been framed as "Who Speaks for Hinduism?" This topic was discussed in a special issue of the *Journal of the American Academy of Religion,* and a broad range of scholars struggled to address this conundrum of Hindu religious identity.[20] The dozen or so contributions on this matter ultimately boil down to the two perspectives that have informed my own presentation—descriptive versus normative. Perhaps not surprisingly, many of the contributors opted, even if not explicitly, for the normative perspective. Their arguments are relevant to our own concerns. It is a broader question that is relevant for all religions—who speaks for the religions and who is best suited to represent them. A good argument can be made for theologians being the appropriate spokespersons, even if the task and form of theological reflection may change from tradition to tradition.[21] Each tradition has its specialists, those who are in charge of explaining the tradition, of making sense of it, and also of sharing and teaching this understanding. If we consider Judaism, do we turn to the layman (the practicing or nonpracticing layman?) or to the religious teacher, rabbi, or scholar, for an authoritative view of what Judaism is? The answer seems obvious. Why, then, should not the same apply to Hinduism? Granted, there are differences among Hindu teachers, but there are similarly differences between Jewish teachers as well.[22]

This is, of course, an idealistic view. It implicitly carries over social and hier-archical structures of one tradition to another. Hinduism may not operate like Judaism and Christianity and its scholars and philosophers may therefore not enjoy the same authoritative status. Given Hinduism's orthopraxic nature and the great diversity of understanding it accommodates, we may not be able to sug-gest one class of people as those who hold the keys to the ultimate or true under-standing of the tradition. Still, the question is powerful and this one particular answer does make sense. Let those who understand the tradition, or who claim to understand it, rather than those who simply practice it to one degree or another, speak for the tradition.

In another way this remains an idealistic portrayal. It already assumes some distinct notion of Hinduism to which scholars, teachers, and theologians belong. It overlooks the complexity of traditions, higher and lower, interweaving in seem-ingly endless permutations. The gap between the wealth of data on the ground and the theoretical discourse of theologians may be such that many Hindus may not recognize what is taught as their own. But is that a failure of theology or of education? Who holds the keys to a proper understanding of Hinduism? Indeed, is there such a true understanding?

These questions have not yet found their final resolution. Any reference to Hinduism in a comparative or dialogical context is thus implicated in these ques-tions of Hindu scholarship and Hindu identity. Accordingly, my own application of Hinduism will reflect some of the complexity in the term's usage. Indecision about and complexity of some of the fundamental issues involved in a Jewish view of Hindu worship can be attributed directly to the tensions resulting from the question of who speaks for Hinduism.

One final point should be added to a contemporary consideration of Hinduism that is particularly relevant both to the discussion of "Who Speaks for Hinduism" and to broader issues of contemporary Hindu identity, as well as of Jewish-Hindu relations. As we shall note below, some scholars have suggested that Hinduism and Judaism have some basic resemblances that make them closer to each other than other religions. These include their ethnic component and their nonmis-sionary nature. According to many, probably most classic, Hindu understand-ings, one cannot become a Hindu. Perhaps one of the characteristics that indeed distinguishes forms of Hinduism exported to the West is that these Hinduisms more readily accommodate converts and hence appeal to and draw members from other religious communities. If my understanding is correct, this was not the case for millennia, and seems to be a characteristic of more recent iterations of Hinduism.[23] If, in former times, to be Hindu was also to be South Asian, eth-nicity is less and less a factor in the constitution of Hindu identity.[24] This fact is of the greatest importance to the Jewish-Hindu encounter. A later chapter of this study will examine issues of identity and the challenges posed to Judaism by conversion of Jews to forms of Hinduism. It is important to recognize that this dimension of the encounter is itself entwined in the complex problems relating to Hindu identity, the legitimacy of its different forms and practices, and the continually changing expressions of Hindu religion.

6

Judaism and Hinduism: Insights from the Comparative Study of Religion

An encounter between religions is built upon the actual contact between individuals or groups from one religion and those of another. In this sense, Judaism's encounter with Hinduism is very recent, at least in terms of mass exposure and multiple possibilities for contact and encounter. This is not to say that there has not been any contact between the two religious traditions for the past two millennia or more. Rather, it is to suggest that the type of encounter that we see over the past decades is qualitatively different from those of earlier generations, some of which are discerned by historians of the traditions. These concern the traceable influence of ideas through which one tradition impacts another. While the present-day encounter is based on personal contact, the historian may point to contact that is not necessarily between people, groups, or living realities, but between ideas, concepts, images, and literatures. When it comes to tracing the Jewish-Hindu encounter in literary and philosophical terms, it is obvious that such an encounter is hundreds, maybe even thousands, of years old. The extent of literary, philosophical, and religious influence has not yet fully come to light.

Indian wisdom was transmitted primarily through Arab sources to Europe, where it was assimilated also by Jews, who belonged to the broader European culture. It is only recently that the question of the extent of Hindu influence on Jewish sources is being posed.[1] A gradually emerging field of study, designated as Indo-Judaic studies, seeks to trace the history of contact and influence of ideas between Judaism and Hinduism.[2]

A recent conversation I had with Moshe Idel, a leading scholar of Kabbalah, highlights the question of the extent of historical contact and how little we know about it. I mentioned to Moshe that I am working on Judaism's encounter with Hinduism, and that Nathan Katz had shared with me his own exchange with Idel. He was told by Idel that Yogic breathing techniques and mantras had made their way into the works of Abraham Abulafia. Idel replied to me by saying that in his view, we have not yet fully assessed the extent of Hinduism's impact on the

Kabbalah. He considers this impact to be much more far-reaching than hitherto assumed. He added that prior to studying Kabbalah, he had spent much time reading about Hinduism and that this prior formation was crucial in shaping his own vision of Kabbalah. The energetic understanding of Kabbalah, which is one of the hallmarks of his own reading of that tradition, is indebted to his study of Hinduism and to the possibilities this opened him up to. However, he has not articulated the relationships between the two traditions in a broad theoretical way, and the reader of his works will only encounter the occasional suggestion concerning the historical influence of Hindu sources on Judaism.[3] It thus seems that more time and more work will be needed before we can make available a fuller appreciation of the extent of Hinduism's conceptual, literary, and religious impact on Jewish sources, primarily in the medieval period.

Examining the literary sources of Judaism and Hinduism can also take us beyond the question of historical contact and influence. The two traditions can be studied and juxtaposed not only for purposes of identifying points of encounter, but also for the benefits of understanding that emerge from a comparative study. One of the major activities undertaken in the academic study of religion is comparative study. The comparativist approach is not dependent on the establishment of direct historical relations between traditions. In theory, anything can be compared with anything else. Of course, this poses the question of the meaning of the comparativist approach, when it should be applied, and how to appreciate its outcomes. These issues are fundamental to the comparative study of religion and are topics to which constant attention is being paid by the scholarly community.[4] Accordingly, we may consider applying the tools of the comparative study of religion to Hinduism and Judaism, independently of the question of historical contact between the two religions. In that case, what we learn will be in the realm of the phenomenology of religion and bring to our attention fundamental similarities and differences that will help shed light on and increase our understanding of both traditions. Perhaps the best example of this type of study is Barbara Holdrege's extensive comparativist examination of Torah and Veda, the core scriptures of the two traditions.[5] Holdrege does not rely on historical contact between the traditions in order to tease out the similarities between them. Hers is the most developed example of a growing scholarly trend that applies the comparativist approach to the study of Hinduism and Judaism.[6]

The comparativist approach, and to a certain extent the attempts to trace points of historical contact between the traditions, might have remained an intellectual exercise, of interest to the Academy, but not much beyond.[7] Viewed, however, from the perspective of Judaism's present encounter with Hinduism, these studies take on a new meaning.[8] Historical studies suggest various ways in which Judaism coped and adapted itself to earlier historical contact. Comparative studies provide us with the tools to approach the present-day encounter. They are something of a map that travelers on the path of encounter and dialogue may use. They suggest the broad contours of the religions, their commonalities and differences, and their possible points of convergence. In short, comparative studies provide a kind of theoretical foundation that can serve the present-day encounter.

Needless to say, not enough work has been done by comparativists to cover all that could be of consequence to the present encounter. However, some key insights have been articulated and I shall spell those out presently. But before doing so, I would like to point out that the relationship between academic comparativist exercises and the personal encounter of Jews with Hinduism (and to a much lesser degree of Hindus with Judaism) is a reciprocal movement. Graduates of the Israeli travel to India, as well as Jewish travelers from other countries, are feeders for the academic study of religion.[9] They carry into the Academy their interest, their experiences, and the impressions of their own personal encounter. We should therefore expect that in the coming years, possibly even decades, increasing attention will be paid to broad comparativist issues, as well as to attempts to retrace points of historical contact between the traditions. As I shall suggest in what follows, today's academic study is increasingly part and parcel of the broader encounter between Judaism and Hinduism.

As we seek to explore some of the comparativist insights, and how they relate to the challenges of dialogue and encounter, I would like to share some words of Charles Mopsik, following his own comparativist reflections on Kabbalah and Tantra:

> It is simply astounding that one's consciousness could interest one's neighbor and that the animation of one's modes of thought, when confronted with the conceptions of a religion under study, is capable of enriching parallel reflections and work. To compare is a constant endeavor of reflexive thought. Between systems of thought there can only be a living dialogue of knowing subjects; it is never a matter of an entomologist comparing the wings of butterflies.
>
> The principle aim of a study like this should be a kind of language of translation, which would permit the passage from one conceptual idiom to another. In this, the comparative scholar is only the precursor of a dialogue—for which he would have prepared the vocabulary and assured the syntax—between the religious consciousness of interlocutors in search of a common language. On this score, a long way—whose stumbling blocks should not be minimized—remains to be travelled between Jerusalem and Benares.[10]

Comparison and dialogue are distinct activities, but one paves the way for the other. Mopsik suggests one particularly important function of the comparativist scholar. He, or she, is a translator, allowing a transition from one conceptual idiom to another. We should not underestimate the importance of such translation work. One of the main challenges of dialogue and encounter are the overcoming of the sense of foreignness and strangeness. People entering a dialogue require the help of the scholar of religion to better understand what they are seeing, to not be led astray by external appearances, and to translate what they see into a cultural language they can understand. The work and the insights of historians and comparative scholars are thus crucial resources for the future of the Hindu-Jewish encounter.

The comparativist not only sets the stage for dialogue, he or she may actually be engaging in a type of dialogue that holds much promise. "Comparative Theology" is a subdiscipline of the study of religion that is very much on the rise.[11] The distinct contribution of Comparative Theology is that the comparativ-ist exercise is not limited to historical study, but seeks to clarify the theological meaning of two traditions, through a constructed conversation between them. While the conversation can be undertaken by two partners and thus constitute a dialogue, it can also be undertaken by a single scholar, who brings the two tra-ditions into conversation with one another. Hindu-Christian studies have ben-efited greatly from the theoretical and methodological advances made by Francis Clooney, a Jesuit priest and scholar, who has spent decades studying Hinduism and who, probably more than any other single author, has helped develop the con-temporary paradigm of Comparative Theology. The practitioner of Comparative Theology conducts a kind of interreligious dialogue within himself and within his own study. This is made possible when theological concerns become more central to the study of religious and theological texts than historical or literary concerns. The concern with the theological import of the text leads to an engage-ment with it on a theological level. A theological conversation and exchange ensues. This conversation may be an imagined conversation, which would pave the way for a real-life dialogue, serving it as a resource.[12] Alternatively, it may be conceived as a conversation taking place between two parts of the scholars' own religious consciousness. Not surprisingly, the work of Comparative Theology is closely related, in the lives of some of its practitioners, to issues of multiple reli-gious identity.[13] They manifest within their own person the encounter between the traditions that they seek to advance through their comparative theologi-cal work. I might add that practitioners of this method of study and reflection are typically Christian. I am not familiar with a Jewish scholar of Comparative Theology, and certainly not one who has engaged Hinduism in such a compara-tive theological encounter. In part this is because the discipline of Comparative Theology is still young and partially because the Jewish study of Hinduism too is still in its nascent stages. Furthermore, Jewish identity construction as well as the academic ethos of the Israeli Academy do not lend themselves easily to such dialogue and engagement taking place within the scholar's own internal world and religious imagination. Nevertheless, the existence of this mode of bringing together two traditions through engaged comparative reflection is sure to find an echo among Jewish scholars, perhaps even in relation to the Jewish study of and dialogue with Hinduism. Until it does, dialogue can still be served by application of, meditation upon, and extension of insights gained through the comparative study of religion. Let us now turn to some of those insights.

I would like to begin with some of the earliest comparativist remarks I have been able to locate, comparing Judaism and Hinduism. These were made by an important scholar of comparative religion, who was also one of the founding fathers of modern interreligious dialogue. A bishop in the Church of Sweden, Nathan Soderblom was also a great believer in the spiritual power of the com-parative study of religion and the testimony it offered to the living God manifest-ing Himself in all religions. His book is accordingly named *The Living God*, and its core insight is that the living God can be found in all religions.[14] In it is found a most insightful comparative presentation of Judaism and Hinduism. Actually, Soderblom does not present Judaism and Hinduism in the sense that we would use the two terms. Rather, he presents Mosaic religion on the one hand and vedantic religion on the other. It is, in some ways, a strange comparison to make, and we can excuse it when we take into account that it was acceptable in the religious and scholarly world of 80 years ago. Judaism did not cease with Mosaic religion, and it is obvious that there is more to Hinduism than Vedanta and the Upanishads. In fact, some of what Soderblom has to say would be offset by broadening the scope of Hinduism and Judaism. Despite how partial Soderblom's perspective is, he is still able to deliver some helpful and fundamental insights. What makes his analysis and insights so pertinent is precisely the position Vedanta occupies within contemporary presentations of Hinduism. Judaism in its turn still retains fundamental dynamics and emphases that were established in the biblical period. Hence the continuing relevance of Soderblom's analysis, despite its predefined scope. That Soderblom's insights could emerge from a very circumscribed view of both traditions may indicate how representative and characteristic they are of both traditions and of their eventual relations. In fact, one could go as far as to argue that contemporary Israeli and Jewish travel to India and its encounter with India's spiritual tradition are to a large extent driven spiritually precisely by the encounter between the two perspectives portrayed by Soderblom. Thus, these comparative insights could end up functioning as a map for real-life encounters 80 years and more after they were articulated.

One of Soderblom's opening statements is of great relevance for the continuing self-understanding of both Judaism and Hinduism and for their relations with other religions, as well as with each other. Israel and India are the two people, the two cultures, that are most closely related to religion. Major religions found their expressions respectively in Israel and in India, and these religions in turn inspired other religions.[15] India and Israel, or Hinduism and Judaism, are thus placed alongside one another as two foundational cultures, two centers of spirituality. We might take a moment to reflect upon this presentation. Consciously or not, we carry within us some sense of center and periphery, origin and growth, when we consider world religions. Jews certainly do, and they are located at the center. Traditionally, this has been conceived as the *historical center*, giving birth to other religions, the *geographic center*, in relation to the holiest of sacred spaces, and the *eschatological center*, to which all will gravitate in the eschaton, when Israel's message, teaching, and God will be known by all. While India has not received explicit attention in traditional Jewish views of center and periphery, in time and space, it too would be considered part of the periphery of humanity that will ultimately come to be absorbed within Israel's holy center. To speak of two centers, of two major cultures, and of two spiritual and historical sources from which all of humanity's religions draw is thus a very different perspective from the one that is typical of the Jewish religious view.

India and Israel are two parallel civilizations. Each contributes in its own way to humanity's spiritual evolution. Each has its own merit and values, and indeed, as Soderblom goes on to suggest, each represents a different type of religion. But the starting point is that neither represents absolute religion, final truth, or the only valid form of expression of humanity's religious life. This is an important perspective to consider as we embark upon a Jewish consideration of Hinduism.

It seems to me we are bound to approach it differently when we consider it a major world religious civilization, paralleling our own in import, scope of influence, and power of spirit, rather than just one more form of error, idolatry, or mistaken human religious invention. For the open-minded student who seeks to find the meaning of the present encounter of Judaism with Hinduism and to develop a historical and spiritual appreciation of the Hindu tradition as a basis for understanding the present encounter, one would do well to consider the starting point of the coming together of two ancient civilizations, each having its own unique religious profile and identity. Such a perspective provides a more appreciative framework that invites a consideration of the present encounter as the coming together of two equally respectable partners in dialogue.[16] It also makes it easier for us to identify complementarity, ways in which one religion may challenge the other, and consequently what it is that draws young Jews to Hinduism today and where the future enrichment of both religions, through the encounter, might take place.[17]

Soderblom suggests three characteristics that are common to Vedanta and to the prophetic religion of the Old Testament. The first is the unity of God. Both recognize that God is one. The second is the spirituality of God. This can take various expressions, either the recognition that God is beyond physical reality, which is recognized as an illusion, or that God cannot be contained or represented through physical means. The third is that God is the ultimate value, He is all, His being is sufficient for our happiness. These common recognitions express themselves in different ways in both religious cultures.

At the same time, Soderblom suggests the following profound differences between the two religious cultures. Tolerance and intolerance are a point of distinction between the exclusiveness of the Mosaic religion and the polytheism of Hindu religion. It is common for Hindu thinkers to present tolerance as one of the virtues and defining features of Hinduism. It is interesting to see how Soderblom too considers the attitudes of tolerance and intolerance to be no less important than the theological differences between the religions. Even when a higher religious insight arose in India, including the recognition of the ultimate unity of God, this higher insight never forced the choice of accepting it at the cost of rejecting another, lower, form of religious understanding. The lower was allowed to remain and flourish and was declared to be necessary and appropriate on its own level. Not so in the case of the Jewish religion.[18]

Mosaism's intolerance is related to other aspects of its particularity. One of its most striking features is the recognition of the activity of God. Communion with God in Israel is expressed in action and not in internal states. Hence, the powerful dramatic appeal and emotional intensity of the Bible. Soderblom in fact highlights the narrative quality of biblical theology and sees in it a constitutive element of the Jewish religion. While solitude and contemplation also find their place in biblical religion, we are never given a method of meditation intended to transport the soul into certain states of feeling.[19] Ultimately, even in solitude it is God who is active, rather than man who performs the appropriate exercises that might bring him into closer communion with God. Psychological analysis of states of mind and practice of internal control of the mind are the domain of the Hindu religion, not the Mosaic. Man's attention is not focused upon himself, but upon what God has done and will do. Accordingly, for the Jews, God appears as will. There is no need to search for Him through ascetic exercises. He is the Ruler of the universe and no one can escape Him. Soderblom concludes that religious exercises have less significance for biblical religion than they do for Hindu religion. Of course, this assumes a view of ritual that we may contest, one that is informed by Soderblom's own Protestant background. Still, even if we do consider the mitzvot to be a form of religious exercise and training, it seems clear that their primary significance draws from the fact that they are a way of fulfilling the commanded will of a personal God.[20] God's will is made manifest in a moral life, through love, and—once again revealing Soderblom's Protestant ethos—not through sacrifice. Trust and obedience are the hallmark of biblical religion. Old Testament ethics have scarcely any room for self-education. The training of the soul is not a major concern for prophetic religion. Contrast this with India, where patient observation of sense perceptions and states of the soul and the detailed instructions on the path of self-discipline are of central concern. What emerges is indeed a contrast between outward- and inward-directed religion.[21]

With will and obedience occupying the primary place they do, history becomes a major arena for the revelation of God and for His recognition. This is where we recognize how dramatic, living, and tangible are the religious life and the revelation of God. The prophets do not move in a timeless world of psychology and intellectual conceptions. God draws near through current events.

Ultimately the differences between the religious types portrayed by Soderblom are those between ascetic mystic and prophetic revelation. Religious exercise on the one hand, and fellowship with the living God on the other. The typology of prophecy and mysticism as constitutive of the differences between Judaism and Hinduism continues to be echoed in contemporary scholarship, and it remains one of the important perspectives through which each tradition continues to challenge and inspire the other, as we shall see presently.[22]

The various differences may be summed up with reference to a founded religion, which Judaism is and Hinduism is not. Judaism was created, it did not simply become. A founded religion confronts people with a choice between the old and the new, which is precisely what Judaism has done in relation to its predecessor religions and to a large extent in relation to all religions, Hinduism included, since.

While presenting these differences between the two types of religion, Soderblom is careful not to lose the balanced perspective in speaking of both. His concluding words accordingly are that "we are rather led to the conclusion that both mysticism in general and the particular revelation point to the reality and activity of God."[23] These two fundamental forms of religious life, mysticism and prophecy, thus complement each other and constitute two pillars or two primary expressions of the religious life of humanity, offering testimony to the presence of the living God.

Soderblom's analysis grows out of a comparison of biblical sources with upanishadic and vedantic teachings. It is worth noting that one of the most recent comparative exercises raises similar fundamental questions, despite a much more nuanced appreciation of the spiritual resources of Judaism. Braj Sinha explores notions of the divine anthropos and the cosmic tree in Jewish and Hindu sources.[24] The materials he works through certainly offset Soderblom's exclusively biblical emphasis. Sinha compares what seem to be equals, mystical traditions of both religions. Nevertheless, fundamental dynamics that distinguish between the traditions come across regardless of the specific literary corpus under examination, or the historical period studied. Surely the formative impact of biblical sources is such that structural differences distinguish the traditions, regardless of the particular stratum of tradition one studies. Accordingly, Sinha raises very similar concerns to those raised by Soderblom, that is, the Hindu tradition poses a fundamental challenge to the Jewish tradition precisely regarding the relation of the prophetic and mystical elements within the tradition.[25] Can mystical experience be recognized as a form of revelatory experience? Judaism, in turn, poses a prophetic challenge to Hindu mysticism: How does the mystic come back to this world from the realm of the transcendent? How is the world then engaged? The lack of a clearly formulated prophetic model within Hinduism makes this an acute challenge to the Hindu mystical tradition.[26]

I would like to now move from the earliest attempts to characterize the Jewish and Hindu religious traditions to one of the most recent attempts to do so. Jews usually think of Judaism in relation to either Christianity or Islam and often assume that Hinduism is distant and has little in common with Judaism, a view that is based on the failure to consider Hinduism as anything but a form of idolatry. Against such common perceptions, it is worth examining the typology of religions offered by Barbara Holdrege, whose work on Veda and Torah I have already referred to.[27] Holdrege seeks to identify other paradigms in the study of religion than those articulated from within the Protestant background that informs much of the modern study of religion. In so doing, she turns to Judaism and Hinduism as two traditions that can provide alternative categories for the study of religion. In the process, she also highlights similarities between them, leading her to identify the two religions as typologically similar.[28]

When making comparisons, one must specify what one is comparing. Significantly, unlike many of those who engage in comparisons of Judaism and Hinduism, Holdrege appeals neither to the Kabbalah nor to the vedantic tradition. Rather, she appeals to rabbinic Judaism, with its emphasis on ritual and its performance, and to Brahamanical Hinduism, with similar emphases—two elite textual communities that have codified their respective norms in the form of scriptural canons. But it is not only scripture and ritual that make these two communities similar. In both cases we are dealing with embodied communities, in which priority is given to issues of practice. Holdrege highlights the orthopraxic nature of both Judaism and Hinduism, where priority is given to right (ritual) action, rather than the correctness of belief. In fact, proper action provides the basis for enormous leeway in religious beliefs. Multiple systems of belief can be constructed, in both cases, upon the foundations of an agreed-upon ritual practice.

Both communities approach issues of religious identity in very similar terms. Clearly, law and religious observance play a paramount role in identity construction. Beyond that, we are dealing in both cases with identities embodied in ethnic and cultural categories. A particular ethnic community, a sacred language, social structure, and practices that are constituted in relation to the word embodied in scripture all make up the community's religious identity. Religious identity is not established in relation to general beliefs, but in relation to membership in particular ethnic communities, whose identities are themselves closely related to the geographic boundaries associated with these communities, whether or not these geographic boundaries are the present boundaries within which the community lives. All these lead to a further characterization that provides a common basis for Jewish and Hindu identity. Both are non-missionizing communities. Given the ethnic, territorial, and ritual dimensions of these communities and their identities, both may be characterized as non-missionary. In the broader framework of world religions, this is an important characterization. In fact, by the end of Holdrege's analysis, Judaism and Hinduism end up being the only two members in this class of religions. Hinduism and Judaism thus emerge as two religions particularly close to one another, when seen in the broader context of world religions. That mission and identity are among the defining features, proposed by Holdrege, is relevant to an appreciation of the contemporary convergence of interest of Hindu and Jewish religious leadership.[29] I will return to this point when analyzing the declarations of the two Hindu-Jewish leadership summits.

Holdrege's Hinduism, or rather the form of Hinduism that she highlights, is at odds, in many important ways, with modern and contemporary forms of Hinduism, expounded in the West and increasingly in India itself.[30] That Hinduism is indeed often missionary. Significantly, it highlights ideas, a worldview, and the correct view of reality. Its teaching is not circumscribed ethnically, linguistically, or geographically. Indeed, one might go as far as to say that two different forms of Hinduism are encountered by Judaism, depending on the time and place of the encounter. This is where the general rubric of "Hinduism" is so misleading, for it assumes a unified reality that never existed. For purposes of comparison and encounter we seem to be dealing with disparate, perhaps even contradictory, realities when we consider different forms of Hinduism and their relation to Judaism. Vedantic, philosophical, and mystical Hinduism are encountered mainly in the West, mainly through great teachers and their writings. Brahmanical Hinduism is encountered in the homes, villages, temples, in the law manuals, and traditional ways of Indian society, primarily in India itself, and secondarily in the Indian diaspora. Each of these meets Judaism and challenges it in different ways. And, as is often the case, these two types are not necessarily encountered in their pure form, but through any number of permutations that combine these ideal types.

It seems to me that both the comparative-descriptive work and the actual encounter with Hindu religious life can take place in relation to one of the two types. It seems to me further that this presentation of two types of Hinduism allows us to more readily identify not only the points of theoretical intersection between the traditions, but also the points of mutual enrichment that occur through the present Jewish encounter with Hinduism. Most of the encounter between Hinduism and Judaism, whether that of scholars or of members of both communities, takes place in relation to one of two primary foci: ritual practice and mysticism.[31] Similarly, most of what has been written concerning the relation between the two traditions falls under one of these categories.[32]

Sacrifices are the classical and most fundamental form of ritual. We find some interesting comparative discussions of sacrifice in Jewish and Hindu contexts.[33] Some of the Hindu polemic against Christianity has even been reconstructed in the context of an imagined Jewish-Hindu exchange. Interestingly, the polemic against Christianity picks up on tensions between Judaism and Christianity and brings to light Jewish notions expressed in its own polemic with Christianity. A consequence of applying this polemical strategy is the identification of affinities between Judaism and Hinduism.[34]

Temples and sacrifices are one of the elements of Hindu religion that strike Israelis the most. Thus, Melila Hellner-Eshed, herself a scholar of Judaism, speaks of the encounter with this dimension of Hinduism as one of the most important elements in her frequent travels to India.[35] I might add to this the testimony of my own son, Neriya, and his fascination with sacrificial practices in a Hindu sanctuary in Nepal. Neriya had just completed his study of the entire Talmud, including the portion of the Talmud that deals with sacrifices and Temple rituals. I was surprised by how interesting he found Hindu sacrificial practices. But then it was really the first time he could witness the kind of activity that he had spent so much time studying, but could never witness, as Judaism no longer practices animal sacrifices. The enormous difference in the details of the ritual, not to mention the theological chasm regarding the recipient of the sacrifices, seemed to matter less than the phenomenological similarity of engaging in similar types of religious activity. It seems to me that this is indeed one of the great discoveries that India holds in store for the Jewish student, especially the religiously erudite student. In India one encounters forms of religious life that are still practiced with fervor and vitality, long after they have become subjects of mere theoretical study in the Jewish house of learning. Such encounter has the potential for bringing renewed spiritual interest and vitality to the approach to these subjects in a Jewish context. Let me quote Hellner-Eshed:

The greatest novum was probably my encounter with the Indian Temple culture. So much of what I had learned in the Bible and in rabbinic literature regarding the Temple, was now present to my eyes. The Bible's descriptions of the Tabernacle and the Temple, the priests and the offering of sacrifices, the holy, the fire, the descriptions in tannaitic literature that describe the world of the Temple, whether these represented what they saw with their own eyes, or whether those represented the Temple as it was portrayed in their mythical imagination, full of longing—all these suddenly seemed real. The visit to India made me encounter a culture of temples that had not undergone an external crisis and had not been exiled from its native locality, an ancient culture, that continued to exist and be transformed throughout hundred and thousands of years, and in its heart temples, of all sorts....Encounter with Temple culture, beyond the wonder it had in and of itself, was for me a kind of encounter with images that remind me of things that belong to the culture and the history of my own people, that were not accessible to me in such a direct and unmediated form, but only through the mediation of biblical and tannaitic texts. This encounter brought me to a new understanding of the power and the feeling of certitude that the presence of a Temple, where the reality of the Divine[36] is so direct and available, makes possible.[37]

Thus, one important fruit of the encounter emerges from both the comparative and the testimonial sources—bringing new life, vitality, and understanding to portions of the tradition shared by both religions. Rituals are particularly relevant in this context. We Jews are not always aware of the spiritual power of the rituals we possess, some of which we can no longer practice. It is only when these are encountered through the parallel reality of India that we can transform our view and enliven our understanding. Recognition of the commonalities fundamental to Judaism and Hinduism can thus lead to a renewed appreciation of aspects of Jewish life, tradition, and heritage.

The second arena in which one notes comparative work, continuing interest, and the promise of much future mutual enrichment is the area of mysticism. Interest in the mystical dimension as common ground or meeting ground is mostly motivated by the vedantic perspective of Hinduism, but not exclusively so. To some degree or the other, anyone interested in the spiritual, rather than ritual, parallels and encounters between Judaism and Hinduism gravitates toward the Jewish mystical tradition, in search of these parallels and a common language. Perhaps this is less a result of the actual contents of the kabbalistic tradition and more a consequence of the application of the intuitive distinction between law and ritual, on the one hand, and spirituality and mysticism, on the other. To the extent that one conceives of these as distinct domains, possibly even in tension with one another, one will consider Judaism in such terms as well, and therefore turn to its mystical resources as parallels to the mystical resources of other traditions. It is thus conceivable that some of the attention that kabbalistic and other materials from the Jewish spiritual tradition receive by writers who explore parallels between Judaism and Hinduism says as much about the writers and their presuppositions as it does about the Jewish mystical tradition itself.[38] In theory, some of what these writers seek by way of parallel may be found in other bodies of Jewish literature, such as pietistic or philosophical literature. Especially given how philosophical the Hindu tradition itself is, it seems striking that no comparative work has been undertaken between the two philosophical traditions.[39] The image of India as a land of wisdom and the possibility of approaching Hinduism as a wisdom tradition, that we shall explore later, would lend further credence to an attempt to contrast the Jewish and Hindu philosophical wisdom traditions. Instead, what little comparative work has been done seems to have been undertaken exclusively in relation to Kabbalah. We find some serious study of Kabbalah alongside repeated appeal to the tradition of Kabbalah, by authors whose knowledge of it is secondary and not extensive.[40] It may therefore be that the appeal to Jewish mysticism is a common conviction, maybe even a prejudice, that characterizes seekers and writers who consider that the Kabbalah is the literature to which they would have turned as seekers and to which they should turn as scholars and writers. Maybe over time this will turn out to be an opinion that is in need of redressing through a more balanced appreciation of both Jewish and Hindu sources, seen in context. In the meantime, however, let us note some of the attention that Kabbalah has received in the context of comparative Jewish-Hindu studies.

The list of comparative studies that contrasts themes in Judaism and Hinduism is not very long. I doubt that it has as many as 20 items, and if the number is greater, then certainly not by much. Probably at least half the comparative studies refer to Kabbalah, when relating to the Jewish side of the equation. If my impressionistic statistics are correct, this is an extremely high percentage. Kabbalah studies certainly do not amount to half of the total of studies written in the context of Jewish studies. It is also worth noting that a good portion of the most extensive comparative work undertaken to date, Holdrege's study of Torah and Veda, is devoted to kabbalistic materials. I have already noted the comparison undertaken by Braj Sinha, between kabbalistic and vedic and upanishadic presentations of the cosmic tree and the primordial man.[41] We also have attempts to engage in comparative presentations of individual mystics and their biographies.[42] Some of the works comparing Hinduism and Judaism, with special emphasis upon Kabbalah, will be dealt with in detail further along in this study.[43] One might also note that other than Holdrege's study of Torah and Veda, the only monograph-length study relating aspects of Judaism and Hinduism is a work titled *The Holy Name: Mysticism in Judaism*. This is a very problematic work, certainly not a scholarly comparison, and it will be dealt with in detail in a later part of this book.[44] But for present purposes it is telling that the author turns to the Jewish mystical tradition as the way of introducing or bridging the two traditions.[45]

One should not assume that only scholars with second-hand knowledge engage in such comparative work. The earliest collection of comparative Jewish-Hindu studies, *Between Benares and Jerusalem*, edited by Hananya Goodman, made an explicit effort to bring a scholar of Kabbalah and a scholar of Tantra in dialogue with one another. The dialogue is created by the very juxtaposition of the same theme, Unity and Union, in both traditions. The scholar of Kabbalah, Charles Mopsik, also engaged in important comparative observations, relating to Kabbalah and Tantra.[46] And it is not superfluous to remind ourselves again of Moshe Idel's recent sharing with me, in which he acknowledged the centrality of Hinduism to the history of Kabbalah, as well as to its phenomenology. Idel noted the energetic dimension of Kabbalah, which is best understood in light of Hindu traditions. The comparison with tantric sources is almost mandated, if we seek to account for the place of sexuality in the practice and theory of both traditions. But perhaps more than anything we must recall the centrality of the Shekhina in the kabbalistic tradition. The centrality of the Shekhina for kabbalistic reflection cannot be overstated. She is the heart of the kabbalistic process, for the major kabbalistic schools. The workings, power, and history of the divine feminine are the soul of Kabbalah and its spiritual quest. While an important attempt has been made to point to the parallel rise in the centrality of the Shekinha in kabbalistic literature and the rise of the figure of the Virgin Mary in medieval devotion,[47] it seems to me quite obvious that the most significant parallels to the Shekhina will be found not in the Christian milieu, but rather in the context of Hindu representations of the Divine.[48] Whether such parallels are best attributed to historical influence or to common fundamental insights relating to the nature of the Divine, stemming from similar or parallel spiritual experience, is a matter for future research and reflection. For the time being, we possess two preliminary studies that point to phenomenological parallels and that provide entry points into what seems to me a vital area requiring more sustained study.[49] As these and other issues come into clearer focus, we will be able to speak with greater clarity about the comparative parameters of Hindu and Jewish mysticism.[50]

7

The Passage to India: The Quest for Spirituality

It is impossible today to consider the attraction that India holds for Israelis and Jews without referring to the term "spirituality." It may well be argued that this term holds the key to the encounter and to its importance. For Indian spiritual teachers this is indeed the message that India has to offer the world. Swami Vivekananda has famously contrasted the material West to spiritual India.[1] India is thus constructed as a beacon of spirituality, emanating into a world caught up in materialism. Clearly, this juxtaposition may be relevant for many seekers, including Jewish seekers, who find in the religious forms they encounter in India an alternative to the materialism of the culture that surrounds them. Nevertheless, it would be a gross oversimplification to portray Judaism's encounter with Hinduism simply as an encounter with spirituality and an opportunity to redress imbalances in another religion or culture.

Let us consider how we use the term "spirituality." Vivekananda's usage juxtaposes spiritual and material, suggesting that India is spiritual. Surely, the contemporary visitor to India is not going to be confronted by a nonmaterial culture or society. If anything, the opposite is the case. Indeed, much of what drives Israeli traffic to India are some of the material possibilities—licit and illicit—that the subcontinent makes possible. The past 20 years, during which mass Israeli exposure to India took place, are, if anything, a time of surging ahead materially for the subcontinent, not a time of rediscovery of its spiritual values. One of the things that struck me the most when I first visited India was not just how material India really is, but how it is no different in terms of its ailments, worries, and need for spiritual guidance than the West. The teachings of Sri Sri Ravi Shankar, my first host in India, took on a new context, when considered in his native India. It was no longer the Indian guru who offers spiritual solutions to the ailing West. Indian society was as much, if not more, in need of the same medicine that was being offered to foreigners. Problems of modern life and society were as relevant to urban India as they were to New York and London.

The following anecdote is telling. One day I found myself on an Indian airplane, in the middle seat, between a Hindu businessman and a Christian diplomat. Some problems kept us on the ground for a very long time, and this provided an occasion for conversation. Most of my exchanges were with the Christian diplomat and they revolved around spiritual issues and my own interfaith work. Toward the end of the flight the Indian businessman made what for me was a startling comment. He said: "I have been on hundreds of flights, and this is the first time that I witness or participate in a spiritual exchange on board." I objected this could not be possible. After all this is India, a land renown for its spirituality. He replied saying that in fact India is as material as any other place. However, there is always the openness for spiritual engagement, deeply embedded within the culture, so that when spiritual voices are heard, one is receptive to them. This may be the most succinct way of capturing the spiritual-material paradox of present-day India.

The recent wave of Jewish exposure to India cannot be subsumed under the spiritual-material dichotomy, if for no other reason than because many of the people who take part in it are already involved in significant ways in pursuing a spiritual life. What leads them to India is not the quest for an antidote to modern materialism. The answer is better found through a comparison of the type of religious life that characterizes their Judaism and the kind of spiritual life to which they have exposure in India. To appreciate this let us return to Soderblom's description of the differences between the foundations of Judaism, Mosaic religion as he calls it, and the spiritual tradition of Hinduism, as it is expressed through the Upanishads and the philosophy of Vedanta. Soderblom points out that the Divine is encountered in Israel through the will of God, orienting life and society and finding expression in history. Soderblom's description may be augmented by reference to the collective nature of the Jewish covenant and Jewish religion, that is, to the community that has received the particular revelation and that follows the exclusive faith demands of Mosaic religion. Following the revealed will of God, made manifest in history, through membership in a community, is a fair characterization of the starting point of Jewish religion. This may be contrasted with the examination of states of mind, and soul, exercises in self-training and in orienting one's life toward awareness of internal states, leading to transformation of consciousness and union with the Divine. This juxtaposition of prophecy and mysticism, even if simplified, can provide us with a key to what India has to offer the Jewish seeker and how that is indeed related to spirituality.

What religion means, how it is practiced, and how it is represented can lead to nearly opposite experiences in both religions. I am not suggesting that Judaism does not have subtle psychological analysis, training of the mind, and complex metaphysical understanding. Nor am I suggesting that Hinduism is devoid of the public expressions of religion, its social structures, and the ways in which religion can fail to touch the heart and soul. Much of brahmanical Hinduism, to which Holdrege has introduced us,[2] and the greater part of what goes on in Hindu homes and temples may be no more "spiritual" than its Jewish counterpart. But at the very least we have here a public-relations issue, probably more. Jews often tend to emphasize, in terms of identity, in terms of practice, and in terms of education, those very elements of their religion that highlight community, history, and outward-oriented activity. In other words, most of religion is lived in the outer world and in relation to it. By contrast, Hinduism can be presented and constructed highlighting precisely the opposite qualities, the interior, subjective dimensions of consciousness, their evolution, and ultimately the subjective quest for God and encounter with Him. In part, the difference stems from the complexities of presenting Hinduism(s) and Judaism(s). While it is almost impossible to present Judaism without its objective, social, active side, it is perfectly possible for both scholars, like Soderblom, and practitioners, like most contemporary Hindu religious teachers, to present the message of their tradition as the internal quest for God, for interiority—in short, for spirituality. Thus, the Jewish encounter with Hinduism takes on a particular flavor when it comes to spirituality. In this context "spirituality" should be considered not as the antidote to materialism, with the concomitant axiological valuation of good and bad, positive and negative. Rather, spirituality may be found as the alternative, but more important—complementary—form of religious life and practice that fills in the very gaps and addresses the very needs that for many are left unanswered by the public and outward expressions of Jewish religion.

It is notable that the term "spirituality" is completely absent from Soderblom's presentation. The term was not yet in vogue when he wrote. Today, we cannot talk of the encounter between these two religions without using the term and without considering its implications. But it is precisely because the term touches on an area of great significance and is, at the same time, taken for granted that we should devote a moment to consider its different uses. Let me preface the following by saying that "spirituality" is one of the least defined terms in our religious vocabulary that, consequently, different people use in different ways, and that the attempts to define it in scholarly literature are so numerous and diverse as to make one give up on the possibility of a single agreed-upon usage of the term.[3] In what follows, I refer to three uses of the term. We have already encountered one use, that represented by Swami Vivekananda who contrasts materialism and spirituality. Some contemporary Hindu teachers continue to use "spirituality" as a reference to the spiritual life in general. I have remarked on several occasions how Mata Amritanandamayi uses "spirituality" in the broadest, and consequently least precise, sense.[4] When used in this way, it is difficult to argue that Hinduism has anything that is so singularly unique, compared to Judaism. Both traditions espouse the spiritual life and teach that the spiritual and religious life is superior to the material life; both traditions espouse fundamental values, all of which could be subsumed under "spirituality," when we conceive of it in such broad terms.

There is a second sense of spirituality that grows out of medieval uses, found in Jewish literature, especially as it reflects Arabic usage. *Ruhaniyut*, the conventional translation for spirituality, is used to describe the capturing of energies, astral realities, and things that transcend the physical, through the instruments of religion, or through other physical means.[5] This usage belongs to a former period and literature and is not usually carried over to ordinary contemporary usage. However, it is particularly relevant to the present discussion and to a certain extent can also account for the dynamics of the Jewish encounter with Hinduism, in terms of spirituality. The usage assumes a twofold approach to reality, a physical basis or substratum, and a spiritual-astral, energetic, or a level otherwise transcending the physical. Unlike the first usage, which refers to the material and spiritual as ways of living, as values and as philosophies, this usage recognizes that the religious and spiritual life itself involves a coming together of the physical and the spiritual, where specific physical acts and objects can be the foundation through which a higher form of life can come through. This energetic understanding is important in that it touches upon an ongoing quest of Jewish religious practice, that of transcending the domain of the physical action or object and grounding a higher spiritual form within the physical order. The fulfillment of the mitzvot is often understood as an attempt to ground in the physical domain a higher form of life, whose quality may be referred to in terms of Ruhaniyut, spirituality. The quest for Ruhaniyut is accordingly a quest for complementing or transcending the mere physicality of classical Jewish religious practice and recognizing it as a vehicle for higher spiritual reality. It seems to me that precisely such a drive is characteristic of much of what religiously minded and observant Jews are seeking when they explore the spiritual possibilities of India and of Hinduism. Whether they are aware of the methods of transcendence practiced within Judaism or not, they turn to other religious traditions, to other practices, to meditations and various techniques, in an attempt to gain access to another domain of reality that would complement the physical. This complementarity may apply to various forms of daily living and being in the body, as well as to the physicality of the Jewish religious life, to which they are accustomed and which they seek to transcend, by enriching physical practices with new energetic qualities. To the extent that India plays a role in this quest, it is because one of the dimensions of "spirituality" in the Indian context involves the kind of energetic nuance that one encounters less frequently within Judaism.

If the second dimension of "spirituality" was energetic, I would refer to the third dimension of "spirituality" in terms of awareness and consciousness. Let us return, once again, to Soderblom. What characterizes India, according to Soderblom, is the careful psychological attention to states of mind and soul, to internal spiritual processes, to spiritual progress. This awareness leads, in turn, to regular and structured exercises and methods that help take the mind from one state to another. This focused, intentional, and self-aware dimension of internal spiritual practice is closely related to spirituality, as the term is used nowadays. In biblical materials, Soderblom notes, there are no ladders of ascent, no exercises, no systematic instructions on how to progress internally toward the interior spiritual high places. This forms a powerful contrast between the aspects of Hinduism and Judaism described by him. Now, Jewish spiritual literature has come a long way since the biblical period, described by Soderblom. Interiority has found more articulate and systematic expressions, internal states have been identified, named, and discussed, and manuals of instruction have been composed to guide the seeker on the path of the interior spiritual life. And yet, the overall economy of the religion did not change. Judaism has been able to make room for this kind of self-aware interiority and closely guided spiritual process, but it is always experienced within the broader conventions through which the religion is constituted. More significantly, these complementary teachings and processes are beyond the reach of many Jewish seekers, either due to assimilation, ignorance, or due to the fact that they are practiced only within fairly small circles of kabbalists and hassidim, almost exclusively male. They are therefore contained sociologically, religiously, and even in terms of gender in ways that do not make them known or accessible to all. Most rabbis serving communities, even Orthodox Jewish communities, would not be aware of these spiritual treasures of Judaism, and even if they are, they would only know of them through second-hand anthologies and translations, not through direct experiences or living relationships within a community or within a master-disciple relationship. All this suggests that these spiritual practices are not part of the common perception of Judaism. Spiritual seekers who wish to bring a more systematic and self-aware quality to their internal growth will, therefore, naturally find it easier to do so outside the framework of the core practices of Judaism. The spiritual traditions imported to the West from Hinduism are excellent candidates for filling this vacuum in the common perception of Judaism.

I would like to now turn to how the term is being used in the academic context of the study of spirituality, an emerging area of study, that has gained much prominence over the past several decades. It is within the emergence of this sub-discipline that multiple definitions for what "spirituality" is have been offered. There is significant overlap between the different definitions, with meaningful nuances distinguishing the different understandings. For purposes of the present discussion, I would like to share the working definition of "spirituality" proposed by Sandra Schneiders, one of the leading figures in the academic study of spirituality. Clearly, her own definition may be heavily informed, as is the entire field, by Christian spirituality. Nevertheless, the concerns and fundamental questions, as well as the proposed answers, cut across religious traditions and make it possible to use insights that grow on the soil of Christian spirituality in a broader comparative context. Schneiders defines spirituality as follows: "Spirituality is the experience of conscious involvement in the project of life-integration through self-transcendence toward the ultimate value one perceives."[6] This definition of spirituality is helpful for an understanding of what makes so much of Hindu spiritual practices what they are and of the secret of their appeal for Jewish audiences. Experience is a key word. The starting point of this definition is experience, rather than practice, ritual, or philosophy. The experience is experienced as something conscious. Appeals to consciousness and self-awareness are the very foundations of so many of the systems of meditation and practice inspired by Hindu tradition as to be considered constitutive of these methods. Self-transcendence is another important feature of this definition. The term itself does not, in and of itself, carry metaphysical baggage. It can relate equally to social groups, to ideals, and values, etc., and need not refer explicitly to metaphysical transcendence. But in the Hindu context this is the most common form of transcendence, and coupled with experience and self-awareness, we have a potent combination of core elements that define a particular approach to the spiritual life and make that approach highly appealing. It is fair to include other elements of Schneider's definition in an assessment of Hindu practices as well—life integration and ultimate values. The former is the focus of many methods and practices, not the least of which is the practice of Hatha Yoga, which is founded upon an understanding of the integration of body and spirit. That these elements are integrated into methods and systems that seek to take the believer to what is perceived as the ultimate value goes without saying. Now, it is perfectly possible to construct Jewish practices in similar terms, to see them as fulfilling the very goals referred to by Schneiders. But this may not be as obvious to spiritual seekers, especially if these values have not been recognized as constitutive of the Judaism they know. Hindu practices conform more readily to such a definition. If what one is seeking is indeed a "spirituality," consisting of self-awareness, experience, life integration, self-transcendence, and ultimate value, many seekers will more readily identify this experience in the forms of Hinduism presented to them than they would in the common forms of Judaism. In this description lies an assessment of a process, a problem (for Judaism), and possibly also the strategy that Judaism should follow in addressing this issue.

The above discussion assumed that Jewish seekers are able to satisfy a thirst, a need, or a personal quest through their encounter with Hindu spirituality. The model is then one of question-need and answer-fulfillment of that need. This model can be played out variously, and there are obviously great differences in how different seekers might be enriched by their encounter with Hinduism in terms of spirituality, particularly in the sense developed by Schneider. I would like to note here how one Jewish seeker found a way of moving back and forth between the traditions. I have already mentioned Elhanan Nir, a teacher of Hassidism and an Orthodox Jew, in whose spiritual life India has played an important role. Nir offers us one model of how spirituality can be lived between the two traditions. One tradition poses the question, the other answers. This model could be variously applied, and probably it is often the case that the question (search for God, spiritual reality etc.), is posed by Judaism and answered (in terms of method and path) by Hinduism. Nir himself applies the paradigm differently. Hinduism poses the questions, the challenges. These challenges allow the seeker to recognize that the answers are present within Judaism and thereby to develop a deeper appreciation for Judaism. Nir describes his own process in response to the questions posed by J. Krishnamurti: "Is there a time of non-movement? Is there timeless action?" Nir is awakened to the realization that Shabbat is the time that is beyond time, a traffic island in the din of the roads, a time not contained in the framework of time.[7] But in a significant twist of thought, Nir concludes with the afterthought: "On second thought: India is apparently the Sabbath of the Western World." Nir's approach is thus non-apologetic and fully open to the spirituality of both traditions and to their complementarity and mutual enrichment. Nir describes ways in which he experiences or considers Jewish and Hindu spirituality to be complementary, like the question and answer model. One teaches how to ascend; the other teaches how to descend back into the world.[8]

Regardless of how this is conceived, the basic process is one in which the Jewish spiritual quest is carried out, for some even fulfilled, through a profound encounter with Hinduism. This is, by now, a social movement and an ideological process that can be described. It is carried out not only in India, but also in Israel, among the alumni of the rite of passage to India.[9] Shalva Weil has commented on some of the spiritual festivals that have come into vogue over the past decade. One of them, playfully titled boombamehla, echoing the Hindu celebration of the Kumbh Mela, provides an outlet for the spiritual needs of the young generation of alumni. The festival brings together Hindu and Jewish elements of practice and celebration. Weil goes as far as to consider these practices syncretistic. Weil argues that the core concern that is emerging is spirituality, and it is the search for spirituality that is impacting Orthodoxy, as well as broader Jewish society.[10]

Turning to India for spirituality, posing the questions from within Judaism, and seeking the answers from Hindu sources, and vice versa, may be taken as a sign of crisis. Of course, crisis contains opportunity and holds within it the promise of growth. While this type of spiritual encounter may be driven by the desire for growth, it is nevertheless fed by dimensions of crisis within Jewish spiritual reality. Talk of spirituality might veil what could be considered the greatest aspect of Jewish spiritual crisis and an important component in the spiritual turning towards India. This is the crisis of God and the ability to find Him within Judaism. I would like to devote the following reflections to this issue.

Different people would identify the crisis that Judaism is presently experiencing in different terms. Some would see it in terms of identity, others in terms of continuity, still others might conceive of it in terms of either learning or practice. In the present context, I would like to argue that Judaism's deepest crisis concerns God. Judaism is a religion that centers around God, but that has lost touch, to a large extent, with the living God.[11] God has not lost touch with Judaism, nor have the people of Israel lost their faith in God. But Judaism has lost, to a significant extent, the awareness of God at its center and the ability to structure the entire life of the religious community around access to the divine presence and its grounding in the community's life. This loss has deep historical roots, and it may be a consequence of the destruction of the Temple, the loss of prophecy, and a long history of exile. This loss is, to my mind, contained in what kabbalists speak of when they refer to the exile of the Shekhina.

Jews are faithful people and people of faith. But their religious life is presently constructed in such a way that other religious values occupy a place of primary significance, often eclipsing God's centrality within the economy of the religious system. The Zohar speaks of the union of the Torah, Israel, and God. They are, says the Zohar, all one.[12] In one way this could be taken as a beautiful way of expressing the unity of all values within the Divine. In another way, the union these values enjoy with the Divine could lead to their becoming primary foci of religious attention and devotion, at the expense of God as the ultimate goal of the spiritual quest. To a large extent, this is precisely what has happened. Torah study and excellence in the observance of the mitzvot have become hallmarks of religious achievement. Jewish religious society values learning and intellectual prowess, often at the expense of direct relationship with God. It is not simply a matter of valuation, but of how education is structured, what goals are set before future religious virtuosi, and consequently of what type of greatness is produced. Religious education has little to offer by way of training to achieve closeness or communion with God. Prayer education is almost nonexistent. In the early school years it consists of training in how to perform the prayer rituals successfully. But there is virtually nothing in religious training concerning how prayer should function from a spiritual perspective, how it should lead to communion with God and to self-transformation in God's presence. The amount of attention paid to proper performance of detail and to excellence in performance and learning in general is completely disproportionate with any instruction that would relate to the interior aspects of the religious and spiritual life.

Not all Jews are religiously observant. For those who are not, much of Jewish life and identity are channeled through the other great religious ideal—Israel. Israel, the people, their life, history, international present and future well-being, and, above all, their continuity are the issues that are uppermost in the minds of Jewish organizations and international leadership. If we wish to find the fullest spiritual meaning of these concerns, it is readily available to us through statements such as that of the Zohar, which affirms that involvement with Israel, its life and well-being, is tantamount to engagement with the Divine. For those who seek to live a life divine and to cultivate a spiritual language that would allow them to care for the community at large without removing themselves from their divine pursuits, such a language is readily available. Indeed, Judaism offers an integrated spiritual vision that includes individual and community, past, present and future, reflection and action, spiritual and earthly—all in one integrated worldview and spiritual path. The path itself may have the needed integrity and balance between its various components. But as it is practiced, we recognize great imbalances. These amount to the emphasis on parts of the system at the expense of the whole and, above all, at the expense of what should be its true spiritual center—God.

The exile of God, His hiding, the difficulty in finding or accessing Him—regardless of how we conceptualize the crisis—seem to me to be at the heart of the crisis of Jewish spirituality. And it is only when we are able to confront the fact that we are in crisis that we may consider what the Jewish encounter with India seeks to heal. What has been already stated above may now be reformulated. It is not simply that Jews find a kind of spirituality in India that addresses a deep hunger in their souls. More fundamentally, India provides opportunities for a direct approach to God that is often lacking in Judaism. It is this approach to God that is perhaps the hallmark of India's spiritual life and the source of Jewish attraction to India's religious life.

When we Jews conceive of the goals of the religious life, few of us would place communion or relationship with God at the top of our ladder of quest, let alone consider it as the only thing worth desiring. We seek happiness, family life, the well-being of our spiritual group, a life of values, learning, and overall flourishing. God plays a meaningful part in this package of ideals. But for very few God is actually the central focus of their Jewish quest. And here India provides so many opportunities for an alternative testimony that it comes to represent that in the eyes of many. Indeed, the very goal of the spiritual life, as stated by so many spiritual teachers of the Hindu tradition, says it all: God realization. Perhaps not all realize what God realization means. Perhaps very few attain it. But it is a central governing ideal that informs the lives of thousands, if not millions, of spiritual seekers. Hinduism, as encountered through various teachers and religious groups, offers God at the center and a systematic path to reach knowledge and awareness of God. I submit this is what draws Jewish seekers to Hinduism and that this is indeed what Hinduism may have to offer Judaism. God realization thus lies at the heart of the Jewish encounter with Hinduism.

The outsider who visits Judaism, its people, and its institutions is impressed by the faith of the people, their dedication, and devotion. The dedication to God's will, His Torah, people and land are impressive. But I think it is fair to say that the outsider will not be impressed by the direct search for God, because that is not what Judaism features as its primary value. It is, however, something that Hindus make the focus of their spiritual path and what they chose to tell others about. God-talk is thus much more direct in Hinduism than it is in Judaism. This may not be exclusive to Hinduism and may possibly be as true of Christianity or other religions. But Jews may have an easier time hearing it from Hindus, with whom they have not shared painful histories and in relation to whom they have not built up psychic defenses that are hundreds of years old.

But perhaps Hindus are even more explicit about their God-focus than are others. God-realization is an explicit aim of many of the systems that Jews encounter. One of the most common practices of Hindus is *japa*, consisting of the repetition of God's names. The quest to keep God's name a constant reality obviously places God very much at the center of one's awareness.[13] But above all, the theological structure of Hinduism makes God more readily available than that of the Abrahamic faiths. We shall discuss below the implications of the view of God as omnipresent and all-pervading. Such a view of God allows one to recognize God in all and to find Him everywhere. Most forms of Judaism think of God in very transcendent terms, even if they employ a religious language that speaks of God in personal terms. Even those traditions of Judaism that think of God in pantheistic terms do not turn that insight into the governing approach to Divinity, readily available for worship and contact. Thinking of God in terms of His omnipresence, as all-pervading in all forms of life, orients religious thought and practice in such a way as to drive home the recognition of God's accessibility. In terms of spirituality, this may be the one element that more than others defines Hindu spirituality, as compared with Jewish spirituality. For Jewish spirituality, as theorized in many forms of Judaism and as experienced in virtually all, access to God is a challenge, an issue, if not a problem. For Hindu spirituality, by contrast, the starting point is God's accessibility. Placing God as the conscious focus of the spiritual path thus accounts for a very different tenor of Hindu spirituality.

Let me try to make the same point in another way. I have clocked hundreds of hours listening to spiritual teachers from the Hindu tradition. God is the focus of all their teachings, with the exception of those teachers who intentionally avoid God-talk, as a means of selling their products or methods.[14] I have also clocked thousands of hours with Jewish teachers. They, by contrast, almost never speak of God. They will speak of God's things, but not of God Himself, as though He was beyond their knowledge and personal experience. A handful of hassidic masters are the corrective to this broader tendency, but operating as they do within the broader Jewish intellectual and cultural milieu, their own approach to God is usually more reserved than that of Hindu teachers. I personally have been motivated enough to seek out those few teachers and schools in Judaism that do talk of God. Many have not been motivated in the same way, or they have not found them and of those who have not found them in Judaism, many have made it to Hinduism or Hindu teachers, who could make up for what was lacking in the Jewish formation.

A recent exchange I had with a Hindu devotee in India was very moving. My conversation partner, in his 70s, following a life of disciplined spiritual practice, was sharing his pain that he had not yet reached God realization. It was, after all, the great goal of life. It is what should be available to all. Anyone who is sincere, said Vinod, should be able to reach God realization. Why had he not? His reply: because his sincerity is lacking. Hence, he must try harder to serve others with a pure spirit. Then, maybe one day he too will see God. I was profoundly touched by his humility, sincerity, and above all by the content of his quest. I had never heard a Jew talking like that. Pious Jews have spoken to me of not having perfected their moral character or of not having achieved the level or extent of Torah learning they would have liked. But to speak of the goal in terms that relate directly to God—never.[15] I believe Vinod is not an exception. He speaks for lakhs, maybe crores, of believers.[16]

I would like to conclude this section by sharing a testimony of an Israeli writer, who speaks of the impressions of her first visit to India. The writer, Rivka Miriam, is active in Torah study and various literary and religious fora. Her Torah knowledge allows her to relate to her experience in India in terms taken from classical Jewish sources. Her testimony confirms the overall direction that I have been suggesting and points to what might be the secret draw of India and Hinduism for Israelis, and Jews in general:

> And now to Divinity. Meeting its expressions in India brought about a transformation in me. We Jews employ the common expression "there is no place that is devoid of Him." In India I discovered a world where indeed so it is. I discovered a world in which there is no one who does not believe. I discovered a world where one sees Divinity in every tree and in every stone. But also in every deed and in every matter. The entire world is full of His glory.
>
> Seeing Divinity in India brought about a transformation in me. Indeed, there I saw a place full of faith. Another, different, way to believe, a path that may have been uprooted from us when, as the Talmud tells, the evil inclination for idol worship was uprooted.
>
> And perhaps together with that uprooting a part of faith as such was also uprooted.[17]

Faith is the all-pervading reality, a faith in the all-pervading Divinity. God is seen everywhere. This gives life to what are otherwise texts, words, and ideas found in Jewish sources. Miriam paraphrases Isaiah 6.3 in light of the Mussaf Kedusha text, proclaiming the entire world is full of the divine glory.[18] Significantly, she appeals to a kabbalisitc source to affirm that there is no place devoid of the divine presence.[19] Once again, the religious reality of India makes sense in light of kabbalistic language and insight. Miriam experiences India as a place full of faith and that faith is transformative. Miriam struggles with the relationship between this faith and idolatry and our own complex loss/gain, upon removal of the inclination to worship idols, based upon a story narrated in the Talmud.[20] It is significant that idolatry enters the overall assessment of the Indian religious reality. Indeed, idolatry is the flip side of the all-pervasiveness of faith in India. The faith draws; idolatry repels. We should not lose sight of the powerful testimony: India is experienced as a place of faith, a place of encounter with God, and hence also a place of potential spiritual transformation.

Appendix: Yoel Glick's *Living the Life of Jewish Meditation: A Comprehensive Guide to Practice and Experience*[21]

The recent publication of Yoel Glick's guide to Jewish meditation is nothing less than an event on the horizons of Jewish spirituality and deserves particular attention in the framework of the Jewish-Hindu encounter and its consequences for Jewish spirituality.[22] This is the most comprehensive manual of Jewish meditation for the market of general (Jewish) spiritual seekers. It offers some of the best formulations I have ever seen of the nature of meditation and the processes of the spiritual life. It is replete with resources, texts, and practices that are sure to enrich the life of a spiritual seeker. What follows is not a review of this work, its structure, or its concept. I will concentrate on one aspect that is a great novelty of this work and that in many ways is also the key to its originality—drawing on Hindu sources in presenting Jewish meditation.

While this is a work of Jewish meditation, it is framed within a broader spiritual horizon that may be termed universalistic and that draws on the wisdom of all religions, finding in them spiritual resources that complement and enhance the fundamental Jewish vision it seeks to put forth.[23] The justification for this is Glick's own spiritual journey, making this work relevant to the broader phenomenon of Jewish exposure to Hindu spiritual traditions. Glick shares with us something of his biography,[24] which includes years of discipleship with a woman swami spiritual teacher,[25] visits to India, and, as we see from his work, extensive readings in the works of great modern Hindu spiritual teachers.[26] While he does not speak of himself as having lived as a Jew and a Hindu, Glick affirms the nearly equal impact of both traditions on his spiritual person:

> My friend urged me to write such a meditation manual. He felt that my own spiritual journey made me well suited for this task. He pointed out that I had a rich background and understanding of Judaism and Jewish sources, as well as a strong grasp of Eastern teaching and practice. I had studied the sources and lived the life. And I loved and appreciated both of these beautiful traditions.[27]

We are introduced to Glick's methodology through his introductory discussion of silence. In his introductory discussion, Glick justifies the need for meditation through the dichotomy of speech and silence. Appealing to the Ba'al Shem Tov, Glick highlights the value of silence as necessary for the spiritual life and as the core of the practice of meditation. While making this appeal, Glick is also aware of the fact that Judaism's prayers rely on words, and are often verbose. Silence is lacking.

> It is essential for our approach to meditation to be simple and direct. We want to focus our practice on inner experience rather than manipulations of the mind; to cultivate serenity and silence while we seek out the living presence of God.
>
> There is a lot we can learn in this regard from the Eastern religions. The East has thousands of years of unbroken meditation practice. Inner silence is an integral part of their religious life. Hinduism and Buddhism have developed the art of meditation into a spiritual science. This science provides clear principles and disciplines that deepen and advance the practice of meditation.
>
> Throughout the book, I will draw on Eastern sources and make parallels between the Hindu, Buddhist and Jewish traditions. I will make use of the Wisdom of the East to shed light on Jewish teaching and practices, to vitalize and illuminate them in whole new ways. [28]

This discussion encapsulates the method and reveals its assumptions. The goal is to illuminate Jewish teachings, which are the ultimate focus, concern, and method taught by Glick. However, something is evidently lacking in Judaism. In the most obvious way, we note this in the lack of silence, hence meditation, in Judaism. This in turn requires us to search elsewhere, in order to bring this knowledge into, or back into, Judaism.[29] The method of turning to Eastern traditions in order to illuminate Jewish teachings is fundamental to the book. It suggests one way in which the two traditions address each other in the framework of spirituality. We note that Glick does not represent a case of someone who has gone into Hinduism and then come back to Judaism. Such cases will be discussed in a later chapter of the present work. Rather, he is someone who, while maintaining Jewish practice, has expanded his spiritual understanding and draws from Hinduism's wisdom. His self-understanding is that what is drawn is nothing but what is already present in Judaism. Hence, Hinduism and Buddhism serve the purpose of illuminating Judaism's true teachings.

In terms of spirituality this may be the ideal balance. It does not involve struggle to affirm Jewish identity, nor does it involve multiple religious identities, as in the cases we shall discuss later. Nowhere does Glick self-identity as a Hindu. Rather, he has a love for the tradition and draws from its teachings inspiration and illumination for Judaism.

The discussion of silence makes it clear that Glick's project takes place within a framework of crisis. The lack of silence and the need to locate it elsewhere may be considered in relation to the crises discussed in the body of the present chapter. But this also raises the question of how we know what is authentically Jewish. Glick never enters into a discussion of the place of silence and speech within the spiritual economy of Judaism, compared to that of other religious traditions. Some students of Kabbalah emphasize Kabbalah's linguistic centrality, raising the question of whether Kabbalah might be distinguished from other methods of mysticism, precisely because of its emphasis upon words, rather than upon silence.[30] In theory, one might juxtapose speech and silence as different modalities of spirituality and note the predominance of the one or the other in either

Judaism or Hinduism.[31] We might wish to do this if we were after an academically informed definition of what constitutes Judaism, or Jewish spirituality. This is not the path taken by Glick. Glick takes for granted the centrality of silence to the spiritual life. This leads him to identify some Jewish teachings and sources he considers representative. He recognizes the lack of silence and he seeks to make up for this lack by learning from Eastern traditions.

This example teaches us something fundamental about Glick's method. He neither takes Judaism as it is as his frame of reference, nor does he present Hinduism as it is as his point of departure. Rather, he offers a view of the spiritual life as such. This view does not necessarily conform to one or the other of the traditions or their particular expressions in a specific body of teachings or the life of a particular community. The method is eclectic, drawing on multiple religions and sources within each religion, chosen and presented by Glick to the degree they conform to his spiritual vision.[32]

Where is this vision taken from? The reader who goes through the book may legitimately pose the question of what is the ultimate source of authority or frame of reference that Glick draws from. The sources are inspiring and indeed illuminating, as he claims. But the broader frame of reference resembles nothing one can find in any typical or recognized presentation of Jewish spirituality. Nor are we dealing with some summary presentation of Hinduism, garbed in Jewish texts. The creation before us is unique. Drawing on multiple authorities, it lacks a clear voice of authority, despite the fact that it is presented through the authorial and authoritative voice of Glick himself.

What, then, is the source of Glick's vision? Where does he take it from? I believe here we come to a point that is of great significance for the very enterprise of a Jewish-Hindu dialogue of spirituality. The meaning of the dialogue and its fruits seem to go beyond present categories, structures, and emphases. Something new is created and the crucible within which it is created is the spiritual life of the individual. A genuine spiritual journey will thus yield some novel statement, recognizable in its parts, but new in its overall structure and message.[33] What we have then is Glick's own synthesis of his spiritual life. It is heavily informed by the formative teaching relationships to which he refers, but at the end of the day it goes beyond them, integrating a program of reading and experience into a novel statement that is individual, original, and unique.

If we contrast this with the work of Bokser-Caravella that will be analyzed in chapter 10, this is a much more mature approach. It does not seek to simply read one tradition in light of the other. It engages in a genuine give and take that can only be worked out through the deep personal engagement of the author and his own creative synthesis.

For some readers this is a great feat, an achievement of interreligious spirituality. Other readers may be concerned by the great subjectivity that informs this essay, pitched as an objective description of the spiritual life. At the end of the day we are hearing Glick, who refracts all wisdom, Jewish and Hindu, yet other than his having undertaken a journey and summarized its outcome for us, the reader is not provided with any grounds for believing or disbelieving Glick's synthesis of two religious traditions in the light of spirituality.

The subjectivity of the process does not preclude some very interesting experiments in reading the two traditions in tandem, against the background of a neutrally presented view of the spiritual life, projected beyond both traditions. The book opens with a presentation of the notion of spiritual centers as the locus of the true spiritual life and where spiritual evolution takes place.[34] These provide the foundation for the practice of meditation. Glick begins his discussion by appealing to "the science of yoga" and naming these centers by their Sanskrit name, *chakras*. But he immediately proceeds to identifying the chakras with kabbalistic *sefirot*. While the parallel is not original to him,[35] it is significant in terms of the spiritual dialogue between Hinduism and Judaism.[36] It is difficult, however, to determine whether Judaism is made to conform to Hinduism, whether Hinduism is cited in order to shed light on a Jewish teaching, or whether both contribute to some self-standing view of the spiritual life that owes to both traditions but that does not seek to replicate either.[37] This and other instances in the book present us with teachings that are intellectually interesting and provide spiritual vision, but that at the end of the day require some faith in the author or in the system he presents to us. Perhaps at the end of the day the question of sources and authority should not matter that much to readers of the book. The book does not seek to make its mark in the realm of theological contribution, let alone of comparative religion. It is a guide to experience and to forming a spiritual life around that experience. For readers of this work, for Glick himself, and probably for the entire enterprise of seeking spirituality through a Jewish-Hindu encounter, the proof is in tasting. If meaningful experience is gained through which a deepening of the spiritual life occurs, why worry about what might seem like academic questions of provenance, historical accuracy, or even religious authority.

This leads me to the next case of Hindu-Jewish spiritual influence, articulated in Glick's chapter on mantra meditation.[38] This is a fascinating chapter, both intellectually and spiritually, but it raises some fundamental questions concerning Glick's project. Chapter 8 is titled Mantra Recitation. The chapter certainly does not conform to the pattern of Hindu sources illuminating Jewish practice. It is, rather, the reverse. This chapter constitutes an attempt to translate Hindu practices into Jewish form. Glick's discussion does not offer a fully developed account for why one might wish to do this, given the guiding principle of Eastern teachings illuminating Jewish teachings. Yet we can reconstruct such reasoning between the lines. For one, Glick offers us a historical reading of certain biblical passages that he considers as phenomenologically equivalent to mantra practice. Similarly, he appeals to synagogal rites involving group chanting and the recitation of litanies as further parallel. On a more fundamental level, Glick seems to consider chanting as a fundamental means of religious expression and therefore as something that is universal to religious cultures. If we might not readily recognize mantra/chanting as Jewish practice, we simply need to search deeper.

Pioneers of Jewish mediation in contemporary times have already charted the path and some attention has been given to mantra recitation in works on Jewish meditation by Rabbi Arye Kaplan.[39] Mantra meditation is the default form of Hindu meditation, and therefore early attempts to provide a Jewish answer to Hindu meditative practices led to the creation of mantra-based Jewish meditations.

Glick follows a similar course, but with much greater depth. He does not simply try to create a Jewish equivalent to mantra recitation. He attempts to find correspondences to the entire theory of mantra practice. Working through the teachings of the "science of yoga," Glick seeks to find correspondence in Jewish sources to the six components of mantra practice. Working through the six dimensions of mantra, Glick offers us a fascinating exercise in interreligious translation and in developing a robust Jewish practice, supported by a theory of mantra that provides background to this work, even if it is not always made explicit. In terms of the contribution of Glick's work to a Jewish-Hindu encounter, this discussion poses some of the most interesting questions. These touch upon a view of Judaism and upon the meaning of interreligious translation and borrowing. In terms of a view of Judaism, it presents us with the challenge of when to highlight similarities and when to pay close attention to fundamental differences. Should Jewish practices that bear some similarities to mantric repetition be presented as precedents and parallels, or should the more obvious gap between the practices of the two religions serve as the orientating principle? Should litanies and the recitations of lengthy prayers, even if repetitive, be considered on a par with the more focused practice of mantra? Can prayer practices that are by their nature short and time-bound be offered as parallels to a practice that is at its heart a form of continual prayer and is structured in practical terms accordingly? For this reader, the differences outweigh the similarities. I personally prefer that the characteristics of rituals and practices of each religion be featured more starkly. Rather than reconstructing a common ground to all religions and seeking to find it in Judaism, it seems to me more honest to engage in conscious borrowing, despite core differences, if such borrowing can be undertaken responsibly.

While I take exception to Glick's theoretical assumptions, preferring a more critical reading of difference between the traditions, the attempt at practical borrowing across traditions that has inspired some of the mantric recitations offered by Glick is rich in potential for inspiration. It suggests the power of borrowing in practice, even where differences in theory are recognized. To me, adopting a central Hindu practice within Judaism would be a case of religious borrowing that should be recommended in view of its results, while recognizing differences in historical and depth theological structures. If mantra recitation is beneficial and a practice that aids in the spiritual life, why not import it to Judaism, provided such practices of import are carried out responsibly. Some of the issues that are relevant to a theory of responsible borrowing and translation emerge from Glick's discussion:

A. Glick's discussion raises the fundamental question of what does it mean to translate. Glick translates core terms relevant to a Hindu mantra-theory into Hebrew. But the terms do not have any cultural resonance in their translated Hebrew context. In my view, more is needed to translate across traditions than linguistic translation. Translation is an act of finding correspondences and drawing out parallels between different systems. It is these parallels that allow for meaningful translation. Creating new Hebrew terms that correspond to Hindu terms but that have no religious or cultural depth places a veneer of similarity that obscures depth differences.

B. Closely related is the question of cultural context. How readily can clusters of religious theory and practice be transported from one tradition to another, without due cultural context. It is difficult enough to extract a practice from its broader religious and theological moorings and parachute it into another religious environment. Yet, Glick is not content with finding some Jewish equivalent to TM, as various rabbis were in the 70s. He seeks to capture the full meaning of mantra and to cast it in Jewish terms. But precisely because he has such high standards, more and more elements from the broader Hindu context are imported, and these end up having little meaning within a Jewish context. Most obvious is the dependence of mantra meditation on a spiritual teacher. Glick writes:

> One of the first questions that we need to address is, which mantra is right for us? The best way to discover our mantra is to find a teacher who can guide us to the right choice. A spiritual mentor will be able to discern what mantra will resonate with our soul. In fact, the whole concept of taking initiation arises out of this relationship. The teacher selects a mantra according to our spiritual nature. He or she then transmits its spiritual power to us at the moment of initiation.[40]

The teacher's choice is fundamental to the Hindu use of mantra. Carrying this view wholesale into Judaism suggests that one can find a Jewish teacher who is capable of providing mantra meditation. But how can one find such a teacher when mantra meditation is not practiced in Judaism? And what can the readers of this book do with such instruction, when, as we know all too well, there simply is no one to go to, that is, unless one considers going to non-Jewish teachers who might provide a Jewish mantra.[41] If this were a Hindu "how-to" of mantra chanting, it would be a detailed, thoughtful, and well-articulated introduction to the practice. But reading all this in a Jewish context, one is left wondering who does this really serve, and can one simply transport an entire cultural practice to a different religious ground?

C. Translation also raises the question of theological context and even of theological propriety. Hindu mantras are names of God or different gods, or aspects of God, depending on one's understanding. Glick is aware of this and finds the equivalent of a mantra's association with an aspect of the Godhead through the notion of *Parzuf,* which he offers as an equivalent to *devata.* This is daring, but it is not problem free.[42] It assumes a theological correspondence of the terms that has to be constructed, but as his project is neither one of comparative religion nor of constructive theology this construction is presumed or taken for granted.[43]

Returning to the previous point, in terms of the Jewish culture, which this serves, the idea has next to no meaning. While constructing a formal parallel with the teachings of yoga, this parallel does little more than establish the parallel. It has little meaning in practice and could be seen as entering complicated theological ground that touches on the proper under-standing of God without ever making it a subject of conscious reflection.

As stated, I would wish to draw a distinction between theory and practice. While I have reservations concerning Glick's theoretical grounding, I find his practical offerings (which for him may be closely related to his theoretical foundations) of great interest. Glick offers us several fascinating and original exercises in mantra meditation, some drawing from Hinduism, some from Christianity.[44] Reviewing them, one can recognize the potential for powerful spiritual moments, through the practice of this recitation. Yet, these mantras and the practices suggested by Glick have little to do with classical Hindu practice of mantra recitation and with the attempt to translate and find correspondence in the *theory* of mantra between Hinduism and Judaism. What Glick offers us is at a remove from the view of mantra as a lifelong friend that he espouses.[45] What we have are sound or recitation-based, fairly brief, meditation exercises and one can intuit their potential benefits for practitioners. But neither the actual mantras nor their form of application correspond to Glick's theoretical discussion.[46]

This gap is interesting and may tell us something about Glick's project. On the existential and experiential level he has experimented and experienced certain things using mantra-like techniques. This has likely taken place in the framework of conscious attempts to imitate or integrate mantra practices into Judaism. But complementing the experiential dimension is a more theoretical discussion, in which Glick tries to ground or justify his forays into Hindu sources from within Judaism. This leads him to constructing intricate arguments that are as interesting as they are problematic. Lacking cultural context, lacking a real referent in a Jewish context, lacking the ability to practice in a sustained way, they remain theoretical exercises in Hindu-Jewish translation that may offer some theoretical enrichment but likely will never carry significant weight or impact in their entirety. Ultimately, Glick's work raises the question of how borrowing from another tradition might take place both responsibly and effectively. The different kinds of suggestions and arguments that are put forth throughout the book represent a range of possibilities for how two traditions might be brought into theoretical conversation and how such rapport might support borrowing of practices.

In the final analysis, Glick's work opens up for us an interesting discussion of how borrowing from another tradition might take place. Perhaps Glick's contribution lies not so much in having provided a formula or a pattern for successful borrowing but in the very fact that he has put the question of conscious and intentional borrowing, in the context of the spiritual life, openly on the table. Taking religious borrowing for granted, Glick experiments with different instances that allow us to continue reflecting on how such practices might be carried out in a way that honors both traditions, their internal coherence, and the higher spiritual aspiration that is recognized as common to both.

Another attempt at translating or converting a Hindu practice is converting Ramana Maharshi's meditation of self-enquiry: "Who am I?"[47] Glick suggests parallels with teachings of Rabbi Nachman of Breslav and Rabbi Natan of Nemirov. He then takes the theoretical parallel and translates it into what is consciously a new practice, creating a new formula of spiritual empowerment that could have the same transformative power that Ramana's formula does. Combining Rabbi Nachman's teaching with the formula, he offers what amounts to a Jewish version of one of the most popular practices in certain circles of Hindu spirituality, Ramana's process of self-enquiry. Unlike the case of wholesale importing of mantra-theory into a Jewish framework, the attempt to create a specific technique that would be equivalent to something known from India is less theoretically charged. At the end of the day, it is either useful or not. Only those who attempt to practice it can tell.

What is the rationale for the kind of religious borrowing that Glick engages in? It is important to state that Glick never suggests engaging in Hindu practices *as such*. He never recommends the use of a known Hindu mantra. Rather, some of the forms of the spiritual life known in Hinduism are imported through translation. What is taken is the structure. The content is provided through Jewish sources. Glick is creative in his suggestions more than he is reflexive about them. He does not offer a theory or an explanation for this kind of borrowing and translating, and it would seem he takes their value for granted. There is room to query this and to ask what theory justifies these practices. I can think of three elements that could provide a theory for Glick's attempts.

The first is the recognition that something works for others, and if it works for others then, in principle, why should it not work for us. In other words, the approach is empirical and results-based. Given that so much of Hindu spirituality revolves around the practice of mantra, it is a fair assumption that if we could successfully import it to Judaism, it could enrich our spiritual lives.

The second assumption is that spiritual processes can be divorced from their concrete expressions. Translating a practice from one tradition to another, by keeping its broad parameters, while altering its content, assumes that the content is somehow secondary. Hindu names of God are, in this view, secondary to the actual practice of chanting mantra, which itself can work equally well with other content. A meditation of self-enquiry can be as beneficial using the formula that its initiator discovered as the one presently proposed. It also assumes practices can be extracted from their broader religious context. A meditation does not depend on the power of the person who revealed it, and with all the esteem and appreciation for Ramana Maharshi, it is not he who empowers the meditation but something objective that can be extracted, translated, and applied within a different context. Similarly, the practice of mantra is not, in this view, dependent on the personal initiation of a guru, but has potency of its own, even though efforts should be made to find analogues to the traditional Hindu framework within which mantras are transmitted. At the end of the day, the principles of the practice are more important than the religious frameworks that sustain them and can therefore be transported to another religious landscape, with new context-appropriate content driving them.

I think there is a third perspective that informs Glick's broader project, though it need not be applied to all the details of his interreligious borrowing and inspiration. It is that Judaism is in the process of recovery of something it has lost.[48] This brings us back to the sense of crisis discussed above. Glick does not hide this view of Judaism in crisis, and so he says in an interview with Alan Brill:

> Q: Is there currently a Jewish realized being who is teaching meditation that we can learn from?
>
> A: Sadly, there is not. We are producing lots of wonderful scholars and even the occasional spiritual genius but no enlightened beings. Enlightened beings and those who seek to attain that state are the soul of a religion. It is time for us to admit that we have a problem, instead of just saying how good we are at this worldly activity.[49]

Hinduism is in some way a response to this crisis, because it allows us to reclaim something of our own. The argument is not historical; it is spiritual and metaphysical. Through Hinduism, or perhaps more correctly through application of the spiritual principles lost to Judaism but kept alive in Hinduism, Judaism can reclaim its own authentic spiritual heritage. The great spiritual masters of the hassidic tradition upon whom Glick relies are of course witnesses to the viability of the Jewish tradition. Yet, while they confirm the theoretical possibility of a high spiritual life, they, or their successors, can no longer, for historical or sociological reasons, provide access to this quality of life. This life must be recovered in other ways, and interreligious borrowing provides the way.

This approach is, in and of itself, not novel. It is precisely the approach taken by Abraham Maimonides to justify his incorporation of Sufi practices into the synagogal rite and into the spiritual life of Judaism. A sense of crisis and loss, associated with the destruction of the Temple and exile, creates a situation where what is genuinely ours is in the hands of others and must be reclaimed.[50] For Abraham Maimonides the argument is historical—they took directly from us. But that would seem to be secondary. The argument can be made with equal effectiveness on spiritual or phenomenological grounds. Abraham Maimonides was head of Egyptian Jewry in the twelfth century and therefore enjoyed enormous prestige and authority. One may consider what it is that makes a strategy such as this successful. Is it the authority behind it? One could well argue that at the end of the day it is the quality of spiritual life and experience that counts most. If the spiritual life of the community or the individual is enriched by integration of elements from another spiritual path, that is all that counts. Living in a consciousness of loss and crisis certainly opens one up to the quest for true and fulfilled spiritual life and for seeking it wherever it may be found.

There is something common to the projects of Glick and Abraham Maimonides. At the end of the day, their spiritual vision serves as the arbiter of what constitutes true spiritual life and true Judaism. The examples seen in another religion provide a yardstick for spiritual possibilities, higher than those presently lived in Judaism. These are somehow self-authenticating, in terms of their value and testimony to what is a true Judaism. Consequently, a truer Judaism is recovered in the construction of a spiritual life that owes much to another religious tradition. For Glick, the place of silence, the significance of meditation, the myriad techniques, and above all the centrality of a God-centered life are all components of a worldview that is constructed in the self-validating subjectivity of the spiritual seeker who crosses religious traditions, discovers their common spiritual core, and ultimately restates and reconstructs what it means to practice a spiritual life within Judaism.

8

Saints: Encountering the Divine in Humanity

Spirituality is never lived in the abstract. It finds expression through institutions, actions, and, above all, in the lives of people who practice a spiritual path and whose practice serves as a model for others. People who have attained a certain level in the spiritual life also become instrumental in the spiritual lives of others. They become teachers and facilitators of the spiritual life of others. Very often, the spiritual life is mediated through such personalities. Such role models, teachers, and facilitators exist in all traditions. Each tradition configures them differently and understands them in light of its norms and unique patterns of thinking. Looking at the lives of exemplary men and women across religious traditions is thus both an exercise in observation and description and an application of thought structures, through which what is seen is understood and interpreted.[1]

When a Jewish person looks at the lives of holy people in India, he is thus confronted and challenged on two levels. The first is the ability to recognize and to accept that extraordinary holiness and spirituality can be found in practitioners of Hinduism. This fact is itself far from obvious. Recognizing holiness in another tradition implies a measure of recognition and acceptance. Even though our sources recognize the existence of *Zaddikim*, saints, among the nations of the world,[2] in practice little has been made of such recognition.[3] Recognition of saintliness may be broken down to recognition of exceptional personal piety, proximity to God, capacity to perform miracles, the answering of prayers, and more. None of these figure in any significant way in Jewish appreciation of other religions and their spiritual virtuosi. In fact, the opposite is more typical. Those considered saints in one tradition tend to be played down, if they are acknowledged at all. Prophets are deemed false, miracles are deemed magic, prayers are considered unanswered, etc.[4]

When religions are in a situation of competition and conflict, it is extremely difficult to concede the possibility of holiness and to recognize the lives of saints in another religious tradition. The present state of relations between the world's religions challenges us precisely on this point. As dialogue and respect grow, we are increasingly challenged to recognize the signs of positive and fruitful spiritual lives, as these find expression in all religions. The fact that Judaism has not had significant historical dealings with Hinduism means that the barriers to the recognition of spiritual excellence, born of competition between the religions, are lower than in relation to other religions. This certainly makes recognition of saintliness—whether by seekers or in the framework of a broader evaluation—less charged. When Jews encounter Hinduism, they often do so in relation to the lives, teachings, example, and spiritual facilitation of religious virtuosi, saints.[5] And they do so without the instinctive protective mechanisms and distancing traditionally associated with Jewish attitudes to Christianity. The novelty of the encounter, the changing context of dialogue, and the greater openness that characterizes Jewish society on the whole all add up to a new challenge, the likes of which we may have never seen before—the challenge to accept, recognize, and come to terms with the fact that special religious lives are lived to fruition through another religion.

A significant part of the challenge that Hinduism poses is that much of it is encountered through and around religious virtuosi, some of whom are indeed extraordinary persons.[6] I believe one of the first challenges that faces serious open-minded Jews who engage Hinduism is to accept the fact that some people, even if few in number, have attained extraordinary spiritual heights through their practice of Hinduism or, more broadly put, within the spiritual context of the religious life of India.[7] How we deal with Hinduism will vary greatly depending on whether one is able or unable to acknowledge this. Certainly, my own thinking has been formed by my impressions of some Hindu religious figures. For me, their sanctity and spiritual achievement are beyond questioning and hence an important point of departure for theological reflection upon other religions in general, and Hinduism in particular. The challenge of accounting for another religious tradition changes radically the moment one is willing to admit that great spiritual heights, perhaps even greater than those seen in one's immediate vicinity or even within Judaism as practiced today, have been or are realized in the lives of individuals of another tradition. In fact, it may take only one such person to transform one's theological views, or at least to change one's spiritual horizons, so as to include others. Even if we postulate that for every true teacher there are a hundred impostors, and that for every guru who is a model there are many fallen gurus, this does not change the fundamental theological challenge. It only makes the question of discernment more urgent and calls us to cultivate spiritual tools for recognizing true from false spirituality. Those tools would have to be applied in relation to our own great teachers too and would therefore not be a means of distinguishing one religion from another, but rather the higher from the lower, or the authentic from inauthentic forms of the spiritual life, as these manifest in all religions. The same intellectual honesty that calls us to apply criteria to help us discern and recognize true spiritual teachers within Judaism also calls us, and certainly has led me, to recognize the authentic spiritual lives of saints outside Judaism and, in the present context, within the spiritual framework of the religious life of India.

Most Jews who encounter Hinduism as a religious tradition do so in the context of one of the many Hindu outreach groups or offshoots and configurations of Hinduism. These are usually centered around exceptional religious figures, teachers, gurus. The situation would be analogous to how one might have come to encounter Judaism in the eighteenth and nineteenth centuries in Eastern Europe, as the hassidic movement was spreading. These figures account for much of the draw of the religion. More significantly, the central role of these individuals structures the religion in specific ways, both practically and theologically. A Judaism that acknowledges the centrality of the *Zaddik* is different in major ways from a Judaism that does not. Similarly, a Hinduism that is centered around the example, inspiration, power, and spiritual facilitation and leadership of a key individual is very different from one that is not.

This point is perfectly clear in the context of Judaism. I came to appreciate just how central it is to Hinduism when I stayed with a Hindu family in Hyderabad. This family's residence is a hub for visiting gurus and spiritual teachers. When I stayed with them, the head of one important ashram, Swami Satchitananda of Ananda Ashram in Kerala, was convalescing there following medical procedures. He was visited by another major Hindu religious personality, Mata Amritanandamayi. Talking with members of the extended household, I learned just how particular is the configuration of Hinduism that centers on holy men and women. For those who were not reared in such a form of Hinduism, like the daughters-in-law of the extended household, joining the family was in effect discovering another way of being Hindu. The Hinduism they had previously known was centered around temples and their worship. Structuring the religious life around gurus was presented as an explicit alternative to temple-oriented Hinduism. Both are recognized as legitimate, though for this particular family saint-oriented Hinduism was clearly of a higher order. It was, for them, a way of being Hindu that was consciously and explicitly an alternative to the form of Hinduism practiced by most Hindus.

In this regard there may be a meaningful difference between Hinduism in the West and Hinduism as practiced in India. Within the Indian landscape, gurus, teachers, and teaching as such occupy a meaningful position, but they do not necessarily define Hinduism. In fact, it may be that most Hindus in India practice their Hinduism without explicit appeal to great religious figures of the present or the recent past. This would also be the case for many Hindus in the Diaspora. However, one way in which diasporic Hinduism distinguishes itself is by its awareness and attachment to teachers and gurus. Ever since Swami Vivekananda traveled to the United States in the late nineteenth century, the West has hosted many Hindu saints. If some saints did not travel, their disciples certainly did, spreading the message of Hinduism, with particular emphasis and attachment to these teachers.

Configuring Hinduism around a particular teacher, a guru, provides a focus and theological emphasis that is particular. As the saying goes, the medium is the message. Indeed, the holy person is often the message. Let me illustrate this with the case of the BAPS branch of Swaminarayan Hinduism. This active and ever-growing form of Hinduism constructed a major museological and spiritual complex, first in its native Gujarat, in a town called Gandhinagar, and later in Delhi, as part of its outreach.[8] A visitor to Akshardham learns much about the specific form of Swaminarayan Hinduism, its founder, and its vision. But the explicit message of the place, as expressed in a movie, which is one of the features of Akshardham that sums up it message, is "guru." Significantly, the message, perhaps in a clever act of public relations, but more likely in a movement that exposes the theological common ground of this movement and other forms of Hinduism, is not the divinity of Swaminarayan himself, but rather the need that everyone has to find a guru, who could lead one on the spiritual life. Granted, the movie goes on to state that they have a guru, who is, supposedly, available to all—Pramukh Swami, the head of this branch of the Swaminarayan faith. His heart, as they say, is wide enough to contain the entire world. But more important than the identification of an appropriate guru is the recognition of the very need for a guru.

That this should emerge as the key message of a costly, contemporary spiritual complex suggests both the centrality of the idea to some configurations of Hinduism and how this message is not universally recognized or practiced. After all, had all Hindus been attached to one guru or another, there would be no need to have highlighted this message as a major message of this outreach complex. The need for a guru is a message that is characteristic of a spiritual and highly evolved form of Hinduism that seeks to leave its mark and to shape broader practice that often manifests a lower degree of spiritual awareness. Holy men and women are thus important in theory but not universal in practice.

To a large extent, knowledge of and attachment to Hindu saints are a distinguishing feature that sets apart different forms of Hinduism and what allows some practitioners to speak of higher and lower forms of Hindu practice. This is largely because saints will manifest spirituality in ways that common folk's daily religious practice cannot. Saints also provide teaching. A form of religion that consciously incorporates teaching and spirituality will obviously be very different from one that is mainly ritualistic. In this sense, it seems appropriate to speak of higher and lower forms of the religion, using knowledge, spirituality, and personal spiritual growth as the yardsticks for distinguishing higher from lower.

The fact is then that within Judaism's contemporary encounter with Hinduism, saints play a major role. Probably all participants in official dialogue subscribe to belief in saints; most of them are even considered by their followers to be saints themselves. Which leads us to the next level of complexity in this discussion. If the first challenge addressed the reality and the very existence of these men and women, the second challenge is posed by Hindu belief in these individuals. How a saint is understood is never a purely descriptive matter. Understanding the spiritual lives of extraordinary individuals will always appeal to a particular worldview, in light of which those individuals are appreciated. The encounter with Hindu saints is therefore not only a challenge in terms of the very recognition of the existence of saintly people in another tradition, but even more so in terms of the specific theology attached to those individuals.

Saints are appreciated within the framework of the broader religious worldview within which they operate. In the case of Hinduism this has implications for the recognition of the divinity that is manifest in the spiritual teacher. Nuances may vary, but the core issue, and herein lies the challenge from a Jewish perspective, is the recognition that the teacher is divine. There are different ways of approaching and understanding this statement. On one level, this is a question of respect, etiquette, and appropriate approach. The guru is approached *as if* he were God. The "as if" approach is, of course, reminiscent of various midrashic statements that inculcate a religious attitude by means of "as if" statements that narrow down and remove the divide between the human and the Divine.[9] However, in the Indian context, the recognition of the divinity of the teacher is more far-reaching than a rhetorical device for the inculcation of a worthy and respectful attitude. In many senses, the teacher is, or can be, seen as divinity proper. Divinity, while being absolute and transcendent, is also understood as being capable of incarnating itself. The teacher, as mediator of divine life and teaching and as model of spiritual perfection, is the most natural target for being considered an incarnation of the Divine. On the Jewish side, we recognize a fundamental disdain from the divinization of the human person. Hence, the attitude found among many Hindus in relation to their spiritual teachers may be considered very much at odds with basic Jewish sensibilities.

Several factors may be considered in the context of future reflection on this core issue. From the Hindu perspective, this issue is related to the broader understanding of the Divine and creation. The divinity recognized in the holy person is recognized in every person, and in fact in all of creation. It is thus a specific, if central, manifestation of a fundamental religious worldview. This worldview has to be brought into closer dialogue with strands of pantheism or panentheism in Jewish thought; for example, some of the teachings of the hassidic masters, and famously that of R. Shneur Zalman of Lyady, often cited in this context. One must also bear in mind references to great spiritual personalities as divine in the Jewish tradition, beginning with the archetypal example of Moses. Phrases such as "man of God," applied to him, and epithets such as "the divine," applied to several later figures, such as R. Isaac Luria and R. Moshe Alshech, beg a clear definition of where one might distinguish philosophically between how far Judaism can go in its recognition of the association of the Divine with the holy teacher and how Hinduism conceives of this relationship.[10]

On the theological level, saints and the attitude to them are significant to determining whether the orientation of worship in a given religion is toward God, understood exclusively, or whether the approach to God can accommodate other manifestations and expressions of the spiritual life. The tension between different forms of Islam is suggestive. As is well known, the Wahabbi authorities that govern the religious practice of Saudi Arabia forbid all expressions of the Sufi cult of saints. To them, expressions of piety and devotion in relation to saints compromise divine unity, while for Sufis the cult of saints is a prominent part of the religious life. Similarly, within Judaism some groups, particularly hassidic and oriental Jews, have a highly developed cult of saints, while others lack it completely. What is at stake seems to be the question of exclusivity of approach to God and the possibility of recognizing Him in some way in relation to His saints. Obviously, there will be different understandings of the relationship between God and the men and women who enjoy particularly close relations with Him. However these relations are understood, they assume some form of sharing of power and life between God and His saints, in and through whom He is known and made manifest. While we may expect stronger and weaker understandings of how saints share in divine life, it seems that weaker and stronger understandings are closer to one another, regardless of their differences, than those forms of religious life that completely deny power to special religious virtuosi are to the weaker understandings. In other words, once the crucial step of according special status to saints has been made, those traditions that have this trait in common have in fact developed a common spiritual language that makes them in some sense closer to one another than they may be to forms of their own religion that completely deny spiritual reality to saints.

In terms of Judaism and Hinduism, this suggests that depending on the kind of Judaism one espouses will be one's reaction to one of Hinduism's major spiritual expressions. Approaching Hinduism from the non-Zaddik-oriented forms of Judaism will likely lead to viewing gurus, and all that takes place in relation to them, as one further expression of Avoda Zara. By contrast, a hassidic understanding of Judaism, or even one that maintains awareness of rabbinic theological roots and how they highlight the role of the Zaddik in various ways,[11] will have a much easier time accepting the special status accorded to unique spiritual individuals. It may even be able to reconcile theologically what might seem to many irreconcilable. At the very least, the theological gaps between the two religions can be considerably narrowed.

A discussion of the different theological understandings of the holy person in Judaism and Hinduism touches on fundamental understandings of the religious life. How far can man go in becoming godlike? What is the role of the saint in relation to God? Is s/he an intermediary? What is the status of mediation, and when does union with God, or the status of special closeness, take one beyond mediation to another form of relationship with God? This issue is one of the most important theological agenda items that must occupy the theological attention of a future Jewish-Hindu dialogue. As an initial observation, I would like to suggest that most Jewish understandings of the function of the Zaddik resort to mediation. As mediation is understood as the root of Avoda Zara, that is, worshipping the intermediary rather than the ultimate,[12] recognition of Zaddikim could run the risk of Avoda Zara were the boundary between spiritual recognition and worship crossed.[13] It is important to note that the Indian model is not one of mediation, but of union, manifestation, and incarnation. Accordingly, the saint is not thought of as an intermediary between the community and God, but rather as a form of divine manifestation. This fundamental difference is also relevant for other issues relating to Avoda Zara and is therefore one of the important theological issues to be worked out between Judaism and Hinduism.

It seems, however, that the real issue is not a matter of theology or worldview as much as of practice, ritual, and local custom. We are thus confronted with the question of the relationship between practice and theory, or how a philosophical understanding of reality can, or cannot, mitigate, contextualize, or otherwise help us come to terms with practices that, considered in their own light, would be considered idolatrous.[14] It is, in fact, Hindu practice that takes us from the realm of the attitudinal to the realm of those concrete manifestations in action that pose the greatest challenge. Let us take the most salient example—the ceremony of waving of lights. This ceremony is performed in the context of the Hindu temple before the images of the Divine enshrined therein. In the context of relations with the teacher, it is performed before a living teacher. Some teachers make this ceremony a regular part of their communal life and ritual. For example, Mata Amritanandamayi has the lights waved before her every time the community gathers for evening song and prayer. As there is no image that is worshipped, she herself is recognized as the Divinity and accorded due respect. Others only have such ceremonies performed on specific and exceptional occasions. Another teacher, Chandra Swami, avoids all forms of idol worship and almost all forms of ritual, preferring instead a more philosophical and interior approach to the Divine. Yet, until recently, on his birthday he had the lights waved before him. This gesture, as well as all gestures of ritual, regardless of their recipient, are expressions of a culture and its particular mind-set. Is this simply the culture's way of affording recognition and giving respect, or does the act inherently express recognition of the divinity, thereby constituting a form of worship, with the attendant implications, considered from a halachic perspective? The matter is further complicated by the fact that every individual may have lights waved before him or her on their birthday. The boundaries between custom and ritual, respect, and worship, the exceptional individual and all people blur and blend, making it hard to arrive at an unequivocal view of the phenomenon. Perhaps the very attempt to address this question through an "either-or" mold is itself an expression of an external gaze that fails to capture the spirit of the culture within which this gesture is performed.

From the perspective of Jewish sensibilities, the issue is not only that of Avoda Zara and whether Hindu understandings and gestures are or are not to be considered Avoda Zara. There is also something in the attitude that can be very disturbing, especially when practiced carelessly and with what might be considered immature zeal and enthusiasm. I have time and again been struck by the ease with which a teacher might be proclaimed, and proven, to be god. For instance, one of the swamis accompanying Mata Amritanandamayi commented to me once on her indefatigable strength. Her ability to pour out love to the masses for days on end, without caring for her own basic physical needs, far exceeds the stamina of her own devotees and attendants, who must therefore take shifts. Who but god, argued the swami, would have such powers? The leap from the powerful and miraculous to the Divine is made with an ease that leaves the Jewish observer ill at ease. It would have been pointless to reply that exceptional power is just that and that it endows its possessor with many attributes, but not necessarily with divinity. Unless, of course, all power is Divine and all life is Divine, in which case what is realized in the saint is not unique to him or her, but is in fact the power of the Divine underlying all things.

I recall another disturbing moment when the Western disciples of Chandra Swami started, in almost clandestine fashion, to refer to him as bhagwan, in other words: Lord, a recognition of the teacher as an incarnation of God. I queried Swamiji on this issue, which he dismissed as the zeal of devotees. In the Hindu context the zeal of devotees easily leads them to regard their teacher as god, at time even leading students of different masters to compete with one another in the piety of divinization. Several years later I queried him again, when he was addressed publicly by one of his disciples in this manner. His reply pointed to the Indian mentality and the ease with which it recognizes divinity, saying that in common parlance anyone may be addressed as bhagwan. In fact, he added, Mr. Alon too is divine.

Ultimately the problem is not simply one of correct or incorrect understanding of the spiritual teacher. Understandings can be reconciled and rituals can be interpreted. I believe the real problem is that with divine status comes immunity from moral error and consequently spiritual corruption for the teacher, for his community, and ultimately for Hinduism itself. I noted the problem when disciples of Sri Sri Ravi Shankar, in a gathering of religious leaders, referred to him as a living God. Beyond how odd it seemed to all non-Hindus, this posed a moral problem. As mouthed by those well-intentioned disciples, the implications of this attitude was that he was beyond criticism. Such an attitude has also been shown by disciples of various gurus, whose names have become associated with scandal of one sort or another. Thus, Sri Rajneesh was called bhagwan. This teacher encouraged sexual licentiousness and developed a type of practice that is far from the conventional ideals of Hinduism as practiced by most of its teachers.[15] No doubt, part of what made this possible was the ascription of divinity to him. Another case is that of Satya Sai Baba, possibly India's biggest guru, until his recent demise. This miracle-working saint has been accused of pedophilia. The charges have been aired by the BBC and the *Times of India*, and the accumulated evidence makes the charges hard to dismiss offhand, even if unproven in a court of law. Believers may respond in one of two ways. They may, along with Sai Baba's spokespersons, simply deny the charges. In that case, the a priori reverence, and in particular the ascription of divinity, could function as a block to moral judgment. They can also function in a more dangerous way, covering up moral wrongs with a spiritual veneer.[16] The moral dangers are obvious.[17]

The situation in Hinduism is in some ways similar to what we find in Judaism, in relation to messianic expectation. The constant expectation of the coming of the Messiah pushes important individuals in the direction of identification with messianic reality. Thus, great masters are turned into "Messiahs," "Messiahs sons of Joseph," and "Messiahs in potential." Similarly, Hinduism is always on the lookout for the manifestation of the Divine. Great souls, aspects of divinity, are understood as incarnating for the well-being of humanity. These souls are the spiritual teachers we encounter. The promise is great: teaching comes from God. The power to reform and transform is grounded in God's ongoing care for humanity, to which He sends teachers time and again. But the dangers are just as great. As there are false messiahs, there are also false *avatars* and false ascriptions of divinity to teachers, who do not make the grade spiritually. A teaching that in its pristine form could be understood is subject to the human psychology of believers and the human frailty of spiritual teachers.

It would be all too easy to chose those teachers who have been termed bhagwan, to point to their flaws and to therefore dismiss everything that has taken place and that continues to take place in relation to gurus as erroneous and idolatrous. That, however, is the easy route. The harder path is the one that recognizes that though they may be few and far between, within Hinduism, personalities of such outstanding quality have emerged that their followers have been led to consider an encounter with them is indeed an encounter with God. Beyond the cultural trappings, ritual language, and frailty of human psychology we must also recognize that India has consistently produced great lives who are moral exemplars and spiritual giants. That they are viewed as divine is, above all, a testimony to how deeply the Divine is sought in this culture. This testimony should not be obstructed by the many challenges posed by the common Indian attitude to the guru and his divinity. At the end of the day, holy men and women are Hinduism's most powerful witness, as well as one of the greatest challenges, to a Jewish understanding of Hinduism.

9

The Wisdom of India: Ancient Images and Contemporary Challenges

The encounter of cultures happens in rich and complex ways. It is also conceived in varying and changing ways. An encounter between cultures can never be reduced to one single dimension or factor that captures its import. Any attempt to frame the encounter, to highlight what another culture is or represents, to focus upon particular challenges and problematics is already informed by a conceptual agenda. How cultures are juxtaposed and how their point of encounter and ensuing challenges are conceived already betrays a certain understanding of what is important to a given culture. The changes in how one culture imagines another, how it portrays it, and what it deems important in it provide an important lens through which we learn about the imagining culture as much as about the encounter of the two cultures. Because cultures are complex, we may expect different and changing conceptions of how they interact and what they mean to each other as these emerge over time. Let us examine how such changes are expressed in the Jewish view of Hinduism.

There are multiple dimensions to the Jewish-Hindu encounter. As scholars have noted, the earliest contacts were based on commerce.[1] Commerce remains an important aspect of present-day relations between Israel and India. While this may not be the aspect that interests us the most, when we think of Judaism and Hinduism as religious entities, it does illustrate how encounters are defined by the perspectives that are brought to bear by participants, and by how they conceptualize both the other and the nature of the encounter.

One may think of various dimensions of Hinduism, and each will lead us to conceptualize the encounter in different ways. We have already noted some of these. Spirituality is one dimension of encounter. In contemporary times this is perhaps the predominant one, with much attention turned to India as a resource for contemporary spirituality. A spirituality-based encounter is already a way of conceptualizing what is important about a religion, both one's own and that of the other. Saints also constitute a form of conceptualizing the encounter, by focusing it upon the human person, his or her potential, and the testimony of different religious traditions to what it means to be fully human, or to what human flourishing is.

The present chapter focuses on yet another way of conceptualizing the encounter between Judaism and Hinduism. Its significance lies in the fact that it is probably the oldest way of conceiving of the contact between these cultures, bearing testimony to what India has meant to the Jewish imagination for almost 2,000 years. The dimension that will be discussed here remains an important aspect of the encounter. It provides a way for both partners to understand themselves, their uniqueness, and the contribution they may make to each other. It further allows us to reflect upon the enduring challenges of the encounter for Judaism's own growth and development.

India is a land of wisdom. It has many sages. Love of wisdom leads its sages on to the spiritual life, including the disciplines and sacrifices it entails. This is probably the most concise summary image of what India means to classical Jewish literature. This composite picture, one that obviously compromises many important exceptions, emerges from texts of late antiquity as well as from the testimony of writings in the Middle Ages and the Renaissance periods. The focus upon wisdom is, in and of itself, far less threatening than the focus on idolatry, and therefore allows for a much more open and accepting attitude toward India and its spiritual reality. Let us study the various expressions of this view of India as a land and culture of wisdom.

The earliest reference to India in terms of wisdom draws on conventions common in the hellenistic world. Probably the earliest such reference is found in Josephus. In his description of the events at Masada, we find the following speech, placed in the hero's mouth, leading up to the collective suicide of Masada's warriors. Josephus composed two speeches, that he placed in the mouth of Eleazar ben Yair, the Masada leader.[2] After the first speech that fails to convince his listeners, Eleazar offers a second one. The focus of the second speech is death, which one must not fear. This leads Eleazar to reflect on the immortality of the soul, and this in turn takes him to India:

> Let us look at those Indians who profess the practice of philosophy. They, brave men that they are, reluctantly endure the period of life, as some necessary service due to nature, but hasten to release their souls from their bodies; and though no calamity impels nor drives them from the scene, from sheer longing for the immortal state, they announce to their comrades that they are about to depart. Nor is there any who would hinder them; no, all felicitate them and each gives them commissions to his loved ones; so certain and absolutely sincere is their belief in the intercourse which souls hold with one another. Then, after listening to these behests, they commit their bodies to the fire, so that the soul may be parted from the body in the utmost purity, and expire amidst hymns of praise. Indeed, their dearest ones escort them to their death more readily than do the rest of mankind their fellow-citizens when starting on a very long journey; for themselves they weep, but them they count happy as now regaining immortal rank.[3]

What Josephus knows of Indian sages he knows as part of a broader hellenistic background.[4] What is important is how he uses it. Indians provide an ideal. They are philosophers, and they put their philosophical understanding to practice in the most extreme way. Not only is the view of Indian sages positive; they are actually considered role models. Of course, emulating them is qualified by the fact that the speech is placed by Josephus as being spoken by a representative of the fourth philosophy, one that he himself opposes. Nevertheless, we do not get the sense of distancing oneself from these teachings. Rather, the Indian sages are an ideal and are upheld as such. It may not be superfluous to point out, in the context of the present discussion, that one of the earliest references to India takes place in a context of cultural borrowing. India provides an inspiration for religiously, or philosophically, motivated action that cannot be sustained with examples and precedents from the Jewish tradition proper. And the author seems to have no problem leaping over into a foreign culture in order to make his point. The fundamental objection that the testimony of another culture is meaningless and its values foreign does not seem to have any place in this rhetorical piece. Philosophy seems to provide a commonality for all humanity. This allows an inspiring speech to be made, leading to action that is far from traditional.

The view of India as a land of wisdom continued to dominate Jewish perspectives on Hinduism throughout the Middle Ages.[5] This view cannot be detached from the broader Muslim context, through which religions are viewed. Indeed, it seems that situating earlier Jewish views on Hinduism within a Muslim context holds the key to how Hinduism is viewed and what aspects of it are privileged.[6] For Muslim thinkers, prophecy is the most important yardstick for measuring a religious tradition, their own as well as those preceding them. What is striking for them in Hinduism is precisely the lack of prophetic tradition, hence the consistent portrayal of India as a culture of wisdom. Wisdom is thus juxtaposed with prophecy.[7] It is a fair generalization that most Jewish references to India and its religious culture are indebted to this way of conceptualizing the religions. This also holds the key to Jewish superiority in relation to Hinduism, as well as to the ways of viewing it in a positive light.[8]

The image of the Indian sage as one who has a true God but lacks prophecy emerges time and again in various medieval Jewish sources.[9] This seems to me the basis for Saadiah Gaon's (tenth century) reference to Brahmins in the course of a discussion of the claims of Christians and Muslims for the abrogation of the Torah.[10] Saadiah can use the Brahmins in the context of a theoretical appeal to Adam and his traditions precisely because they are outside the framework of prophecy and represent a theoretical other, hence a test case for his argument.[11] In another context, the Brahmins are portrayed as saying: "We do not behave according to law or prophet or image or god...We recognize from ourselves the cause and principle of wisdom, and our mind teaches us the way we should work."[12] Accordingly, both the language and the themes placed in Jewish writings as spoken by Brahmins reveal similarity in worldview. Common faith emerges in relation to monotheism, creation, the value of Wisdom, praise and trust of God, and the truth of human impermanence.

While many authorities view the religious tradition of India positively, some view it negatively. Yehuda Halevy is a case in point. Halevy speaks of the people of India and how they "arouse the indignation of the followers of religions through their talk, whilst they anger them with their idols, talismans and witchcraft."[13] The contrast that Halevy sets up is precisely the contrast between religions founded upon revealed scriptures and a religion that is not based on a book, but on magical practice, astrology, and the like. A recent analysis of Halevy suggests that it is precisely the lack of revelation that creates the space for alternative practices, and thus one may suggest a causal relation between lack of revelation and magical practices.[14] Underlying Halevy's classification of the religion of the people of India is the same typology, contrasting revelation and human wisdom.[15] However, in Halevy's hands the distinction becomes more extreme, leading to the contrast of revelation and evil and false human wisdom, typified by magic and sorcery.[16]

The various references to India as a land of wisdom are important not only for what they have to say about India, but also for providing us with a positive precedent for appreciating it. The importance of these references also lies in the fact that once again we realize how the assessment of another culture, or another religion, is indebted to the choice of categories through which it is viewed, and how culturally determined and time contingent these categories are. Thus, the Middle Ages provide us with an important paradigm, one of several possible paradigms, for how Jews have thought about Indian religion and culture. The wisdom paradigm, contextualized in Greek lore and further developed in light of the Muslim emphasis on prophecy and its centrality, offers us one way of viewing the religious culture of India.

The legacy of the Middle Ages is one of the resources for contemporary attitudes to India and its religious traditions. Indian sages being viewed in a positive light led to some positive evaluations of Hindu wisdom. An important bridge, in this context, is Menashe ben Israel, the seventeenth-century rabbi from Amsterdam:

> Similarly, when he (Abraham) went down to Egypt and lived there, he taught this philosophy, after which he sent the sons of his concubines away from Isaac while he was yet alive towards the East to their holy land, India. They also disseminated this faith. Behold, you may see there the Abrahamites, who are today called Brahmans; they are the sons of Abraham our patriarch and they were the first in India to spread this faith, as Appolonius Tionius, who spoke with them and King Yercha face to face, testified...And they spoke the truth, for from the seed of Abraham this ideology was created anew. From there, the new belief spread all over India, as is evident from the writings of that period. Their faith is, however, often thought of as Pythagoras' innovation, since it had disappeared for a few years, but he was not the originator. Also, this was the code followed by Alexander Polister who heard and studied it from the prophet Ezekiel who was his mentor.[17]

Underlying this passage is a reading of Genesis 25,6, according to which Abraham gave gifts and then sent off the sons of his concubines to the East. This verse has a rich history of interpretation.[18] Menashe ben Israel, writing in Renaissance times, relates to more concrete knowledge about Hindus and their beliefs.[19] The description of Hindus and their practices is received positively by him. In a classical inclusivist move, he is able to contain the beliefs of the Hindus within his worldview, by suggesting they originate with the teachings of Abraham. Gen. 25,6 thus provides a key for affirming the validity of Hindu teachings as having Abrahamic origins.[20]

This positive evaluation of Indian wisdom by Menashe ben Israel provides the theoretical foundations to one of the most interesting attempts to relate Hinduism and Judaism, made by Rabbi Matityahu Glazerson. Glazerzon authored a book titled *From Hinduism to Judaism.* [21] The quote from Menashe ben Israel is used by Glazerson as the book's motto. Relying thus on Menashe ben Israel allows Glazerson to approach Hinduism in an open and positive manner. In fact, it is probably the most favorable and positive treatment of Hinduism by any Jewish author. This is made possible through the twofold strategy of concentrating on Hinduism as wisdom, rather than worship or religion, and approaching that wisdom as our own, in the inclusivist mode already mentioned. The book's logic runs as follows: Hinduism teaches; we find these teachings in Judaism as well. This conceptual scheme is repeated time and again and provides the book's basic mode of thinking. The basic premise is that Hindu teaching is valid. Glazerson's job is to demonstrate that there is no need to go to Hinduism in order to obtain that wisdom and that it is fully available in Judaism as well. Hinduism emerges as valid and meaningful for non-Jews. In Glazerson's scheme, Jews are endowed with a special soul and therefore can only find their spiritual fulfillment through the observance of the mitzvot and by following Judaism. Hinduism is thus a valid way of wisdom (Glazerson never uses the word religion in this context), but it is inadequate for Jews. The problem with Glazerson's deep logic becomes apparent when put this way. What makes Judaism perfect or appropriate for Jews is that it is more than a set of wisdom teachings and practices; it is a religion in the full sense. Hinduism is never acknowledged as such. The comparison is made in a partial way that works in Judaism's favor.

That Glazerson's argument is partial should not lead us to minimize his achievements. Glazerson is able to highlight what is positive, in his eyes, in Hinduism, while bracketing all that most rabbinic figures find problematic in Hinduism, namely the foreign worship. Constructing this argument and developing it as extensively as he does is an important strategy that must be respected. In part, Glazerson does so because this is the Hinduism that his readership has encountered. His educational work focuses on bringing back to Judaism those spiritual seekers who have had meaningful religious experiences under the umbrella of Hinduism. Most of these seekers were never involved in living Hinduism as native Hindus might, but rather practiced some rarefied or distilled form, imported to the West, in the service of Western seekers. Their practice of meditation, exercises, breathing, and the likes was complemented by a set of teachings that emphasized the wisdom aspect of Hinduism, thereby presenting a Hinduism that is indeed more of a path of practiced wisdom than a full religious path. Glazerson is not simply ignoring parts of Hinduism. He is responding to specific presentations and constructions of Hinduism that have crystallized in various contemporary movements. The strategy of acknowledging, owning, and going beyond functions for him far more effectively than the theoretical alternative of rejection.

It is hard to guage to what extent Glazerson really took his key from Menashe ben Israel and then went on to substantiate it through his encounter with

Hinduism, or whether he was seeking a strategy that would allow him to take an inclusivist stand toward Hindu teaching, thereby facilitating the reentry of thousands of returnees back to the fold of Judaism. My sense is that his use of Menashe ben Israel is not cynical or calculated. A historically naive view of the spread of wisdom teachings is helpful to contemporary challenges. Once accepted, it allows Glazerson to load it with its fullest possible meaning. For all its naivete and despite the fact that it presents Hinduism as only a part of what it is, this remains the most interesting and positive approach to Hinduism found in contemporary literature.

Similar in strategy, though much less elaborate, is a recent contribution by Rabbi Yitzchak Ginsburgh.[22] Speaking to Jewish seekers who have returned from India, Ginsburgh puts forth an inclusivist view that sees Hinduism as basically positive, yet inadequate for Jews. Ginsburgh too provides a foundation for positive appreciation of Hinduism by seeing it as wisdom originating in Abraham's gifts to his children and appeals to the wordplay of Abraham and Brahmin.[23] The inclusivist perspective is nicely captured through the wordplay associating Jew and Hindu: יהודי – הודי. It is only one letter that distinguishes the two. Ginsburgh is able to affirm the spiritual quest, as it takes seekers to India as a necessary step in self-discovery. Nevertheless, there remains something incomplete in Hindu teaching. Mantra meditation is positive, yet inadequate; Hindu pantheism features only one side of a theological paradox.[24]

As we follow the trajectory that sees Hinduism as a wisdom tradition, we note important differences between the different historical stages. It appears that only with the passage of time, as more and more is known of the real India, does the encounter become increasingly real. The ancient and medieval projection of India was based on hearsay and on the popular view of a distant culture.[25] This popular view was shaped more by contemporary concerns and ideals than by an actual encounter. Not a single one of the noted authors of the Middle Ages seems to have visited India or read any of its writings. They did, however, integrate Muslim reports and views on India into a Jewish view of India and Hinduism.[26] Significantly, this brought India into the scope of meaning and relevance, within which Judaism and the Torah's commandments were appreciated. We note, for example, Ibn Ezra's Torah commentary relating to various commandments from a broader cultural framework that includes India in its horizons.[27] While India is presented in ways that may not represent it faithfully, through the filter of another culture and its historians, it nevertheless is within the frame of common meaning. This in turn can potentially generate a respectful attitude.[28] Menashe ben Israel seems to represent a further stage in moving toward real historical contact. His references to India are based on actual contemporary reports, which he then assesses, in light of his worldview. Finally, Glazerson encounters Hinduism through the lives and teachings of the young Jews who had been exposed to it and who are making their way back to Judaism. The trajectory of viewing Hinduism in terms of wisdom is one; its manifestations become increasingly real, as Judaism's encounter with Hinduism becomes more real, immediate, and urgent.

There may be one exception to the statement concerning lack of contact with actual Hinduism. This is the case of the famous traveler Benjamin of Tudela.[29] In contrast to most authors of old, Benjamin does not focus on the wisdom, but on the ritual practices.[30] The Hinduism that Benjamin sees is the precise opposite, or complement, of that presented by Glazerson. This Hinduism is interpreted by Benjamin in light of biblical pagan worship, as his choice of language suggests. It is hard to draw conclusions from this fact, but it is still one worth reflecting upon. Does the immediate contact with Hindus impress the observer so that worship is highlighted at the expense of wisdom? Does Benjamin provide us with an example of the one-sidedness of many Jewish observers, who only see ritual and fail to consider the wisdom of the religion? And could Glazerson and Benjamin be representatives, from within Judaism, of the fundamental problem of multiple Hinduisms, taking on multiple expressions and manifestations, which is precisely what makes a uniform approach to Hinduism so complicated? Finally, both writers may be approaching what they encounter through the lens of their own tradition, that in turn colors their view and judgment. By applying biblical verses to the practices of southern India, Benjamin may be not simply describing, but also prejudging and interpreting. In fact, the biblical sources may be driving what he sees and how he describes it. Similarly, Menashe ben Israel's view of the Abrahamic Hindu truth colors Glazerson's judgment, leading to comparisons and identifications that are at times too facile. In their disparate ways, at different points in time, both authors provide us with a reminder of how we must try to understand the phenomenon of the religious other as closely as possible on the other's own terms and not to jump to interpretation, let alone description, in terms that we are predisposed to and comfortable with, drawn from our own tradition.

Recognition of India and its religious tradition as a repository of wisdom is probably the most persistent view of India found in Jewish literature. It is about as old as rabbinic Judaism itself. This should tell us something important in terms of the Jewish encounter with Hinduism. Regardless of how well previous generations knew the religion of India and whether that knowledge was direct or mediated, wisdom is a recognized way for engaging Hinduism. Given that many, possibly most, Hindus will feel comfortable with a description of their tradition in terms of wisdom, and that they would probably even consent to distinguishing it from revelation, as used by the Abrahamic faiths,[31] we have here an important element for contact and mutual understanding that is by now a fundamental aspect of the Jewish tradition's view of India and its religion. For the contemporary encounter this could mean two things. The first is an important dimension of positive appreciation and recognition of Hinduism, as demonstrated in Matityahu Glazerson's work. The second is far more challenging, and is to a large extent a matter for the future. In order to introduce this second aspect of the significance of recognizing Hinduism in terms of wisdom, I would like to turn to a passage from A. J. Heschel. In *God in Search of Man*, Heschel writes:

> Had Jerusalem been located at the foot of the Himalayas, monotheistic philosophy would have been modified by the tradition of oriental thinkers. Thus, our intellectual position situated as it is between Athens and Jerusalem is not an ultimate one. Providence may some day create a situation which would place us between

the river Jordan and the river Ganges, and the problem of such an encounter will
be different from that which Jewish thought underwent when meeting with Greek
philosophy.[32]

Heschel's words seem prophetic. Indeed this providential moment has
arrived, and only decades after Heschel surmised about this possibility. Heschel
recognizes the potential of the encounter with Hinduism for Jewish philosophy.
Heschel poses the initial challenge: What would be the problems and challenges
that the philosophical encounter with Hinduism would generate? These challenges are not seen by him as a threat, but as part of the growth and development
of Judaism, as it seeks to articulate its uniqueness and its identity, in the course of
encounters with other religious civilizations.

While the present encounter with Hinduism is now well on its way, very little
has actually been undertaken in terms of the philosophical dialogue envisioned
by Heschel. With the exception of one or two authors, who have tried to formulate their understanding of Judaism in light of insights gained through exposure
to Hinduism,[33] we lack as of now serious attempts to tackle the philosophical
and theological challenges of the encounter. I imagine that a certain critical time
and critical number of travelers and people who have been exposed to Hinduism
must be attained, before the encounter can impact Jewish theological thinking.[34]
Given the speed, breadth, and intensity of travel and encounter, we may not be
far from attaining the kind of critical mass that would impact Jewish theological thinking. I personally know of several rabbis and teachers of religion whose
travels have served as a resource for theological and spiritual enrichment.[35] One
present-day teacher, in particular, offers a kind of synthesis of Jewish and Hindu
wisdom as spiritual food for the contemporary Jewish seeker.[36] My sense is that
the time is not far off when Heschel's prophetic insight will become a reality.
The philosophical and theological encounter that lies ahead may thus hold a key
to future regeneration of Jewish theological thinking, as it seeks to articulate its
core understanding in dialogue with a new religious universe. This religious universe is already welcomed by many as an alternative to Western philosophy and
culture and may prove to be a potential context for Jewish spiritual transformation and regeneration, much as earlier Jewish encounters with other cultures led
to their own novel articulations of Judaism.

In this context, we do well to recall that Judaism is the latest "Abrahamic"
faith to explore its relations with the religions of India. Both Christianity and
Islam have done so for centuries. The paradigms have ranged from coercion and
competition to spiritual transformation through dialogue and acculturation.
The twentieth century saw several important Christian figures, who sought to
state their Christian identity within the context of Hindu reality, thereby leading to new theological and spiritual statements of the reality of Christianity. Key
figures in this movement include Bede Griffiths, Swami Abhishiktananda, and
others. Of particular note, in this context, is the recent work of Francis Clooney.
His *Hindu God, Christian God*[37] is a good example of the kind of theological
creativity and regeneration that is made possible through the deep spiritual
dialogue with Hinduism. As noted already, there is, as of yet, nothing even

roughly equivalent to Clooney's work on the Jewish side.[38] I would think that as the encounter deepens and broadens, we may expect similar Jewish theological explorations to emerge.

In what follows, I would like to trace some key ideas that could be relevant to such a future theological dialogue and to its possible impact on a Jewish theological and spiritual regeneration. In tracing these ideas I find myself relying on my own experience and the questions that have occupied my attention. But I draw no less on some of the experiences and challenges faced by my Christian friends, as they have sought to state what is unique and particular in their tradition, vis-à-vis Hinduism.[39] What follows is of necessity impressionistic and suggestive. I hope it is nevertheless helpful in adumbrating some of the areas where a future wisdom-based dialogue can lead to philosophical, theological, and spiritual creativity and rejuvenation within Judaism, through its developing encounter with Hinduism.

Jewish religious thought has long ceased tackling in fresh and original ways some of the core issues that should be of concern to any religious thought. The accumulated achievements of nearly a thousand years of philosophical, theological, and mystical creativity have to a large extent come to a near standstill. There is very little theological creativity in contemporary Jewish thought. It seems the questions have been settled, or at least addressed, and one is often content to quote positions and solutions articulated by earlier masters. Most present-day efforts are aimed at addressing various social ills, the challenges of implementing a Jewish vision for the state of Israel, and the various concerns of the Jewish people worldwide. I cannot think of a single Jewish thinker who has made a significant contribution to our understanding of God and the spiritual life for nearly 70 years, since the passing away of Rabbi Abraham Isaac Kook.[40] Even the changes in our worldview resulting from advances in scientific thought have not led to broad, serious reflection on core beliefs and how they are to be understood and articulated in present times.

It makes sense to me that the encounter with Indian religious thought can stimulate a fresh wave of reflection on issues of fundamental religious concern. The challenges of the encounter with Western society over the past century or more have not brought about meaningful development in religious thought because the focus of Western philosophy and culture has not been upon matters of ultimate religious concern. We have been challenged in our social thinking, in all that concerns the human being and his or her dignity, and by the traumatic and challenging events of history, as these have applied to the Jewish people. But, other than the challenge of theodicy to religious thought, we have not been challenged in ways that would require, or provide the opportunity for, fresh theological articulation of Jewish faith. This is likely to take place only in dialogue with another religious culture, one that Judaism has not been previously in dialogue with. Here the encounter with Hinduism, as well as with other Eastern religions, provides an important opportunity for spiritual and theological regeneration.

Let me spell out what I think are some of the issues that could be part of such a future conversation and how Judaism might be challenged to restate its faith. We begin with the recognition that religious systems form an integrated whole, where various religious insights and understandings cohere into a system that has its own logic and that is complete and whole unto itself. Therefore, religious systems should be considered in their totality. A specific religious cognition should be appreciated in relation to the overall parameters of the religious system. While religious systems may be similar to one another in many specific faith claims and spiritual recognitions, they draw them together under different governing principles. The differences between the faith systems concern the system as a whole, but they extend to the specific faith claims, including such claims that could have provided common ground with another tradition. Let me illustrate this. Jews and Hindus believe in God. Jews and Hindus express this through worship. Jews and Hindus recognize the specialness of the human person and the spiritual opportunities and obligations that are particular to the human person. Jews and Hindus attach great importance to proper action and right living. All these commonalities may be taken for granted. Indeed, they may be overlooked or go unappreciated by members of the faith tradition who choose to highlight all that is different at the expense of fundamental religious commonalities. Thus, for many Jews, who view Hinduism as a form of idolatry, the fundamental commonalities suggested just now are not at all obvious. We therefore need to recall them. But even once we have recognized fundamental commonalities, each religious system, and its subsystems, Judaisms and Hinduisms, configures the various metaphysical and spiritual recognitions in different ways. Key spiritual insights are clustered into wholes that condition both faith and practice differently in both traditions. It is here that the mutual engagement between the traditions becomes fascinating and a source of potential enrichment.

In considering what the Jewish encounter with Hinduism could mean theologically, I would like to focus attention on two core issues—the relationship of God and creation and the understanding of the Divine and its inner life. All that is challenging in Hinduism for Judaism, in both theoretical and practical terms, can probably be traced back to these two issues. The challenge is of course reciprocal. In what way does a Hindu understanding either challenge a Jewish understanding, or enrich it, possibly revealing a deeper affinity between the two? By contrast, in what way does Judaism consider itself as having a message that might be relevant to the fundamentals of the Hindu worldview? Regrettably, to the best of my knowledge, there is not a single attempt to state what Judaism has to offer, as an inspiration or as a corrective, to a Hindu worldview. Hindus are, in this respect, much more self-confident in the universality of their message, considering it is either already articulated in another tradition (following a common trope in the widespread Hindu view of other religions) or is the fundamental spiritual truth, that all religions should be teaching. While Judaism obviously affirms fundamental truths regarding the nature of God and His purpose for creation, common references to Hindu religion tend to belittle the spiritual value of the religion and to identify it with simplistic idol worship. Consequently, Judaism's "message" to Hinduism remains quite unsophisticated, if not primitive—outgrow your idol worship, rather than offering a nuanced spiritual response, alternative, or affirmation to the core spiritual recognitions expressed through Hinduism.

What is the relationship between God and creation? There are multiple voices within Judaism on this issue, reflecting in part the different environments within which theological notions were formed, possible opponents in relation to whom theological ideals were expressed and the profound spiritual and experiential insights of individual authors. It would be fair to say that the default Jewish position seeks to distinguish God from creation. Creator and creation are divided through the act of creation and the metaphysical implications it carries for both. It would be equally fair to say that most Hindu philosophies either bridge that gap in significant ways or perhaps do not even recognize it. A common way of expressing the Hindu position appeals to God's attributes. Some of these would seem to be common to both traditions, like the notions of God's omnipotence, omniscience, and goodness. But for many Hindus we would need to add one more fundamental attribute—God's presence as an all-pervading Being, whose being pervades all of life, the entire universe. Herein lies a great challenge. What does it mean to speak of God's presence, or stronger yet, His all-pervading presence? If God is all-pervading, does that make everything Divine? Where does the human person, and his will, come into play? How autonomous is creation from the creator? And if we do assume the fundamental divide between creator and creation as the default Jewish position, does that mean that creation is completely distinct and separated from divine reality. This is by no means the position of all Jewish thinkers. The kabbalistic school finds various means of affirming divine sustenance and life force within creation. Still, on the whole, Jewish thinking tends to separate God and creation, where Hindu thinking tends to identify them. At its philosophical heights, this makes Hindu thinking monistic, recognizing the unity of all existence, as distinct from the monotheism of Judaism, the recognition of the one God.[41]

Let us move from metaphysics to psychology, education, and the spiritual life. What type of religious personality is formed when we operate with one view or with the other? Can we be enriched either by the theory or by the practice of a religious worldview that posits the relationship between God and creation in ways that are different from our own conventions? And can engagement with these very issues allow us to recover or to better appreciate various sources or possibilities within our tradition that we might not have considered previously?[42]

These issues are not simply fine points of metaphysics, worked out by one tradition or another. Some of today's most pressing issues can be traced back to the fundamental question of God and creation. Contemporary environmental concerns have highlighted the question of the attitude to creation as a fundamental issue of religious thought and as a significant issue for dialogue between religions. A common accusation against the biblical tradition is that it separates man from nature, commanding man to conquer nature, thereby leading to its exploitation and to man's alienation from nature.[43] That this charge is very much oversimplified has been adequately demonstrated.[44] But there does seem to be another, even more fundamental, divide that affects our attitude to nature, and that is the division between God and creation. How God's relationship with creation is envisioned has moral consequences that are nowadays immediate, rather than the subject of theoretical metaphysical speculation.

The moral consequences do not refer only to nature and creation. They concern a fundamental vision of the unity of life and the unity of all beings. While such unity can be established in various ways, recognizing the continuity of expression between the divine life and creation is the most important and fundamental strategy for achieving this.

It is also worth recalling that today's religious thought, and this is probably true for all religious traditions, is more challenged by today's significant other—science—than it is by any individual religious tradition. It stands to reason that different approaches to the question of the relationship of God and creation will yield different perspectives for religion's encounter with science. Creation may speak to us in other ways and provide other kinds of testimony, perhaps even revelation, if our view of it is less divorced from divine reality. It is my impression that on the whole, Indian religious thought has been more successful in tackling the science/religion challenge than Jewish religious thought, which has been mostly either defensive or ignored the challenges of contemporary science.[45] This may be traced back to fundamental attitudes to creation and to its religious significance.

Jewish and Hindu positions that seem to be placed on opposite sides of a great metaphysical divide may in fact be closer to one another than what initial inspection suggests. Let me illustrate this by considering one of the classical Jewish statements of faith, found in Maimonides' legal code. In fact, this is the statement that opens Maimonides' Mishne Torah. I turn to Maimonides, rather than to the tradition of Jewish mysticism, precisely as an indication of how unexpected the similarities may turn out to be and how much common ground might exist between classical Jewish and Hindu views.

Let me quote the opening of Mishne Torah:

1. The foundation of foundations and the pillar of wisdom is to know there is a primordial Being, and that He brought about all that is. And all that is (exists), of heaven and earth and what is between, exist only on the account of the Truth of His Being.
2. And if one were to consider that He did not exist, naught else could exist.
3. And if one were to consider that all beings other than Him are not (or: do not exist), He alone would exist, and would not be annihilated on their account. For all that is needs Him, but He, blessed be He, does not need them, nor one of them. Therefore His truth is not like the truth of one of them.
4. This is what the prophet says, "But the Lord God is Truth." He alone is the Truth and none other has Truth like His Truth. This is what the Torah has said: "There is none else beside Him" (Deut. 4,35), meaning: there is no true Being like Him, besides Him.
5. The knowledge of this is a positive commandment, as it says "I am the Lord your God"(Ex. 20,2). Whoever considers that there is in existence another god, other than Him, transgresses the commandment "Thou shalt not have another god upon my face"(Ex. 20, 3) and denies the principle that is the great principle upon which everything depends.[46]

I turn to this text probably because of the power of one occasion when I contemplated it. I remember reading this text closely in the ashram at a time when I was engrossed in reading, thinking, and dialoguing with the vedantic worldview. Several things struck me. The first, and most obvious, was how easily this text could have been composed by a vedantin. God alone is. All else is secondary and derivative of His existence. In truth, God alone exists. Nothing is real as God is real. God alone is Truth. God alone is Being. These are the most fundamental teachings that the student of this Hindu philosophy encounters regularly. And the Hindu would surely agree with Maimonides in placing these teachings as the foundation of all other knowledge. This is the core knowledge. All else is derivative of it.

Things do not become culturally specific until we encounter the appeal to Scripture, first in the appeal to the prophets in 4, and then to the ten commandments in 6. What Maimonides has done here is to make the ten commandments announce first and foremost the most fundamental philosophical truth, one that can well be appreciated outside Judaism and its particularity.[47] The universal metaphysical truth is couched in the terms of Judaism's basic Scripture and core revelation.

Reading this text with vedantic eyes is not only an exercise in recognition of common truths. It is also an exercise in highlighting ideas, as they are seen through the lens of another religious tradition. Truth and Being are core notions of vedantic philosophy. They are understood as core attributes of the Divine. They also designate the realm that is being addressed and what it is that is important to know and recognize about God.[48] The actual content may be close, perhaps even identical. But reading this text in light of another tradition colors it in particular ways that provide it with meaning and resonance.

It would be unfair to stop at this parallel. More is at stake than simply discovering fundamental truths that two religions have in common. We need to move on and to ask: How central a role does this teaching play in the spiritual formation of each of our traditions? Here is where one important distinction emerges. Many well-educated and pious Jews may never read this text, and if they do it may not play a formative role in their thinking of God. By contrast, reflection on these ideas is the spiritual bread and butter of Vedanta. It is the philosophical basis and the fundamental spiritual and psychological training. In the context of the Mishne Torah these are the opening lines, important as they may be, to a legal code that is vast, occupying 14 full volumes. Many readers have little recourse to its opening chapters, a programmatic effort Maimonides made to include philosophical understanding within classical Torah curriculum and within the framework of Jewish law. For the vedantin, these issues are what spiritual teaching is all about, and their elaboration, exploration, meditation, and realization are the goal and the path of the spiritual life. Surely, there have been Jewish authorities and schools that have paid a great deal of attention to these questions and that have made contemplation of these issues and training in their realization significant aspects of their spirituality. This is as true for the Jewish philosophers as it is for some mystical schools. The vast literature of Habad (Lubavitch) Hassidism, with its library of hundreds of volumes, many of which engage such issues in great detail, comes to mind. Still, we recognize an important difference in the overall economy of these ideas and how they play out in the respective systems.

If I were to overstate my case, I would say: one system's introduction is another system's focus and goal. If so, a Jewish encounter with a Hindu perspective, in light of such a text, can do more than simply provide a common language or a means for recognizing the ultimate spiritual validity of a Hindu position. It can also serve to regenerate and deepen the Jewish understanding, as it takes stock of its own treasures, their value, and how they can provide a basis for an entire spiritual path, orienting the life of the individual and focusing the goal of a religious worldview.

But are the differences simply differences in emphasis? The answer is no. What could serve as a common foundation is later elaborated and developed in ways that are contradictory. The point of divergence touches upon the relationship between God and His creation. What is the nature of the reality of all that exists? How are we to understand the statement that all that exists, exists only on account of the Truth of His Being? For Jews this means that God alone exists. The existence of all else is secondary and derivative of God's Being, but ultimately not real, not true. Hence, in the ultimate sense, God alone exists; nothing else. The vedantin would well agree with this, with one major difference: All that exists exists because it shares in God's existence. Therefore, all Being participates in this Truth, as it derives its life from God and shares in His life. Recognition of the all-pervading God, whose life fills all of creation, and for whom creation serves as its outer expression, leads to a radical difference in the view of creation in terms of its relation to God, Being, and Truth.

The difference could be considered small or huge, depending on the reading we offer, which in turn depends on the type of Judaism we espouse. That everything may be recognized as divine is very different from Maimonides, but not so different from some of his later applications. The tradition of Habad Hassidism is particularly strong in its emphasis on there being no other reality besides God, affirming this through the very proof text brought by Maimonides, Deut. 4,35. How broad the metaphysical gap is would depend on the positions we adopt and how we identify with the development of these ideas within Judaism.[49]

Things look very different, however, when we come to the practical applications of these philosophical differences. What are the implications of the recognition that all life shares in the divine life for worship? Put differently, whom is one worshipping? If all is one, and God alone is, one cannot worship anyone or anything but God. From this perspective, idolatry, as a worship of another god, would be an oxymoron. It is not really possible to worship anyone but God and all worship that is not directed at Him or does not recognize that it is directed at him is simply an expression of ignorance.[50]

What all this suggests is that philosophically Jews and Hindus could understand each other much better than one might have thought. What gets in the way is often the external worship. Even if profound commonalities in spiritual and metaphysical outlook can be found, the common foundation may be applied in radically different ways in both traditions. That everything may be worshipped and that nothing may be worshipped except for God may both be derived from the same set of metaphysical foundations, as these are variously applied. These differences should not be minimized. But they should be taken for what they are, differences applying to the realm of the practical, the realm of worship, rather than fundamental differences in worldview, or at least irresolvable differences between two religious worldviews. Recognizing the fundamental affinities in worldview has important attitudinal consequences. Whether we affirm our differences, hold on to a particular viewpoint or message as the message of Judaism, or even declare Hinduism to be Avoda Zara, any move we make must be undertaken in a nuanced way.

The move from philosophical premises to the realm of worship leads us to the second fundamental issue: understanding the Divine and its inner life. Here we encounter differences that may be more significant or perhaps theological challenges and opportunities that may be greater. What do we mean when we say "God"? That is the question that is at the heart of the divide between different religions and between various philosophies and religious approaches found within them. As religions talk to one another they may chose to recognize the God worshipped by another religion as the same or as a different God. If the other god is not recognized, his worship is considered idolatrous.[51] If the other's God is recognized this would, in some cases, lead to syncretism; in others it leads to recognition of the validity of another religion. There is yet another possibility, recognition of the other tradition as a form of inspiration or enrichment for theological thinking. Jews have for some time struggled with the question of whether the God they worship is the same God worshipped by Christians and Muslims. In the case of Islam, encounter with Muslim theological reflection on God resulted in a great enrichment to Jewish theological thought, as a consequence of the exposure to the reigning philosophical paradigms that provided a theological common ground for Jews and Muslims. Indeed, philosophy seems to have the power to stimulate fresh theological reflection and thereby to deepen and enrich religious thinking. This could also be the case with the present Jewish encounter with Hinduism, and the exposure to a philosophical discourse and religious worldview that Judaism had not previously been exposed to. There are important ways in which such a discourse touches directly upon the question of what we mean when we say "God."

Jewish monotheism with its emphasis on God as the only God may make it superfluous to engage in further contemplation upon the nature of the Divine. Indeed, for most practitioners, and even authorities, the understanding of God remains remarkably simple. While philosophers of the Middle Ages have problematized our ability to speak of God in human language in meaningful ways and while kabbalists have developed intricate systems for describing the life divine, most Jewish discourse on God maintains an intuitive simplicity that is best attributed to the relational framework within which it is experienced and conceived. Liturgically, hence conceptually, one focuses on God in relationship to Israel, rather than on God's nature and similar abstractions. Alongside complex systems, a simple faith is maintained, which is both a secret of enduring faithfulness and a source of contemporary religious crisis. Hinduism too knows such polarities. They are, in fact, far more extreme. On the one hand is popular piety, an orthopraxic and ritualistic Hinduism that lacks any philosophical superstructure and conceptual complexity, and on the other hand are fully elaborated systems that attempt to account for the meaning of what we speak of when we speak of God. The suggestion that there can be enrichment on the theological plane by revisiting fundamental religious understandings relating to God and how He is understood in both traditions is of particular interest when juxtaposing the views of Vedanta with the typical Jewish approach to God.[52] I suspect that the Indian philosophical tradition has the potential to impact and transform the consciousness and thought structures of that broad span of everyday Judaism that is not colored by a particular spiritual or ideological affiliation, be it kabbalistic, philosophical, or otherwise. This is probably the source of the fascination with Indian spirituality and thought that so many Jews and Israelis exhibit. In most cases it is not an encounter of the nuanced theological tradition with its counterpart, but the encounter of a refined tradition on the one hand with a popular middle-of-the-road version of another tradition. Given how contemporary Hinduism and contemporary Judaism are broadly configured in the public eye and on the educational front, it seems that the encounter with Hinduism will, very often, open up practitioners of Judaism to a depth of reflection on God to which they may have been previously unaccustomed. Heschel's suggestion that the encounter with Hindu civilization could have significant impact on Jewish thought should thus be seen both in relation to the wisdom tradition itself, as it encounters an ancient and meaningful alternative, and in relation to a broad section of Jews, perhaps majoritarian, whose accumulated religious understanding could be seen as a projection of what Judaism has come to be.

Probably the most important notion that one encounters in a Hindu context, which is relevant to the present discussion, is the distinction between relative and absolute, or in other formulations, between form and formless. God can be thought of in both dimensions, and part of the richness of Hindu religious thought is precisely how it juxtaposes these two dimensions. Differences between various schools of philosophy hinge precisely on the issue of the relationship between form and the formless, and a series of ensuing consequences that different philosophical understandings have for the life of worship and for the expectation for spiritual liberation. But what is common to just about all schools is the recognition of a tension involving a dual perspective on God. Following the previous discussion on God and creation, we realize that Hindus may relate to any aspect of creation as divine. This includes aspects of nature, as well as what are considered to be particular manifestations of God, through individuals who come as teachers and as manifestations of the Divine, known as avataras. In fact, the term "manifestation," which is a stock term in Hindu religious discourse, only makes sense against the background of this twofold approach to the Divine as relative and absolute, in and out of form. To speak of God in manifestation is thus an attempt to bridge the gap between these two different aspects of God.[53]

This twofold approach to the Divine is not simply an attempt to make sense philosophically of polytheism and iconic ritual. In fact the concerns over God and form go beyond the question of worshiping God in form. They touch upon understanding God, different paths to Him, and the very meaning of relationship with Him. The Hindu terms are *nirguna* and *saguna*, with and without attributes. God can be approached in His aspect as absolute, without attributes, qualities, or through qualities, form, and manifestation. Perhaps this distinction overlaps, at least partly, with Western notions of the transcendence and immanence of God. From this distinction arise very different paths and different spiritualities. Is one's approach personal or impersonal, is it based on relationship and love or on contemplation of an absolute Truth?[54] Many of the differences between the various forms of the religious life of Hinduism can be traced back to this fundamental question.

Now, Judaism grows out of a relational matrix, that of the covenant with God. It is therefore perfectly natural to think of God in relational terms. Relational language is closely related to the anthropomorphic and anthropopathic language that presents God in Scriptures (biblical and rabbinic) as a character, possessing human attributes.[55] It seems to me that Jewish history on the whole reinforces the notion of Jewish particularity, which in turn points to relationship with the Divine, which in turn reinforces a saguna image of God in Judaism. There is, of course, the philosophical alternative, symbolically associated with the figure of Maimonides, that speaks of God apophatically, in terms of the *via negativa*, denying meaning to any positive ascription of attributes to God. That this tradition never became dominant may not be only on account of the difficulties in identifying with a philosophical position, nor due to the ascription of new meaning to divine attributes in the Kabbalah. More fundamentally, the tenor of the entire religious system is such that thinking beyond attributes, relationality, subjectivity, and particularity are so counterintuitive as to remain of necessity minoritarian.

We now come to the point of appreciating some of the possible consequences of the encounter with the Hindu dual perspective of saguna and nirguna. For one, it challenges our religious thought to think beyond the relational and personal parameters that have become second nature, as though there was no meaningful alternative religious language. Second, it places Jewish opposition to worship in form, what Judaism considers idolatry, in a broader theoretical matrix. Judaism may not worship in form, but its approach to God is still saguna, hence implicated in form. For Hindus, this is a frequent strategy to justify the worship of idols or manifestations of the Divine. For Jews, this is a humbling thought.[56] Third, it calls us to re-own and to take more seriously an entire tradition of religious reflection that has been almost left by the wayside—the Jewish philosophical tradition. Finally, it poses the challenge of whether the teachings of the Kabbalah do or do not seek to articulate a similar duality in the nature of the Godhead. Kabbalah speaks of God as *ein-sof*, the infinite. Ein-sof manifests through or in (in kabbalisitc terms emanates) divine powers, known as sefirot. These are the divine attributes, and it is here that the anthropomorphic language of the Bible becomes appropriate. So, does the Kabbalah really teach the same thing as the vedantic tradition, and as some of Hinduism's core scriptures, or are there fundamental differences even in this realm?[57] Now, each of these questions, addressed as it is to a different aspect of Jewish thought, mentality, and canon, is another way of applying Heschel's insight. The attempt to either provide a response to these challenges or to think the issues carefully through is, in fact, opening the door to fresh religious reflection. Such reflection would take place in dialogue with a serious religious system that has thought through issues of God and the world and would invite Judaism to articulate its message and self-understanding in light of such reflection.

It is obvious, but still bears stating, that my entire presentation is one-sided. Following the ancient image of India and its wise men, I have been asking how this wisdom could inform our own religious thinking. The exercise has been characterized by relating to only one direction. How could it be stated in a more reciprocal way, taking into account a possible Jewish contribution to Hindu religious thought? I have no doubt this is possible. However, my own reflections are one-sided because of the very one-sidedness of the present exercise;[58] it would take a Hindu to think of what Judaism can offer to Hindus. At the very least, it would take a Jew who has worked through these issues in careful and thoughtful ways. I am not familiar with a single serious Hindu attempt to engage Judaism, nor of a Jewish statement of what it might offer Hinduism, in a theological dialogue. We have a common view that does not recognize the challenge, because it is caught up in a caricatural view of Hinduism, respectful treatments of Hindu thought, that are aimed at the Jewish believer (Glazerson), and almost no Hindu attempts to tackle Judaism as a meaningful religion.[59] The Hindu side has its own obstacles that make it difficult to undertake the task. I am not referring to the complexities of studying Judaism as a historical and theological tradition. There is no reason why the process of study cannot be reciprocal. But first Judaism must be recognized as a distinct religion. Often enough it is not, and is collapsed into Christianity. But more seriously, conventional Hindu theology of religions does not seem to recognize any religion as distinct and worthy of specific one-on-one dialogue, which might be the cause of transformation within Hinduism itself in a mutually transformative engagement. Contemporary Hindu theology of religions is mostly fed by Vedanta principles that apply implicitly the dichotomy of relative and absolute to all world religions. Hinduism itself is relativized in relation to the absolute, as are all other religions. The Truth, Brahman, Vedanta, these are the values that are seen as absolutes. Worship, rituals, myths, etc., are all relative expressions of the path to the absolute. Seen in this light, all religions are, at least in theory, equally valid paths to reach the goal. This reading leaves little room for one religion to seriously challenge another theologically.[60] Vedantins hold the key to absolute reality and within their worldview can accommodate all manifestations of the religious life of humanity. Other religions are not there to inspire, challenge, and transform. They are simply further instances of well-known principles that have been articulated adequately within Vedanta's philosophy.

It may be that Judaism feels itself to be in crisis, and its practitioners sense they need the wisdom of India, while Hinduism is at a self-confident point in its own collective self-awareness. If so, one can well envision a turning of the tides, as the quick pace of change erodes the stability of thousands of years of Indian religious life. Dialogues may be most fruitful precisely where the engaged parties identify the point of crisis. Judaism is keenly aware of its theological and spiritual crisis. The passage to India plays heavily into this process. Hinduism may locate its crisis point elsewhere.[61] It may therefore find other aspects of Jewish life and wisdom helpful for its own growth and survival.

Whether or not a theological dialogue along the lines discussed above can be of any really transformative value for Hindu thinking will, in the final analysis, depend on the spiritual journeys of individual Hindu thinkers, who engage other traditions. I suspect that once Hindu thinking takes place outside the classical establishments of India, with their foolproof reasoning and closed theological systems, and shifts into the academy and the theological realms it opens up, we may discover greater reciprocity in the exchanges of wisdom. I also suspect that once a more serious theological dialogue, rather than a cultural one, or spiritual apprenticeship, starts to emerge, the Hindu side will find itself affected in some way, other than on the social and educational planes. But all this must come from the Hindu response to a dialogue that in truth has not yet begun.[62]

10

The Encounter within: Hinduism and Configurations of Jewish Identity

Profile of the Present Jewish-Hindu Encounter

The present encounter with India and with Hinduism provides us with unique opportunities to examine the challenges and opportunities related to identity and the making or keeping of boundaries between two communities.[1] There are several aspects that make the present encounter with Hinduism unique, compared with other encounters that Judaism has known in relation to other religions. It is precisely the uniqueness of the present encounter that allows us to consider it a test case, through which fundamental questions related to identity formation and maintenance, in relation to another religion, can be worked out.[2] Let us consider the particularity of the present encounter with Hinduism:

A. *Historical context.* For thousands of years Judaism encountered other religions under conditions that included religious competition, which was expressed as an immediate challenge by the surrounding culture to the integrity of Jewish identity. This included the threat of conversion, forced or otherwise, as well as various limitations placed upon Jewish practice. Religious persecution plays a defining role in Judaism's attitude to neighboring religions for close to two millennia, and it is complemented by persecution and threats to well-being that are founded upon Jewish identity, even if they do not directly address religious observance. Jewish-Hindu relations, by contrast, carry no memory of religious persecution. The story of the Jews in India seems free of religious persecution, and the Jews seem to have been welcomed in that culture, adapting themselves to its social norms and conventions, while maintaining their religious way of life. There is therefore no bitter memory that continues to poison present-day relationships.

B. *Novelty of the encounter.* While small-scale encounter has taken place for millennia, most of the present-day encounter with Hinduism is perceived by its participants as being novel. With almost no literary record of earlier encounters and almost no rabbinic or literary positions that would shape this encounter specifically (as opposed to general and nonspecific references to Avoda Zara, as these abound in the literature), participants in the present encounter approach India and Hinduism almost tabula rasa. They therefore feel they are charting new ground, and in exploring this new territory there is often a sense of freedom to explore boundaries. Explorations within such a context therefore allow issues of identity, its formation, and boundaries to be explored under more neutral conditions, which could teach us important lessons pertaining to broader issues of identity.

C. *Previous encounters.* All previous encounters of Judaism with other religious civilizations have taken place in situations of common living. For millennia Jews have been guests in host cultures. Earlier periods saw Judaism struggle to contain the potentially harmful effects of religious minorities living within a Jewish majority culture. While majority-minority relations have changed over the millennia, the basic reality within which other religions were assessed was one of common living and its ensuing challenges. Distant cultures were a rumor, a theoretical concept, or perhaps rather a construct, but not a real challenge. The encounter with Hinduism, except for the tiny community that has lived in India for generations, has never been an encounter with neighbors. It has always been an encounter of travelers. What is unique about the present-day encounter is a direct consequence of the ease of travel and the extent of present-day Jewish travel to India. It is, to a significant extent, an encounter of travelers. Jews, whether from Israel or from elsewhere, come to India as travelers and their encounter is framed by the conditions of travel—short, well-defined periods of visiting another culture, maintaining clear awareness of its otherness and the temporary nature of the encounter. In this situation, the concern for loss of identity to the surrounding culture does not play in the same way. Rather, travelers will seek to receive something from the encounter with India and Hinduism that they can later integrate into their lives, upon returning home. If the visit to India is anything more than just a time of "chilling out" following an arduous military service, it will be a time of seeking to obtain tools, skills, or experiences that will then be integrated into one's life back home or otherwise help shape an identity that is defined primarily in relation to home. This situation therefore makes some form of impact, inspiration, or borrowing, a regular feature of the encounter of today's Jews with Hinduism. It consequently makes the question of identity and how it is maintained in view of such borrowing and inspiration particularly relevant to the encounter, providing an excellent test case for theoretical reflection on identity maintenance and its boundaries.

The encounter of travelers is characterized by several formal features that make it distinct in relation to earlier encounters with other religious civilizations. By definition, an encounter of travelers takes place in more than one locality. It takes place both at home and away from home. Even if the actual encounter takes place outside, in a foreign land, its impact and its legacy play out at home. Home is the ground of preparation and the space to which one returns, following a departure to a space outside, where the actual encounter takes place.[3]

An encounter of travelers is limited both in terms of space and time. One does not travel forever. Travel is always time bound. A time-bound exposure to another religion makes such an encounter much safer than the continual threat of exposure to a neighboring religion. A time-bound exposure may therefore make participants more daring in the choices they make and in the experiences they are ready to open themselves up to. Time-bound travel is thus a testing ground, a liminal time and space, wherein identities may be redefined, transformed, or affirmed.

D. *Absence of political implications.* Perhaps because so much of the encounter is carried out by travelers, there is little political impact to the encounter. Clearly, the extent of the present-day encounter is a direct consequence of the establishment of political relations between Israel and India. But the substance of the encounter is, on the whole, free of a political agenda. Jews and Hindus meet, whether in India or in the diaspora, without an immediate political agenda that has to either be upheld or is threatened in the context of the relationship. It is fair to claim that this is not the case with all encounters between Jews and other religious cultures, today or in the past. Obviously, living within a host community or hosting a religious minority bears immediate political consequences. Indeed, Jews existed within host cultures through specific political arrangements, within which their rights, including those pertaining to their religious rites, were defined. The situation in relation to Islam is particularly relevant. Jewish existence as a minority within Muslim society was conceptualized and carried out through a well-defined political system that was founded on Muslim superiority and toleration of religious minorities. This system was upset with the departure of Jews from Muslim countries and the establishment of the state of Israel. A significant part of Arab hostility to the state of Israel, since and preceding its establishment, draws on the difficulty in redefining power relations and the implications such redefinition would have for a sense of Muslim supremacy.[4] None of this pertains to the encounter with Hinduism. Even though Hinduism and Judaism are two religions that are associated with states that are in some way aligned to them—Israel and India—the political dimension associated with the states plays at best a marginal role in the encounter.[5]

E. *Secular-religious dimensions.* All previous encounters with other religions took place in a context that was defined primarily through religion. The present encounter is simultaneously an encounter with a country where the regime is officially secular and with a culture where Hindus are a dominant majority. It is both an encounter of *Israelis* with India and Hinduism and an encounter of *Jews*. While religion, spirituality, and identity are obviously important to the encounter, it is nevertheless not necessarily an interreligious encounter. This complexity makes the entire encounter somewhat slippery, inasmuch as it does not fit neatly into precedents created by previous encounters with other religious cultures. It also puts it beyond the reach of traditional religious authorities. While the Israelis who visit India often experience spiritual realities that will significantly impact their own Jewish identity and religious practices, the entire process is outside the realm of normativity and beyond the reach of the authority of people who traditionally guide religious communities. In fact, the entire encounter is surprisingly, perhaps shockingly, outside the realm of any religious counsel, advice, supervision, and regulation. With the obvious exception of those religious groups that have created centers in India, through which they care for the religious and personal needs of Jewish travelers, there is to the best of my knowledge no organized (or even unorganized) framework, or even recognized authority, who can provide counsel and guidance to the challenges that accompany the encounter. The mixture of internal boundaries of Israeliness and Jewishness, religious and secular, makes this encounter more complex and elusive. Questions of identity ultimately play out across the various identity definitions of participants. Both Jewish and Israeli identity are impacted. I believe that the present encounter with India and Hinduism is the first time in history that challenges to identity and opportunities for its definition and construction are not strictly religious and take place through a complex weaving of religious and national identities.

F. *Accessibility of knowledge and information.* Encounter with another religion is an encounter both with people and their living religious realities and with the ideas, scriptures, and knowledge base that are representative of that religion. Hinduism is probably the first religion that Jews encounter under conditions characteristic of the information age. If earlier periods saw control of knowledge by authorities, thereby setting some of the parameters for encounters between religions, Hinduism is being encountered en masse under conditions wherein free access to ideas and texts goes hand in hand with ease of access to the places in which Hinduism is practiced.

G. *Judaism in crisis.* The encounter with Hinduism takes place at a time considered by many as a time of crisis for Jewish identity. The reason why rabbinic authorities cannot guide travelers to India is that there is a crisis in the relations of trust and authority between most travelers and those who are entrusted with Jewish religion, its protection, and furtherance. This crisis is part of a broader crisis of identity, meaning, and affiliation that afflicts large parts of the Jewish people and of Israeli society. Crisis is not simply a description of the situation; it is part of the self-awareness of many in leadership situations, as well as of their flock. There is a crisis concerning why one should be Jewish and how this should be maintained. There is a crisis concerning the practice of religion and the need for, and a perceived lack of, spirituality. As noted in an earlier chapter, there is a crisis concerning God and how He is reached and experienced. India appears in some way as an answer to these crises. While the answer to how exactly the encounter with India aids, or aggravates, these crises, is not clearly articulated, the testimonies of many travelers do suggest that the encounter with India has had a beneficial impact on their sense of identity and on their religious practice. However, the ways in which this has taken place are neither clearly formulated nor within the reach of conventional religious authorities. Religious crisis thus intersects with the present encounter with Hinduism in multiple ways, making the encounter messy, as well as fruitful, and threatening, as well as beneficial.

This novel situation confronts Judaism in ways that are particularly challenging. The theoretical sources and resources of tradition in relation to other religions are articulated from a place that is imagined as a place of wholeness and integrity. From within an imagined perfection of self, our tradition reflects on others. The sense of imagined integrity and wholeness has given way, in so many sectors, to a sense of crisis and search that it becomes much harder to respond to new religious encounters by simply applying the tried and tested answers of old. It may be for this reason that so many traditional voices remain silent concerning one of the most interesting religious phenomena of our time—exposure to Hinduism and its impact on Jewish self-understanding, observance, and identity. Significantly, those Jewish communities that operate from within a paradigm of wholeness and integrity of tradition are also those that maintain most strongly the approach to Hinduism as Avoda Zara, as witnessed in the sheitel crisis. By contrast, those that share the sense that Judaism, and in particular their own communities, is undergoing a crisis will be more aware of the identitarian dimensions of the encounter and will therefore often highlight another aspect of the encounter with Hinduism—spirituality. We have already seen that the encounter can take place under various headings. There seems to be a correspondence between what one privileges in the encounter and one's view of tradition and community today. Those who operate within from a sense of crisis will, according to this suggestion, be more open to encountering the spiritual dimension of Hinduism and consider its possible benefits for Jewish life and practice.[6]

The aggregate of factors described makes the present-day encounter with Hinduism unlike anything Judaism has ever experienced before, in relation to another religion. As a consequence, the possibilities and opportunities that are opened up are more nuanced, more complex, and, above all, more elusive than those that governed encounters with other religions. These factors are crucial as we consider the impact of the encounter on Jewish identity.

As stated, the present-day encounter with Hinduism is not exclusively an encounter with another religion. It is also an encounter with another country and another culture. Religion, philosophy, and various practices of spirituality blend within a broader cultural encounter. At the same time, the identity that encounters India and is transformed by it is not only Jewish identity, but often Israeli identity, with the varieties of Jewish shadings of identity that characterize it. Looking at some of the research on the meaning of Israelis' travels to India and the impact it has had on them, one is struck by the occurrence of the language of "self" and "other" and how central the discourse of identity is to these discussions.[7] One study examines the image of India in Israeli literature.[8] India is imagined as the arena for encounter of the self in all its power and reality. An examination of Hebrew literature since the 1930s suggests that Israel no longer provides a space where the reality of the self can be encountered. This sense of self was lost. Its recovery points to India. To retrieve the lost sense of realness one has to enter the symbolic space of the archetypal other. Thus, India is conceived as Israel's archetypal other. It is likely that it is precisely the "clean" history, devoid of charged confrontations, that allows India to assume this position in the Israeli imagination. Thus, India becomes the symbolic locus that constitutes a lost home for Israeliness and functions as the sphere where, miraculously, the latter can be repaired.[9]

Laurie Patton and Shalom Goldman have surveyed the place of India in Israeli literature and movies. In attempting to understand why India fascinates the Israeli imagination, they raise several possibilities.[10] The first has to do with how India is positioned as an alternative to Jewish culture. India allows exploration of, but not commitment to, the rules of the mystical path. It seems to provide a nondualist antidote to the dry intellectualism of talmudic debates. The perceived absolute authority associated with Judaism is replaced with the directness of experience, without sullying it with the political power of haredim. In this understanding, India functions as a kind of alter ego, in terms of Israeli or Jewish consciousness. Extending their claim further, one may suggest that the passage to India really is a quest for those parts of the self that cannot be made manifest within one's home space.[11] Patton and Goldman attribute this to the politicization of religion in Israel. They also note that in reality, all those aspects that Israelis flee from in Judaism are also found within Hinduism, as practiced by native Indians, as opposed to how it is perceived by the traveling Israeli. India would therefore provide an opportunity for rediscovery of parts of the self that have been lost, but at the same time also constitutes an invitation to reintegrate those dimensions, much as Hindu religious society itself incorporates parallel tensions and complexities.[12]

These suggestions lead to an interesting observation I heard in the name of Melila Hellner-Eshed. She noted that while American Jews turn mostly to Buddhism as their preferred other religion, Israelis turn to India and to Hinduism.[13] She accounts for this by the distinction between different quests. The turn to Buddhism serves the quest for peace of mind. The turn to Hinduism serves the quest for God and for living religion in a way that is an alternative to how religion is practiced in Israel. If this observation is valid, it lends further support to the suggestion that the turn to India is really a turn to the self, or a turn to the missing parts of oneself.

This brings us back to two dimensions of the encounter with India, which have already been noted. The first is the sense of crisis that is characteristic of Jewish communal and spiritual life. The second is the turn to India as a part of the quest for spirituality.[14] As Patton and Goldberg suggest, Jews do not turn to India for those expressions of the religious life that they can find back home, but for those that they consider are lacking in Judaism. The most obvious rubric under which one can classify this dimension is "spirituality."

We come then to the point where we must consider the possible relationships between spirituality and identity.[15] The question here would be, what degree or what form of borrowing and inspiration, derived from Hinduism, is compatible with the concerns for maintaining Jewish identity. Here we ask the following boundary question—not what are the boundaries of legitimate faith,[16] but what boundaries need to be maintained in order to establish or uphold Jewish identity. Implied in this formulation is also the possible recognition that some boundaries are permeable and allow contact, borrowing, and a restatement or regeneration of spiritual life, in light of contact with another religion.

Spirituality and Jewish Identity

In terms of challenges to identity, Hinduism, or perhaps the Hinduism that many Jews encounter, is in a very special position to engage, and challenge, the concerns for maintaining Jewish identity. Informing the concern for Jewish identity is a recognition of the importance of particularity and the commitment to maintaining the particularity of identity, through the dual expressions of ethnic belonging and religious observance. When Jews consider Jewish identity as a value, they rarely pose the question of its instrumentality. The particularity of Jewish identity is understood as a value unto itself. Maintaining the Jewish people, its continuity, and even its faithfulness to its ancestral ways, to its covenanted lifestyle, and to its commitment to God, depending on the shadings of how particularity is justified, is rarely thought of as serving some goal beyond itself. In fact, part of the crisis of Jewish identity and continuity is precisely the inability to articulate what purpose such particularity serves beyond itself. True, one may always appeal to the instrumentality of the covenant community as a means of reaching out to the rest of humanity, in fulfilling the divine plan for humanity. While this is a valid answer, Jewish life reflects little concern for fulfilling such instrumentality. Jewish life, whether religious or communal, tends to revolve around itself. Even for those religious communities that have made *Tikkun Olam*, social action as part of a religious vision of healing and rectifying the world, a focal point of their religious orientation, justifying particularity in terms that are non-self-referential remains a challenge. Differently put, whatever our sense of the mission of Judaism may be, it remains an overarching reading of the meaning of Jewish life and rarely gets translated into the consciousness and daily practices of Jewish communities. It is possible that precisely this inability to either articulate or to consciously live, let alone live up to, the vision of Jewish particularity and its mission makes the challenges of maintaining Jewish identity all the more difficult. One of two responses ensues. Either one relaxes one's hold on the understanding or practice of particularity or one becomes attached to it as an ideal that must be affirmed as a value unto itself, regardless of how its ultimate purpose is integrated within the fabric of Jewish life.

What does the encounter with Hinduism do to this sense of Jewish identity? For most Hindus, there may not be a significant difference in the approach to identity from that just described in relation to Jews. Most Hindus live their identity as part of a self-defined group, formed by the boundaries of caste and related creed. A global view of Hinduism might reveal profound similarities with Judaism, in terms of identity construction and the quest for its maintenance, particularly under the pressures of contemporary life. However, the Hinduism that Jews are drawn to is often of a different ilk. It draws on a philosophical worldview that juxtaposes relative social norms to absolute reality and the conventional practices of religion with the higher goals of spirituality. It is precisely such a way of constructing Hinduism that appeals to many Jewish seekers, providing for them an image of what they cannot find back home.

I would like to illustrate this particular approach to identity through a conversation I had with Chandra Swami, a swami who receives quite a number of Israelis and Jews in his ashram and who has visited Israel several times. At one public gathering,[17] I posed to Swamiji the following question: "What would you like your disciples, ideally to be: Hindu, vedantin, religion of their choice or birth, above all religions, or at home in all religions?" The question followed an earlier one, in which I asked Swamiji to describe himself in terms of his own self-identity, along lines similar to those that this question frames in relation to his followers. It was meant to explore precisely the issue of religious identity and how it is impacted by the contact with a spiritual teacher who belongs to or who comes out of the Hindu tradition. Clearly, the importance of this question for me was an expression of its centrality for the Jewish community. I therefore sought to explore whether the swami's followers were in some way compromising their identity, in case they belonged to another religion and what his own understanding and expectations were in terms of the fidelity and continuity of his followers' identity with their (earlier) religion.

Swamiji replied as follows:[18] "I like the people who come to me and ask me for guidance to be spiritual persons, rather than to be strict religious persons. Spirituality is the essential element of all religions. In all the religions there have [been] great saints and sages, who are respected and revered by all the seekers of truth. There is nothing wrong for a Muslim to go to Mecca, for a Hindu to go to Haridwar or Benares, for a Christian or Jew to go to Jerusalem, for the sake of pilgrimage. There are some seekers in all religions who prefer to go within (inside) themselves for pilgrimage instead of going to Mecca, Jerusalem, or Haridwar." And in a follow-up note, he stated: "Outgrowing your religion does not mean giving up your religion."

This brief exchange almost sums up the entire situation of different Jewish and Hindu views on identity and spirituality. My own formulation, heavily indebted to Jewish concerns for identity maintenance, seeks to clarify whether Swamiji's Jewish followers would in some way be compromising their Jewish identity and to what extent his views or teachings might encourage them to do so. I also raise the possibility that his teachings might propel them to take their religion more seriously, in a manner akin to reports of the Dalai Lama pushing Jewish people who wish to join his own religious tradition back to their own tradition.[19] Chandra Swami's response indicates that the sensibilities that inform my question are foreign to him. There is no concern for identity and its preservation. There is only concern for authentic spirituality. Accordingly, he prefers his disciples to be spiritual, rather than religious. "Strict religious persons" in the above quote, should be construed as: people who fulfill rituals with minute and careful attention, without feeling any concern for the ultimate end and purpose of the religion. Pitting religion and spirituality against each other in this way is founded on the fact that there are people (and this is obviously true for both Hinduism and Judaism) whose religious life concentrates on performance and ritual without corresponding attention to interiority, intention, and spirituality. National, ethnic, or collective identity do not figure at all in his thinking. This is obviously a particularly Jewish concern, given the centrality of the ethnic component to the construction of Jewish identity.[20]

Chandra Swami's answer also expresses an entire way of thinking regarding ritual and spirituality. Ritual is fine, external acts are fine. However, they are instrumental and the ultimate purpose is the achievement of the spiritual state. When that state is achieved, it can replace the external act. Individuals are free to continue engaging in such external acts as pilgrimage and the like. There is nothing wrong with that. Nor is it truly necessary. The spiritual seeker will be just as happy with performing the pilgrimage internally. As religious practices become metaphors, the internal spiritual life ends up replacing the external life of religious observance, making practical observance superfluous, a purely personal and voluntary matter. Spirituality thus operates as a domain that grows out of religion (read: particularity, ritual, observance), fulfills it, replaces it, and ultimately transcends it. An instrumental view of religious ritual is presented in terms of spirituality, leading to the ultimate shedding off of religion. As the final quote indicates, spirituality allows you to outgrow your religion. This is not the same as giving the religion up. But it certainly relativizes the importance of those aspects of the religious life referred to here as 'religious." Identity and fidelity are maintained inasmuch as one is not called to give up one's religion, as in the case of conversion to another religion. Rather, the lower parts of religion are subsumed in its higher aspects.

This is a very particular challenge to particularity and identity. It does not assume replacing one identity with another. It is clear that Swamiji does not suggest that Jews should become Hindus. To the extent that age-old fears concerning encounter with other religions and their effects on Jewish identity were formulated under conditions of substituting one identity for another, we certainly have a different case here. It is almost universally true that none of the Hindu-born movements or teachers to whom Jews have been attracted espouse trading Jewish identity for Hindu identity. The challenge or threat to identity should be considered not a horizontal, but a vertical challenge. In other words, the particularity of identity loses its meaning, relative to a higher vision, a higher truth, which is understood in light of some form of Hindu teaching, usually vedantic. Recognition of this higher truth or spiritual vision is understood from within the Hindu matrix, conceiving of the spiritual life as a gradual approach toward a higher spiritual reality, wherein the strictures and obligations that apply to common religious practice are transcended. The Hindu ideal of *moksha* and its social counterpart in the institution of the sannyasin, the renunciant who goes beyond conventional social boundaries and their corresponding ritual obligations and limitations, is founded on such a hierarchical view. The Hindu social and religious system contains simultaneously strong boundaries and the means for transcending them. Spirituality is used in contemporary Hindu-talk to refer to the particular domain that permits transcending of boundaries. The entire thought structure is fundamental to Hinduism, and it finds expression not only in its philosophical theory but also in its social institutions and hierarchy.

The application of this system of transcending and relativizing the religious life has been extended in this quote by Swamiji, as well as in the teachings of many contemporary Hindu teachers, from an internal Hindu social-religious thought structure to a view of other religions. Accordingly, all religions are subject to the same dynamics of fulfillment and transcendence, through the attainment of spirituality. I think it is fair to say that this structure is particularly attractive to Israeli and Jewish seekers. It provides a refreshing alternative to the overemphasis on ritual and observance that makes up so much of traditional Jewish practice. It suggests a spiritual path and goal, instead of mere observance, and it liberates them from the heavy baggage that their previous exposure to Judaism places upon them.

It seems to me that herein lies one of the more serious challenges of the encounter with Hinduism. This entire thought construct is very alien to the Jewish approach to observance, identity, and the understanding of the spiritual life. Fundamental to the Hindu view is the recognition that ritual and observance are instrumental and can therefore be transcended. The Jewish view of ritual does not necessarily dispute their instrumentality, but it does not consider that a point comes on the spiritual journey where one has arrived at the destination and therefore leaves behind the means that transported one to that point.[21] Observance is a continuing commitment and no matter how high one is considered to be on the spiritual path, one remains bound by it.[22]

Observance is closely bound to identity. Observance of the mitzvot upholds and reinforces Jewish identity, even as it propels the practitioner forward in the spiritual life. It is understood as having cosmic and theurgic significance, impacting the entire world and the internal life divine. Consequently, one does not imagine a time when all that is relative—ritual, identity, nationality—will be transcended. Or rather, thoughts of such transcendence are postponed until a messianic future, concerning which we do find speculations of transcending the need for ritual.[23] As long as the world has not been redeemed, as long as we await the coming of the Messiah, we cannot think of having reached a goal that would make religious practice superfluous. The difference in approach may indeed be attributed to a fundamental difference between a religion that thinks in terms of history and its process and a religion that thinks in terms of metaphysics and personal salvation. The former cannot announce having arrived at the goal outside historical processes. The latter can declare a state of human perfection to be the goal and the consequent end of the need for religious practice.

What is thus at stake, from a Jewish perspective, in the involvement and entry into a Hindu perception of the religious life is the threat to all that is particular, bound to mitzvot and related to the specific identity of the Jewish people. The threat as such is far more subtle than the temptation of conversion or the appeal to abandon one's religion. It is the threat of gradually falling away from the Jewish path, without ever formally renouncing it. In fact, Jews who occupy important positions in Hindu-based movements are often proud of their Judaism and maintain their Jewish identity.[24] However, the identity they maintain, as shall shortly be argued, is primarily ethnic. The spiritual path is defined by the Hindu-based practices and road map.

Previous eras saw confrontations of Judaism with other religions in horizontal terms, when all who were involved in such confrontations were fully identified with the Jewish community and followed its practices, at least in theory. The present-day situation is far more complex. The challenge is, as just suggested, vertical. But it is also horizontal, in the sense that there is the danger that encounter with a Hindu-based movement will draw the attention and energies of the individual member, leading him or her to follow that path in practice. While it is not formally a matter of choosing one identity over another, and the individual person might proclaim loyalty to or affiliation with both religions, in terms of practice and in terms of priorities, expressed in time and attention, there is clearly a choice of one over the other. But what makes today's situation much more complex is that the starting point in terms of Jewish identity is so much weaker or diversified. Attitudes to other religions as identity threats were formulated in an era when identity was strong and the shift from one identity to another was dramatic, often requiring great effort or pressure. Jewish identity today is, as already acknowledged, in crisis. For large parts of the Jewish people it is a weak identity, expressing itself through minimal affiliation and minimal corresponding observance. Even for those who may come from a more observant background, such as many of the Israeli travelers, identity is much less monolithic or taken for granted, in an age colored by postmodern sensibilities. Consequently, the shift to Hindu-born movements or spirituality often addresses personal needs and challenges that were created precisely because of weak, complex, or problematic Jewish identities. Affiliation with a Hindu spiritual path is therefore for the individual a solution to a problem, often generated within the Jewish context, rather than, as it might be for the collective, a problem in and of itself.

Recognition of the background of crisis and of complex and shifting identities and affiliations of Jews in today's world makes it impossible to simply condemn or reject spiritual journeys that take individuals from Judaism to Hinduism. In any event, such rejection is meaningless, because those for whom one would be making such statements are not listening to us. The situation requires a far more nuanced approach that takes into account the internal Jewish need and recognizes what it is that spiritual seekers find in a Hindu environment. Following that, one might reflect on various ways in which Jewish identity and practice might come together with Hindu-based spirituality. Various options already exist, based on the life choices made by individuals. We would be well served to take those into account and to consider the consequences of the encounter with Hinduism for Jewish identity in light of norms and patterns that have already developed. What follows, then, is a presentation of three models of encounter and contact with Hinduism that may be recognized in the experience of individuals. In light of the following presentation, we will be in a better position to think of the challenges and possible promises for Jewish identity that the encounter with Hinduism holds.

Constructing Religious Identity: Identity Markers

As a prelude to this discussion, we do well to consider ways in which identity is expressed. It will be easier for us to weigh these three models when we take into account some of the identity markers through which association with Hinduism is expressed:

A. The most obvious manifestations of affiliation with Hinduism are expressed in the performance of rituals and the adoption and propagation of a Hindu worldview. Identity is established through the quality and intensity of affiliation with a religious path. Intense practice of Hindu rituals, practices, and a full commitment to a Hindu worldview would accordingly amount to adoption of a Hindu identity.

B. Usually, such deep immersion in another religion is never a private matter. It involves affiliation with a religious group, order, or community. Therefore, communal affiliation should be considered an additional factor that governs identity formation. It seems fair to state that one of the main driving forces of any religion is its communal aspect. Community is important not simply as a means of fulfilling precepts and rituals of the religion. Community is often at the heart of the religion and of its practices.[25] Religion always organizes community in some way and belonging to a religion means belonging to a community in some way. When members join a new religion, it is often the community life or community aspect that draws them to that religion, even if the outward or formal reasons offered for joining that religion are couched in theological or soteriological terms. In terms of how religion actually functions in the lives of believers, we cannot underestimate the importance of community. Community is the great hidden driver that hides behind many a visible expression of the religious life. Accordingly, community also impacts one's religious identity. To belong to a community is a form of staking one's territory and stating one's identity. While one may ask what constitutes belonging to a community and indeed one may come across various shades and degrees of affiliation, this does not detract from the basic reality that membership in a group or an organization can serve as a strong identity marker.

C. In certain cases there is little room for doubting that one indeed belongs to another religious group. I refer to cases in which one not only belongs to another religious group, but actually has a leadership role within that group. Leadership implicates one in a religious organization, its faith and doctrines, in ways that are profound and certainly mark one's own identity as well as how one is perceived by others.

D. To these considerations one may add several additional ones, relating to external expressions of identity. One of them would be adopting a new name. Interestingly, the rabbis suggest that one of the markers for Israel's faithfulness to their identity, during their exile in Egypt, was maintaining their names.[26] When a Jewish person takes on a Hindu name, a definite statement is made in terms of identity.

E. Similarly, dress functions as an external identity marker. Hindu tradition often finds outward expression through a dress code that is particular. In part it is purely a matter of culture. But to some degree, this cultural expression also has religious significance. Special clothes are associated with specific stages or forms of the religious life. Adopting those clothes, as well as additional bodily markers, delivers a message through the body and its expressions. This message is never purely religious, in a spiritual sense. It is also a social, cultural message that ultimately defines the identity of the individual through the particular dress, and how it is understood and interpreted within society.

F. To all these objective criteria, we must add an individual's subjective sense of identity. One self-identifies as belonging to a group or a religion. One's self-identification is clearly an important consideration. However, it cannot stand on its own, divorced from the external and recognizable identity markers, listed above. Surely, if one self-identifies as a Hindu, and takes on a Hindu name along with Hindu religious practices, one's self-identification both undergirds and enhances one's identity as a Hindu. The issue becomes more complicated when external identity markers point to Hinduism, while subjectively one continues to maintain a Jewish identity.

This brings us then to the very heart of our discussion—the encounter between Hindu and Jewish identities in the life of an individual. Here, we may consider three possibilities for negotiating Hindu and Jewish identities.

Model A: Adopting a Jewish Identity, Following the Encounter with Hinduism

This model assumes, at least implicitly, that different religious identities are incompatible. Thus, affirmation of one's Jewish identity comes at the expense of association with Hinduism, and vice versa. Consequently, one must be either Hindu or Jewish. The first model describes Jews who following a meaningful engagement with Hinduism return to Judaism, more or less casting aside the experiences and lessons gained through their contact with Hinduism. In sociological terms, a large portion of those who belong to this class, perhaps most of them, are Jews of American origin, who encountered Hinduism through the wave of gurus who came to the West since the 70s. Having had meaningful experiences with Hinduism at a formative point in their lives, these individuals ultimately found their way to Judaism. It is possible that the experiences they had within a Hindu context opened them up spiritually, providing a training and an introduction to dimensions of the spiritual life that they had not encountered in their pre-Hindu Jewish life. On the whole, members of this class are part of the ba'alei teshuva movement, people who self-identify and who are recognized as returning to their former Jewish roots. Unlike converts, who assume a new identity, these returnees are Jews by origin, who in some cases lapsed in their observance, but in most cases were never aware of the spiritual treasures of Judaism. Having cultivated aspects of the spiritual life outside Judaism, they then made their way back into Judaism, embracing a form of Judaism that is stricter, more committed, and more intentional in terms of seeking spiritual fulfillment than the Judaism practiced by their parents.

While the ba'alei teshuva movement cuts across different parts of the Jewish world, its American expression, probably more so than any other geographical counterpart, provides numerous points of intersection with Hinduism. By comparison, few Israeli ba'alei teshuva return to Judaism via Hinduism.[27] The Israeli experience is better described through the third model, suggested in the following discussion. The difference between Israeli and American ba'alei teshuva is most likely a consequence of the strong presence of the various Hindu schools in America, where many Jewish followers were drawn to each and every Hindu group that implanted itself in America. Interestingly, to date, no Hindu group has been truly successful in implanting itself in Israel. While Israelis have been open to receiving techniques from Hindu-based movements such as Transcendental Meditation, Art of Living, and, more recently, Amritanandamayi's global service mission, heavier engagement with Hinduism has not taken root in Israel, as it has in the United States and Europe.[28] It is reasonable to suggest that the reason is identitarian. Israelis have been quick to absorb spiritual techniques and practices that promise improvement in one's overall functioning. They are, however, quite resistant to accommodating the otherness of an alternative religious path. Concern for identity and its integrity seem to me the best way of accounting for such resistance. Within the State of Israel, maintaining Jewish identity is a supreme cultural value. There is consequently great reluctance to embrace a lifestyle that is expressly non-Jewish. In the United States, by contrast, individuals are much more free to join religious communities that involve adoption of a Hindu identity, within the broader matrix of a society that upholds religious freedom and does not show the same concern for the particularity of one specific identity. We thus find the movement of ba'alei teshuva returning to Judaism, following their exposure to Hinduism, as a primarily American phenomenon.

This movement was aided by the presence of several personalities who served as bridgeways to Judaism. Involvement with Hinduism was a phenomenon of the Hippie generation and those rabbis who catered to that generation were also the bridge from Hindu to Jewish identity for many Jews who had been involved with Hindu movements. Rabbi Shlomo Carlebach was a major figure in this context. I know of quite a number of his disciples, "chevra" as they are called, who prior to returning to Judaism had been members of the religious communes associated with such figures as Swami Muktananda, Swami Satchidananda, and others. Significantly, Carlebach's attitude to those Hindu teachers was, as far as I am aware, always respectful, always collegial. I personally recall him speaking of Swami Satchidananda with great respect and awe. His ability to recognize saintliness in Hindu teachers was part of his overall approach that was nonconfrontational and nonderogatory in relation to people in general and people of another religion in particular. This made him a safe teacher, one who could be trusted with respect for one's former spiritual path, even as one advanced toward a fuller Jewish way of life, under his inspiration.

The same may be said of the other figures who aided Jewish returnees from an engagement with Hinduism. Rabbi Zalman Schacter is another rabbinic figure who showed great openness toward other religions, their masters, and practitioners. Rabbi Matityahu Glazerson, who authored the only book on Judaism and Hinduism,[29] catered to this particular group from within a more standard Orthodox orientation. Nevertheless, as suggested in an earlier chapter, his work is striking in the respect it shows Hinduism. Rather than denigrate it, he upholds its spiritual teachings as valid, while suggesting Jewish practitioners have something additional they need to attain, for which Jewish practice is necessary. The most recent case of applying this attitude is Rabbi Yitzchak Ginsburgh. Ginburgh, a prominent Lubavitch rabbi, provides spiritual inspiration for many of the Lubavitch emissaries working in India, who cater to Israeli travelers. His educational approach is one of viewing Hindu teaching as valuable, but ultimately inadequate for the Jewish seeker.[30] His students guide seekers back to Judaism and have established, under his guidance, educational frameworks for Jewish "graduates" of India.[31] With the aid of such figures, ba'alei teshuva were able to return from Hinduism to Judaism, adopting or affirming a Jewish identity, in lieu of the Hindu identity they had temporarily assumed.

The story of these returnees has been studied in detail by Judith Linzer.[32] Linzer's study is based on interviews with 20 individuals. Of those, 7 moved from Judaism to Eastern Religions. The path of the other 13 led from various Eastern practices to Judaism, mostly Orthodox Judaism. It is hard to derive conclusive data from Linzer's study, with specific reference to the move of ba'alei teshuva from Hinduism to Judaism. Her sample is simply too small.[33] Nevertheless, one does obtain some significant impressions and these are corroborated by my own observations, in various personal situations with which I am familiar. The impression is that the returnees have gone through a stage of exposure to Hinduism, or Hindu-based groups, as a way of discovering spirituality and their own deeper sense of a spiritual self. They are then led to explore this discovery within a Jewish context. What they carry with them back to Judaism is more in the nature of a spiritual drive and a quest for and commitment to spirituality than anything specifically Hindu. Hinduism frames their experience and continues to define their horizons.[34] But it is no longer part of their practice, and more often than not, also no longer part of their ideology.[35] As Linzer documents,[36] many of them seek to bring something from their experience back into Judaism. But precisely this desire raises the question of whether the graduates of various Hindu groups who have made their way back to Judaism have actually brought something back to Judaism through their previous engagement with Hinduism. Is their practice more meditative? Is it more self-aware? Does it show greater passion and enthusiasm, following their exposure to practices of *bhakti* in a Hindu context? In short, is their Judaism richer for having once been involved with Hinduism? Linzer's study does not attempt to answer this question.

I would like to share my observations on this matter, acknowledging they are impressionistic, based on many individual cases with which I am familiar. It is my strong impression that the answer to the question just posed is negative. Very little of their former Hinduism is carried over into the Judaism to which they return.[37] There is little attempt to integrate or to search for a synthesis between the two religions to which they have been exposed.[38] At most, one can say that given their interest in and predisposition to a certain quality of spiritual life, the groups to which they will affiliate themselves within Judaism will be groups that cultivate those qualities. Hence, many returnees find themselves within hassidic groups, or the forms of Judaism that evolved around the figures of Rabbis Carlebach and Schacter. The rabbis who were able to reach these ba'alei teshuva and to point their way to Judaism also helped shape the kind of Judaism they practice, drawing largely on hassidic spirituality, enthusiasm, and practice. Having found something that may be considered equally satisfying, these returnees opted for one religion at the expense of the other. Their former Hindu life was largely cast aside, something to be forgotten, ignored, and in some cases never to be spoken of again. In part this may be because of how Jewish authorities overall shun any form of alternative religious affiliation.[39] Even those rabbis who serve as bridges and who show respect for other religions point to a life that is singularly shaped by Judaism, suggesting it has all the needed riches to nourish one's spiritual life. Other teachers, to whom the ba'alei teshuva would later be exposed, are far more extreme in their condemnation of anything smacking of another religion. Religious authorities therefore leave little room for creative construction of identity, drawing on multiple religious resources.

To this must be added the recognition that ba'alei teshuva typically find themselves in a position of inferiority, in relation to surrounding Jewish society. This society is typically Orthodox in its observance and boasts a high-level of Jewish learning. The returnees are at a double disadvantage, having to learn both practice and traditional sources often at a late stage in life. Psychologically, ba'alei teshuva carry a kind of inferiority complex in relation to surrounding Jewish figures and authorities. They do not consider that theirs is an experience that can in some way enrich the Jewish people. Rather, their past is often considered something to be ashamed of, at worst, or at best to be ignored. What matters are the norms of piety, learning, and practice of the surrounding Jewish environment, and in relation to these they are clearly at a disadvantage due to their late arrival on the scene. Given such insecurity, it is unreasonable to expect any positive contribution from their Hindu experiences to their present Jewish experience. At the most, having had their spiritual appetites satisfied once, they are now able to satisfy them again, in the context of Judaism. But for virtually all intents and purposes, the status, experience, and contribution of returnees from Hinduism to Judaism is no different from that of returnees from ordinary secular life to a newly discovered spiritual life within Judaism. The exposure to Hinduism leaves almost no visible traces in their lives as serious Jewish practitioners. In terms of identity, one can therefore not speak meaningfully of the impact of Hinduism upon their identity. Hinduism provided an important station on their spiritual journey, but no longer defines their identity in any meaningful way.[40]

Model B: Adopting a Hindu Identity

The second model also assumes fundamental incompatibility of different identities, leading to the eventual choice of one identity over the other. The cases covered by this model are those where Hindu identity is preferred over one's Jewish identity. Jews who have had a meaningful exposure to Hinduism opt for Hinduism as their primary form of religious expression, assuming a Hindu identity. Hindu identity would be established through a critical configuration of the identity markers, presented above. In some cases, all identity markers are present, making the identification of an individual's identity as Hindu fairly easy. However, as will become apparent through the analysis of several test cases, it is often the case that identities are not clear-cut. In fact, identity is often a messy thing, when it concerns identity as shaped and defined by the encounter between different religious traditions.

The most extreme case of assuming Hindu identity is to all intents and purposes identical with the classical Jewish *mumar*, the convert who has assumed a different religious identity. However, whereas in former ages social pressure and forced conversions were a primary drive in Jews adopting Christian and Muslim identities, in the relatively new encounter with Hinduism, it is mainly the spiritual encounter and the quest for a life not found previously within Judaism that drive the adherent to adopt a Hindu way of life, hence a Hindu identity. But within this difference in circumstance also lies the major distinguishing point between the identitarian implications of adopting the ways of another religion in the earlier cases and in the case of Hinduism. The classical Jewish mumar renounced his Jewish identity. The present-day Jewish follower of Hinduism rarely does. Let us look at some individual cases as a way of presenting the phenomenon of adoption of Hindu identity, as well as of the potential complexity of identity in relation to one's original Jewish identity. That Jewish identity itself is composed of the twofold aspects of religious and ethnic-national identity greatly complicates a consideration of Jewish and Hindu identities.

The twentieth century has seen several Jewish personalities who have found their place within a Hindu religious framework. Some of them have attained great renown within the Hindu framework. In a letter from Gershom Scholem to the young student Danny Matt, the former rebukes the latter for having visited India, but having failed to visit the most famous Jewish woman since the Virgin Mary. Scholem is referring to the Mother of Pondicherry, affirmed as divine by Sri Aurobindo.[41] If the Mother is second in fame, she is first in status, as, to the best of my knowledge, no other Jewish woman has ever been declared divine. Nor has any Jewish woman, or man, occupied such a central position not only in the administrative hierarchy but in the spiritual life and organizational unfolding of any Hindu organization.

Mirra Alfassa is the name of the Pondicherry Mother.[42] A review of her life suggests that she brings little that is Jewish to her Indian context. Coming from an atheistic and communist background, she carries no meaningful Jewish teaching, training, or practice. Her Judaism is thus primarily ethnic. As I have learned from Boaz Huss, her path to India, as that of several other figures in the first part of the twentieth century, passes through the study of the occult and esotericism. An important station in her occult studies is the spiritualist teacher Max Theon. Theon was a Polish Jew, who taught a brand of esotericism, the cosmic movement, that purported to have kabbalistic affiliations, but whose actual substance resembles little of what we know of Kabbalah. Interestingly, the symbol of the Star of David containing a lotus within it, which was the symbol of Theon's school, was carried by the Mother into the design of Sri Aurobindo's symbol.[43]

The Mother seems to have made very little of her Jewishness.[44] Thus, we can find her saying: "I belong to no nation, no civilization, no society, no race, but to the Divine."[45] Manifestations of her Jewishness seem to appear mainly in times of crisis for the Jewish people. Aurobindo and she are outspoken about the fate of the Jewish people during World War II.[46] Similarly, during the time of the Six Day War, in 1967, she expresses strongly pro-Israel positions. Her Judaism as a Hindu figure thus corresponds only to the degree of her Jewishness in her earlier life. It is an ethnic or national identity that finds no religious expression and that seems to come to the fore mainly in situations of extreme national crisis.

There might be one further aspect to her "Jewish" contribution, even if it does not strike us as immediately Jewish—her contribution to organization and education. Alfassa was the primary force behind the organization of Aurobindo's ashram, the educational initiatives that it launched, and the creation of a new ideal urban settlement—Auroville. Quite apart from her internal mystical life, this woman contributed greatly to the practical and administrative life of an emergent community. I note with interest that a similar path may be identified with reference to several other Jews who have assumed a Hindu identity, one in which their Jewish identity plays a very minor role, if it is present at all. Thus, Maurice Frydman, Swami Bharatananda, played an important role in a variety of projects related to India's material development, social organization, and political emancipation.[47] More recently, the Jewish Swami Radhanath, seems to follow a similar trajectory. With little meaningful Jewish background, he plays an important role in ISKCON and has taken initiative in a variety of contemporary social projects. This includes inspiration for the founding of the Bhaktivedanta Hospital in Mumbai, for initiating ISKCON's Midday Meal Program, which feeds 1.3 million poor school children, in coordination with the Indian government, and for cofounding a hospice in Vrindavan. The story he tells in his autobiography[48] of his promising to do something for India if he is only allowed entry at the border certainly captures the spirit and contribution of this Jewish swami to contemporary India. That such a high percentage of Jewish swamis and teachers, over half of the small number of individuals studied,[49] should contribute in such active ways to Indian society raises the question of whether such contribution might not itself be a way of their expressing their Jewishness. Heirs to a culture of charity and social action, with little emphasis on specifically "religious" values, they put the great ideals, as well as organizational and educational skills, received from their paternal tradition at the service of another great religious culture.

There are a number of other Jews in prominent positions in various Hindu organizations nowadays.[50] Apparently, a Jerusalemite is in an important position of governance in Rajneesh's ashram in Pune. In cases known to me personally,

I can think of several Jewish people who either run or have important leadership positions in Hindu organizations. One is Sadhvi Bhagawati, whom some describe as the CEO of Swami Chidananda's Parmarth Niketan. In her introduction to the latter's book *Drops of Nectar*, she makes some comments that indicate her awareness of fundamental differences between the Jewish culture within which she was brought up and the path and identity that she had come to embrace through her close association with Swami Chidananda.[51] Bhagawati never renounced her Judaism. This is probably the case for all modern Jewish converts to or practitioners of Hinduism. Hinduism, as a religion that claims tolerance as its virtue, might never require renouncing another identity. Thus, Jewish-Hindu practitioners will rarely if ever be found disowning their maternal religion. Rather, Hinduism is embraced as the religion that gives meaning, while Judaism may be nominally or minimally maintained. My talks with Bhagawati suggest to me that she maintains the warmth and openness to Judaism that her reform upbringing instilled in her. Her own spiritual openness, coupled with the interreligious work in which she engages on behalf of her Indian guru, also provides opportunities to learn from Judaism and even to experience various of its ways of approaching and channeling the sacred. These are received in a spirit of openness and interest. As is the case with Jewish attraction to Hinduism, interest and contact with Judaism is upheld through contact with and the inspiration of Jewish religious leaders, whom Bhagawati has become close to, through her interfaith work. A certain sense of belonging to the Jewish tradition and a warmth toward it allows for the occasional symbol or ritual to be incorporated in her practices. However, these do not carry sufficient critical spiritual mass to make Judaism her primary or even defining source of religious identity. Thus, she provides an example of how many contemporary Jews have found themselves within the Jewish-Hindu nexus. Without ever renouncing their Judaism, they have made their Hindu identity primary, while maintaining spiritual openness to Judaism, if and when opportunity arises.[52] There is a novelty in this situation, compared to the age-old situation of Jewish apostates to other religions. Because Hindu identity is adopted with no out and out rejection of the previous Jewish identity, one remains in theory open to what Judaism might have to offer and to its message, as it is encountered. Because previous Jewish identity was weak, and specifically lacking in spirituality, spiritual food is sought in Hinduism, without necessarily undermining those positive elements of the former weak identity.[53] Thus, paradoxically, while previous generations saw stronger Jewish identities collapse, in favor of alternative religious identities, in today's encounter with Hinduism, a weaker Jewish identity is maintained precisely because it involves less, is less demanding, and therefore can be maintained alongside or as a component within the primary and more central Hindu identity.

Similar to the case of Sadhvi Bhagawati is the case of Ma Jaya Sati Bhagawati. Her moving record of an encounter with Rabbi Zalman Schacter Shalomi corresponds to the suggested parameters. A Jewish devotee of the great Hindu saint Neem Karoli Baba,[54] she ran his spiritual center in Sebastian, Florida, until her recent death. In a moving tale, she recounts how this Jewish Hindu leader discovers her Jewishness and experiences Sabbath, through Sabbath celebration with

R. Zalman and in particular his gift of lighting the Sabbath candles.[55] The overall experience is positive. The author is open to the rediscovery of her Jewish identity. Yet, this rediscovery does not amount to a change in her own identity. She is not led to return to Judaism, or to leave her position as the head of a Hindu ashram.[56]

In these instances, Hindu identity remains primary, while at the same time allowing some dimension of Jewish identity to be affirmed and integrated. The possibility for continuing affirmation of one's Jewish identity and openness to spiritual moments, lived through contact with Judaism, is a sign of the times. It is not simply a consequence of weaker Jewish affiliation that continues to coexist alongside the new Hindu identity. It is an expression of broader tendencies of maintaining multiple identities, or multiple dimensions of affiliation with different religious traditions, that is increasingly common and characteristic of an age where religion is freely chosen. Along with free choice comes the option of constructing both religious practice and religious identity in ways that are complex and original, ways that defy the classifications and boundaries of former ages.[57] In the case of Hinduism it takes on the added dimension of greater flexibility and agility in the construction of identity, given the fundamental premise that truth is not contained exclusively within one path or one school. Given such fundamental tolerance, one may be open to the manifestations of the religious life of Judaism, even from within the matrix of a Hindu lifestyle and identity.

In terms of the criteria for identity construction, listed earlier, I would argue that in such cases the self-identity of the individual and his or her willingness to continue to recognize themselves as Jewish should be given far less weight than the accumulated evidence of the criteria deriving directly from the person's actions, embrace of an alternative religious path, and the aggregate of external identity markers that point to an alternative religious identity. While from a pastoral as well as a metaphysical perspective there may be great value in continuing to affirm the Jewish identity, or certain dimensions of Jewish identity of the Hindu practitioner, there is also potential harm in glossing over the choices made by the individual and the serious commitment made to another religious path. In an appendix to the present chapter, I will examine in detail two books, at least one of which belongs to the present category of Jewish converts to Hinduism. As I shall argue in reviewing this book, there is something misleading in the way the author presents his worldview as somehow commensurate with Judaism. While his choice of religion must be respected, as well as his sincere quest for integrating his parental religion with his embraced religion, it is equally important to distinguish authentic expressions of Judaism from misrepresentations and from attempts to cover over meaningful differences in ways that are not respectful of the real issues at stake. Identity seems to me to be one of the main issues at stake. Even if one can reconcile various teachings and practices, there remain some irreconcilable differences in terms of identity. Attempts by Jewish converts to Hindu religion to present their own religion as commensurate and contiguous with Judaism may be interesting philosophically, but they are misleading in terms of the different, and competing, identity claims of different religious communities. Jewish converts to Hinduism may have what to teach Judaism and what to bring to it, through their exchanges with Judaism. But such potential enrichment should not be confused with continuity of identity. In all the above cases of Jews who opt for another religion, as this manifests through their practice, through their names, and through the priorities according to which their spiritual energies are expended, we must accept their choices and consider them as Hindu. If in metaphysical terms we may be led to affirm the continuity of Jewish identity, regardless of one's practice, in terms of a given interreligious encounter, in cases where Jewish identity is maintained only through claims of (ethnic) self-identity and a minimal contact or openness to Judaism, we should consider those practitioners as Hindus. To consider them as Hindus does not mean that we bring to these individuals the full charge traditionally associated with apostates. Rather, we must learn to appreciate their novel identity for its beauty and riches and to accommodate those individuals in their particularity, with full sensitivity to the moments of their encounter with Judaism. Open and appreciative as our affirmation of their life choice may be, it should not detract from the fact that they are operating from the matrix of another religious identity, a Hindu identity.

Model C: Affirming Hinduism and Judaism—Shades of Multiple Religious Identities

The third model describes those individuals who, in some way, amount to a movement and seek to affirm simultaneously their Judaism and their Hinduism. What defines this group is that they neither reject their Hindu associations, as does the first group, nor is their Jewish identity defined minimally, primarily on ethnic grounds, as in the case of the second group. They thus consciously maintain a positive and engaged attitude to both Hinduism and Judaism. This description is sufficiently broad to describe a wide range of attitudes and positions, regarding how the two religions feed and enrich the spiritual lives of these practitioners and shape their identity. Because the array of positions is wide, we can find within it anything from practicing Jews who engage in Hindu-based meditation to the case of one member of the ISKCON (Hare Krishna) movement, whom I know, who continues to put *tefillin* on daily, even as he continues to direct his worship to Lord Krishna, thereby clearly affirming his multiple religious affiliation. The common denominator of this group is thus attitudinal. It describes the attitude of simultaneous affirmation of elements of both Hinduism and Judaism. In some cases this simultaneous affirmation has identitarian consequences, leading the practitioner to affirm his or her identity as both Hindu and Jewish. In other cases, involvement with Hinduism may be circumscribed in such a way as to have beneficial spiritual impact, without affecting one's identity. In distinction from the second model, where Jewish identity is mostly nominal, drawing primarily on ethnic origins, the third model describes practitioners who maintain some conscious and intentional aspect of their Jewish identity, while practicing some form of Hinduism, fully or partially.

Unlike cases representing the first and second model, which may be personally interesting, but seem to have little interest for broader issues of Jewish identity and spirituality, cases representing the third model inevitably offer us new challenges and new opportunities in terms of Jewish practice, spirituality, and identity. If members of the first group have cast aside their former Hindu identity and members of the second group have not cultivated a Jewish identity that has the power to be shared and to impact the spiritual lives of others, members of the third group seek, in some way, to uphold their Jewish identity, and in many cases to deepen it as they deepen their spiritual lives. This makes their stories more interesting and of greater potential significance for the broader Jewish community, especially when its spiritual crisis is recalled.[58] Clearly, not all cases that belong to this third model have the power to address the Jewish crisis or to shape the future of Jewish spirituality. However, all may be considered as life experiments that seek to work out fundamental dynamics of spiritual transformation, personal and collective identity, and the broader crisis of the individual and community that is typical of our age. As such, each of them provides a case to be studied, a potential lesson, an example upon which we can reflect. Those who are closer to the heart of traditional observance may have a more enduring testimony to offer than others, but all seem to me of great interest, in terms of their testimony to the ongoing quest for an authentic spiritual life and how it is played out in the various shades of multiple religious affiliation.

What follows are two portraits or options that reflect the spiritual explorations of individuals I have encountered in person. Let me begin with the case of Swami Vijayananda, who has already been mentioned in the present study.

Swami Vijayananda was born Avraham Jaakov Weintraub in Alsace in 1914. Having lost his father at the age of four, he grew up in the home of his stepfather, who was the rabbi of Metz.[59] He received a good Orthodox training and was knowledgeable in Judaism in both practical and theoretical terms. However, he chose to study medicine rather than to pursue the rabbinic career his family had designated for him. His independence in relation to his family seems to have extended beyond career choice. His late teens and twenties saw a great interest in the spiritual traditions of both Hinduism and Buddhism, as well as an intense search for spiritual realization, which led him to such figures as Gurdjieff. It seems that he had let go significantly of observance of the mitzvot at this time. His dual interest seems to have focused on the study and practice of medicine and on seeking to practice yoga and follow the spiritual path as it was known to him from writings of Eastern teachers. The war years were spent practicing medicine in occupied France. By his own testimony, communicated to his students,[60] he did not go into hiding, but maintained a bold and fearless attitude, playing down his Jewish identity, without adopting any alternative identity.

Vijayananda's published autobiography begins in 1945, with the liberation of France, when he was already 30 years of age.[61] Significantly, nothing in that autobiography reveals the fact that he is Jewish. It details his spiritual search, which led him in 1951 to travel to India. What was supposed to be a three-month passage ended up being a lifetime journey, as he never again left India. Nor did he ever return to the practice of medicine. He met his longed-for guru in the person of Sri Sri Anandamayi, one of the great saints of twentieth-century India. Under her direction he lived as a *sadhu* and received the name Vijayananda. Looking at his life story from the outside, one would be led to conclude that we have here a case of someone who had traded his Jewish identity for a Hindu identity. However, closer examination reveals the situation is far more complex.

I had the privilege of getting to know Swami Vijayananda for about six years, prior to his death in 2010. During this time period I had about half a dozen serious exchanges with him, touching on his personal life story as well as on the issues that are seminal to the present discussion of Jewish identity and more specifically to the question of multiple religious identities.[62] While nothing in his autobiography suggests this, the stories shared by him in person reveal that in fact he had intended to come to Israel. Prior to traveling to India he had made three attempts to go to Israel, including as a volunteer doctor, in order to serve in Israel's battle for independence. He was rejected by the local representative, who apparently knew his family and sought to protect them from any harm befalling him in the course of fighting. Swamiji still hoped to go to Israel and considered his trip to India as a preliminary trip that would shortly be followed by a visit to Israel. This trip was never realized, as his trip to India was his last travel. He remained in India for nearly 60 years, until he died. The passion to visit Israel, however, remained real and alive for him, and some probes were even made regarding visiting Israel during the years of our acquaintance. It seems that his faithfulness to his guru's instruction to remain put in the location where she put him was the cause for his refusal of the various arrangements his disciples were willing to make in order for him to visit Israel. He knew in himself that if he visited Israel he could not leave it and felt an obligation to remain in India, under his teacher's instructions. His continuing interest in Israel was made manifest in things as trivial as maintaining a subscription to the international edition of the *Jerusalem Post*. He followed with keen interest developments in Israel, on both political and spiritual planes. He was current with noteworthy Israeli music and even taught such songs as "Jerusalem of Gold" to his disciples. He maintained interest in Israel and Judaism, without ever renouncing them.

His small room was cluttered with a variety of spiritual books, many of them *seforim*, Jewish holy books. My second trip to India was preceded by a train robbery in Brussels, where all my religious artifacts were stolen. I was able to obtain the most essential ones prior to my departure, but was still in need of some standard books, used for ongoing worship. Those I found available to me in swami's room and he was most willing to lend them to me. I was surprised to find in his library hassidic commentaries on the Torah, such as the commentary of the *Sefat Emet*, as well as the *Tanya*. I asked him whether he was indeed able to comprehend the text, with its dense rabbinic associations, and he responded positively. He claimed he consulted the book on a periodic basis. Having had some training in Jewish learning, he maintained his love for learning even when he became a swami. Thus, love of the people of Israel and love of Torah were consciously maintained by him throughout the 50 odd years of his spiritual life in India.

I interrogated him once concerning his Hindu identity and he stated emphatically he was not a Hindu. I am told that a visitor once asked him whether he used to be Jewish, to which he proudly replied that he still is Jewish.[63] Even though he wore the sannyasi's robes and bore a Hindu name, even though he lived in an ashram and was considered a foremost disciple of one of India's greatest gurus, still he did not consider himself Hindu. He stated emphatically that he never ceased to be Jewish and that indeed the matter was clearly understood within the relationship with his guru, Anandamayma. What drew him to her and what defined his spiritual path were the spiritual teachings of Vedanta. He was thus a vedantin, but not a Hindu. *Sannyas*, spiritual monastic initiation, was undertaken within the framework of the quest for realizing the ultimate goal of the spiritual life, not as part of adopting an alternative religious identity.

The quest for spirituality is closely linked to the encounter with a formative religious figure. What caused Swami Vijayananda to stay in India and to devote his life to the path of renunciation was the personal contact and impact of a towering saintly figure. In this Swamiji prefigures a generation of seekers that made the same moves decades later. Because of his Orthodox formation, he was able to trace a path that allowed him to maintain his Jewish identity, even while living in the depths of a Hindu religious community, sharing its broader goals. This sense of identity and an internalization of ritual boundaries and how they shape identity are also responsible for how he approached Hindu worship. Swamiji told me he never worshipped God through the forms associated with Hindu worship, even though such worship can be readily defended from the perspective of Vedanta philosophy. This was one of the clearest indications of his different religious identity. Vijayananda used to tell Western seekers who came to him for guidance, whether Jewish or Christian, that they need not worship Hindu images. His reasoning appealed to forms of worship as specific cultural vehicles. Hindu image worship was appropriate for the Hindu mind and Hindu culture. It was not appropriate for Jewish seekers, as it was foreign to their psyche, habits, and broader religious environment. His argument was not metaphysical, nor couched in terms of law or prohibition. Rather, it was couched in psychological and cultural terms.[64] True to Vedanta's capacity to relativize all things ritual and religious in light of its ultimate unitive spiritual vision, Vijayananda was able to contextualize, hence to relativize, Hindu worship, within the specific confines of Hindu religious mentality. He is the only person I have encountered who has taken such a culturally relative position, in relation to Hindu image worship. Someone like Chandra Swami avoids image worship for himself and for his Hindu disciples as well. While he does not consider it metaphysically wrong, he avoids it on spiritual grounds. The case of Swami Swaroopananda, which will be presented shortly, offers the more common option of adopting Hindu ritual practices and justifying them based on vedantic understanding. Swami Vijayananda seems to have found a unique middle path that allowed him to simultaneously legitimate Hindu practices for Hindus, while making them superfluous and even out of place for Jewish practitioners and Western practitioners in general.[65]

Swami Vijayananda's views on image worship lead us to a more fundamental dimension of his religious self-understanding and to a significant point of intersection between his Jewish identity and his vedantic worldview. One of the most obvious identity markers and expressions of religious belonging is the fulfillment of the commandments of the Torah. While Swamiji continued to self-identify as a Jew, maintaining a keen interest in all things Jewish, and to study Torah, he did not practice the mitzvot in any specific way. Clearly, he followed many of the mitzvot inasmuch as a large part of the Torah is concerned with leading a moral life. However, in terms of ritual observance, he did not consider himself as a practitioner of the mitzvot. I believe I capture his attitude correctly by saying that while he was not averse to the fulfillment of any given mitzvah, especially time-related memorials or various practices of Jewish prayer,[66] he did not engage in these in a systematic way that would indicate that they are either binding upon him or part of his spiritual path. Thus, he did not seek to practice Jewish commandments with the understanding he gained through living a spiritual life in the shadow of a great spiritual master and in light of vedantic philosophy. I recall his exasperation following a contact he had with the Chabad emissary to that region of India. That emissary sought to convince him that as a Jew he must assume a life of living according to the Torah. I believe on that occasion he tried to have him put on tefillin. My recollection is that Swamiji would not have been averse to the act of putting them on and may have even done so. However, he was both offended and frustrated at the insistence of the Chabad emmisary that he *must* practice Jewish ritual for his own salvation and perfection. He considered this a lack of spiritual sophistication and intelligence and readily contrasted this with my own openness to accepting him and recognizing him on his own terms, which he saw as an expresssion of greater spiritual intelligence.[67]

His explanation for this attitude is couched in terms of Vedanta and of the classical Hindu understanding of the role and position of the sannyasin, the renunciate. As already mentioned, all rituals and specific religious practices are considered instrumental toward the attainment of proper understanding of reality. Different religions have different rituals, and all of them are equally valid and valuable in achieving the purpose of aiding the individual toward reaching a higher spiritual understanding. Once this understanding is reached, however, ritual is no longer necessary, its purpose having been fulfilled. The social counterpart of this view is that the sannyasi is considered as beyond all rituals and often no longer performs them. Vijayananda thus transported the Hindu view of the instrumentality of ritual and its relativity to his own view of the mitzvot. Clearly, the Chabad emissary could not see eye to eye with him on this. For him, the mitzvot have inherent significance that far exceeds their instrumentality in aiding the spiritual life of the individual aspirant. Failure to perform them is of consequence to the individual, the community, the cosmos, and ultimately the Divine. A fundamental philosophical divide thus separated the swami and the hassidic emissary. This divide is precisely the point at which Vijayananda shaped his own identity and religious practice, in light of Hindu religious thought. Conceding to one of the defining dimensions of Jewish identity would undermine another dimension of his identity, not as a Hindu but as a sannyasi and a vedantin.

It may be that we should consider Vijayananda's attitude to Judaism as something that evolved over time. A comparison between his early and late writings is revealing. Reading his autobiography, first published in 1978, one would not know he was born Jewish.[68] His life story begins in 1944, when he is 30. Nothing is known of his earlier life. Any reference in this work to Judaism or to Jewish teachings takes place as part of a listing of several religions that concur on a given point of the spiritual life. There is not a single case of citing a Jewish teaching in its own right.[69] It thus seems that his earlier writings and public expressions seek to play down his Jewish background, and it only creeps into the discussion through some narrow cracks.

By contrast, the later Vijayananda seems much more comfortable with acknowledging his Jewish origins and identity. This is certainly the case as far as oral communication is concerned. All of our conversations pointed that way, as do various communications that I have received in his name. An examination of transcripts of teachings from the later years confirm this change as well. The second part of his publication is titled *The Conversations of Kankhal*.[70] Published in 1999, it reflects the teachings of the previous 10–15 years. It was not authored by swami, but edited by disciples from transcripts of his daily evening *satsangs*.[71] Despite the editing, one notices that Swamiji is more comfortable sharing Jewish teachings. These are presented directly as Jewish teachings and one significant teaching brings to the attention of his listeners the work of the *Chafetz Chayim* and the importance of avoidance of speaking *lashon hara*, speaking ill of others. It may be, then, that rather than seeing in Swami Vijayananda simply a figure who reconciled multiple identities, we should see in him a figure who through his lengthy spiritual career worked through these issues, until he achieved the balance he felt was appropriate for someone who was born a Jew, who identified as a Jew, but who at the same time followed the path of Vedanta and the instructions of a great Hindu saint.

If we approach his dual identity as a lifelong process, it may be meaningful to consider the symbolic meaning of his burial and the complications it involved. Most Hindus are cremated after death. A chosen few, recognized as great masters, are buried. Vijayananda shared with his disciples that Anandamayi had instructed him to have himself buried rather than cremated. He passed this message on to his disciples, who were going to bury him on ashram grounds, in Khankal where he spent his final decades. However, here they met with great opposition from local Hindus, who did not consider this appropriate, despite their great reverence for him, and despite this request being made on Anandamayi's authority. As a consequence, his body was brought to France and buried there. While Hindu funeral rites were performed, at the end of the day he was not buried in the manner customary to a Hindu or even to a swami (usually burial in a river). He was buried as a Jew would be. Despite organizers of the funeral originally saying no to the possibility, Kaddish was recited at his funeral by one of his nephews.[72] He was thus buried a swami, but a Jew all the same.

Swami Vijayananda cannot be dismissed as a mumar, as someone who has changed one religious identity for another. He never opted out of Judaism. Rather, as he presented it in his later years, he simply understood it in light of Hindu philosophy and its social consequences and applied those consequences to his Jewish ritual practice.[73] In so doing he brought together two distinct identities and worldviews, seeking to integrate them within his person.[74]

Does Swami Vijayananda present a case of dual religious belonging? Yes and no. His affirmation that he was Jewish and not Hindu would lead to a negative answer. At the same time, his stated position vis-à-vis his Jewish observance was grounded in a distinctly Hindu worldview and its corresponding social structuring even if these are affirmed in philosophical terms. What is for certain, however, is that his is a pioneering experiment in religious integration between Judaism and Hinduism, and that this experiment does touch on the fundamentals of identity construction within both cultures. Furthermore, we may also affirm that his personal example is of significance beyond personal curiosity. It allowed him to guide and direct many seekers who came to him. In him they could find a spiritual teacher unlike any other that India had produced. His unique views and his capacity to bring together different worlds and cultures opened paths and inspired many who came to him, Jews as well as Christians. He remains a model to which many present and future seekers could appeal.

Swami Vijayananda provides us with an opportunity to examine much more than the question of multiple religious identities. In what follows, I would like to use him as a test case, our only test case, for thinking through one of the most challenging aspects, and possibly the thorniest, regarding the involvement of Jews in Hindu spirituality, teaching, and practices. While what follows is neither specific to Hinduism, nor is Vijayananda the only figure in relation to whom these reflections may arise, he may provide us with the cleanest and least threatening case, thereby allowing us to reflect on these issues with least interference from habitual attitudes that have been built up over centuries concerning Jews and their practice of other religions. The classical paradigm, already alluded to in our presentation of Vijayananda, is that of the mumar, the apostate. This paradigm developed over centuries of tense competition between Judaism and its neighboring religions, primarily Christianity and Islam. Membership in one community came at the expense of another and the apostate was the traitor, leaving behind not only the ways of his ancestral religion but also his community. Judaism has been, and remains, involved in a struggle for its survival. It is concerned about how it will pass its legacy from one generation to another and what its continuing relevance will be. Under these conditions, thinking of following another religion carries, even if unwittingly, many of the resonances associated with the traditional battles and competitions. For those of us who have been shaped by traditional texts and views, some small part of us will always think of the Jewish person who has opted for another religion as a traitor. At the very least, even if we are able to show sympathy and understanding for the life circumstances and the particularity of the story that led an individual to follow another religion, we will feel sorrow and a sense of loss. The loss may be the loss of membership or the loss of spiritual treasures and opportunities that either the individual or the community he left behind are seen as having lost. It is extremely difficult, perhaps even impossible, for us to think of a Jewish person following another religion in positive terms.

I do not wish to argue that we should rejoice in cases of Jews choosing other religious paths. Nor would I argue that the deep-seated attitudes are wrong, obsolete, or inappropriate. However, there is also room for self-examination of our attitudes on these issues, and Vijayananda might provide an excellent opportunity for doing so. Never having forsaken his Jewish identity, and having avoided Avoda Zara, he went on to develop a spiritual life, wherein he achieved significant results. It is obviously hard to assess how far he had advanced. For his disciples, he was enlightened, whatever that may mean. Various statements he made concerning himself do suggest that he had significant achievements in terms of self-control, overcoming human appetites and desires, calming the mind, and above all, living in the presence of God. Taking these likely achievements as a given, for purposes of this reflection, we must ask: How should we view his life? Should we applaud his achievements, even as we bemoan the fact that in significant ways he was lost to the Jewish people? Should we underplay those achievements, because they were reached outside the framework of Judaism? Or should we concentrate only on his spiritual life, ignoring what we consider a significant biographical fact, namely his Jewish birth and early formation?

One of the young rabbis who visited India, Rabbi Yakov Nagen, met with him, upon my recommendation. Upon his return, he published a short piece in one of Israel's popular websites.[75] In it he described his meeting and shared Vijayananda's existence with the broader public. Toward the end, Nagen shares with us his own struggles, regarding Vijayananda and his Jewishness:

> Following the meeting I reflect upon the advice Vijayananda shared with me [i.e. that one must stick to one spiritual path, one's own]. It is hard to say, concerning someone who spent 55 years in an ashram, that he did not stick to one path. But what about the declaration that that path must be "according to your tradition"? Did he express thereby regret regarding the path not chosen by him? Today he recognizes that the same spiritual understandings that brought him to India are present also in Judaism, especially in the kabbalistic-hassidic tradition. I suddenly imagine what could have been—the Rebbe Avraham Yitzchak, surrounded by grandchildren and disciples, the light of his Torah guiding thousands of our people. I am saddened, for the old man whom I quickly fell in love with and for the people of Israel, that did not have the good fortune to become enriched by someone who possessed a great soul. I feel I must return to him, to talk to him one more time. [76]

This is a very telling quote. It is as positive in its view of the subject as it can get, and also as honest as one could hope, concerning Vijayananda and Judaism. For Rabbi Nagen, his having achieved the greatness he did outside Judaism, which Nagen readily recognizes, is cause for simultaneous joy and sorrow. Joy at the achievement; sorrow for the dual loss—the loss that the imaginary Rebbe (hassidic rebbe, according to the acronym used by Nagen) lost by being outside Judaism and the loss that Israel as a people lost, by not receiving from a great soul. Nagen's reflection shows us how deeply embedded the "Jewish" side of the spiritual path is, in the ideal imaginations of the path that Jews ought to take. His views are respectful and subtle, a far cry from the declaration of apostasy that others might pronounce. Yet they also share in the deep concern for the propagation of the Jewish path, for the individual seeker and for the community as a whole. Even the Jewish preference for family life comes across, in the subtle allusion to the Rebbe's grandchildren.

But let us move from the realm of the imaginary to the real. What really transpired in Dr. Weintraub's life? Can his missed relationship with Judaism simply be reduced to his lack of knowledge, at a crucial point in his life, of the riches of Jewish spirituality? What kind of life would have awaited him had he followed his family's desire and become a rabbi? While knowing next to nothing (aside from some oral stories) concerning the spiritual life of his stepfather, the local rabbi, I daresay that the spiritual life that Vijayananda cultivated far exceeded anything his stepfather could have conceived of. Even had he made his way into the more spiritually oriented sections of Judaism, it is far from clear that his life would have borne better spiritual fruit. In significant ways, Vijayananda had greater spiritual opportunities available to him in India than in the spiritual landscape of Judaism, over the past half a century. The possibility for sustained spiritual practice that his life as a renunciant afforded him should not be minimized. Nothing comparable is available within Judaism. We may idealize the Jewish balance of family and spiritual life. But we should not be blind to the fact that other paths can, if well followed, lead to a more intense spiritual life. Likely related to this very fact is the stature of individuals that he had available to him as inspiration. His spiritual teacher, Anandamayi Ma, seems to have really been on a rare level. Certainly no female within Judaism has come close to such a level, at least not publicly recognized, for centuries, if not millennia. Very few males have. In theory, we might bemoan the fact that he did not meet one of the few spiritual giants who served through the Jewish community during the second half of the twentieth century. While theoretically he might have been equally inspired by, say, the Lubavitcher rebbe, there is an equally good chance that he may have never come into contact with him. In that case, his life would have ended up as one of good service as a medical professional, with little active spiritual work.

We have developed the tools to come to terms with the secular or atheistic Jew, who does good deeds, contributes to society, and is a member of the Jewish community, the Jewish state, or the Israeli army. We lack the tools to appreciate the value of a Jewish person making his way through another religion. Yet, Weintraub-Vijayananda challenges us on precisely this point. Simply put—are we able to recognize his life as fulfilling God's will for him? If so, his life was not a second-best, but the life he was meant to lead. Reading his life, we might reflect on those crucial moments when he was refused permission to come to Israel. Was God's hand at work? And had God intended for him to grow through Judaism, why did he meet an extraordinary teacher and why did she receive him as a disciple, despite prevailing reticence to accept Westerners into the religion or into the order?

These questions can be posed because they relate to an individual life. It is much harder to pose these question in relation to "isms," such as Judaism and Hinduism. Reading a life, we must seek to read it in God's light, over and against the light of the highest principles of our tradition and our faithfulness to it. Read in this light, Vijayananda stands for a much broader challenge, and that is recognizing the possibility that God's plans and the workings of the spirit do not correspond to the boundaries and identity markers that are so crucial to us. Vijayananda thus challenges us, as does an entire generation of youth who follow unknowingly in his footsteps, to consider the relationship and correspondence between our spiritual outlook and our deep-seated processes of upholding and maintaining identities.

Ultimately, Vijayananda can function as a test case not only for the question of whether God might want an individual Jew to come to know Him through paths other than Judaism, but also for whether the individual Jew has what to offer to others through such a path. We are comfortable with the contribution of Jews, identified ethnically, to all fields of human activity. We take great pride in Jewish Nobel Prize winners, scientists, doctors, musicians, novelists, film-makers. We are comfortable speaking of the Jewish genius and, with the possible exception of a narrow segment of the Jewish people who insist on viewing life exclusively through halachic and narrowly defined Jewish lenses, take pride in the achievements of Jews in all segments of society. There seems to be one single exception—religion and spirituality. Here most people find it nearly impossible to take pride in the achievements of a Jewish person through another religion. The lengthy history of religious competition and the exclusionary ways of affirming Jewish identity seem to make such recognition an act of betrayal. Yet, it is precisely here that we must consider the deeper meaning of the crisis of Judaism. If Judaism is in crisis this may mean more than simply that we cannot reach all of our youth and that some of our membership is either drawn to or lost to other religions. As all crisis is also an opportunity for discovery and new openings, this crisis may mean that Jews are either contributing to or otherwise growing positively in relation to other religions in ways that previous generations could not have imagined. In thinking of the broader spiritual implications of the phenomenon for which Vijayananda is ultimately only a metaphor, we must ask whether it is appropriate to continue viewing it exclusively as loss, apostasy, and cause for regret, or whether we may discern deeper divine purpose, sense, and will behind it.

In reading Nathan Katz's *Spiritual Journey Home*,[77] I came across a story that captures the two sides of the issue—concern for identity on the one hand, and reflection on God's plans on the other. Katz narrates a conversation he had with Elie Wiesel. Katz shares with Wiesel his sense of loss regarding Jewish teachers who have gone East and are now teaching as Buddhists and Hindus. Katz, much like Rabbi Nagen, suggests that "maybe it was not too bad for them, but surely it was too bad for the Jewish people to lose such spiritual and intelligent people." Wiesel's response is startling: "Maybe not". Wiesel goes on to explain: "From what you have told me, I suspect that there may be some very deep *tikkun* going on. But this goes much deeper than politics. Their *tikkun* is to repair the very Jewish soul." This is an amazing quote, one which Katz himself is not sure how to understand. Seeing the phenomenon in its fuller scope, Wiesel realizes more is at stake than the story of individuals, and that a deeper sense of mysterious providence guides this broader movement. The term used by Wiesel is Tikkun, often employed in contemporary American Judaism for social involvement, but having its roots in kabbalistic reflection on cosmic and divine rupture and repair.[78] The Jewish soul finds its healing or rectification through those individuals who either bring something from it into other religions, or bring back to the soul sparks received through encounter with those religions. Wiesel does not specify which direction of influence generates the Tikkun, but it is clear that the exchange—whether understood in terms of energy, teaching, or otherwise—is neither an accident, nor a sin, but part of a divine plan, going back to the roots of the Jewish soul.

It is obviously much easier to offer such reflections in relation to the past, in describing events that happened, especially if we are dealing with a recently deceased figure in his 90s. It is much harder to adopt such a perspective when educational and pastoral concerns are at the forefront, such as when guiding youth or students. Nevertheless, from a theoretical perspective it seems sufficient to pose the question in relation to one single figure, in order to make clear what is really at stake in the entire discussion of identity. The fundamental drive for exclusivity and for faithfulness to our tradition, born of the Jewish concept of election of Israel, leads us to assume that a life of Jewish religious practice will always, almost regardless of grade and circumstance, be superior to a life lived within another religion.[79] We also identify this as God's will. But if God's will has to be discerned through historical circumstances and their complexity, then we must consider whether this unequivocal identification can be sustained under all circumstances. We seem to have already partly come to terms with the theological possibility that God's will is not fully coextensive with the mandate of Torah and Jewish religion. More than a hundred years of dealing with secularism has forced us to this recognition, however fully or partially we acknowledge it. The present reflection sought to explore whether we are able to extend this logic to another religion as well. Swami Vijayananda offers us the opportunity and the challenge of struggling with this issue. Surely, we do not wish to compromise Jewish identity and its integrity. But then we should also give at least some consideration to the complementary concern—we should not compromise God's centrality in our view of life and how God's purposes unfold in the life of the collective and the individual.

Let me move on to another example of what could be considered multiple religious identity. Swami Swaroopananda is an Israeli who has been involved for most of his life with the Sivananda Yoga Center in Tel Aviv. The center is part of an international network of yoga centers, founded by Swami Vishnudevananda, himself a disciple of the celebrated Swami Sivananda. Since the late 70s, the Tel Aviv Yoga center has drawn spiritual seekers, offering courses in yoga, complemented by the spiritual teachings of Vedanta. Swami Swaroopananda, to whom the following paragraphs are devoted, is but one example of a broader phenomenon characteristic of this spiritual center. Its adherents are drawn into the spiritual life, based on Hindu principles. However, these are practiced along with Jewish ritual practices. The center was visited frequently by Rabbi Shlomo Carlebach, who was friendly with its members, though I doubt he ever engaged fully the consequences and implications of the group's theology and practices. Members of the group observe Shabbat and Jewish holidays, though not necessarily with all halachic strictures. Swami Swaroopananda was for many years the local swami in charge of the group. Recognized by the international authorities for the spiritual and administrative talents he possesses, he has risen in the organization's hierarchy and now is one of a small group of individuals at the organization's helm.

I have known swami for over 30 years. We learned from the same spiritual master. We belong to the same age group and there is a sense of spiritual camaraderie between us, which is not disturbed by the different expressions of the spiritual life that we both practice. During these years we have been on retreat together, have spoken and shared, visited each other, and maintained a respectful and affectionate relationship. His case, as well as that of the Yoga Center as a whole, is particularly fascinating, and challenging, in terms of a discussion of a composite Jewish-Hindu identity. For all intents and purposes we are dealing with a Hindu group. Swami Swaroopananda is no longer Roni; he wears orange robes, though often the orange shades are manifest in civil clothes that do not betray the religious identity behind them. He practices various Hindu rituals, and these include the worship of God as it finds expression in the Sivananda Ashram itself, and consequently in the various centers established by Sivananda's disciples. That is, alongside a high vedantic philosophy, the ritual life involves worship of the Divine through the many forms that are recognized and worshipped in India. Hindu mantras are chanted and, all in all, the spiritual practices are a reasonably faithful Indian export.

At the same time it is clear that Swami Swaroopananda and others strongly identify themselves as Jews. This self-identification is more than ethnic. As Israelis, they could have been content with the identification as Jews provided through membership in the Israeli state and its institutions. But as spiritual seekers they relate to their Judaism much more seriously. I have seen the laying of tefillin, the recitation of daily Jewish prayers, and intensive study of Torah, with particular emphasis on kabbalistic works (and I imagine the degree of comprehension would exceed that of Swami Vijayananda). Both individually, for Swamiji, and collectively, the group self-identifies and practices Judaism as a spiritual path, either alongside Hindu practices or within a broader Hindu frame of understanding.

This last phrase gives occasion to thoughts of potential significance. To what extent is it necessary or important to establish the exact nature of the relationship between the two components of this group's identity? Is it significant for purposes of Jewish identity whether Jewish religious practices are practiced alongside Hindu, as parallel and complementary tracks, or whether one frame of reference is primary, providing the interpretive framework for the rituals and acts proscribed by the other? If so, then this would provide a means of assessing this group from the vantage point of Jewish identity and practice. That is, if we deem it important to focus on an individual or a group's stated path, that which provides the frame of interpretation for its various activities, then it might be that we will be called to make the determination of whether the primary interpretive spiritual framework is Hindu or Jewish. In that case, the group will be considered as one or the other, having absorbed elements of the other faith.

However, I am not at all convinced that the interpretive primacy of one religious framework is all that significant in helping us confront the challenges of multiple religious identities. Judaism is largely orthopraxic. Over the generations it has comfortably coexisted with multiple philosophical schemes. As Heschel astutely observed,[80] there is something of a historical accident in the fact that Judaism migrated to the West, leading to its encounter with Greek philosophy and eventually with Christianity and Islam. Had it migrated to the East, the kinds of syntheses we would have seen over the ages could have provided us with precedents for the encounters that have arisen over past decades. Jewish practice can be reconciled with multiple systems of orientation and signification. One could therefore equally argue that it is not the broader system of understanding that provides meaning for the acts of worship but rather it is the acts of worship that help identify one's religious affiliation, regardless of the theoretical superstructure that is imposed upon them. In that case, the fact that individuals practice Judaism seriously is what should count, rather than the philosophical worldview to which they subscribe.

The practices of Swami Swaroopananda and the Tel Aviv Sivananda Yoga Center are discussed here from the perspective of identity, but they touch not only on matters of spirituality but also on the subject of Avoda Zara, to which a separate volume has been dedicated. In what follows I shall consider the question of Avoda Zara from another angle than the one that occupies our attention in *Same God, Other god*. That work focuses on the status of Hinduism as Avoda Zara primarily for Hindus. The question at hand concerns the meaning of Hinduism as Avoda Zara for Jews. Before expounding on this further, some words are in order regarding the identitarian implications of Avoda Zara. In understanding why Avoda Zara plays such a central role in Judaism's foundational texts, we can opt for one of two fundamental explanations. One has to do with truth and the concern that worship not express religious, theological, metaphysical, or even moral error. According to this understanding the problem with Avoda Zara is that it is *wrong*.[81] The other possible explanation of what is wrong with Avoda Zara has to do with identity. Avoda Zara is a problem because it belongs to the realm of the *other*. Our own identity is established in relation to whom we worship.[82]

One of the halachic options in viewing other religions is that different criteria apply for Jews and non-Jews. Recognizing the legitimacy of a different religious approach for non-Jews suggests there is room for legitimate or acceptable otherness. The otherness in the identity of another religion is not threatening by its very existence. It only becomes a menace when it is applied within. Accordingly, a distinction would have to be made between otherness outside and otherness within.[83] This concern accounts for the greater strictness with which Avoda Zara is approached when it comes to Jews.

With these comments, let us return to Swami Swaroopananda and the Yoga Center. Avoda Zara and spirituality are both relevant to a consideration of the Jewish and Hindu dimensions in the identities of Swaroopananda and the Yoga Center. In terms of spirituality, it is fully clear to me that Swami Swaroopananda would have never entered Jewish thought and practice as deeply as he has without the impetus, inspiration, and example of the spiritual life, made known to him through the paths of yoga and Vedanta. Originally a secular Israeli, he found his own way into Judaism (as distinct from back to Judaism, in the case of the ba'alei teshuva) through involvement with a Hindu path. He and his collaborators[84] have in a sense made this a spiritual path, bridging Judaism and Hinduism. One may legitimately claim that their path to Judaism passes through Hinduism. Unlike the American ba'alei teshuva discussed earlier, their Hindu identity is not discarded upon entry into Judaism. In terms of depth of practice of Judaism, their practice is far deeper and more engaged than that of Swami Vijayananda. The latter applied the same vedantic philosophy and the same status of a renunciate he shared with the Tel Aviv swami to other conclusions.[85]

But the Tel Aviv Sivananda Yoga Center also takes the opposite stand in relation to Hindu ritual than that of Viyananda. The latter, largely due to his Jewish roots, avoided all contact with Hindu idols. He was thus simultaneously above Jewish and above Hindu ritual. The Tel Aviv Center is on the opposite pole, practicing simultaneously Jewish and Hindu rituals. Consequently, the various pujas, mantras, and rituals that would be seen in a Hindu temple can be seen as part of their ongoing practice.[86] Hindu rituals, directed to images of Hindu deities, are incorporated in the Center's yoga teacher training course. This has been a source of great suffering for students who wish to be certified as yoga teachers, but who are forced to partake, even passively,[87] of Hindu rituals as a prerequisite for such certification.[88] Rather than being sensitive and open to the possible challenges of bridging religions and of borrowing and drawing from each other, and making room for different course participants to find their own comfort zone on this sensitive ground, the Yoga Center's institutionalization of a certain form of training and the incorporation of Hindu rituals within that training suggest that the kind of balance between Hinduism and Judaism that the leadership has found suitable for itself is now considered normative. I must be clear on this point. The leadership does not consider that it is forcing people to worship idols. In fact, the last thing they would seek is to be engaged in Avoda Zara. Rather, they consider that their own way of understanding Hindu practice, in light of vedantic philosophy, absolves their practices from the charge of Avoda Zara. Perhaps because ritual is ultimately nonessential, it can be defended and maintained, despite protestations of participants.[89] While one can follow this kind of reasoning, one cannot ignore the fact that it also produces pain and suffering among students of the Yoga Center. It seems to me that the best way to capture this suffering is precisely in terms of identity. Even if in philosophical terms, the worship, by Jews, of Hindu deities can be accounted for, and even if one could construct, under duress, a halachic viewpoint that exempts it from the charges of Avoda Zara,[90] there remains something fundamentally distasteful, foreign, threatening, and inappropriate in Jews worshipping Hindu images, especially when this is done, actively or passively, under pressure. The problem is precisely one of identity. Jewish practice has for so long been opposed to image worship that it has become a defining feature of Jewish identity. Its identitarian dimension is even more pronounced for Israelis whose Jewish observance is weak and who therefore retain certain features of Jewish observance as particular markers of identity. Forced participation in Hindu pujas thus goes against the grain of feeling or self-identitying as Jewish. The problem is perhaps one of insensitivity, even more than of theological or ritual error. Having found their own balances between Jewish and Hindu practices, these are seen as the norm, to which future students will gradually grow through increased understanding, rather than as an ongoing challenge that each individual seeker must confront, as he or she makes his or her way through the complex and sensitive terrain of multiple religious inspiration.

At the end of the day Swami Vijayanada and Swami Swaroopananda offer us two models for integrating Jewish and Hindu identity. Both must be appreciated against the background of the larger spiritual crisis of the Jewish people. Both point to the fact that Jews have found spiritual inspiration through Hinduism.

One model maintains Jewish identity while the other deepens Jewish involvement. At the same time, one avoids all rituals, for better or for worse, so to speak, while the other cultivates a deeper feeling for the rituals of both traditions. The issue is clearly not to choose one model over the other. Both bring to our awareness the complex landscape of pursuing a spiritual life, while maintaining multiple religious affiliations, or multiple identities.

I would like to now move on to a more moderate expression of the challenge, as witnessed in the experiences of Israeli seekers who travel to India for spiritual purposes. A window onto the experiences of Israeli travelers can be found in the collection of essays *From India Till Here*. The collection records the religious impact that the encounter with India has had upon thoughtful Israelis, some of whom occupy positions of educational leadership and who are fully identified and committed practicing Jews. One response to the encounter, and less challenging at that, is that of enlivening our understanding of our own tradition. Visitors to India encounter in India an intensity of spiritual reality they feel is missing in Judaism. This encounter inspires them to rediscover the missing depths of Jewish spirituality and to search for similar intensity of religious experience within Judaism. Whether it is the Sabbath, prayer, or sacrifices, encounter with certain dimensions of Hindu practice turn out to be an incentive for deeper commitment to or appreciation of a spiritually informed practice of Judaism.[91] Receiving inspiration and returning home with it is not threatening in terms of identity. It may have been threatening before the travels were undertaken, as one did not know what they would ultimately yield. But this constitutes a safe return. It also does not require negotiating the continuing presence of Hindu elements in one's practice or identity.

There is another response that is typical of many travelers. Elements of Hindu practice are imported. Most commonly, yoga and meditation are picked up in India and later practiced in Israel. This is not fundamentally different from borrowing specific items that are Hindu or Hindu-based on a limited basis, as encountered en masse in such movements as Transcendental Meditation. These are cases of limited borrowing that express an openness to Hinduism, or some of its offshoots, without implicating one's identity. One is borrowing from Hinduism, without in any way *becoming* Hindu. This would seem to be the safest form of multiple religious affiliation. What makes it possible is precisely the reduction, or distillation, of an entire religious tradition or teaching into a technique. The power of technique is that it can be exported and cross the boundaries of a specific religious tradition. The genius of many of the gurus who reached out to the West was in their ability to offer Westerners a technique.[92] While those who follow these teachers are in fact introducing some dimension of Hindu practice into their life, this should be considered a low degree of religious borrowing and in some cases even of multiple religious belonging.

The significance of borrowing a technique exceeds the act itself. Individuals who undertake the practice of meditation obviously consider it significant and impactful in their lives. Meditation practice becomes a source of meaning and significance. It holds the key to personal transformation. In light of such borrowing, some religious tradition, represented through a teacher, a practice or a book, becomes significant in the life of the person. Undertaking a practice is rarely done in complete neutrality. It is accompanied by deep appreciation for the teacher, and consequently for the tradition from which he or she comes, either in terms of the specific chain of teachers, the scriptures that inform their work, or the religious and spiritual heritage of Hinduism as a whole. Borrowing a practice means one is willing to have one's spiritual horizons shaped by another religious tradition and one considers that such shaping is permissible, beneficial, and probably not a source of significant conflict of identity. Serious engagement with and appreciation of another religious tradition is on some level a commitment to that tradition. However limited the scope of this engagement might be, it does take the practitioner into the realm of multiple religious affiliation. Multiple religious affiliation, according to this understanding, need not consist of equal and simultaneous commitment to two traditions, such as described with reference to the Tel Aviv Yoga Center. Suffice it that more than one tradition is the source of significant spiritual understanding. An inevitable consequence of that is that one tradition is read and interpreted in light of the other. Meaningful engagement with another tradition may even occur on a philosophical level, without ritual implications.[93] Thus, it may be argued that no act of borrowing from another tradition is free of identitarian consequences. We are shaped by whatever we are engaged in and the choice to be informed, in theory or in practice, by another tradition is transformative personally, forcing one to redefine oneself, making room for the positive influence of the other religion.

Jewish-Hindu Identity: Parameters of Dual Religious Affiliation

It is time to evaluate the phenomenon of multiple religious belonging in light of the various cases and reflections offered above. One opening comment is in order. The entire discussion of multiple religious identities is a one-sided discussion. I am not familiar with Hindus attempting to integrate aspects or elements of Judaism into their practice. True to general ignorance of Judaism, as distinct from Israel, on the subcontinent, it is Jews who find Hinduism fascinating and draw from it rather than Hindus who turn to Judaism.

A discussion of Jewish-Hindu identity in terms of multiple religious identities should be limited to the third type of encounter we described. I do not consider the first two types as cases of multiple religious affiliation. The ba'alei teshuva were inspired by Hinduism, but Hinduism is no longer meaningful or operative in their spiritual lives. Jews who consider themselves Jewish only by virtue of their ethnic identity should similarly not be considered as having multiple religious identities. For purposes of the present discussion, I would offer the definition that multiple religious affiliation assumes two religious traditions inform one's religious horizons. The two traditions find some expression in practice. They exist in some kind of creative tension with one another, leading to continuing efforts to understand the one in light of the other, to harmonize between them, or between those aspects that are studied or practiced. Both are sources of significance. Regardless of how deeply one is engaged in one or the other, a situation of multiple affiliation assumes that the tradition, through its representative, teaching or technique, is approached with the kind of respect and reverence that only the insider has toward her tradition. With that respect, a positive appreciation is developed for broad sections of the tradition, usually much broader than the scope of the actual teaching or technique that is practiced. Specific individuals, usually teachers, are respected in both traditions as role models and authoritative voices.[94] It is up to the practitioner to reconcile all these into a coherent and integrated worldview. Better yet, the process of spiritual growth and transformation of the individual practitioner takes place through an attempt to integrate in her life, heart, and being the spiritual lessons and fruits that she continually draws from both traditions.

I would consider the above a minimal definition of multiple religious affiliation or belonging. This definition provides an emphasis that is process oriented, focusing on attitude and psychological orientation. Consequently, the practitioner who is only practicing some form of meditation or technique that is derived from Hindu sources, without thereby opening up to the broader Hindu tradition as a source of signification in her life, would not come within the purview of the present discussion.

Among multiple religious practitioners we can identify various shades. Ultimately, each of the seekers makes his or her own way, thereby generating a potentially endless range of shades and nuances of multiple religious affiliation. Working through multiple identities is not a matter of theory that can be controlled by strict guidelines, determining the boundaries between the permissible and the nonpermissible. It is, rather, a kind of spiritual art, open to continuing inspiration, and transformation, based on a continuing process of growth and learning. Within the range of shades and options we could, however, distinguish between weak and strong senses of multiple religious belonging. Various criteria may be applied to distinguish between different forms of multiple religious belonging. One criterion may be to determine whether one tradition is primary, while the other is secondary. Accordingly, Jewish travelers to India maintain a strong Jewish identity, while broadening their spiritual horizons in a way that makes Hinduism a meaningful religious presence in their lives. Conversely, Swami Vijayananda and Swami Swaroopananda seem to draw primarily on Hinduism, in one or another of the expressions of its religious life. Their Jewish identity and practice are either maintained or enhanced, while they continue to be primarily sustained by practice and theory that are informed by Hinduism. A second means of ascertaining primary and secondary would draw on the various identity markers listed in the opening to the present discussion. Group membership, public identification, and taking up the clothing and name associated with another religion would obviously point to a strong sense of membership in that religion. A third way might be to pose the question of who interprets whom. The religious system that offers the interpretive framework through which the practices derived from the other religion are understood would be primary.[95]

Once we are able to suggest criteria for identifying a primary and secondary religious affiliation, we can move toward a distinction between strong and weak forms of multiple religious identity. It is perspective that determines our taxonomy. The distinction is being made from within a Jewish framework. Were it being conducted from a Hindu framework, we would arrive at a mirror image of our proposal. What I propose then, is the following. Cases in which Judaism can be recognized as the primary religious tradition, and elements of Hinduism are integrated within it, would be considered weak cases of multiple religious belonging. By contrast, where we find Hinduism as the primary religion, with Judaism nevertheless playing a meaningful role on the spiritual horizons of the individual or the community, we have a case of strong multiple religious belonging. It is recognized that as multiple criteria are used to determine identity and as these criteria operate simultaneously in relation to two traditions, there may be cases of uncertainty as to how we might classify a given identity. Whether Swami Swaroopananda is primarily Jewish or primarily Hindu might depend on the factors through which we make the evaluation. At the end of the day, the distinction between strong and light cases is purely heuristic. Its significance does not lie in the classification, but in the educational and theoretical challenges that it opens up. Weak cases can be more readily integrated in pastoral and in public terms. They challenge us less than do strong cases. From the perspective of public Jewish life, the concerns of the community and even the dictates of halacha, it is easier to integrate a weak sense of multiple religious affiliation than a strong sense. We lack the public, social, halachic, and pastoral tools to accommodate a strong sense of multiple religious affiliation, suggesting the primacy of Hindu identity. One may even claim that from the perspective of Jewish public life and policy a weak sense is welcome, while a strong sense is unwelcome. A weak sense of multiple belonging can be limited to inspiration and borrowing that would amount to enrichment of the spiritual life of Judaism. A strong sense, suggesting the primacy of Hindu identity, undermines Jewish membership and practice. Even if it does not involve formal conversion to Hinduism, it comes dangerously close to the age-old concern with conversion. Obviously, religious identities and movements do not follow our educational guidelines, let alone halachic prescriptions. Individuals make their way in the spiritual life in complex and surprising ways. We must develop a positive appreciation for these journeys and find ways of accommodating them. At the same time, we should develop the pastoral tools of discernment and guidance that would aid spiritual seekers to maintain the primacy of their Jewish identity.

In concluding this discussion I would like to raise the following theoretical question: Is it possible at all to successfully maintain multiple religious identities? The question might be posed in relation to any two religions; however, the answers will differ depending on the specific religions under discussion. Therefore, the question should be posed here in relation to Judaism and Hinduism. What is unique with regard to Hinduism is the great fluidity in Hindu practice, self-understanding, and identity construction. Hinduism is so fluid that it becomes almost meaningless to pose the question in this manner. The answer would largely depend on the specific configuration of Hinduism. Swami Vijayananda could be considered legitimate because of a specific configuration of practices, disciplines, and relationships that did not make it even necessary for him to be called a Hindu, let alone to convert. Disciples of Chandra Swami can practice the same form of spiritual life as their Hindu counterparts, without compromising their Jewish practice. The same is not true of followers of more strictly defined groups, especially those that place a premium on forms of worship involving image worship. Thus, the case of Stuart, the follower of Krishna who continues to wear Zizit and to don his tefillin daily, is one unlikely case of attempting to maintain multiple religious identities. Still, it is an attempt that suggests that in some way both traditions remain meaningful, and that the individual gropes to find a way of remaining loyal or at least connected to both as meaningful sources of inspiration, growth, or personal religious identity.

Given the great variety of Hindu ways of constructing identity, much would depend on what form of Hinduism one is upholding along with Judaism. The key to successful maintenance of multiple identities would seem to be first and foremost avoidance of Avoda Zara. While, as attempted above, certain practices may be justified in vedantic terms or tolerated in halachic terms, it seems beyond dispute that taking up worship of idols and images compromises identity in some way. Consequently, I would not consider Swami Swaroopananda a successful case of upholding multiple religious identities, from a Jewish perspective, even while I maintain respect and appreciation for the spiritual path he is on and its benefits, also in terms of his Jewish practice and that of his followers.

Another key to successful maintaining of multiple religious identities would refer to the totality of Jewish life that is lived by the individual. The fuller the Jewish life, the more readily integration of Hindu elements may be a source of inspiration and spiritual enrichment, rather than a menace to identity. It stands to reason that cases of a weaker double belonging would go better with a fuller Jewish life, thereby pointing us in the direction that successful dual belonging is possible primarily in cases of weak double belonging.

Can appropriation of significance and affiliation ever be completely problem free? Is it possible to envision a sense of multiple religious belonging that is fully harmonious with Judaism? I would offer two answers in response. The first is that it may indeed be possible. Weak cases of double belonging in which Judaism maintains its primacy, while Hinduism provides either a philosophical framework, a technique, or spiritual inspiration may be considered as successful multiple religious belonging, precisely because a clear hierarchy exists between the different religions. The second answer is that it may be that at some point a conflict will arise. This is obviously the case for stronger cases of Jewish-Hindu identity, but conflict could arise also in cases of weak double identity. The arising of conflict does not invalidate the multiple belonging. It suggests what I think could be a helpful distinction. It may be that one may not be able to *fully* be both Jewish and Hindu. Both Swami Vijayananda and Swami Swaroopananda fall short of ideal Jewish observance. Yet, they maintain their Jewish identities in ways that make their double belonging *meaningful*. All too often we apply criteria of strictness, excellence, and totality to our subjects of discussion. Perhaps the question is not best posed by asking whether one can be *fully* Jewish and Hindu. Rather, given the reality on the ground, we may be better off posing the question of whether one can be *meaningfully* both Jewish and Hindu. To this I would have to respond positively, with reference to all the cases that conform to this model. Recognition that this is not only a reality that takes place but that it is meaningful for the participants in such a process as well as for today's Judaism is one of the great challenges that we face and one of the important recognitions to arise from Judaism's present encounter with Hinduism.

Appendix: Works of Jews Who Have Opted for Hinduism

Following this discussion of identity on the Hindu-Jewish axis, I would like to review two works. Both were authored by Jews who have become deeply involved with Hindu religious movements, and both offer us a window to the processes of defining identity and of constructing a worldview that seeks to integrate the Jewish and Hindu influences in their lives. The first book is by a Jewish convert to ISKCON (Hare Krishna), Steven Rosen.[96] Rosen has been a follower and student of this particular form of the Vaishnava tradition for over 30 years. He has published numerous books and edits a respectable journal, the *Journal of Vaishnava Studies*. The fact that he carries two names may encapsulate the entire story. He is both Satyaraja Dasa Adhikari and Steven Rosen, and he is publicly known by both names.

In 1990, Folk Books, a book label that Rosen set up and that carries his works, published a work titled *Om Shalom: Judaism and Krishna Consciousness*, further subtitled *Conversations Between Rabbi Jacob N.Shimmel and Satyaraja Dasa Adhikari*. The book presents itself as a record of a series of publicly held exchanges on spiritual matters between a Vaishnava Hindu and an Orthodox Jew. When I started reading the book I was thrilled. Here was a dialogue of substance. The themes exchanged between these two figures were interreligious dialogue at its best. Questions concerning the approach to God, the power of chanting, the centrality of God's name, and a host of others that are fundamental to the religious life are the subject of what is in and of itself a fascinating discussion. My initial impression was that this was possibly the best interreligious dialogue I had ever followed. Indeed, this dialogue suggests that a very special kind of dialogue could take place between Judaism and Vaishnava thought, which would emphasize other aspects of philosophical and theological encounter than the more prevalent dialogue with Advaita Vedanta. In many ways this could be a more "religious" dialogue, touching the heart of such core religious dimensions as worship, piety, devotion, and more. As the horizons for such a unique dialogue emerged from Rosen's book, I became more and more enthusiastic about it.

But then came my suspicions and these increased as I advanced in my reading. Early warning signs were the moments when the rabbi appeared ignorant of Jewish tradition, referring to kabbalisitc teachings, while acknowledging that they were actually beyond the scope of his knowledge (even though the book's blurb presents him as having specialized in Kabbalah).[97] Then came my own engaged disappointment at how the rabbi failed to respond adequately to various points, even if response to those points did not require extraordinary knowledge; even I could have done better. Then came the moments of surprise and incredulity. It simply did not seem reasonable that the rabbi went to the Hindu temple of

Pakshi Theertam (as well as to other temples) and that he should be offered as a witness to a persistent miracle that the faithful ascribe to the temple (pp. 67–68). That such a visit should be a public event, accompanied by other members of the faith seemed even less likely, considering the prohibition on entering houses of Avoda Zara. The book's blurb made the tale of the visit to India most unlikely. Rabbi Shimmel is said to have developed a broad appreciation for the mysticism of other religious paths, based on his own studies of the Kabbalah. This appreciation has taken him to India, where he studied among the Jews of that land. That seemed highly unlikely. The Jews of India were probably never a source of teaching on Judaism for anyone but their own flock. And by the 1980s when the undated dialogue took place, there would have barely been on hand enough Jews to show the visitor around, certainly no one with whom the rabbi could study.[98] As the dialogues moved on I was also struck by the increasing passivity of the rabbinic interlocutor.[99] If in the earlier portions of the book the rabbi had teachings, differences, and meaningful objections to the teachings of Satyaraja Dasa, by the end of the book he had become a passive listener, who was cast into the role of an open-minded and excited student, with the Hindu voice providing all the teaching. It all seemed too much.

But the breaking point came with the book's conclusion. In an appendix (p. 207), both authors offer a joint statement, as though this were the result of their own interfaith summit. The appendix states:

It is the contention of both Rabbi Shimmel and Satyaraja Dasa that all disparity between Judaiam and Krishna Consciousness can be minimized by the sincere recitation of the holy name. Despite various differences, this is one thing that practitioners of both religions can wholeheartedly engage in, and in this way join together, resolving superficial discrepancies.

Perhaps such spiritual camaraderie will never come to pass. But both traditions do exhort adherents to chant the holy name above any other spiritual practice. So, at least on this principle, there is an option for peace and harmony, for a concerted spiritual effort. This belief in the superexcellence of chanting is grounded in the Bible and in vedic literature as well. In an attempt to establish this fact, then, we conclude this book by presenting a series of scriptural quotations that show the primacy and efficacy of the chanting process. This listing may serve to induce sincere souls to find a common platform for engaging in God Consciousness.

This was the final giveaway. Beautiful and inspiring as the call may have been, it was simply impossible that a rabbi would sign such a statement. The lengthy list of quotes from the Bible and from the Siddur does not include any postbiblical text (other than the Siddur) in support of chanting or approaching the divine name. Indeed, this is one of the key differences between Jewish and Hindu practice. Postbiblical Judaism expresses its reverence for the Holy name by avoidance. One must not express the name, and therefore chanting of the name is one of the practices that is found in almost all religions, with the singular exception of Judaism. To issue such a call simply goes against the grain of anything that a rabbi would have been taught and would uphold.[100] It was obvious, the statement was fake, and so was the entire book.

It was time to check the facts. Who was this Rabbi Shimmel? The book's blurb described him as having considerable literary work to his credit in the field of traditional religious commentaries. A search of the Hebrew University's catalogue revealed that no such personality exists, regardless of how this name was spelled in either Hebrew or English. Google too had never heard of him, nor of his rabbinical academy, except for the reference to the publication by Folk Books. I now understood why the work was copyrighted by Steven Rosen, rater than by both authors and why the way of contacting both authors was through Folk Books. The fact was that Rabbi Shimmel did not exist. He was a literary figure, created by Rosen for purposes of this book.[101] The book that purported to be a dialogue was a sham.

An earlier work by Rosen engages in a Hindu-Christian dialogue.[102] There, however, the Christian interlocutor is a known personality. My attempts to reach the Christian author were unsuccessful because, I was told by the person who answered the phone bearing his name, he was now in an old-age home. It didn't seem sufficiently urgent to determine whether both works of Rosen were similarly executed, or whether it was his inability to identify a Jewish conversation partner that led him to invent a fictitious personality.[103]

Having determined the fictitious nature of the entire enterprise did not mean the book was devoid of value.[104] On the contrary, it was now possible to frame the book in its appropriate context and to appreciate it for what it was. One could, of course, argue that this was simply a cheap missionary tactic. By "dialoguing" with Judaism, Rosen was able to elicit from its spokesperson various statements that would serve his missionary purposes. Thus, when Rabbi Shimmel states that, having studied the world's religions, he found that Vaishnavism is the best religion, after Judaism, this unlikely moment of recognition could be taken as a pitch for legitimating Rosen's faith, thereby facilitating its appeal and increasing its success in recruiting converts. However, had *Om Shalom* simply been a missionary tract, it would have read differently.[105] For one, there should have been much greater polemic effort invested in undermining Jewish teaching. But *Om Shalom* is quite respectful and on the whole nonpolemical. It seeks to teach, to engage in ideas, not to prove the truth of one system at the expense of the other. It is as though Rosen is content for Vaishnavism to come out second best in Shimmel's eyes; he does not need to prove himself right, only legitimate. This might, of course, be a very realistic missionary tactic. But my reading of Rosen's work is that he is really interested in working out ideas, not in proving himself right.

But *Om Shalom* is more than just a theoretical exchange of ideas. It seems to me that Rosen's urgency in authoring this book, even if he could not find a suitable Jewish dialogue partner, stems not only from the desire to engage the ideas, but to somehow give an account of two components of his own identity. Ultimately, *Om Shalom* is a dialogue between the two parts of Rosen's personality. It is his own way of coming to terms with his Judaism and of making sense of who he had become. Read in this light, *Om Shalom* offers us a valuable window to the questions of Jewish identity, as it is experienced by Jewish converts to other religions. Seen in this light, what can we learn from *Om Shalom*?

Perhaps the first and most obvious lesson is that it is important for Rosen to engage Judaism as part of his account of his own faith. Rosen is clearly thoughtful and intellectually engaged. To simply reject Judaism and to wholeheartedly embrace Hinduism seems out of the question. He must not only account for his choice but also come to terms with his Judaism. Rosen thus teaches us how important it is for the Jewish convert, or rather for a certain type of Jewish convert to Hinduism, to make sense of his choice also in terms of Judaism. In terms of identity one might recognize here a mature move that seeks to integrate and reconcile identities, rather than preferring one over the other.

It is fascinating to read the book, once we can recognize it for what it is. The book opens with an introduction by Rosen's mother, arguably the most "Jewish" move that an author could make. The brief introduction encapsulates the book's concerns, as these are projected into Sylvia Rosen's words.[106] In essence, the introduction is an apology for her son, who chose to follow the path of Krishna Consciousness, rather than that of Judaism. Placed in the mother's mouth, it suggests acceptance of this move, in Jewish terms. The choice is highlighted against the background of practices that could be critiqued within Judaism, such as the use of a *shabbes goy*. In other words, there is an implied criticism of Judaism, and what are seen as its imperfections provide the background against which Rosen's choice is justified. And yet, Steven's choice is presented as a vote in favor of what ISKCON had, and that he found missing in Judaism—a path to God. While acknowledging that pure devotees must exist in Judaism, they were beyond his reach, while ISKCON presented him with a path that allowed him to find God. Thus, Judaism is not put down; rather, the spiritual opportunities afforded by encounter with another religion are highlighted.

Rosen finds an interesting way of justifying his choices in Jewish terms. In Krishna Consciousness he has found a way to reach the goal of Judaism. Thus, a pattern of end and means establishes itself, where Judaism's goal is achieved by means of Hinduism.[107] But Rosen's claim goes much further than that, and it is here that its implications for Jewish identity become obvious:

> The word "Jew," Steven told me, is derived from *yehudah*, which means "one who exalts the Lord." Originally, then, a Jew was merely one who glorified God—this is according to the deeper implication of the word, divorced from its ethnocentric connotations. But in order to glorify the Lord properly, Steven suggested, one must look toward a practical—living—example, a person who is one hundred percent dedicated to God. (p. 3; italics in the original)

By playing on the term *yehudi*, Rosen empties it of its ethnic meaning and makes it a purely spiritual matter. This spiritual turn allows him to identify himself as a Jew in essence, since his quest is, after all, to glorify God. Personal circumstances have brought him to recognize his Hindu teacher as a role model. There is no claim for metaphysical superiority of Hinduism. One would assume, from this presentation, that Judaism and Hinduism are *theoretically* as effective in attaining their common goal. The problem is simply that Hinduism provides us with the role models that Judaism does not, at least in his case. This is a strategy that is respectful, in the same way that his teacher, Bhaktivedanta, was respectful of other religions. Vaishnavism is practically superior, not theoretically. While the ultimate appeal is to life circumstances that provide Rosen with the opportunity to fulfill his Judaism through ISKCON, in terms of the broader argument he makes, he ultimately points to Judaism's crisis and to the difficulty of reaching God consciousness through Judaism. Judaism's crisis justifies Rosen's approach to God through Hinduism, a means of fulfilling Judaism's deepest quest.

This attitude is refracted also in the call to chant God's name regardless of one's religion, which constitutes the closing declaration of the book. It is not that Hinduism is superior to Judaism, as much as that in Hinduism there is available a path through which one can practice the chanting and glorifying of God's name. But provided one chants God's name, regardless of how He is called and through which religion He is approached, one achieves the spiritual goal. This is the core of Bhaktivedanta's interreligious views, and it allows Rosen to affirm Judaism in principle, while choosing Vaishnavism in practice.

While Rosen's construct is laudable in one way, it is highly problematic in another. Rosen, as his mother informs us, has made a discovery, unknown to any of us, according to which there is an original and a secondary, later, meaning to what is a Jew. The primary meaning is spiritual; the secondary is ethnic. Rosen can maintain his Jewish identity through recovery of the original meaning of what a Jew is: someone who praises God. Unfortunately, the price of maintaining Jewish identity is a historical construct that is false and that does gross injustice to the covenantal and historical foundations of Israel's faith. Judaism is cast as simply another version of the same thing that one attains through Hare Krishna, thereby losing its particularity, for better or for worse. Coming from Bhaktivedanta the move is deeply respectful of other religions, Judaism included. Coming from Rosen, in the framework of justifying his choices in Jewish terms, it is deeply distorting. And herein lies the problem. The goal of upholding some kind of affiliation with Judaism comes at the price of deep distortion, which in its own way is deeply violent toward the tradition.

The argument for congruity of Hare Krishna and Judaism is repeated again, in the mother's words:

> Steven felt that this was Judaism in the strictest sense of the term. It was Judaism as it should be—beyond mundane ethnicity and unwarranted sectarianism. To hear him tell it, he had found the Absolute Truth and the essence of spirituality. (p. 4).

The mother goes on to affirm the legitimacy of her son's choices on theological grounds, couched in maternal love:

> As I listened to Steven's explanation, I became proud. Maybe I was just being a sentimental mother. But in his soliloquy on Krishna consciousness he didn't contradict the basic tenets of Judaism in any way. On the contrary, as he explained to me that the Vedic tradition was originally monotheistic and that "Krishna" was one name for the Lord—although He has millions of names—I began to see that the teachings of Krishna consciousness very much paralleled the teachings of Judaism. (p. 4).

Now it is not only the essence of Judaism that is attained, but differences are minimized to the point that the two religious systems are simply equivalent to one another. Placed in the mother's mouth this appears to me to say much more about Rosen and his way of integrating his identities than about how he might seek to convert Jewish readers of his work to Hinduism.

The introduction goes on to minimize differences between religions as consequences of culturally varying orientations, while the essence remains the same—developing love for God. The ultimate acceptance in mother's words is framed as follows:

> I see that my son, seventeen years later, is happy, healthy, and productive. He has a lovely home and satisfying work. He's finally a *mensch!* Who could ask for more? (p.6)

In terms of "Yiddishe mama theology," this is clearly a knock-out argument. When, in her concluding paragraph "Sylvia Rosen" claims that

> his being a devotee doesn't seem to get in the way of his Jewishness…Actually, it augments it, since the essence of Judaism is to love and honor God with all of one's heart, mind and soul (p. 6),

she has opted for a definition that has replaced the ethnic dimension of Judaism with its essence, which is deemed compatible with devotion to Krishna as its fulfillment. The terms of reference are no longer recognizable to anyone within the Jewish community, but they do point to the interest that exists to continue affirming Steven's Judaism, even if in ways that are very counterintuitive.

The concern for reconciling Judaism and Krishna Consciousness is raised time and again throughout the book. While one cannot argue that this is the book's exclusive concern, it is certainly one of its leitmotifs.[108] In one way Rosen exposes us to a range of arguments for why his adoption of a particular path should either be accepted on Jewish terms, theological terms, or logical-philosophical terms. But on a more subtle level, he constructs the book's rhetoric in such a way as to undermine objections to his adoption of another religion. Some of his arguments are thoughtful;[109] others merely resort to cheap rhetoric.[110] While his interlocutor never endorses Rosen's choice, the format of dialogue, coupled with the gradual objections to notions of Jewish particularity and its implications for the faithfulness of the individual Jew, leads the reader to a point at which Rosen's choice is either accepted, respected, or at the very least opposed with less vehemence than it would have been prior to reading the book. Thus, the dialogue serves as a clever, even cunning, way of legitimating Rosen within a Jewish framework.

One may say the same of the entire work. The work engages the great themes of spirituality that Rosen considers important for the spiritual life, attempting to situate the Krishnaic perspective within Jewish horizons, while engaging Judaism on the grounds that are most important for Rosen. While this is of great interest, it is also distorting. While, to Rosen's credit, Judaism is rarely out and out misrepresented, it is given a slant in accordance with his interests. Whether it is making vegetarianism more central than it is,[111] or working through Jewish objections to the corporeality of God, Judaism is made to look closer to Gaudiya Vaishnavism through the fictitious voice of Rabbi Shimmel and through the dynamics of the dialogue than any real dialogue partner would have permitted.

Fascinating and distorting may be the two words that sum up this work. I am willing to give Rosen the benefit of the doubt, or the credit, that slants, distortions, and misleading presentations of Judaism are not intentional, nor do they necessarily serve a missionary agenda. But if so, what is the purpose of the book and how should we classify it? It seems to me the book combines several purposes, reflecting a complexity in the psyche of its author. On the one hand, it is a piece of religious propaganda, reflecting the author's missionary zeal, or interest in making his religion understood by others. On the other, it is a framework for working out issues of the author's identity and his own positioning vis-à-vis his maternal religion. From yet another perspective, it is the product of a mind curious about religious ideas and their comparative dimensions. Scholarly concerns combine with personal and ideological concerns to produce a work that cannot be narrowly classed, probably in the same way its author cannot.

What can *Om Shalom* teach us about the Jewish-Hindu encounter? Rosen defies the neat categorization suggested above. In terms of practice, commitment, and affiliation, he belongs in the camp of Jews, secular Jews, as he emphasizes (p. 55), who have opted for Hinduism, leaving behind their Judaism. His Judaism is ethnic, something that will always remain in his heart (p. 6), but not something that will inform his practice or life. At the same time, Rosen has a deep need to affirm his choices in Jewish terms, arguing for the legitimacy of his choices from the essence of Judaism, from the love of God. Rosen is clearly a student of religion. He and Rabbi Shimmel continually quote from books on religion and on Judaism.[112] An avid reader, he feels the need to make sense of his choices in terms of Judaism. Ideas are thus important to him, and he spends much time comparing, reconciling, harmonizing ideas, and at the very least reducing tensions between them. The combination of a passionate and dedicated convert to Hinduism and a curious mind with a comparative scholarly bent is precisely what makes this book fascinating reading. But does it also make it a case of multiple religious identity? Here I would have to offer a negative reply. Even though Rosen seeks to make sense of his life choices in terms of Judaism, this could not be considered a case of double religious affiliation. Rosen does not practice Judaism. Its canon of meaning and how it offers significance are not determinative for him. He has but one source of authority and one system that he considers normative. All the rest is intellectual and spiritual curiosity.

The mixture of motives ultimately makes Rosen's book dangerous, even if in ways that are more subtle than the danger posed by outright missionary work. The danger stems from the deceit of his project and from the twisting of truth that it inevitably leads to. A rabbi who is none other than Rosen himself ends up playing into Rosen's agenda, thereby either misrepresenting Jewish ideas or offering positions and responses to Rosen's views that are weaker than what a real interlocutor might have.

Rosen represents a very unique personal journey. Starting from knowing next to nothing about his own Judaism, he moves on to cultivate a rich spiritual life in Hinduism. He then sets out to learn about religions, including Judaism.[113] *Om Shalom* is the attempt to synthesize the knowledge he has gained. But, in contrast to the next author we shall study, all of Rosen's knowledge of Judaism is book knowledge. Repeatedly, he acknowledges the theoretical presence of experience and people who possess it within Judaism. But there is neither trace of experiences born of practice, nor of encounters with living practitioners. Rosen contrasts a world to which he was drawn through example, personal charisma, and deep experience with another that is only represented through book knowledge. The result is as distorting as it is sad. Had Rosen attempted to explore and live both *spiritual* realities, he would have provided an outstanding case of multiple religious affiliation. As it is, he has produced an interesting, if curious, book, that speaks much of his intellectual and rhetorical skills, but really tells us much less than we would have liked concerning the real significance and potential of the Jewish-Hindu encounter. It is my impression that the book has enjoyed little circulation. For someone like myself, who, like Rosen, is fascinated by religious ideas, Rosen's book is fascinating. As to the readership whom Rosen might have hoped to reach, it really is a good thing that his book went largely unnoticed.[114]

The second book I would like to review in this context is Miriam Bokser Caravella's *The Holy Name: Mysticism in Judaism*. The book was first published in 1989 by Radha Soami Satsang Beas in India.[115] The double dedication on the opening page tells the entire story:

> To the memory of my father,
> Rabbi Ben Zion Bokser,
> who instilled in me a love for God
> and a spirit of open-minded inquiry.
>
> To Maharaj Charan Singh,
> My beloved master,
> Who initiated me into the path of Sant Mat,
> Bestowing on me the gift of his radiant love.

Ben Zion Bokser was a noted rabbi and author. Unlike Steven Rosen, Miriam Bokser grew up in a house of Jewish learning, where mystical learning and religious devotion were present. Judging by the fact that the book is co-dedicated to her father, we are not dealing with a rebellion or turning against him.

The second dedication forces us to consider the inclusion of this work in a discussion on Judaism and Hinduism. The book is co-dedicated to the leader of the group that published the book, RSSB (Radha Soami Satsang Beas). One could argue that RSSB is not properly speaking a Hindu group. Opinions differ on this matter.[116] RSSB is part of a larger family of religious movements, originating in the mid-nineteenth century, from the teachings of Shiv Dayal Singh. The movement, whose various branches mostly share the common Radha Soami element in their name, is variously portrayed as a philosophical movement, a (heteredox) form of Sikhism, a synthesis of Hinduism and Sikhism, or a new religious movement. Someone with a strong Jewish formation might be attracted to it precisely because it may be formally presented not as a religion, because its points of friction with Judaism are minimal (no image worship, no alternative scriptures), or simply due to the power of the encounter with the teacher or with the teaching. We do not know why Bokser was drawn to the movement, nor whether she considers it a religion, let alone a form of Hinduism. Nevertheless, for purposes of the present study, one can justify including this work in a discussion of the Jewish encounter with Hinduism for several reasons.

As we have already come to know, Hinduism takes many shapes and forms. While many, especially in recent decades, consider Sikh and Hindu identities to be distinct, many others see them as a continuum, wherein Sikhism is part of the larger family of religions growing out of Hinduism. Given the great variety in the construction of religious groups and their identities, the same would hold true, by extension, to an offshoot of Sikhism, or to a new religious movement that grows on Hindu soil.[117] Phenomenologically, this work certainly belongs in a discussion of Jews who seek spirituality in Eastern religions. The phenomenology of Bokser's process and the worldview she constructs fit overall with the patterns typical of encounters of Jews with Hinduism. Most significantly, the centrality of guru to her worldview and experience is fully commensurate with the place that the guru occupies in the various schools of Hinduism.[118] This alone, in my view, justifies treating this book within the framework of a discussion of Judaism and Hinduism. To this should be added the entire worldview, which is heavily colored by a Hindu orientation. Fundamental to her worldview is belief in karma, reincarnation, and an understanding of the cosmos and the evolution of the individual soul that are completely Hindu. When taken together with the centrality of belief in the incarnate guru, they make her work appropriate for analysis in the present context.

Unlike Rosen's book, which sought to bring Judaism and Krishna Consciousness into dialogue, even if Rosen represents both dialogue partners, Bokser Caravella offers a synthetic worldview that obviously draws on both aspects of her spiritual formation. Bokser also contrasts the two systems at various points. However, her contrasts lead to identifying the two, rather than to an elucidation of their commonalities as well as differences.[119] Her book is not offered either as a testimony of her synthetic spiritual achievements, nor as a treatise that seeks to expose and engage the tensions and challenges of receiving inspiration from multiple religious sources. Rather, her work presents itself as *Mysticism in Judaism*, plain and simple. This shows a high degree of engagement, possibly even commitment to, Judaism, wherein the author is called to offer her summary views on Jewish mysticism. But precisely herein lies the problem with the work and, in a manner similar to that of Rosen's work, its danger. Under the guise of presenting Judaism, Bokser presents a hybrid religion, Judaism, as she understands it through the teachings of RSSB. The effort would have been noble, in and of itself, had Bokser shared with us how she came to a deeper understanding of the Jewish sources in which her father specialized, in light of her personal experiences and encounters with her Indian guru. The power of a personal testimony that illuminates how two traditions shed light on one another and how she has grown through these multiple religious sources of formation could have been truly inspiring. Even a less personal engagement with the ideas of the two systems brought into dialogue with one another in an honest and open way would have been edifying. But this is not the path chosen by Bokser Caravella. Instead, she has authored a book on mysticism in Judaism, wherein Judaism is made to speak the language of RSSB.

RSSB is the truth, and Judaism is now interpreted in its light, with little regard for the original meaning or historical complexities of Judaism itself. The way in which Caravella has integrated the different strands of her identity are no longer visible to the reader, who is presented with a synthetic view of her beliefs, packaged as Judaism. Needless to say, this is deeply misleading. In its own way it is even more misleading than Rosen's work. Rosen at least attempted to separate two religions and to bring them into dialogue with one another. Bokser seems to be so taken up with the teaching of her master and his path that she has little regard or concern for maintaining the distinctiveness of each of the traditions under discussion. As a consequence, the actual contents of her work on Jewish mysticism end up starting with Judaism but moving on to the teachings of RSSB, presenting the latter contiguously, as though they were the teachings of Jewish mysticism. The outcome is a misrepresentation of Judaism.

Having grown up with not only a strong basis of Jewish learning but also with a healthy critical and self-critical approach to tradition, one wonders how Bokser Caravella came to present this hybrid form of religion simply as Jewish mysticism. The theoretical options are the same as those we saw with reference to Rosen. Much depends on who the author envisioned as her audience. Did she write it for a RSSB audience, seeking to impress them with the compatibility of Judaism to their worldview, or for a Jewish audience, seeking to inspire them, or draw them to the teachings of truth she had come to learn through RSSB? Or did she simply write this as a personal account of her faith, without clearly identifying her audience or establishing the purpose for which this book was written? One possibility is that she has simply provided us with a peek into her internal spiritual workings and how her multiple religious affiliations have been synthesized into one coherent worldview. In that case, the work would be a testimony to one way of constructing a multiple religious identity, and an uncritical way at that. The other possibility is that the work seeks to win Jews over to a certain worldview. It presents Judaism, understood from a Radha Soami perspective, with the hope of not only illuminating Judaism through insight gained from Radha Soami spirituality but of actually winning converts to the movement. In that case, it is really a missionary work.[120] Let us then have a closer look at the work in order to better appreciate its profile and intentions.

Bokser is explicit about her intended audience. She has written the book for spiritual seekers from a Jewish background who would benefit from her own search.[121] Having described herself as growing up in Judaism, but feeling there was something beyond, which was foundational to all religions and that therefore went beyond the particularity of Judaism,[122] we would assume that her intended audience are Jews, who either seek to transcend the particularity of their Judaism to a broader recognition of the ultimate spiritual truths of all humanity, or who might be encouraged to do so, through exposure to her own process. Bokser launches her process through querying whether Judaism was really her primary identity (p. xiv) and moves on to refer to Judaism as her background (p. xvi). Thus, in terms of identity, we do not have here an attempt to reconcile two identities, as much as to revisit the former identity, now become background, from the perspective of the spiritual understanding gained later. This latter is considered truth and possesses the interpretive power to interpret Judaism. Consequently, the spiritual teachings to which she was exposed through her contact with Maharaj Charan Singh are taken to be universal and as having been taught throughout history in all countries and civilizations (p. xv). If this universal truth is the substance of the teaching of all religions, then all that remains is for Bokser to reveal the teachings of truth, to which she has been exposed, within the history of Judaism. This is the purpose of her book. Needless to say, having thus defined her purpose, there is no room left for difference or individuality in relation to different religions. A possible critical perspective that might distinguish, critique, or choose between religions is lacking.[123] The purpose of the book is thus quite simple—to demonstrate the universal truths that Caravella has discovered in the history of Judaism, or differently put: to demonstrate that the real meaning of Judaism or Jewish mysticism is found in the teachings she came to appreciate through her encounter with Maharaj Charan Singh.

Bokser Caravella is aware of Jewish concerns regarding change of religious identity. Following her statement of purpose, she therefore continues:

> There is no need to give up one religion and adopt another in the quest for spiritual knowledge. Mystics come at all times and may appear in any religion, and there may be more than one true master living in the world at the same time. My purpose in writing this book is to awaken in the seeker the desire to find a living spiritual master who can guide him on the path back to God.

This seems like a clear disclaimer of any missionary intention. The author simply seeks to provide inspiration, and the seeker may then fulfill his spiritual quest by finding a master who can take him on the path herewith described, regardless of the religious identity of the master, in other words: even within Judaism. This disclaimer may be of theoretical significance, but it is largely neutralized, if not belied, by the entire project of the book. The book points to a path and a living master, while addressing a public that may be seeking just that, unable to find it within Judaism. The conclusion would be obvious, allowing Caravella to make a nod to the concerns of Jewish identity, while pursuing a program that is likely to point the way to masters of her tradition rather than to launch a seeker on a search for a Jewish master.[124]

The theoretical perspective from which this book is written accounts for its title, thematics, and presentation. The centrality of the divine name in the theology of RSSB is reflected in the title of the book, where mysticism in Judaism is only a subtitle. No sooner has Caravella launched her description of biblical history, we learn that worship of the one God is attained through coming in tune with God's divine creative power, the inner holy Name resounding within all living beings (p. 3). Here the book's thesis has already been stated in brief. It remains for the rest of the book to unpack it.

The process of juxtaposition of Jewish and Eastern mystical sources, wherein Caravella finds the two systems offering similar teachings, is of great interest in and of itself. The readings she offers, according to which the teachings of Jewish mystics are understood in light of those of oriental mystics, are often spiritually enriching and could provide the basis for fruitful discussion and exchange.[125] What is lacking, however, is a critical evaluation of whether this is *the* meaning, as she suggests, or whether a more complex process of elucidating the meaning of these texts might be enriched by some of her suggestions. The difference between the two methods is precisely the difference between the essentially dogmatic sharing of truth and the more open-ended process of sharing wisdom gained from different religious traditions. As a consequence, the entire book flattens potentially enriching differences by jumping to perceived commonalities, identifying the teachings of two distinct mystical traditions, proclaiming them essentially as one and the same. Judaism, then, ends up teaching karma, and this conclusion, as many others, is never problematized by the author.[126] One system is simply a refraction of the other.

Because the book shares the truths of the spiritual life, some of the discussions are drawn exclusively from the Indian side, with little or no input from Jewish sources, even though the official task of the book is to present Jewish mysticism.[127] For example, the chapter on control of mind has next to no reference on the subject from Jewish sources.[128] In part, this is an indication of the limits of Caravella's knowledge. Better knowledge would have made this chapter fascinating reading, especially in a comparative context. An honest presentation of the subject matter should have led to reflection on why is it that materials for any given chapter are drawn exclusively from the resources of the Indian saints. It is precisely this critical reflection that is lacking. Caravella tells the truth, known from the Indian path of Saints, presents it as Judaism, and has little concern for how much support she is able to muster for her thesis.

This method perforce leads to corruption in the presentation of Judaism. One notable corruption concerns the core theme of the book—the name of God. The divine name is indeed a subject of much mystical speculation in Jewish sources. However, Caravella presents Jewish teachings on the divine name not based on the Jewish understanding of the name, but based on what the "mystics" (read: Indian) teach us about it. Accordingly, there are outer and inner names. Significantly, all Jewish names are relegated to the external realm, while the inner name, which is the core of the spirituality she practices, is what was experienced throughout the ages. Not only do we have here a corrupting influence of one system as it superimposes itself upon another, but such a reading does injustice to the system by lumping together all Jewish names for God, and considering the most sacred name of God, the tetragram, as belonging to the realm of outer names.[129] As a consequence of such superimposition, Caravella cannot really account for the Jewish prohibition on pronouncing the divine name and ends up implicitly arguing with it, presenting it as meaningless, in view of the distinction between exterior and interior names.[130] Thus her presentation rides roughshod over the testimony of the Jewish sources themselves. The same holds true for other fundamentals of Jewish faith. Revelation of the Torah seems to be reduced to the mystic experience of the revelation of the inner name, rather than the receiving of the Torah, as conventionally understood. Rather than expand revelation to a full meaning, such as a mystical tradition might teach, and as her proof texts from the Jewish tradition suggest, Bokser seems to replace outward revelation with inner mystical experience.[131] Needless to spell out how violent this interpretation is to the Jewish tradition itself.

Throughout, Caravella is unable to cope with the particularity of Judaism. The universality of the path of the Saints makes more sense to her. The same was true of Rosen. But Rosen used this very fact to justify his choosing a path outside Judaism. Bokser Caravella copes with all particularity by allegorizing it. Thus, the particularity of the Jewish story loses its meaning. It becomes but an allegory for the soul.[132] Jewish particularity is but an example for the universal principles known to her from elsewhere. Better knowledge of Jewish sources would have revealed to her that indeed exile and redemption had been spiritualized by hassidic masters and that the readings she offers of the Bible have been offered within the tradition of Jewish mysticism.[133] However, better knowledge of the tradition would have also made her aware of much more complex relationships between the external and the interior, such that do not allow for easy dismissal of the external and objective in favor of the mystical. Precisely herein lies the difference between genuine Jewish mysticism and Bokser's overlaying Judaism with a mystical veneer, drawn from another tradition.

Caravella's entire presentation of meditation and the spiritual path is another instance of superimposition of an external model on Jewish evidence. The method and the path are Indian. Various Jewish sources are woven together. They rarely prove her point. Rather, they are integrated into her running presentation, suggesting an affinity, that, upon closer examination, remains unproven.[134]

Where Caravella really departs from Jewish teaching is in her discussion of the master, the guru. Her understanding, typical of the Radha Soami school, is that the master is God incarnate. It is this, in large measure, that justifies consideration of this school as part of Hinduism. Bokser argues for the acceptability of this notion, suggesting God can take human form, so He can be perceived by others.[135] She is conscious of the problem of Avoda Zara. In a work whose stated purpose is to present Jewish mysticism, we end up entering into an apologetic for why guru worship should not be considered Avoda Zara. Whether her argument is convincing or not, true or not, is completely besides the point. What matters, for present purposes, is just how corrupting of Judaism this presentation of *Mysticism in Judaism* really is. Consequently, her appeal to important hassidic texts as if they describe the Zaddik as God incarnate fails to note the most important distinction between the hassidic teachings and those of Radha Soami religion.[136]

Bokser's reliance on the Bible and her attempt to describe Judaism through the lens of her tradition lead to the following telling conclusion of one discussion:

> In summary, although it may not be possible to determine which of the many biblical figures were masters of the highest order, it appears that Moses definitely was, some others almost certainly were, while many others were spiritually evolved souls who had master-disciple relationship with their followers and imparted spiritual knowledge and benefit to them. (p. 187)

Attempting to read the Bible in light of spiritual knowledge known to us is an important exercise. So is the attempt to present Judaism's spiritual side, as distinct from common perceptions of Judaism as an external religion. However, one is struck by what amounts to spiritual hubris in the attempt to define, pronounce, rank, and rate spiritual figures of old, in light of the canons to which Bokser has become privy. The strange note struck by this summary is a symptom of the deeper problematics of her entire project.

Chapter 7, titled "Rituals and Prayers" shows how problematic Bokser's project really is. If one had to sum up, in a sentence, what the great thrust of Jewish mysticism is, one could offer the following formulation: Jewish mysticism seeks to uncover the higher mystical meaning behind Jewish ritual and the Jewish way of life. The project of the greater part of Jewish mysticism is to bring to light how central and essential ritual is, thereby buttressing its observance, against possible antinomian trends, based on pure philosophical or spiritual understanding.[137] Bokser's knowledge does not seem to go that far. Instead, she presents not the meaning of the *observance* of rituals, but the meaning of the rituals themselves, such that would allow one to dispense with them. Consequently, she does away with the objectivity of time and space-related rituals, making them purely internal.[138] Sabbath is ultimately but meditation, and pilgrimage to the Holy Land is entering the third eye. What started out as a presentation of mystical truths as she would have uncovered them in Judaism ends up as a thorough rereading or, better yet, a reading away of Judaism, in light of the truths known to the author and her masters. If nothing else, this presentation alone makes the title *Mysticism in Judaism* a sham.

The chapter called "The Way of Life" brings several precepts that are fundamental to Radha Soami, including vegetarianism, abstention from alcohol, and daily meditation, discipline, etc. Bokser makes no effort to distinguish between the teachings of Jewish mysticism or tradition and the core injunctions of her own school. She offers very thin connections to Judaism, and only biblical references at that. These teachings are presented as though this was the truth, and by implication also the truth of Judaism.

Looking then at the entirety of Bokser Caravella's work, we may revisit the questions we set out earlier. Is this a case of multiple religious identity? I am forced to say it is not. It is a case of attempting to read one tradition in light of the other. The Jewish tradition is background, but it is not a commanding voice. It has no real control or impact on Caravella's religious worldview. The latter is derived exclusively from Radha Soami teachings. Judaism is but one example for the knowledge she receives from RSSB. No care is taken to respect Judaism in and of itself. The entire work rides roughshod over Judaism. The author either presents one system as another, or argues with Judaism in light of truths known to her from outside of Judaism. A genuine double religious identity struggles to harmonize two sources of authority and meaning. Caravella seems to know of no such struggle. Her struggle is at best a struggle at marketing—how to present Judaism as an expression of the truths of Radha Soami.

I do not read the work as a genuine struggle to reconcile two worlds. There are no points of tension; never does the personal voice of the author come through, except as background to why the work was written. There is but one reality, to which Judaism is made subservient. This is a Radha Soami book, not a Jewish book. This affirms the suggestion raised above concerning the work—it's ulti-mate purpose is missionary, in the sense of spreading the teachings and truths of a given school or religion to members of another school or religion. In the process we do encounter some interesting and enriching insights, along with the occasional spiritual inspiration. But even more than that we encounter misrep-resentation, corruption, and falsification of Judaism, in the name and under the authority of Caravella's line of teachers.

Both Rosen and Bokser Caravella suffer from a similar problem: corrupt-ing their presentation of Judaism, in the context of its juxtaposition with their Indian-based faith. I would still distinguish between the two. Rosen's corrup-tions are milder, and they may be less intentional and less conscious. His for-mat is one of dialogue, in which he seeks to present the two religions as distinct. The project is his way of making sense of Judaism, and its relation to Krishna Consciousness, and many of his errors can be traced to his second-hand knowl-edge of Judaism. Caravella, by contrast, seeks to identify the commonalities of both religious systems. Her zeal for recognizing commonalities leads her to superimpose one system upon another, making her work completely unreliable. It may simply be a matter of my own theological tastes and fancies, but overall I find Rosen's work far more interesting and stimulating. His dialogues chal-lenge us to consider fundamental issues that are often taken for granted, in light of another religious system that is presented in its own terms. In the process, we are challenged to consider a host of issues that makes for fruitful dialogue. Caravaella reads her agenda into Jewish sources, and the process is overall far less original and intriguing. We are taught, rather than challenged, and what we are taught does not touch core issues that would serve as major divides between religions. Coming out of a Sikh tradition, her teacher's message is much closer to Jewish sensibilities than the teachings of Gaudiya Vaishnavism. Less challenging in this case also means less interesting. Had she chosen a different strategy, one that respects and works through the uniqueness of each system, the outcome might have been very different.

I first came across Caravella's work at Chandra Swami's ashram. Salma, an Israeli friend who regularly frequents the ashram, shared the book with me and asked me for my opinion of it. As a seeker, she was intrigued by it and drawn to reading it. Having read it closely and considered its message I would have to return to Salma and discourage her from reading the book. I am in favor of shar-ing wisdom and inspiration across religious traditions. I am not in favor of cor-rupting one tradition in light of another. The audience for whom this book was written would not be capable of discerning where such corruption has occurred and would consequently be misinformed about their own Judaism. I would rather they read the works of her teacher, Maharaj Charan Singh, than the work of Bokser. That would provide inspiration for the spiritual life, without corrupt-ing and misrepresenting Judaism.

The lessons drawn from Caravella's book may be representative of the approach to Judaism that we can expect from members of the second group discussed here—Jews who have adopted Hinduism. Like Rosen, Bokser returns to Judaism, only to investigate it in light of her newly found truths. The outcome in both cases is corruption, serious corruption. The Jewish encounter with Hinduism has already produced some thoughtful works by individuals who seek to genuinely integrate inspiration from both traditions.[139] But such works are authored by those who seek to uphold and be responsible and accountable to two traditions. Apparently the lesson we must draw from the study of these two works is that for those who have adopted one religious identity at the expense of another, the possibility of revisiting their Jewish roots is no longer viable, as far as intellectual honesty and spiritual integrity are concerned. Allegiance to one source of authority, outside Judaism, of necessity corrupts one's reading of Judaism. This is a lesson worth noting on both intellectual and pastoral grounds. It is, alas, a sad lesson, but nevertheless an important one, pointing to one significant dimension of the Jewish encounter with Hinduism.

But there are other lessons that emerge when we consider the joint testimony of these two works. Despite differences in the specific theologies and schools to which the two authors belong, we can point to some important similarities that deserve our attention. In both cases, the core of the involvement with another religion comes from the personal relationship that the author experienced with the guru. For Bokser this is a core theme of her book. For Rosen, he has offered his personal testimony to this in another context.[140] Let us take as our starting point the assumption that both Maharaj Charan Singh and Bhaktivedanta Prabhupada are individuals of great spiritual height, achievement, charisma, and value. Let us also take as a starting point the realization that personal encounters with spiritual teachers are a prime entry point into the religious life. Why, then, do Jewish seekers need to go to India, or to encounter Indian gurus, in order to meet individuals of a certain caliber? Do they not have the opportunity to do so within Judaism?

The sad reality is that they probably do not, or at least not readily. Rosen is quite straightforward in acknowledging that comparable figures must exist in Judaism, but that he simply has not had the opportunity of meeting them.[141] Jewish religious leadership is, in this regard, quite different in its expectations, training, and profile from Hindu leadership.[142] Rabbis are trained as scholars and community leaders. Few of them are trained in spiritual excellence. Expectations inform the formation of leadership, as well as what followers find in a leader. Consequently, it would have been extremely difficult for either author to come across a Jewish equivalent to their Indian guru. Bokser's father was a noted conservative rabbi. With all due respect to the movement and the important figures it has produced, I think it is not exaggerated to say that it is likely that it has not produced a single spiritual personality that is comparable to either guru under discussion. The same holds true for Reform Judaism and, on the whole, for Modern Orthodox Judaism as well. In other words, the overwhelming majority of religious leaders in the United States (and for that matter anywhere else) are different in type and quality from the individuals who inspired our two authors. Had our authors sought equivalent personalities, they would have in all likelihood had to turn to the ultra-Orthodox, and particularly the hassidic world, which, for all its faults, at least has the capacity to produce certain religious personalities that might seem a match to Indian gurus. In this context we must not overlook considerations of gender. Even where these options do exist, they exist mainly for males. That Jews are drawn to certain religious personalities whom they seem unable to locate within Judaism, or that they can only locate with great difficulty, is one obvious and important lesson that emerges from this reading.

This recognition should provide a wake-up call, though the authorities who are in charge of rabbinic training have limited ability to address the issue. It is a consequence of deeper systemic issues, as these affect each of the major Jewish denominations. Such issues can only be resolved through comprehensive long-term changes, and the attraction to gurus is therefore only a symptom for larger issues that need to be addressed. Some consider that the situation today is better than it was in the 70s or 80s, when Bokser and Rosen made their way to Indian spirituality. Judith Linzer, who studied the move from Eastern religions to Judaism, did so as a participant-observer and her work includes her own personal reflections on the state of Judaism. As such, she is a great fan of "Renewal," a movement largely indebted to Rabbi Zalman Schacter. In it she finds an appropriate response to the challenges arising from the encounter with Hindu and Buddhist spirituality. I myself am not as convinced as Linzer is on this key issue. Perhaps I give too much credit to Hindu religious personalities, or I give too little credit to those formed in Jewish Renewal. Either way, while that movement does address some of the spiritual concerns that led youth to Hinduism, as far as the concern for leadership and spiritual excellence goes, I do not believe that it can provide a satisfactory alternative to the spiritual models that Jewish seekers encounter in the person of Hindu spiritual masters, at their best.

Another common lesson that emerges from the reading of both books is the interest in mysticism. Both books place a heavy emphasis on the mystical dimension of Judaism, as the possible counterpoint that they seek to address in dialogue, or in correspondence, to the religion they have come to own. This suggests that spiritual seekers feel more nourished and drawn to the mystical resources of Judaism than simply to a way of life, a social vision, a community life, or an intellectual agenda. Learning and knowledge of the Jewish mystical tradition are much more broadly available today than they were 30 or 40 years ago, when these individuals, as well as those studied by Linzer, were making their spiritual way. It is hard to know whether as a consequence of that Jews are less drawn to Hinduism today than they were several decades ago. Certainly, in terms of the Israeli draw to Hinduism, this is not the case. Perhaps the reality is more complex. It may be that with greater access to Jewish mystical sources, Jewish seekers in India may be able to engage Indian spirituality in ways that are more complex and nuanced than they were 30 years ago. It may be, and this may be an impression only, that today's seekers construct more complex models, drawing on multiple sources of inspiration, creating complex multiple religious identities, where the seekers of the previous generation ended up opting for one religious identity, mostly at the expense of the other. If so, the testimony of these books, both published over 20 years ago, may no longer be relevant for today. To the extent that mystical knowledge and spirituality have become more common, the passage to India may no longer be an either/or option. Indeed, as Elhanan Nir's thoughtful work might suggest, India may provide the experience and personal contact with individuals who reflect some of the ideals that the Jewish student has already encountered through her study.[143] India, then, becomes a means of realizing something that is considered Jewish, rather than an alternative to Jewish life.

There is a third lesson I would like to draw from the reading of these two books. If guru and meditation provided experience and if mystical teachings provided a conceptual framework and a broader spiritual path, there is a third dimension that comes across as common to both books: their interest in metaphysics. Both authors invest significant attention in constructing a metaphysical worldview that endows their chosen path and their life with meaning. Both include in their work a detailed presentation of Jewish history. This juxtaposition of history and metaphysics leads one to reflect upon the balances that characterize our education and our (if there is a common "our") own worldview. History continues to define what is most important for the Jewish people. By contrast, metaphysical concerns have all but disappeared from the horizons of most contemporary Judaisms. We may teach the history of Jewish philosophy or the history of views on eschatology or the afterlife. But most of what passes as Judaism, in the seminary world as well as in the pulpit, shows very little interest in metaphysics, the afterlife, the human soul, and other related issues that defined Jewish thought for centuries. This may be part of the secret of those sections of Judaism that are able to maintain spiritual vitality and bring forth religious personalities that are a match to their Indian counterparts—their metaphysical worldview remains more or less intact, unaffected by the challenges of modernity and contemporary social challenges. What is interesting in both works is that it is not simply that the authors found an experience of God they could not previously locate within Judaism. Rather, they found an entire spiritual and metaphysical worldview that they were willing to buy into as a way of making sense of or structuring their own personal experience.

The final point that emerges from the reading of both works is the continuing challenge of Jewish particularity. Both authors struggle expressly with the limitations of Jewish identity, and how it contrasts with universal ideals, the universality of religious experience, and the perceived commonality and spiritual affinity with members of other religions. Part of the attraction of the new religion is that it is perceived as less narrow, regardless of its own strictures and disciplines. Jewish particularity is understood at best as a mission, but it lacks positive content that is commensurate with the spiritual life of both authors.

Particularity is indeed one of the most challenging theological issues for Judaism.[144] But it can be variously constructed. It is noteworthy that oftentimes the more spiritual the brand of Judaism, the stronger its understandings of particularity are, such that leave little room for positive appreciation of the spiritual life of practitioners from other religions. Serious theological and pastoral concern with understanding Jewish particularity must seek to incorporate a positive appreciation of other spiritual paths and not construct Jewish particularity on a negative view of other religions and a stereotypical views of non-Jews. Such a possibility may be more within reach today than 40 years ago. It certainly seems within reach when we consider prospects for a future Jewish theology of other religions. Constructing our identity on the negativity of other groups and religions can only work as long as one does not have serious exposure to those groups. In a world in which free access to knowledge, ease of travel, and open exchange between religions are the norm, negative identity construction could drive people away, rather than draw them to Judaism.

Most of the commonalities that emerge from these two books point to work that is beyond the capacity of most religious leaders, and probably even schools, to deal with in the short term. However, this last point, concerning positive identity construction, which does not come at the expense of the other, seems within reach. With the exception of the ultra-Orthodox, all Jewish denominations are increasingly aware of their own religious and educational work taking place within a broader multireligious and multicultural environment. Awareness of the other may manifest in theoretical or practical ways, but either way it impacts one's sense of identity, broadening the horizons from which one understands oneself. This is a positive and important development. Recognizing the harmful impact of negative, or limited, identity construction, as it is refracted in these two works and their testimony of the perceived state of affairs in the Jewish community, serves as a reminder to the importance of the good work that is already taking place.

11

The Encounter Becomes Official: Hindu-Jewish Summits

The twenty-first century has seen a series of defining moments in Jewish-Hindu relations, all in fairly close succession. The decade opened with the sheitel crisis that provided public testimony to how Hinduism is viewed among the ultra-Orthodox almost exclusively through the lens of Avoda Zara. But shortly after these events new ground was broken in a series of high-profile public meetings and summits between Hindu and Jewish religious leaders. The first of these was a meeting between Chief Rabbi Jonathan Sacks of England and Ramesh Kallidai, secretary general of the Hindu Forum of Britain. The meeting that took place in 2004 was not strictly speaking a meeting of religious leaders. Accordingly, it did not focus on issues of major religious significance, let alone differences.[1] The common denominators to which the Chief Rabbi appealed in his statement were broad enough to give expression to the goodwill of the moment, without implicating him in any meaningful theological statement. Thus, the Chief Rabbi is quoted as saying:

> We both honour our past while living in the present. We both seek to honour our traditions while contributing as members of British society. We both cherish our communities, our families and our children.

In this statement, the Chief Rabbi naturally practices the most fundamental form of interreligious dialogue, especially in situations that are primarily diplomatic and geared at serving the needs of coexistence: identifying commonalities in lifestyle, culture, or even faith and offering them as a platform that can uphold coexistence or serve the common purposes of both communities.

This same strategy informs many of the contributions that were made a number of years later at meetings that were as notable for their very occurrence as they were for their substance. In 2007 and 2008, two Jewish-Hindu summits, featuring noted religious leaders of both religions, were held.[2] The meetings were organized by the World Council of Religious Leaders and its secretary general Bawa Jain. They brought together the Chief Rabbinate of Israel with the Hindu Dharma Acharya Sabha, a recently formed body that brings together the heads of many of India's leading schools and religious groups in an effort to develop a united Hindu voice on theoretical and public issues.[3] The body owes its creation to Swami Dayananda Saraswati, one of the foremost and well-respected exponents of vedantic philosophy, who has centers of teaching in India and in the United States and who has the authority, charisma, and standing to drive such a major initiative. Swami Dayananda is also the driving spirit behind the Jewish-Hindu summits. Having worked closely with Bawa Jain for many years in the inter-religious field, he sought to advance his Jewish-Hindu encounter project with the help of the latter. The partners on the Jewish side were the Chief Rabbinate of Israel, together with the American Jewish committee. A key personality in executing this project was Rabbi David Rosen, Judaism's foremost representative for diplomatic interfaith initiatives, who serves both the American Jewish Committee and the Chief Rabbinate in interfaith work. Identifying the players in these groundbreaking meetings is essential to understanding their purpose and to assessing the achievements of the two summits.

Before entering a detailed discussion of the contents and achievements of the summits, we should state the obvious and objective facts that may be more important than whatever was said, or not said, during those summits. The summits were a milestone in the very fact that they took place. They brought together high-ranking representatives of both religions who are recognized and who lent the summits a high degree of representativity, hence legitimacy. Perhaps even more significant than the fact that the summits took place is the fact that they took place in a way that was reciprocal. Time and again, the present work has pointed to lack of reciprocity in Jewish-Hindu relations. While Jews have shown great interest in Judaism, Hindus are barely aware of Judaism as a religion.[4] We have surveyed numerous writings of Jews on Hinduism, but barely any works of Hindus on Judaism.[5] There is an ongoing movement of Jews who seek spirituality in India. There is nothing parallel on the Hindu side. The summits of religious leaders are thus moments in which the two religions, through their leadership, come together in a public display that is fully reciprocal. The meaning of such reciprocity is, of course, dependent on the substance of those meetings and their public reception in both communities. As the following analysis will suggest, here we again find ourselves in a situation that is nonreciprocal, except that in this case lack of reciprocity pulls in the other direction, namely to the stakes being higher on the Hindu side. Nevertheless, in terms of public symbolism, setting of agenda and establishing patterns that can carry relations forth to the next stage, there is no doubt that the meetings were both a significant accomplishment and a source of potential future development. One might even go as far as to say that the moment at which the encounter finds expression through the meetings of official leadership is the moment when the encounter has come of age and must therefore be reckoned with seriously in the future.

Observers of the Hindu-Jewish summits have paid attention either to the very fact that these groundbreaking summits occurred or to the two statements issued in these summits. A thorough evaluation of the achievements and challenges posed by these summits requires more than applauding the two declarations. We must ask what the goals of the summits were and to what degree were they achieved. What were the expectations of participants and to what degree were expectations more or less parallel or reciprocal? What is the relationship between these two summits and other dimensions of the Hindu-Jewish encounter, described in the present work? What impact have these summits had and how are they seen by the participants and by their respective communities? In short, what was *really* achieved at these two important summits?

We are able to attempt an overview of the summits and their achievements thanks to the detailed information provided by the World Council of Religious Leaders, which organized these meetings. On its website are featured several valuable documents, through which I shall attempt to address the questions just raised.[6] In addition to the two declarations, the site features detailed transcripts of the proceedings, along with ample photographs of the two events. The report on the first meeting (henceforth 1, referenced by page number) is 73 pages long, and the report on the second meeting (henceforth 2, referenced by page number) is 76 pages long. In addition, various press clippings and additional information make up a third document (henceforth 3, referenced by page number). Thus, a total of about 175 pages document the processes and proceedings. Roughly half of this is text, and most of it is relevant to our subject matter, making it an important resource for the study of present-day Jewish-Hindu encounter in its most public and official form. Moreover, the records of these meetings allow us a glimpse into the workings of interfaith dialogue, its dynamics and transformative processes, as well as the various limitations placed upon it by context and circumstance. For nearly all participants, this was the first occasion to encounter a member of the other faith. Given that we are dealing with leaders who have a deep commitment to their own faith and a healthy interest in the other, these proceedings are a rare opportunity to observe fundamental dynamics of interfaith dialogue at work.

Welcome Messages and Discussion

The proceedings are prefaced by a series of welcome messages. These are significant for an assessment of the mind-set and expectations of participants. The first fact of note is that among the 9 welcome messages of the first meeting and the 2 welcome messages of the second, there is not a single Jewish message. This could, of course, have some practical explanation, related to the dynamics of convening the meeting. Nevertheless, the fact is suggestive. It points to what I think will emerge from the following analysis: while the summits are of interest to both parties, they serve the needs of the Hindu side in particular and are driven by it. This, of course, accords fully well with the fact that the initiative for these meetings comes from Swami Dayananda. It leads us to then ask what was the motivation for the meetings, on the Hindu side. Swami's welcome message (2,7) may encapsulate the purpose of the meeting in one phrase: "I am very sure the outcome of the discussions will mutually help us in preserving and promoting our ancient religious traditions." While he recognizes the importance of mutual knowledge, this too is tied to the practical ends that bringing together leadership on both sides might achieve: "The more we know each other, the more we can work together on important issues affecting both the religious traditions."

What are the issues and what are the concerns? In conversations I held with Swami Dayananda prior to the first summit, it was clear that his main concerns have to do with the continuing survival and advancement of the Hindu tradition. He considers the Hindu tradition to be under threat, and it is this context of threat that leads him to take various initiatives. One could argue that forming a body of Hindu religious leadership, the Hindu Dharma Acharya Sabha (henceforth HDAS), the Hindu partner to the dialogue, is itself a way of promoting the cause of contemporary Hinduism and its struggle for survival and flourishing. Swami Dayananda is a man of broad spiritual, intellectual, and worldly horizons. Aware, as he is, of the fragmented nature of Hinduism and its leadership, he seeks to address weaknesses inherent in the structures of Hinduism and its religious institutions, especially when these are compared with structures of other religions, by creating new structures that would serve Hinduism today. The creation of a body that brings together for the first time the major leaders of diverse "Hinduisms" is itself a major achievement. The push to have this very body dialogue with a body that is perceived as having representativity and recognition on the Jewish side is further expression of the drive for preservation that led to the creation of the HDAS.

What are the threats to preserving and promoting Hinduism that Swami Dayananda seeks to address? First and foremost is the threat of conversion. My conversation with him took place in Montreal, five years after 9/11, at a conference called "World's Religions after September 11." Swami gave a rather lengthy talk devoted to the theme "Proselytization and Religious Freedom."[7] It was obvious from that talk, as well as from my personal exchanges with him, how deeply concerned and hurt he was by ongoing Christian missionary efforts in India. While open to the possibility of genuine conviction leading to conversion, he strongly opposed a variety of missionary tactics that compromised integrity and authenticity by using external incentives to advance the goal of gaining membership to another religion. The perception of an endangered Hinduism informs and drives the Hindu leaders' dialogue with Judaism as well. Judaism is viewed by Swami Dayananda and other members of the HDAS as similar to Hinduism in fundamental ways. Both are nonmissionary,[8] both have suffered persecution, and both continue to fight for their survival. A dialogue with Jewish leadership is thus a way of joining forces between two religions, similar in fundamental ways, struggling with similar challenges.

Underlying the dialogue is thus a perception of basic similarity between Judaism and Hinduism, both in terms of fundamental characterization and in terms of common challenges. These two dimensions inform much of what the Hindu leaders have to say concerning the dialogue, both prior to the event (greetings) and during the meetings. While details of this sense of fundamental similarity may vary from one Hindu spokesman (no women's voices, despite the greater possibilities for women to ascend to leadership and recognition in Hinduism, compared to Judaism) to another, all Hindu leaders approach the dialogue from a conviction of fundamental commonality with Judaism. Reading the Jewish contributions to the dialogue, one does not get anywhere near the same impression that the Jewish leaders are united in their basic approach to Hindu leaders as close brothers, who share a fundamental reality, despite small, ultimately insignificant, differences. The difference in approach stems from deep-seated differences in how other religions are viewed in general. For Hindus, especially vedantins, religions are basically equivalent or parallel means of attaining the same ends, hence there is fundamental parity between the religions. This informs the Hindu attitude to Judaism, almost a priori, independently of prior knowledge, study or examination. By contrast, Jews have imbibed an attitude that highlights distinctiveness of identity, thereby making the affirmation of similarity or commonality a task to be met, rather than a given, a starting point. Even when they are able to affirm such similarity, there remains a gap in attitude and in the ease and depth with which another religion is declared of a kind with Judaism.

Statements by Hindu leaders, in the greetings and proceedings, will provide a clearer indication of the sense of commonality to which I refer. Let us consider some of the following statements:

> Both our civilizations have been the targets of terrorism. Both have been persecuted for many centuries. Our two communities have many common concerns. We are both victims of proselytization and mass conversion programs of our people, and yet both our communities do not convert people from other faiths. (1,8)

Thus, Sri Sri Ravi Shankar. Sri Sri, as he is commonly known, in essence sees the dialogue as a dialogue of victims, pointing to commonalities of victimhood, with pride of place going to concern about attempts at proselytization. Sri Sri is a savvy international leader, who runs a vast international organizaton. He has had extensive contact with Jews worldwide, and his organization, unlike those of most of the traditional leaders who extend their greetings to the meeting, has numerous Jews as members. It is particularly interesting to see him raising the concern for victimhood in relation to conversion to other religions as a common defining feature of Judaism and Hinduism, apparently with little awareness of the fact that he himself would be seen by many Jews as involved in similar activities precisely in relation to the Jews with whom he seeks to partner in this battle. This may be taken as a first sign of something of a cognitive dissonance that characterizes the meeting between these religious leaders. The two groups discuss with one another how to face the common threats of third parties, while completely ignoring the actual dynamics that inform relations between their own members, indeed involving some of the participants in the summits. To be sure, Ravi Shankar is not a Hindu missionary to Judaism. But his movement, which stands somewhere between a religious movement and a series of techniques and practices stripped of a religious context, does draw thousands of Jews and Israelis, and for many of them it provides an alternative means of establishing their religious identity. To the extent that the common ground that is sought between Jewish and Hindu leadership focuses directly on concerns of identity, maintenance of fidelity to one's identity, and the survival and propagation of the respective religious communities, the involvement of Jews in movements such as Sri Sri Ravi Shankar's Art of Living cannot be overlooked. Ravi Shankar's participation in or endorsement of this meeting is not disingenuous. It simply points to a glaring gap in how the meeting is conceived. Hindu and Jewish religious leaders address each other from a constructed perspective that considers the two religions as near aliens, who seek to identify similarities that might allow them to undertake common causes. That the relationship between them on the ground is already half a century old, that it is in many ways messy, and that the messiness involves some of the very participants in this project are all facts that elude the attention of participants in the dialogue.

Returning to Sri Sri's words, the shared victimhood is the foundation for future common action, seen to be the outcome of the meeting of Hindu and Jewish leaders. Issues such as community organization and battling bad images in the press set the agenda for future collaboration between Hindus and Jews. Note the lack of any specific theological, spiritual, or wisdom-related agenda. The goals are communitarian and public. Leaders come together because it serves common interests. Sri Sri's eloquent message is, I believe, a good summary of what the dialogue is, from a Hindu perspective.[9]

Let me offer one further indication of the gap between how the Jewish people are perceived by Hindu leadership and the challenges on the ground. His Holiness Jagadguru Swami Jayendra Saraswatiji, Shankaracharya of Kanchi Kamakoti Pitham, possibly the most important of the four respected teachers in the lineage founded by Sankara, offers the following greeting to participants:

> It is very essential that every human being should feel proud of one's country of birth and one's own religion. As a shining example of this, we have the people of the ancient Judaic faith who are proud of their homeland, and who are very devoted to the practice of their faith. (1,7)

The view of Judaism is highly idealized. Indeed, Indians, if they have heard of Israel, or Judaism at all, have heard of it in elevated terms. Note the close association of country and religion. This betrays both the high esteem that Israel as a state (much better known than the distinct religion of Judaism) enjoys in the Indian popular mind and the legitimate identification of Israel as Judaism's nation-state. The perspective is identitarian and it highlights pride in one's identity. For the Shankaracharya this seems to also be the purpose of the meeting: "reinforcing the feeling of pride for one's religion and country." Jews may have what to teach Hindus in this respect, it seems. Jews are thus appreciated on identitarian grounds and the dialogue with them might strengthen related aspects of Hindu identity. The identitarian perspective is itself interesting. No less noteworthy is the (understandable) lack of awareness that Jews are facing crises on precisely the same fronts that Hindus are, and that their relationships with Hindus are intertwined in ways that are more complex than collaborators in a common battle.

Other speakers reference similarity between Judaism and Hinduism in terms of history,[10] but I would like to move from claims of historical or phenomenological similarity to theological claims. These tie together the two major themes of identity and idolatry as sites for Hindu-Jewish encounter, and it is these two foci that dominate the statements that emerge from the meetings. As a means of further establishing commonality between the religions, both as part of the background for the meeting and as part of the meeting itself, arguments are made concerning the understanding and worship of God in both Hinduism and Judaism. This is a major focus of the actual dialogues, to which I shall return shortly, but it is interesting to first examine what Hindu leaders take for granted as a starting point for the encounter:

> Our religions and traditions are similar. We believe in truth and God. There is not much difference between us. Our religion says "*satchit-ananda*"[11] is God. God is everywhere and God is one, and can be worshipped with and without form.[12]

This is a typically Hindu view of other religions. It is charming for its straight-forward statement of the fundamental similarity between different religions (the statement should not be limited to Hinduism and Judaism): There is not much difference between us. Accordingly, the swami proceeds to present the core formulae that summarize Hindu faith—nature of God, His omnipresence, and His being accessed through and beyond form—as features of a basic understanding of God in Hinduism, which are apparently shared, in his view, with Judaism. They are certainly not considered a source of division, let alone points of an identitarian divide.

Others echo similar understandings. "We have many things in common, most important of which is the belief in one God, who is the creator and sustainer of the universe."[13] And in an even more pronounced way: "We have the same concept of God in both our traditions, and we have the task of transmitting this to the future traditions."[14] Thus, the common charge facing us in relation to future generations grows out of the same God concept. Note: two different statements may be made. The first is that Hindus worship the one supreme God. The second is that Jews and Hindus worship the same God.[15] We note that the Hindu leaders slide from one statement to the other with great ease. "The same God is invoked by the wise in many forms and many names, and worshipped in many ways. This is the message that needs to be given to the world."[16]

Affirmation of the "same God" on the Hindu side, goes hand in hand with certain affirmations concerning God, His nature, and His worship, which seem to the Hindu thinkers to be compatible with Judaism. While none of them has, presumably, studied the matter from a Jewish perspective, it seems that having worked the philosophical issues through to their satisfaction, they transfer the conclusions to their view of Judaism, and further to how Judaism ought to view them. Accordingly, statements concerning the compatibility and identity of the knowledge of God in both traditions are followed by such statements: "There is only one creator, whose truth is hidden in all beings. The name and form of God is not in question; God is all pervasive." or "We are the worshipers of nature as God. We have the same concept of God in both our traditions."[17] To make the point clear: not a single Hindu spokesperson, either in the greetings or in the later discussion of God in Hinduism and Judaism, ever arrives at the conclusion that there might be a difference in how God is understood in both traditions.[18] The harmonious starting point of commonality of theological understanding continues informing the Hindu perspective. Since for the assembled Hindu voices,

God is one while His manifestations are many, Judaism is simply one more manifestation or rather it must worship God as known also in Hinduism and must therefore share the basic identity of God with Hinduism. Herein lies the theological foundation for practical collaboration. Returning to the asymmetry found throughout the proceedings, one notes that arguments for similarity and sameness, especially the sameness of God, are made by Hindus, never by Jews.[19] While Jews find parallels to details, throughout the dialogues, these are never elevated by the speakers to a general view of the relationship between the traditions and their fundamental similarities. Hindus, by contrast, apply an understanding of fundamental similarity of religions to their view of Judaism. All that is left for them to do is to find the details that sustain this understanding.

One of the most important ways of establishing similarity is in relation to God. The question of God emerges as a central concern in the conversations between Jews and Hindus. When Hindu leaders affirm God as a commonality with Judaism they do more than provide one more common feature between Hinduism and Judaism, a value or an experience among others. Reference to the same God also touches on a fundamental concern of both sides. On the Hindu side, we note a dominant apologetic streak (apologetic in no way detracts from the seriousness and authenticity of the claims), where Hindu leaders feel the need to affirm their belief in one God, rather than many. It is clear they see themselves as engaged in correcting a misperception concerning Hinduism. The importance of the affirmation of faith in one supreme God may be philosophical, involving the truths internal to the religion, or political, involving Hindu relations with others and their perceptions of Hinduism. In the case of the assembled leaders it seems both factors motivate them to make this a major point of reference. For Jews, this question is obviously central as well. It seems to me that in the framework of the gathering it was never really made clear why the issue is important and what is at stake on the Jewish side. When Hindu leaders affirm they do not worship many gods or idols, the argument could have equally well been made in the eyes of Christian or Muslim leaders. Indeed, as a quote from Swami Dayananda that we shall see later suggests, the question of "one God-many Gods" is framed with a Christian view in mind. The centrality and the consequences of Avoda Zara to a Jewish view of other religions seem to have never been made part of the discussion. For Jews what is at stake is legitimacy, recognition, and validity of the other religion. Working through the issue of Avoda Zara would be the foundation for establishing any meaningful relationship with Hindus. Of course, there is a certain level of relationship that can be maintained with others even if they are considered in breach of the prohibition of Avoda Zara. But the possibilities for relationship change greatly depending on the determination of another religion as free of Avoda Zara. Thus, on the Jewish side the issue is not one of simply clearing up a misunderstanding but the most fundamental decision regarding another faith and how it should be viewed.

Despite the centrality of discussions concerning the nature of the Hindu belief in one supreme God to both summits and their declarations, it seems to me that here too we encounter the lack of symmetry that seems to be a feature of these encounters. In fact, analysis of discussions, declarations, and attitudes regarding the question of God provides us with multiple opportunities for observing the dynamics particular to these two groups and the lack of symmetry of their discussions or perhaps, it is better to state, the incomplete nature of the dialogues that took place at this initial stage of official encounter. Thus far we note the difference between whether one is affirming belief in one or the same God or whether one is discussing the question of Avoda Zara and its consequences. Major differences emerge when looking at the substance of the discussions. Throughout, the Hindus present a coherent philosophical worldview that spells out the relationship between their understanding of one God and the ability to worship many gods, better yet, their recognition that everything is worshipable as a manifestation of God. The Hindu voices, both in the letters of welcome and in the substantive discussion of the subject (2,27–40), are consistent, impressive in their own right, and offer a coherent worldview. Looking at the combined Jewish response one is struck by theological utterings that are more like stutterings, providing isolated responses that are partial, and that never reach to the heart of the matter. With one or two exceptions, the uniqueness of Jewish faith does not come across, but more importantly, it is never argued, justified, or made to stand out clearly in distinction from Hindu theology.[20]

It is interesting to follow the dynamics of what might be the most important conversation of the summits, the conversation on God. The basic dynamics are that Hindus present and Jews query. There is a lead Hindu presentation on God; no such Jewish presentation is offered. Jewish responses to Hindu discussion of God may be classified as three types. The first are the rabbis who simply avoid the theological dimension and who shift the conversation to common values or to lessons they found inspiring. About half the rabbis simply shun the philosophical-theological discussion. This may be because they realize they do not have the philosophical tools needed to engage the Hindu leaders. Probably all the Hindus gathered have had systematic training in their philosophy. Rehearsing the arguments concerning the understanding of God is fundamental to their religion and they will have been trained in this for many years. Jews, by contrast, rarely discuss God. Rabbinical training is primarily legal and hermeneutical. The rabbis who have received some kind of systematic theological training are a minority. Shifting the ground of conversation to values may simply reflect their level of comfort in philosophical dialogue. Thus the opening shot of the discussion provides us with the following Jewish response:

> We greatly appreciate this meeting and see it as great blessing. I am not sure that we can reach an understanding today with regards to all aspects of the philosophical principles, but I am more interested in reaching an understanding on the practical aspects of our respective religious life style.[21]

In another moment of self-reflexivity, a longtime member of the dialogue with the Vatican states:

> I would like to thank the almighty, for the occasion that we are here to speak and listen to you, because we, the rabbinical council, had meetings in Rome and in

Jerusalem with the Cardinals. We made a point of it not to talk about theology, we only spoke about things that we have in common. Yet I thank the almighty, today we diverted a bit from that principle.[22]

Avoidance of theological dialogue has been a guideline of Jewish-Christian dialogue for Orthodox participants. This follows the instructions of the leader of Modern Orthodox Judaism in mid-twentieth-century North America, Rabbi Joseph Dov Soloveitchik. The latter ruled that one may collaborate in practical matters, but one should avoid theological engagement.[23] One of the explanations for this, which appeals to an oral communication attributed to Rabbi Soloveitchik, is that he realized how competent future Christian interlocutors would be in the domain of theology and how poor the Jewish representatives would be. In order to avoid embarrassment and to protect the Jewish side from being and looking inferior, he issued this instruction, which has remained dialogue policy for most Orthodox Jews to date. Whether the reasoning is correct or apocryphal, it is suggestive. A review of the conversations of rabbis and swamis on the nature of God makes it credible.

But there are other reasons for avoiding a theological dialogue. Rabbis may wish to not enter a theological dialogue with Hindus because they would be obligated to state their differences. The context is essentially diplomatic and therefore the codes of diplomacy dictate that one should not push differences to their limits. The voice of Rabbi Shear Yashuv Cohen, who is head of the Chief Rabbinate's interfaith dialogue commission, and who is himself well-trained in Jewish thought and philosophy, is very important, and I bring his words in full:

I agree with my colleague Rabbi Ratzon Arussi that I do not think we should go into elaborate discussion in the definition of our deity. We know that there are differences between our approaches, but the values we can share and benefit from each other, because I do not think that we should try to say that basically there is no difference, there is a difference and we respect the differences.

In one point we had in the Jewish history a very bitter development, one Jew spoke about Pantheism, which means God and the world are one, God and nature are one. He was excluded from the Jewish tradition. Later days, the late Chief Rabbi Kook, who believed in Pantheism, which means everything is in God, and there is no place empty of God, he said it in Aramaic expression "Sovev colalmim, male col almim," means transcendent and eminent. Literally means he encompasses all worlds and is encompassed by them. So there is a difference. Islam and Judaism share one thing in common, for them, there is only one God. They do not even have other names for any other Gods that are manifested by him. We have a committee that meets every year with leaderships from the Vatican; the Holy Trinity can be construed as God manifested himself, but also can be construed there are many Gods, three of them, The Father, The Son and the Holy Spirit. So we have a difference there. The purity of the concept of monotheism gives itself to different expressions and both of us feel that we should not add anything to the One, the One only. I must say that I was surprised to learn that behind the many names of Gods that you find in India, there is one Supreme God. (2,33)

The keyword of this discourse is "difference." If the collective voice of Hindu leadership suggested multiple levels of similarity, particularly in relation to worshipping the same God, Rabbi Cohen is the one and only important voice that argues for difference. The opening sentence is suggestive: we should really avoid theological dialogue because at the end of the day our differences will remain and therefore why expose them. Therefore, let us talk about common values. The strategy for coping with differences is respect, but not downplaying the differences.

Rabbi Cohen has grasped the full meaning of the Hindu position. The Hindu position may be presented as monotheistic, but it is also, maybe primarily, pantheistic. This leads him to some observations on pantheism from a Jewish perspective. He evokes the memory of Spinoza, excommunicated from the Jewish community—"the Jewish tradition"—due to his pantheistic belief. If we follow the allusion through, there woud be no room for Hindu faith within a Jewish worldview. Cohen does not go so far, because he is aware of the possibility of different criteria applying to Jews and non-Jews. But this would certainly impact any discussion of a same God. Following a reference to Rabbi Kook, who held pantheistic beliefs,[24] Rabbi Cohen affirms that Judaism and Islam share a common belief in pure monotheism and that they refuse to compromise it in any way—"not add anything to the One, the only One." The allusion to Christianity seems to group Christianity and Hinduism on one side, with Judaism and Islam on the other. This may have been the great lesson that Rabbi Cohen learned. The lessons the Hindus shared were not wasted. He was surprised to learn that behind the many names of God there is one supreme God. This seems to allow him to classify Hinduism in the same camp as Christianity, itself an important achievement in theological and halachic terms. But it does not allow him to classify Judaism and Hinduism as belonging in the same camp, affirming belief in the same God.

This is the most articulate statement of Jewish belief, in relation to Hindu faith, to emerge from the records of the summit—a lone voice, that would have preferred to talk of values but was forced to state his theological differences, contrasted with dozens of coherent voices that expound Hindu theology. Most of what needs to be said is never said. The Hindus state their faith and account for it. They tell us why it makes sense. The Jews never tell us *why* they believe what they believe. At most, the voice of Rabbi Cohen affirms difference. But we never reach a point of real exchange and real dialogue. We never consider what it means to think of God in one way or another, nor what are the experiential and educational implications of the differing approaches.

Some important contributions are made in terms of terminology. Daniel Sperber, who is both rabbi and professor, and who therefore employs multiple methodologies and disciplines in his approach to the subject matter, raises the important question of terminology.[25] He helps advance the discussion from general talk of "God" to the greater nuance that is characteristic of Hindu terminology and that is of huge consequence to the subject matter. Accordingly, he restates what was already obvious to al Biruni, which is that the theology of Hinduism is better understood by appeal to the notion of angels, alongside God, rather than to a multiplicity of gods.[26] The Hindus affirm the terminological and metaphysical distinction.[27] But some of the most important questions remain unanswered, awaiting future exchanges.

One such question is the distinction between theology or philosophy and worship. Recognizing one ultimate Supreme Being does not resolve the question of the appropriateness or permissibility of worship of others. Let me quote the opening address of Swami Dayananda, from the first summit, a statement that reveals the Hindu starting point, rather than the attempt at a nuanced exchange that characterizes the dialogues of the second summit:

> We have many lineages within the Hindu tradition, but we do not worship many Gods. There are not many Gods. "There is only one God." People are the ones I am really afraid of. They say there is one God, and they say, you are not allowed to worship other Gods. One man was standing by a pond, pulling the fish out one by one and throwing them on the ground. Another man came by and said, "Hey! What are you doing? The first man replied, "I am saving the fish from drowning." Later I learnt that the fellow who was trying to save the fish was a missionary!
>
> We do not bother with this one-God-many-Gods business. In fact, we go one step further and say there is only God. Everything for us is sacred. We take nothing for granted. The light of the sun, the air we breathe, the water, the stars, the solar system, Mother Earth, all is Ishwara, God. This is the view that underlies all the lineages within the Hindu tradition. (1, 14)

One gets the flavor of how entertaining Swami Dayananda can be as a teacher. One also gets a glimpse into the concerns that drove him to organize this meeting. This quote is the inaugural address of the first summit, and these paragraphs are the first substantive statement in that address. In other words, this is the opening shot of the entire enterprise and as such it says much about Dayananda's concerns. His affirmation of one God is neither an exercise in Hindu metaphysics nor an attempt to find common ground with Jews. It is pitched directly at his core concern—missionaries. The battle lines with missionaries seem to be drawn along the axis of one God-many Gods. Accordingly, he ups the ante by attempting to go beyond the divide and proclaiming his lack of interest in the question of one God-many Gods. He transcends it by going beyond the numerical question to the proclamation that there is only God and all is God. This might be an excellent argument in terms that are internal to Hindu philosophy; it may even work in relation to the missionaries. It certainly is not helpful to his rabbinic audience. Affirmation of the One God underlying and beyond all provides common ground with Judaism. As proceedings of the second summit suggest, it comes as a great discovery to Jewish participants and one that does help them shift their view of Hinduism. However, the difference between common affirmation of one supreme God and overcoming the charge of Avoda Zara lies precisely in the question of what is worthy of worship. From the outset, the Hindu side does not seem to have been made aware of the importance of this distinction, and consequently of the remaining challenges in developing a halachic view of Hinduism. As we see time and again, Hindu speakers readily conflate belief in one Supreme Being and recognition that all is God with the legitimacy of worship of all, some going as far as to portray these understandings as common ground with Judaism. Swami Dayananda too seems to think that resolving the philosophical challenge will resolve the core issues on the Jewish side. This may betray his strong philosophical orientation, according to which resolution of the philosophical issues resolves all else.[28] It may reflect previous encounters with Christian missionaries or it may simply betray his lack of previous exposure to how Jews approach this matter. Whatever the reasons, not all is resolved by affirmation of common faith in one Supreme Being, underlying all of creation. The question thus remains: What is worthy of worship, and how does this impact the Jewish understanding of Avoda Zara?

Rabbi Cohen seems to have already alluded to one possible answer in recognizing Hinduism for what it is, while affirming the differences that make it akin, from a Jewish perspective, to Christianity. If so, Hinduism might still be considered Avoda Zara or it might not, depending on the viewpoint adopted. Either way, the implications of identifying common metaphysical ground to a halachic view of Hinduism in terms of Avoda Zara are not automatic. They must be further constructed in light of the various options that have previously been developed in relation to Christianity, or in some other way.

Rabbis participating in the conversation on idolatry during the second summit were obviously aware of these difficulties. They refrained from stating their real views boldly or from stating what was really at stake for them in the discussion. But they were open-minded and curious to gain a better understanding of Hinduism, precisely in order to clarify the issues at stake. The following exchange is possibly the most important one in terms of its halachic significance. While most of the sharing took place on a philosophical level, pointing to belief in a common Supreme Being, the following exchange is informed by proper halachic concerns, even though these are never spelled out:

Rabbi David Brodman: We Jews, thought about the Indians, that your religion has to do with idol worship and today we hear, and not only hear, we are learning something very important. Again, I must be careful because my mentor the Chief Rabbi had said we must be careful because of the differences we have. But to hear things which are so clear and so clarifying, we think that we made a mistake.

I would like to stress one sentence, which we say and I hope my colleagues agree, every morning and a few times a day, we say "Shemah Israel, Adonai Elohenu, Adonai Ehad." Hear Israel, our God is One. But it says, Elukeinu in plural! Elukim, the word God is in plural, Gods. We do not worship, we do not give power to the various expressions of Gods. When we speak about Elukim, Elukim is actually God. My people from my community sometimes say how do we call Gods? There are no Gods, there is only one? But here, I think we understand what you are saying. There are angels, they are expressions of God. There are animals as you say.

I would like to ask you, because we are very near to each other, when you say that you worship, do you give power, absolute power to that expression of Gods, or you say it is just an expression of God without the power? When you pray to it, you do not pray to the animal, you pray to the almighty? Am I saying right?

Swami Adveshananda Giri: We do not pray to the animal or to the physical manifestation, but we pray to the almighty, or the unspeakable, or the unununderstandable almighty in this form.

Anuja Prashar: I would like to say the word worship itself, in the semantic of using English takes away what we are trying to say. When we recognize divinity everywhere even within ourselves, when we worship we connect with that divinity. So it is not in the being or in the form that we are actually observing that divinity or energizing. When you say, do you give power? We do not give power, we do not take power, we connect with the power and that is the form of worship. (2, 37).

This is an important and meaningful exchange. In terms of procedure, it shows dialogue at its best. There is listening and querying in an attempt to better understand each other. There is also the ability to identify the teaching of the other with one's own, thereby establishing common ground. Rabbi Brodman positions himself, and his colleagues, as being in a position of learning. He readily admits having made mistakes and is willing, even if with some reservation, to revise his views. The newfound common ground allows him to revisit the foundations of his faith and to reread the core statement of the *Shema* along the lines of Hindu theology—reference to the one God and to the many angelic manifestations of His being.[29] This is a major moment in the conversation. Revisiting one's scriptures in light of the teaching of the other is a significant achievement of dialogue. Revisiting the core statement of one's faith in that light is truly eventful. In this case, Hindu theology offers a key to resolve a difficulty inherent in a text that is recited daily, but often not understood.[30]

Rabbi Brodman, with tact and intimacy, then engages in the most basic procedure of querying the other regarding their faith. The purpose of the question is not stated, but we recognize that what is stake is the status of Hinduism as Avoda Zara. Brodman's question is to a certain degree informed by Jewish discussions of the status of kabbalistic prayer and what it means to address prayers to one of the divine manifestations known as the sefirot. Even though these are manifestations within the Godhead and not incarnations in the physical world, the query follows similar lines: Who is the approach made to? In Brodman's words: Who is being given power? Framing the question in this way assumes that if God is being approached through another being or form, then Avoda Zara does not apply. The question is ill-formulated, in my view, precisely because it does not spell out clearly enough what is at stake, namely approaching another being as Divinity and the demand to approach God alone in that capacity. The two Hindu responses therefore suffer from the difficulties in the formulation of the question. The first response denies that one approaches the form and insists that one only approaches the absolute. The second denies the validity of the term "worship," thereby supposedly undermining the basis of the Rabbi's question.

I am afraid I am left unsatisfied by the Hindu responses and recognize the limitations set by the format of the meeting or of its transcript. On a purely theoretical level, the answers may be appropriate, possibly even adequate. Certainly, when one takes the case of an animal, they make sense. But as far as addressing the unarticulated concerns of the rabbis, I fear the answers obtained are not representative of most of Hinduism, perhaps even of the speakers themselves, and I suspect they represent an apologetic moment that must be revisited as part of a larger attempt to address Hinduism and the challenges of Avoda Zara. The view that Hindus do not worship, but only connect energetically, is very rarefied. It may fall within the broad range of options that Hinduism makes available. In fact, I recall one Hindu professor whom I invited to Jerusalem during the first years of the Elijah School, T. S. Rukmani, making a similar point (though not necessarily in the context of worship). While some Hindus may approach worship in this way, it is clear that Hindus worship, and they do so intensively in ways that, at least from a Jewish perspective, cannot be dismissed as merely "connecting." Similarly, while one might approach a holy cow not as Divinity itself, but as a manifestation of Divinity, and this may be the extent of what Swami Adveshananda intended, it is hard to make a similar statement concerning the major gods and goddesses of Hinduism. Perhaps a perfected vedantin like Swami Adveshananda is capable of keeping these lines clear in his mind. My conversations with Swami Yogaswaroopananda suggest to me that indeed those well-trained in Vedanta are quite clear in how they approach worship in their minds. But then we are led back to the important questions of how to view Hinduism and who speaks for it.

One important question in the dialogues seems to go completely unanswered. Oded Wiener poses the following question, representing healthy common sense and the basis for a balanced Jewish approach:

> Your description is much deeper than most of the people can understand. All these multi names of God may confuse the simple people. When you talk to your believers, do they understand the meaning, that actually all the symbols are one God, the only God, can they understand it or they accept the symbol as God itself? (2, 33)

In other words, to what extent are these presentations representative of Hindus, broadly speaking, or are they limited to a small class of experts who are able to maintain a more rarefied understanding? To this I would add the question of whether this understanding is shared even among all Hindu leaders. I recall a conversation with Sugunendra Theerta Swami, one of the leaders of the Madhva sect. Following a six-hour puja to Lord Krishna, I asked him why he needed to concentrate on the image of the Lord and what the Lord meant to him. His response was that it was for him a necessary means to go beyond and therefore an important and indispensable part of his worship. The intensity of devotion and worship to the important manifestations of God cannot be checked by the mental recognition that they are simply, almost "empty" vehicles for the supreme power.[31] I doubt that even Advaitins practice this approach to their rituals. I am convinced that few Hindus do, even if they recognize one Supreme Being. Whether most Hindus will recognize the claims for one supreme Divinity manifesting through the various deities is a question that might require serious statistical data to resolve. My view remains divided on this question, even though at times I do accept the claims of swamis that ultimately (all) Hindus recognize there is one God. But the recognition of one Supreme Being in no way guarantees how worship is understood. To the extent that Rabbi Brodman's question is relevant,[32] I fear that it was not duly addressed in the dialogues. Coupled with Wiener's open question, these questions point to future conversations that need to take place.

The dialogues seem to have convinced many rabbis of the authenticity of Hindu views concerning one God. But they do not resolve the problem of Avoda Zara.[33] Looking at the proceedings of both summits, I can identify only one moment of tackling the issue directly. This is in a response by Rabbi David Rosen, given during the first summit. Rosen sidesteps all theological discussions simply by appealing to Meiri, assuming his principles extend to Hinduism as well.[34] Here we have a discussion of idolatry, in Jewish terms Avoda Zara, rather than a discussion of the nature of God. One of the features of the dialogue is the implied assumption, perhaps the blind spot, that assumes the two conversations are equivalent. They are not. There is, obviously, a close relationship between the two.[35] Recognition of one Supreme Being is a necessary condition for resolving the crux of Avoda Zara, but it is not sufficient. In the deepest sense, framing the dialogue in terms of discussion of one supreme God betrays the Hindu agenda and its approach to the question.[36] It assumes that a successful resolution of the problem of one God-many Gods will resolve potential differences between Judaism and Hinduism.[37] While working through these issues was fundamental and while much was achieved due to advances in relation to the question of one God-many Gods, the consequences of this discussion for a halachic view of Hinduism remain mostly unexamined.[38] The discussions that took place posed the questions in terms familiar to the Hindus and resolved them accordingly with a great measure of success. They did not, however, begin to seriously tackle the Jewish *fraagestellung*, addressing what is of concern to the Jews and its practical implications. These remain tasks for the future.

The Declarations

Differences in how the subject matter was approached are reflected in the aftermath of the meeting. But before reviewing that, let us now turn to the declarations that emerged from the two meetings and review them in light of the analysis of the meetings' views and positions. Following the typical preambles, the main points of the first declaration, are as follows:[39]

The participants affirmed that:

1. Their respective traditions teach Faith in One Supreme Being who is the Ultimate Reality, who has created this world in its blessed diversity and who has communicated Divine ways of action for humanity for different peoples in different times and places.
2. The religious identities of both Jewish and Hindu communities are related to components of Faith, Scripture, Peoplehood, Culture, Religious Practices, Land, and Language.
3. Hindus and Jews seek to maintain their respective heritage and pass it on to the succeeding generations, while living in respectful relations with other communities.
4. Neither seeks to proselytize, nor undermine or replace, in any way the religious identities of other faith communities. They expect other communities

to respect their religious identities and commitments and condemn all activities that go against the sanctity of this mutual respect. Both the Hindu and Jewish traditions affirm the sanctity of life and aspire for a society in which all live in peace and harmony with one another. Accordingly, they condemn all acts of violence in the name of any religion or against any religion.

5. The Jewish and Hindu communities are committed to the ancient traditions of Judaism and Hindu Dharma respectively and have both, in their own ways, gone through the painful experiences of persecution, oppression, and destruction. Therefore, they realize the need to educate the present and succeeding generations about their past, in order that they will make right efforts to promote religious harmony.

6. The representatives of the two faith communities recognize the need for understanding one another in terms of lifestyles, philosophy, religious symbols, culture, etc. They also recognize that they have to make themselves understood by other faith communities. They hope that through their bilateral initiatives, these needs would be met.

7. Because both traditions affirm the central importance of social responsibility for their societies and for the collective good of humanity, the participants pledged themselves to work together to help address the challenges of poverty, sickness, and inequitable distribution of resources.

The areas of agreement can be divided into three categories: faith, identity, and common action. Clause 1 discusses faith. It is the only clause to do so and therefore should be seen as the condition that allows the other conclusions to follow. Clause 7 speaks of common action. Clauses 2–6 can be classified as expressing concerns on matters of identity. Looking at the thematic division, then, identity and its preservation emerge as the most important concerns of the joint declaration. If we consider that Clause 1 lays the religious foundations for all that follows and that Clause 7 is almost par for the course for interreligious meetings, and that it neither reflects the substantive discussions nor does it really establish a concrete program of action, the respective significance of the opening and concluding clauses are set in context, allowing the identitarian torso of the statement to emerge as the true focus of this statement. This emphasis is fully in accordance with the vision and purpose that led to the summit. To put the matter more strongly, it shows that the goals, set by the Hindu side, were attained. What that means for the Jews we shall shortly explore.

Clause 1 relies on the strategy of commonality as a basis for relationship and collaboration. This strategy informs the entire project and we have to simply take note of the elements that were chosen to express this commonality. The most important one is the affirmation of faith in a Supreme Being who is creator and who communicates religious paths to different parts of humanity. Concerning this common ground of faith, we learn of the Supreme Being in two contexts— creation and revelation, or a milder form of it—communication of spiritual ways. A historian of religion might be inclined to deconstruct this statement. Some may argue with the very notion of creation in Hinduism. Others might argue that fundamental differences in understanding revelation in Judaism and Hinduism should preclude facile presentation of commonalities. Jews might readily disagree that their tradition teaches that God communicated different ways of action to different people at different times. It is precisely this kind of formulation that got Chief Rabbi Jonathan Sacks into trouble, leading him to revise some statements made in the first edition of his *Dignity of Difference*.[40] However, it would be wrong to argue with this formulation. It is not meant as a statement of theology. The Chief Rabbi of Israel did not sign a statement affirming the validity of other revelations or even for that matter affirming that Jews and Hindus worship the same God (let alone that Hindus are exonerated from the charge of Avoda Zara). The clause should be appreciated for what it is, a general way of suggesting fundamental *structural* (rather than substantive) similarities between the two religions, thereby clearing the way for the rest of the declaration, which should be deemed its heart and core. Accordingly, even though this is a historic meeting and a novel declaration, the theological, let alone halachic, implications of this opening clause should be taken with a grain of salt. At least with regard to the declaration coming out of the first summit, it seems to me that some of the voices describing a major breakthrough, in theological terms, in Jewish-Hindu relations have taken too literal an approach to the statement, without qualifying it sufficiently in terms of both political and literary context.

What the statement is really concerned about is identity. Clause 2 makes no meaningful point, other than to direct our attention to the domain of identity as central to religion, which, however is quite a novelty in the realm of interfaith declarations. Clause 3, framed in terms of heritage, continues to address identitarian concerns, affirming the interest of both groups to pass their tradition from generation to generation. The perspective is thus inward looking. The other is a peaceful partner in what is essentially concern for success in an inward-looking educational and identitarian agenda, particular to each of the religions. Clause 4 identifies the common "enemy," attempts at proselytzation that undermine identity and the propagation of the religions. Thus, Judaism and Hinduism, both nonmissionary religions as we have learned from the proceedings, share the concerns for the stability of their community's identity in the face of threats from the outside.

The second part of Clause 4 seems slightly out of context and breaks the identitarian flow. In purely thematic terms it would have fared better along with Clause 7, in relation to common challenges. We should therefore take note of its inclusion precisely at this point. As the central clause in the statement, it comes midway and expresses the peak expectations of the two communities.[41] What is most important for the Hindus is the battle against proselytization. What is most important for the Jews is condemnation of violence. Hindus become partners in the ongoing attempt to fight terrorism and extremism through the medium of interreligious relations. The two concerns, which are in and of themselves distinct from one another, are tied together through linguistic and conceptual ties. We hear of a "sanctity of mutual respect" (by no means a classical site of sanctity in either tradition), along with the "sanctity of life." Both points broaden the scope of awareness to include others. Other communities are expected to respect the religious identities of those making the declaration. Others who commit acts of violence in the name of religion are condemned.

Clauses 5 and 6 take the identitarian concerns into the domain of education. Commonality of historical suffering (victimhood) is coupled with commonality of commitment to one's tradition. Both point to the importance of education within and making oneself understood outside. Education and better understanding by the other thus serve the mutual interest of both communities in successful propagation and continuity of their respective traditions.

An analysis of the real interests of the declaration thus suggests that preservation of identity, especially within the broader interreligious context, lies at its core. Education and understanding serve the purpose of maintaining identity in the face of threats by other communities and enhance harmonious living in a multireligious world. This adheres fully to the intentions of the Hindu side. What of the Jewish side? What does it *get* out of the declaration? What Jewish interests are served by the declaration? The Chief Rabbinate's participation is closely related to Israel's foreign policy needs. It is only with the encouragement, maybe even pressure, of the Israeli foreign office, and certainly with its active support, that the Chief Rabbinate participated in the dialogue. Were the Jewish side's interests fulfilled by the very fact that the dialogue took place, thereby lending a religious dimension to existing political relations? This is certainly a possible reading of the summits. David Rosen indeed describes the summits as having accomplished precisely this, in his public presentations of the summits and their achievements.[42] The American Jewish Committee's involvement as a partner in the second and third summits makes sense in light of such concerns of the broader Jewish community, as well as the Jewish state. Jews and Israel require allies, and the Hindu leaders provided an important ally in making friends and cementing international and intercommunal relations. In the same way that the Hindus used the dialogue to advance an agenda, the Jews may be said to have used these dialogues to further a political agenda. My reading of Clause 4 and its introduction of condemning violence would fit well with such a political reading of the meaning of the dialogue. Thus, even if the proceedings of the summits touched on a variety of religious and spiritual concerns, the real import of the dialogues emerges in the declaration(s), which point to what brings each of the communities to the dialogue table.

Having identified the driving forces on each side, and how these find expression in the summit's final product, allows us to identify what seems to me the most glaring omission on the Jewish side, an omission that is a true failure of leadership and that raises serious questions concerning the dialogue and its significance for the Jewish community. The statement focuses on issues of identity and expresses particular concern for the propagation of the faith within, in the face of encounters with other religions that would undermine identity and affiliation. It is formulated in India and signed by the Chief Rabbi of Israel. At the same time, literally tens of thousands of Israelis are running (or maybe just sitting in meditation) around India, exposed to Indian spiritual heritage. Jewish leadership has nothing to say about this! The real, on-the-ground encounter with Hinduism seems to be completely divorced from these declarations of identity and adherence to religion. Moreover, some of the figures attending the summit, or otherwise involved with it, host Israelis in their ashrams and often involve them in spiritual practices that these rabbis would not condone. If Hindu identity concerns are addressed through this statement, why are Jewish identity concerns completely absent?

Lest one think that the idea is completely beyond the horizons of the meeting and its participants, let us recall the words of the most influential of today's Shankaracharyas quoted already earlier: "It is very essential that every human being should feel proud of one's country of birth and one's own religion. As a shining example of this, we have the people of the ancient Judaic faith who are proud of their homeland, and who are very devoted to the practice of their faith" (1, 7). Could such a statement not have figured in the final declaration, affirming the importance of each party's adherence to its respective faith, even while drawing wisdom and inspiration from the other? Several months prior to the summit, I had invited one of its participants to an interreligious gathering in India, where the Dalai Lama participated. This rabbi was excited to meet the Dalai Lama, telling me how much he valued the fact that the Dalai Lama directs his Jewish students back to their Judaism, as their proper spiritual path. Would adopting some similar recommendation not have suited the occasion and served the real needs of the Jewish community? Making Hindu leaders aware that, from a Jewish perspective, they may be part of the same problem, and not only part of the solution, would have been proper both for the proceedings and for the declaration.[43]

The total disconnect with the reality of Jews and Israelis on the spiritual path in India tells us much both about Jewish leadership and about the purpose of this meeting. The Chief Rabbinate is precisely that part of the Israeli rabbinate that would consider itself the leadership of those Israelis who travel to India. Yet, it seems oblivious to the actual challenges and dangers that might affect its flock.[44] Instead, it speaks to Hindu leaders as though they belonged to some distant esoteric religion, one with which Jews have had little previous contact, and therefore one that in no way challenges Jewish leadership. The entire tone of the meetings is one of great interest in what is essentially a distant, if not esoteric, religious culture. The importance of the moment is diplomatic and it is largely devoid of theological or pastoral consequences.

Let us now consider the declaration that came out of the second summit:

1. In keeping with the Delhi declaration, the participants reaffirmed their commitment to deepening this bilateral relationship predicated on the recognition of One Supreme Being, Creator, and Guide of the Cosmos; shared values; and similar historical experiences. The parties are committed to learning about one another on the basis of respect for the particular identities of their respective communities and seeking, through their bilateral relationship, to be a blessing to all.

2. It is recognized that the One Supreme Being, both in its formless and manifest aspects, has been worshipped by Hindus over the millennia. This does not mean that Hindus worship "gods" and "idols." The Hindu relates only to the One Supreme Being when he/she prays to a particular manifestation.

3. Central to the Jewish and Hindu worldview is the concept of the sanctity of life, above all the human person. Accordingly, the participants categorically reject violent methods to achieve particular goals. In this spirit, the participants expressed the hope that all disputes be resolved through dialogue, negotiation, and compromise promoting peace, reconciliation, and harmony.

4. As the two oldest religious traditions of the world, the Hindu Dharma Acharya Sabha and the Jewish religious leadership may consider jointly appealing to various religious organizations in the world to recognize that all religions are sacred and valid for their respective peoples. We believe that there is no inherent right embedded in any religion to denigrate or interfere with any other religion or with its practitioners. Acceptance of this proposition will reduce interreligious violence, increase harmony among different peoples.

5. The participants expressed the hope that the profound wellsprings of spirituality in their respective traditions will serve their communities to constructively address the challenges of modernity, so that contemporary innovation may serve the highest ideals of their respective religious traditions.

6. In the interests of promoting the correct understanding of Judaism, Hinduism, and their histories, it was agreed that text books and reference material may be prepared in consultation with the scholars' group under the aegis of this Summit.

7. Svastika is an ancient and greatly auspicious symbol of the Hindu tradition. It is inscribed on Hindu temples, ritual altars, entrances, and even account books. A distorted version of this sacred symbol was misappropriated by the Third Reich in Germany, and abused as an emblem under which heinous crimes were perpetrated against humanity, particularly the Jewish people. The participants recognize that this symbol is and has been sacred to Hindus for millennia, long before its misappropriation.

8. Since there is no conclusive evidence to support the theory of an Aryan invasion/migration into India, and on the contrary there is compelling evidence to refute it, and since the theory seriously damages the integrity of the Hindu tradition and its connection to India, we call for a serious reconsideration of this theory and a revision of all educational materials on this issue that includes the most recent and reliable scholarship.[45]

The ground covered by this second declaration is basically the same as that covered by the first. Its emphases are largely the same, as are the gaps and the issues that the declaration fails to address. The first clause repeats the basic strategy of commonality, identifying God, values, and history as the sites of greatest commonality. Education is once again highlighted, and the purpose of it all is once again framed in terms of community identity. What I have suggested as the Jewish, or Israeli, interest in producing an antiviolence statement finds expression in Clause 3, which is now not an adjunct to another idea, but a self-standing clause that receives its prominence by appearing immediately after the significant, possibly groundbreaking, theological statement of Clause 2. Clause 4 once again tackles the problem of missionary activity, this time through the strategy of joint appeal by both bodies to "various religious organizations in the world." One wonders what religious organizations exist that might serve as the proper address for such an appeal, but the intention and strategy are clear enough.[46] Clause 5 is a novelty, the first reference to spirituality in the declarations. Spirituality is not an aspect of the conversation between Hinduism and Judaism proper, as many Jewish seekers might think. Rather, it is a depth dimension of both traditions that should inform their respective dealings with modernity. This makes the statement much less interesting and possibly as belonging outside the framework of a mutual interreligious declaration. I also do not see it as growing from the discussions of the second summit, as these are recorded, which increases the sense that this statement is not germane to the concerns of the summit.[47]

We are left then with several clauses that are particular to this declaration. I would like to suggest that all of these can be classified under one rubric—clearing up misunderstandings and misrepresentations of Hinduism. Going backwards, Clause 8 addresses the Aryan invasion theory. The theory was deemed important enough to have been featured as a presentation during the first summit.[48] I cannot see why Jews should be implicated in what is purely an internal issue of Hindu self-identity. Many Hindus feel that whether Hinduism grew on local soil or was imported has strong identitarian consequences. They consider the import theory as serving colonial interests and as undermining Hindu unity. Why should Jews be involved in this debate? Imagine the Jewish leaders asking the Hindu leaders to sign a statement condemning biblical criticism. It would seem unimaginable and completely out of context. However, given the concerns for identity that inform Hindu participation in the dialogue with Jewish leadership, we understand why it made sense, in the context of the specific initiative. If the initiative is designed to clear up misunderstandings and to create coalitions for preserving identity, Jewish support for objection to the Aryan invasion theory makes more sense.

Clause 7 is another case of correcting mistaken views of Hinduism. Here, however, enlisting the Jewish side, given the history of the Third Reich, does make sense. While the point mainly serves the purposes of preservation of Hindu identity, it is not without benefit for the Jewish side. The minutes of the meeting tell us of Swami Dayananda's active involvement with reference to contemporary misappropriation of the ancient symbol, which would have been hurtful to the Jewish community and damaging to the relations between the two communities.[49] Clause 6 too is concerned with the matter of proper perception and its relation to education. It states the intention to continue working on this issue, thereby reenforcing its centrality. This brings us then to Clause 2, which, for many observers, is the most radical and most important clause in the declaration.

The first declaration already affirmed belief in one Supreme Being. The second declaration takes this a step further. It clarifies that Hindus do not worship gods or idols, and that they worship the Supreme Being alone. I have already queried how apt this is as a statement of fact, but surely it is up to Hindu religious leaders to faithfully portray their religion. While one rejoices at the theological rapprochement, one also wonders what would happen were one to determine by statistical or factual means that this presentation of how Hindus worship is imprecise. Perhaps we ought to read the statement as saying : The [well informed and properly educated] Hindu relates only to the one Supreme Being when he/she prays to a particular manifestation.

Hindu participants have taken great pride in this clause and seen in it one of the major achievements of the summit. In an article in the *New Indian Express*, Swami Dayananda himself describes the meeting and its achievements:[50]

> The Jerusalem meet concluded with a landmark declaration that Hindus worship "one supreme being" and are not really idolatrous.
>
> The implications of this are profound in content and far-reaching in effect. Judaism was born of the complete repudiation of idol-worship and the rabbinic literature abounds with denunciation of idolatry in an entire tractate of the Talmud devoted to this.
>
> The importance of this issue in the Jewish and other Abrahamic traditions cannot be overstated. Since its first encounter with these religions, due to their incomplete understanding of its Sastras, Hinduism has been perceived by them as idolatrous and promoting many gods, says Swami Dayananda Saraswathi.
>
> The Hindus have, for centuries, experienced the extremely violent consequences of this wrong perception.
>
> The historic declaration made at the Hindu-Jewish Summit at Jerusalem on 18 February, 2008 sets at rest the wrong notion that Hinduism is idolatrous.
>
> The declaration reads: "It is recognized that one supreme being in its formless and manifest aspects has been worshipped by Hindus over the millennia. The Hindu relates to only the one supreme being when he / she prays to a particular manifestation. This does not mean that Hindus worship "gods" and "idols."
>
> The Jewish leaders, in so many words, owned their perception of the Hindu tradition as erroneous and came up with the declaration which the Hindu delegation could happily accept. This establishes that honest and bold dialogue can completely reverse wrong views and erroneous perceptions held over millennia.
>
> It emphasizes that leaders of every religion need to be informed about the basics, vision, and beliefs of other religious traditions, says Swami Dayananda Saraswathi.

Swami Dayananda presents Clause 2 as the great achievement of the meeting. Dayananda is aware of how central the issue of idolatry is to Hindu-Jewish relations. He considers the statement puts to rest the charges that Hindus are idolatrous. It clears up ancient misunderstandings that have led to acts of violence. Thus, the greatest of all misunderstandings has been cleared up thanks to the dialogue and is a sign of the importance of the procedure of dialogue. Whether the summit really achieved what Swami Dayananda claims it did is to a certain extent a matter of expectations and definitions. To the extent that the purpose of the summit is to clear up misunderstandings and improve perception of Hindus, as emerges from a thematic analysis of the second declaration, he is probably right. The proceedings of the meeting do suggest a change in perception and better understanding. The statement does have the potential to redress perceptions. In terms of public image and public relations something significant has been achieved.

The Jewish perception, however, may not be identical to that expressed by Swami Dayananda. That is not to suggest that some Jews may not see eye to eye with him. Thus, Nathan Katz, who belongs to the scholars' committee, writes the following for *Hinduism Today*:

> On the traditional side, leading rabbis and swamis recently overcame one thorny issue that has stood in the way of our mutual affection. For the past 1,500 years or more, what in English is called "idolatry " has clouded Jewish perceptions of Hinduism. Happily, this issue may have been resolved once and for all at a February 2007 dialogue in New Delhi between members of the Chief Rabbinate of Israel, a body which speaks with authority in the Jewish world, and the Dharma Acharya Sabha, a similarly august Hindu group. Led respectively by Rabbi Yona Metzger and Swami Dayananda Saraswati, the rabbis and the swamis issued a nine-point statement of principles, the first of which removed the "idolatry" issue from the table: "Their respective Traditions teach that there is One Supreme Being who is the Ultimate Reality, who has created this world in its blessed diversity and who has communicated Divine ways of action for humanity, for different peoples in different times and places." This acknowledgement by credible rabbis and swamis that the same G-d is the source of their two faiths is a major step forward for our relationship, enabling our traditionally religious members to join our secular ones in this symbiosis of mutual support and enrichment.[51]

I personally think Katz has over-read how far we have come. The rabbis never affirmed the "same God" strategy. Recognition of the same one Supreme Being is not the same as affirming that Judaism and Hinduism believe in the same God.[52] The overlap between the two statements is partial and identifying them is misleading. What is at stake is precisely the distinction between the Hindu concerns—explaining the nature of their faith—and the Jewish concerns—applying the category of Avoda Zara. Success in the former cannot automatically be translated into success in the latter. Accordingly, I am much less optimistic than either Dayananda or Katz on the issue of idolatry being behind us, off the table, finally resolved, or any such formulation.

There are multiple reasons why the statement should be applauded as an important step forward, but by no means the final word. If we seek any correspondence between the statement and the proceedings of the dialogue (though some discrepancy always exists) we note that the rabbis were impressed, surprised, and excited to learn that Hinduism was not completely polytheisitc or animistic. They were happy to learn of the notion of one Supreme Being. But they remained reserved. They continued to affirm that differences remain and these differences are crucial for the subject of idolatry. Or perhaps here is precisely where the difference between "idolatry" and Avoda Zara might emerge. Perhaps in terms of "idolatry" they came to recognize what Dayananda and the swamis sought to impart, that Hindus do not worship idols but the one supreme God. But that in no way resolves the issue on the Jewish side. This is the first, not the final, step. Worship of nature forces, beings, gods, etc., while recognizing one Supreme Being could, but does not necessarily, resolve the halachic problem of Avoda Zara. I don't believe for a moment that any of the rabbis who signed the declaration thought they had resolved the problem.[53] Rabbi Metzger—who has the rabbi who initiated the sheitel crisis, Rabbi Elyashiv, to thank for his position as Chief Rabbi—never ran to the elderly rabbi, requesting he revise his ruling that Tirupati wigs must be burned. In fact, I would even doubt that the rabbis fully understood or subscribed to what they were signing. Clause 2 speaks of recognizing the one Supreme Being in its formless and manifest aspects. This makes a lot of sense to Hindus. It makes little to no sense to Jews. If we were to push the case, we would be forced to claim that rabbis have affirmed pantheistic worship as legitimate and that they recognize notions of incarnation of the Divinity. Nothing of the sort. The rabbis were signing a diplomatic statement, framed for diplomatic purposes, without really entering into its details, let alone its theology. Many of them could not even read it in the original. When the Israeli Chief Rabbis signed this declaration they did so on trust (mainly of David Rosen) and on the faith that it was serving Israel's diplomatic needs. No real change has taken place.[54]

I do not suggest that either the declaration or the meeting were not important. Both remain significant, moments of breakthrough and new beginnings. They may continue to initiate processes that will advance understanding of Hinduism and improve Jewish-Hindu relations. However, whatever was achieved was achieved within a context and through a medium. Hindu leaders may work through declarations. Jewish leaders only sign statements in the framework of interreligious meetings, and the impact of such statements is extremely limited within their communities. Thus, one looks in vain for a version of the declaration on the Chief Rabbinate's Website. The site is in Hebrew, and a sign of how irrelevant the statement is to the daily concerns of the rabbinate and its target audience is the fact that the statement was never translated into Hebrew. The statement is an act of diplomacy, carried out in diplomatic language (that the Chief Rabbis do not even read), and not an internal Jewish revolution. Had it been a true revolution in understanding it would have taken a different literary form, a responsum using internal halachic language. But the meeting *was* nevertheless a breakthrough because one of its participants is in the process of composing a responsum that states essentially what the declaration does. An examination of the minutes of the summits reveals the critical faculties that Rabbi Daniel Sperber brought to the meeting and that he possesses by virtue of belonging to two communities—religious and academic. These qualities have served him as he continues to reflect on these issues. When the English declaration becomes a (Hebrew) responsum we will know that something of real value, in internal Jewish terms, has taken place through the summits. Until then, there is much to be satisfied with in terms of the changed perceptions of individuals, as these are reflected in the minutes of the summits, even if these changes fall short of the final resolution and final clearing up of misperceptions of Hinduism.

The gap between how the meeting is viewed by its initiator and how I suggest members of the rabbinate would actually view it is one more sign of gaps and asymmetry concerning the meeting. This was primarily a meeting for Hindus, serving a largely Hindu agenda. This is also reflected in the aftermath of the meeting and in the attention it received in the press and on the Internet. I have already noted that the Chief Rabbinate never went public with the meeting and that its constituency was not made aware of either the real or the imagined break-throughs of the meeting. Within the Jewish community, its impact was limited to a small number of specialists who are interested in Jewish-Hindu relations or in interreligious relations in general. On the Hindu side, we find both declarations posted on the Hindu Dharma site. This difference in and of itself speaks volumes. The meeting and declarations were taken up by various Indian media outlets. It is interesting to see what coverage the meeting received on the Jewish side. A news item in the *Jerusalem Post* of Feb.7, 2007, highlights fighting religious violence as the message of the meeting, true to Jewish concerns. Other than that, we only hear of the meeting from its sponsors. It is mentioned on the website of the Israeli foreign ministry as well as of the American Jewish committee. In both cases, the entire declaration is not reproduced, in either Hebrew or English. One news agency, interested in interfaith relations, Search for Common Ground, provides a translation into Hebrew of parts of the declaration.[55] Other than that, the meetings go unnoticed by Israeli or Jewish media.

Diplomatic meetings are not the stuff of religious discourse. But they provide important symbols and they can launch important movements. The two Jewish-Hindu summits prove the point. Their discourse stands outside normal Jewish discourse and therefore has little impact within traditional Jewish circles and institutions, even those from which the participants came. At the same time, the meetings provide important symbols, and these can help drive other processes. The great emphasis of both summits was on education and the need for continuing education. Education is a long-term prospect that is not achieved in one meeting, no matter how high level or representative it is deemed to be. The importance and success of the summits should thus be weighed as much in terms of education as in terms of either diplomacy or theology. I would argue that in educational terms the summits were extremely important and successful. They provided an opportunity for participants on both sides to learn. They helped dispel some important misunderstandings concerning Hinduism. They created resources, including statements, that are worthy of study. But above all, they created the drive and impetus for further study. All the individuals who attended were impacted in some way. It is enough that some of them, like Rabbi Sperber, take the message to their communities.

The process of education has just begun. The Jewish-Hindu summits can continue to inspire and fuel future educational processes. But they can only do so if they integrate the real public that is involved in Jewish-Hindu encounter into their own process. If the Rabbinate continues to engage Hinduism in isolation from the processes of Jewish seekers, it will remain irrelevant. If the two processes, on-the-ground meetings of spiritual seekers with Hinduism and high-level diplomatic meetings of leadership, can be brought together, there is promise for continuing change of perspective, deepening of understanding, and transformation of both traditions as they share their spiritual riches and understandings.

12

Hinduism and a Jewish Theology of Religions

The challenges presented by an interreligious encounter, any interreligious encounter, always go beyond the particularities of the given encounter. The encounter not only asks us to consider our view of our conversation partner, but also invites us more broadly to consider our view of other religions as a whole. Hinduism provides us with the opportunity and challenge of revisiting the important questions that are fundamental to a Jewish view of religions, or how it is presently called—a Jewish theology of religions. Hinduism not only offers us a new chapter in Jewish relations with world religions, it also provides us with the opportunity to think through and to revisit the fundamentals of a Jewish approach to other religions.

A review of Jewish positions in relation to Hinduism shows that the range of possibilities that are typically considered as defining the parameters of one religion's view of another are all represented in Jewish views of Hinduism. Alan Race distinguishes between Exclusivism, Inclusivism, and Pluralism, as modes of one religion relating to the other.[1] Recently, Alan Brill has shown how Jewish attitudes to other religions cover the full range suggested by Race and further elaborated the theoretical model.[2] Brill's work does not focus particularly on Jewish attitudes to Hinduism. In what follows, I will suggest that we are able to identify all three attitudes also within contemporary Jewish attitudes to Hinduism.

By exclusivism in this context will be meant the attitude that draws sharp demarcation lines between oneself as possessor of truth, while others are in falsehood. A separate volume is dedicated to a consideration of Hinduism in terms of the halachic category of Avoda Zara. One thing is sure—those voices that do consider Hinduism to be Avoda Zara, like rabbis who instructed to burn wigs whose provenance was in Hindu temples, are best classified as offering an exclusivist perspective. Even though the issue is considered from the perspective of the legal category of Avoda Zara and not from the perspective of the theoretical validity of another religion, it seems to me that one position sustains the other. Determination that Hinduism is Avoda Zara is not technical. It defines an attitude and that attitude is informed by the sense of total invalidity of another religion, which in turn is further strengthened by the declaration that it is Avoda

Zara. Exclusivist in this context may be paraphrased as rejectionist, rejecting any possible validity, legitimacy, or meaning from that religion.

The position that is called inclusivist sees another religion as a partial recognition of truth, and its validity is contained within the fuller truth known through one's own religion. Thus, another religion is valid, but only partially so. This is obviously a more respectful approach, but it nevertheless maintains the fundamental hierarchies of meaning, validity, and truth that characterize each religion's view of reality. Menashe ben Israel presents us with an inclusivist view of Hinduism.[3] Hinduism is considered as the wisdom of Abraham's sons, those he had sent to the East. Hinduism is thus part of the Abrahamic heritage. This allows Menashe ben Israel to applaud the wisdom of the sages of India and to uphold a highly idealized view of India that features wisdom as the primary characteristic of Indian religious culture. This attitude is then taken up by some contemporary rabbinic authorities, particularly those who engage in bringing young Jews back from Hinduism to Judaism. If the exclusivist view focused on ritual, declaring Hinduism invalid on its count, the inclusivist view focuses on wisdom, almost intentionally ignoring the problems occasioned by Hindu worship.

The most surprising articulation of a Jewish view of Hinduism is found in the Chief Rabbinate's declaration on Hinduism. Our earlier discussion explored to what extent that statement may legitimately be read as having successfully done away with the charge that Hinduism is idolatrous. But there is perhaps an even more surprising, and in its own way important, novelty in this statement. Let us revisit the first and second declarations. In the first summit, participants affirmed that

> their respective traditions teach Faith in One Supreme Being who is the Ultimate Reality, who has created this world in its blessed diversity and who has communicated Divine ways of action for humanity for different peoples in different times and places.

It is not only that the two faiths teach faith in the same God, but that God is ultimately the source of both religions. Diversity is a blessing and such diversity includes religious diversity. Accordingly, God is at the root of different religions, and He has communicated paths to different parts of humanity, at different times and places. The statement does not spell this out, but one assumes that each path is suited to the time and place of its recipients. While the statement does not say so in so many words, it is clear that Hindu leaders recognize Judaism as one such path, while Jewish leaders in turn also recognize Hinduism as a God-given path, for Hindus. In terms of Jewish theology of religions this is a revolutionary statement, whose significance far exceeds the willingness of Jewish authorities to take Hindu leaders at their word that they worship the supreme God and not idols. Here, after all, the rabbis are making a statement not of how they view Hinduism, but of how they view God and His plan for humanity. And the understanding they express accords with the finest of pluralistic theologies. Moreover, this pluralism is grounded in divine acts of communication. Unlike typical Hindu models of theology of religion that focus on the effectiveness of different religions in reaching a common goal, this statement grounds a pluralistic view in the divine author and guide. By this understanding, Hinduism is as valid a revelation as Judaism, provided the recipients of the revelation are properly confined to their respective communities.

This is a true revolution in religious thinking. It is so revolutionary that I do not believe it should be taken as representative of the views of its signatories. The same reservations I expressed earlier, concerning the meaning of the second declaration in terms of Avoda Zara, apply here concerning the pluralist potential of the statement. The only reason this statement did not draw the ire of the rabbinical world, in the same way that Jonathan Sacks's *Dignity of Difference* did, is that, unlike the latter, the statement went unnoticed and was not brought to the attention of the colleagues of its signatories. It may even be that it, or its implications, were never fully brought to the attention of the signatories themselves.

Nevertheless, the statement is before us, as a major, foundational statement of Jewish-Hindu relations. Even if one raises doubts concerning what it means for today's rabbinical world, we no longer have control of what it might mean to tomorrow's religious. It shows that a mode of thinking can find expression and possibly take hold even within a classical rabbinical worldview. The novelty of the encounter with Hinduism thus generates surprising theological utterances that will provide the building blocks for tomorrow's theology of religions.

The pluralist option is not limited to this joint statement. This volume's complement, *Same God, Other god*, presents one important rabbinic thinker, whose thought is best classified as pluralist, Rabbi Menachem Meiri. At the basis of Meiri's view is the recognition that religions have purpose, structure, and fundamental commonalities as well as minimal basic conditions that afford them legitimacy. Returning to a comment of one of the Shankaracharyas, made as a welcome statement to the first Jewish-Hindu summit, we note the following statement by His Holiness Jagadguru Sri Swami Svarupananda Saraswatiji, Shankaracharya of Jyotir Math:

> No matter in which corner of the earth it might have originated, religion comes directly from God. The main purpose of religion is to enhance our lives, and uplift our personalities from succumbing to animalistic tendencies (1,11).

This statement could have been penned by Meiri.[4] We have here a clear statement of religion in terms of its goals. All religions are recognized as equally valid and are to be judged in relation to their ability to guide their believers beyond their animal nature. Meiri predicates the legitimacy of other religions on their goals and achievements in the lives of believers, not on their divine origin.[5] Meiri thus leads us from a revelation-based pluralism to a process-and-outcome-based pluralism. We thus move from theology and metaphysics—the affirmation of true and valid revelation—to the realm of phenomenology—the lived religious life and its consequences in the lives of believers. Meiri is here on very common ground with Hindu thinkers, who also approach their religion, as well as other religions, from a phenomenological, rather than a "dogmatic" perspective, in other words, a perspective that focuses upon the faith content associated with a given revelation.

The three perspectives—exclusivist, inclusivist, and pluralist—suggest different basic approaches to other religions, what we seek in them, and how we interpret them. The first seeks to make another religion adhere to its standards and based on that judges it as valid or invalid. It is not in a position to, nor does it have any interest in, learning another religion for its own sake, for what it might teach others and ourselves through its spiritual experience. Large portions of the Jewish world apply this perspective, leading them to examine other religions only in terms of their conformity to standards mandated by the halacha.[6]

The inclusivist perspective has more room to listen to the other tradition. However, it can only do so from the security of being able to identify the same teachings within Judaism. It therefore allows for a more respectful and accepting approach toward the other, but is limited in its capacity to appreciate the other on its own terms. Nevertheless, looking at what the inclusivists, represented by Matityahu Glazerson, have been able to do in relation to Hinduism, one realizes that even an inclusivist approach can be enriching. The very fact of focusing one's attention on the other in the attempt to identify similarities and to contain the other within one's own religious understanding is bound to yield new self-understanding. Even if one claims that all that one is discovering is, and always has been, part of one's self, the self as it emerges through this process is often quite richer than the one that has not gone through the process of rediscovery in light of the other. Therefore, reading works like Glazerson's brings to light themes and emphases that are often completely outside the perspective of common presentations of Judaism. The inclusivist perspective is genuinely engaged in the encounter with the other, and its sincerity is ultimately transformative, even if such transformation is not declared or fully acknowledged and is presented as simply a rediscovery of oneself.[7]

The pluralist option is the one that opens up most fully to receptivity, learning, and transformation between religions. Once the theoretical ground has been cleared, one is free to learn from the other, appreciate the other for his strengths, and possibly receive inspiration as well. While the inclusivist perspective could in theory also lead to instances of religious borrowing, it is more likely that it is the pluralist who will really be open to sharing, borrowing, and receiving inspiration from the other. Borrowing and some degree of multiple religious belonging are not necessarily virtues. They are not proof of the advantage of the pluralist option, nor should they be taken as proof of its drawbacks. One cannot, however, avoid the inference, from accumulated experience among contemporary practitioners, that there is some relationship between multiple religious identification and a pluralist view of religion.

Often we require of our religious understanding to provide the theory, in light of which we might make sense of our complex realities. The Jewish-Hindu encounter demonstrates that various shades of multiple religious belonging have emerged through the encounter of Jews with Hinduism. A pluralist view of religion could be one way of making sense of such practices. And Meiri's views on religion might provide a framework for making sense of how one can not only recognize and legitimate other religions, but also receive the best from their religious and spiritual practices. That the Chief Rabbis based their pluralistic statement on a notion of multiple revelations is both a sign of the problems attached to the statement and of the low standing that Meiri enjoys in the rabbinic world overall.[8] What the Chief Rabbis sought to achieve remains a continuing need of Jewish theology as well as of interfaith relations. Meiri can continue to inspire such efforts.

Religious inspiration and borrowing are potentially transformative, but they are also threatening. Serious interreligious dialogue can accomplish something that is less threatening, but potentially no less challenging. Serious engagement with the other is an opportunity to rethink one's worldview and to restate it in light of that encounter. In order to confront another's worldview we do not need to validate that worldview, let alone adopt a pluralist worldview. If we are not able to validate the other's worldview, or the legitimacy of the other holding a different worldview, we will find ourselves engaging in religious polemics that may be transformative as well, forcing one to revisit and restate one's faith, in refutation of the faith of the other. However, a dialogue based on acceptance and recognition is bound to generate a different dynamic, and will ultimately have more far-reaching consequences. If one really internalizes the pluralist option, this may enhance a genuine dialogue, leading to mutual enrichment.[9] Especially if one's pluralism is grounded in some notion of divine revelation, given to different recipients, this would lead to meaningful sharing that seeks to clarify the particularity of each of the revelations and the ways in which it is best suited to its recipients.[10] If we take seriously the notion that revelation is somehow adapted to its recipients, then human encounter would serve as a paradigm for theological dialogue. Humans meet, come to know one another, seek out their commonalities and differences, and are thereby enriched. The same would be true for the religions, adapted to the blessed diversity of humanity.

13

Summary and a Personal Epilogue

This book has put forth several theses, either explicitly or in how the presentation was structured. Let me summarize these briefly, before concluding on the same personal note that the book opened with. By way of introduction, I should affirm once again what by now is obvious to the reader, and that is that the present work does not seek to describe the encounter from the perspective of some neutrality. Rather, it is an engaged description and as such is carried out from my own specific Jewish vantage point. A Hindu reading of the encounter is important, but, as I shall presently note, remains some distance away, in view of the contours of the present encounter. What have we seen then in the course of our study?

A. In the most basic way, this work has described and argued for the very existence of the Hindu-Jewish encounter as a significant contemporary encounter. The dynamics of Judaism's encounter with Hinduism are unique. A religion only dimly heard of for millennia and for most intents and purposes completely marginal to Jewish concerns has come, within a relatively short time, into the center of Jewish attention. It has engaged masses on the ground as well as leadership at the top. The encounter is vital in its various manifestations; it encompasses ever-growing circles of participants on both sides, but especially on the Jewish side. It plays out interesting dynamics of homeland and diaspora for both religious communities, impacting both in changing ways. It is not an encounter that is about to disappear from our lives and as such it deserves our thought, attention, and reflection as scholars, teachers, thinkers, and religious leaders.

Obviously, there is great importance in the encounter itself. Billions of faithful, who practice the world's third most practiced religion, in India and throughout the world, are, by definition, something that should be of interest and should deserve the attention of Jewish thinkers and leaders. If nothing else, they are important as part of the humanity we seek to form bonds of friendship and service with. But, as I have also argued, there is much more to the encounter than the potential of reaching out in universal friendship.

B.   A second argument of the book, implicit in its structure, is that the encounter is not one thing, one point, one focus, one problem. Both Hinduism and Judaism are rich and multifaceted. There are multiple configurations of each, and the points of comparison, contact, and inspiration are consequently numerous. Which Hinduism, and what aspect of it, interacts with what type or what aspect of Judaism will determine the nature of the encounter, its challenges, and its promises. Recognizing the breadth of the potential encounter, I have suggested several foci for the encounter. These are domains in which contact has taken place and where I see potential for future engagement. These include the exchange of ideas, as it can take place either in a direct theological sharing or mediated through the comparative study of religions. They also include saints, wise men (and women), and wisdom and spirituality. Each of these constitutes a way of conceptualizing what Hinduism might mean to Judaism, what about it is important, and where engagement could take place. It is important to affirm the multiplicity of points of contact in view of a perspective that considers Hinduism exclusively through the lens of Avoda Zara, thereby making all other points of contact irrelevant, if not inappropriate. The volume dedicated to Avoda Zara problematizes the ease with which the category is applied to Hinduism, making the matter at the very least complex, much as the encounter itself is rich, complex, and multifaceted. To have affirmed that there is more, much more, to the encounter than simply the concern for Avoda Zara is one important affirmation of my work.

C.   A third important argument of the book concerns the lack of reciprocity of the dialogue, a fact that bears repeating. Overall, the Hindu-Jewish encounter is characterized by great asymmetry. Jewish interest in Hinduism far exceeds Hindu interest in Judaism. Given declared Hindu interest in all things religious, this is somewhat surprising. It may be accounted for by ignorance of Judaism as a distinct religion and its frequent conflation with Christianity. Alternatively, it may be that those who adopt a certain Hindu theology of religions, and their declared harmony of religions, have little need for the kind of detailed study and knowledge that makes for real encounter. Whatever the explanation, Hinduism and India serve a need for Jews, and no parallel need seems to be served by Hindu engagement with Judaism. Surprisingly, the dialogue of leaders is characterized by lack of reciprocity in the opposite direction, where the needs of Hindu leadership set the agenda and defined the contents of the encounter. One wonders whether it is really possible to conceive of a situation of complete neutrality and reciprocity. While ideally dialogue and encounter assume a high degree of symmetry, it may be that most dialogues are in some way tilted, in view of power relations, spiritual interests, ideology, and other considerations. Mindfulness of lack of reciprocity may be the most important antidote, coupled with whatever attempts are possible to create situations that are more reciprocal.

Reciprocity is crucial. It is not simply that good relationships are reciprocal. A Jewish view of another religion cannot be taken for granted. Often the views and positions that are held in relation to that religion continue stereotypes and attitudes that existed prior to the encounter. For new thoughts, positions, and possibilities to come to light, work is required. In the field of theology of religions this work is driven by theological will. For things religious and theological to move there must be a theological will. Theological will does not grow in a vacuum. It is sustained by encounter with the reality of the other and by the cultivation of relationships. Relational reciprocity is therefore the key to advancement on all fronts. We do not yet know what fuller Hindu discovery of Judaism might bring about. To the extent that Judaism's encounter with Hinduism is relevant to the fulfillment of Judaism's ultimate vision, to a better self-understanding of its position in the world and to its continuing mission, greater reciprocity will play an important role in bringing these fruits of the encounter to maturation.

The key to a successful conversation is that both parties are successfully engaged. One might think that the persistence of certain negative Jewish views regarding Hinduism would be the biggest obstacle to developing a meaningful conversation and process between Judaism and Hinduism. As the preceding pages suggest, Judaism has already come forth with a broad range of options through which a future conversation with Hinduism might proceed. There are enough indications at hand to suggest that even the question of Avoda Zara would not be a stumbling block to meaningful engagement between Judaism and Hinduism. Looking at the Jewish-Hindu encounter in all its breadth, I would venture a different suggestion as to what might be the greatest obstacle. We have seen that Jews have shown massive interest in Hinduism as a spiritual reality. This, as I have argued, has not been reciprocated by Hindus. The one Hindu-driven encounter, and an important one at that, was not driven by spiritual concerns, but by political concerns, related to the Hindu quest for maintaining identity. Thus far, Jews and Hindus have not been involved in the same process in the same way. While they have met, the agendas, roles, and expectations have not been reciprocal.

Let me illustrate this with a personal anecdote, the last one of this volume, that affirms this impression. As I have mentioned, my visits to India involved dozens of hours of talks with Swami Yogaswaroopananda, exploring the core issues of idolatry, the challenge they posed for Judaism, and what they meant for a Jewish appreciation of Hinduism. In the course of dozens of hours of talks, I was barely if ever asked concerning Judaism, its teachings, and its particularity. At one point I expressed my dissatisfaction with the one-sidedness of the engagement. This did not lead to a more reciprocal process, but rather to a theoretical statement accounting for why from the perspective of the particular body of teachings followed by the swami's detailed knowledge of another religion is not really necessary. I am ready to allow for personality differences and to see the reply in no small measure as an expression of an individual personality.[1] Nevertheless, having visited dozens of ashrams, and met with scores of swamis, I do retain the same impression that one gets from the transcripts of the Jewish-Hindu summits: Hindus explain their philosophical worldview while Jews asks questions out of genuine interest. The interest of the rabbi who seeks to reach a position on the acceptability of Hindu practices and that of the seeker who asks fundamental metaphysical questions is only one of degree. Both exhibit a trait that may be characteristic of the Jewish mind and its formation—curiosity, openness, and the desire to know about the other. Such curiosity may be curbed by social constrictions and in particular by the damning judgment that another religious system is idolatrous, or otherwise devoid of value. However, once those obstacles are removed, Jews seem to have a propensity for being fascinated by other religions, exhibiting healthy curiosity and spiritual openness. Hindu participants in the dialogue manifest their openness in another way. It is a more existential openness, perhaps an openness of being, possibly founded on recognition of the deeper unity of humanity and its existential commonality. Such recognition may not be a good driver for stimulating and advancing mutually enriching theological exchanges. Perhaps Jews maintain the sense of distinctness and otherness of the other, which in turn stimulates curiosity and interest in precisely what is considered "other." The Hindus, who are trained to recognize unity in diversity seem more interested in attitudinal, existential, and intellectual affirmation of this unity, than in the exploration of otherness. For most Hindu participants in interreligious encounter there is no real otherness. It is an illusion.[2]

We thus encounter an interesting paradox. Hindus, who come to the dialogue through their concern with identity, are not really interested in otherness.[3] Jews, who affirm their otherness as a fundamental trait of their identity, are more fascinated with the particularity of the Hindu. While Hindus may have to battle wrong attitudes to the other on the political plane, *otherness* as a philosophical and spiritual reality is of secondary importance. Hence, Hindus approach Judaism sure of the commonality between the religions, as though there was little to learn, beyond the obvious harmony and compatibility of which they are already aware. Jews come with the burden of particularity and seek ways to make sense of it. The attitudes brought to an encounter between Jews and Hindus are complementary. They could be mutually enriching, with each side teaching the other not only what its official positions are, but also what its deeper attitudes to the other are. This potential for enrichment has yet to be realized.

For the time being, most of Hindu-Jewish relations are driven by Jews and their interest in and fascination by Hinduism. There are multiple factors that could change this. Increase in travel and commerce, needs of communities in the diaspora, political pressures in intergroup relations, and the global of flowering interfaith relations—all these could help shift attitudes on the Hindu side, making them eventually more similar to and more reciprocal with Jewish attitudes. When such a shift occurs, the Hindu-Jewish dialogue may explode with teaching, meaning, and spiritual opportunities. It is my firm conviction that when both sides are ready to be enriched by the encounter and are willing to take it to its depths, they will surely be gratified by what they discover.

D. The fourth point I mention here concerns theological challenges and opportunities. Our study has suggested time and again that the theoretical conversation between Judaism and Hinduism is only at its beginning. The encounter with Hinduism, as a serious and novel religious other, provides Judaism with the opportunity of revisiting and restating its fundamental beliefs. Any encounter is an occasion for better self-understanding. And any theological encounter is an occasion for revisiting our core spiritual reality and the content of our faith, in light of the particular encounter. Whether we think in terms of truth—the specific set of teachings that might be ascribed to Judaism, or in terms of mission—its purpose, vocation, and goal on the stage of humanity—a new encounter invites revisiting these questions from a new angle. Such revisiting is an occasion for taking stock, rediscovery, or restatement of what our faith is about in fresh ways. If one of the greatest dangers of the religious life is it becoming old and habitual, losing its attraction and vitality of message, an encounter with a religious other is an opportunity to keep faith fresh.

As suggested in the previous chapter, the encounter with Hinduism implicitly summons us to affirm what kind of attitude we expect to cultivate to ward another religious tradition. Our tradition places multiple options before us, different broad general attitudes as well as varying stances taken toward specific issues. The encounter is thus an invitation to affirm the type of theology of religions we espouse—be it exclusivist, inclusivist, pluralist, or some other way of expressing how we view other religions, and Hinduism in particular, from a Jewish vantage point.

The encounter with Hinduism is an encounter with a specific religious worldview that is constructed differently from our own. If we seek to engage it, this forces us to revisit fundamental theological issues. This is not to suggest that we are called to revise our faith. Rather, any encounter is an occasion for examining prior assumptions and for the rediscovery of voices that may be on our margins but at the center of the other's thought. And so, we have noted a series of fundamental philosophical and theological questions that the encounter invites us to ponder. Among them: What is the meaning of divine transcendence and what room is there for divine immanence? What is the relationship between God and creation? What can we say about the inner life of God and the ways God can be known? What are the boundaries, as well as continuities, between the human person and God? What is it that we truly reject as wrong and offensive to God? These are but some of the fundamental issues that we will have to revisit over the years, as our conversation with Hinduism deepens.

While any interreligious encounter is occasion for revisiting our philosophical worldview, the encounter with Hinduism is particularly suggestive in this respect, in view of the enduring view of India as a land of sages. Wisdom is an important, and much underutilized, resource in the Jewish view of other religions. Judaism's classical dialogue partner/ opponents have been playing on the same playing ground of revelation and an entire configuration of religion that we consider similar enough to group these religions together as "Abrahamic." Encountering a new religion, theistic in essence, that speaks of God from a platform that is largely wisdom based is a novelty. This constitutes an invitation to consider what might be the wisdom content that Judaism can either share or engage across traditions. What is Judaism's own wisdom that it could share with Hinduism and what might it discover as commonalities or challenges in Hindu wisdom? The answer will emerge, I believe, over the long run.

E.   The encounter and the promise of spirituality is yet another point to be noted here. One significant dimension, possibly the most significant, concerns a domain that is distinct from theology and ritual, even if it draws on both of these. This is the domain of spirituality. By spirituality is here intended the interior, subjective dimensions of consciousness, its evolution, and ultimately the subjective quest for God and encounter with Him. Self-conscious processes of interiority and advancing the self toward a higher goal of realization or deeper relationship with God are associated with Indian spiritual tradition and constitute an important part of Hinduism's draw. Spirituality is often mediated through teachers who are exemplars of their tradition and of the perceived dimension of spirituality. Thus, the draw to Hinduism is not to an abstract notion but to configurations of spiritual life, focused around specific teachers, chains of tradition, and schools and communities.

In many ways, spirituality is the most universal dimension of religion and one that translates most readily across traditions. Thus, if Jewish seekers find something lacking in their tradition and then discover it in a Hindu context, it is only a step away to rediscover that same quality within Judaism, at least if these seekers are thus motivated.[4] The recognition that spirituality plays an important role in the present encounter is in many ways good news. Not only is Hinduism less threatening; it can actually be considered as having a positive message or contribution to make to the lives of Jews who have explored Hinduism, maybe even to the public life of Judaism itself. Identifying spirituality as grounds for much of the encounter also highlights how different this encounter is from previous encounters, where ritual, theology, and issues of conversion dominated the horizons.

The domain of spirituality also shows just how one-sided the present encounter is. There is no doubt that Judaism possesses enormous treasures, teachings, and paradigms of the same quality that is identified in the Hindu context as spirituality. Yet, spirituality is not the subject of a two-way exchange. Rather, a public image suggests that spirituality's natural home is India or Hinduism. Thus, Jews are seen as in need of Hindu spirituality; a two-way exchange on spirituality to the benefit of Hindus is never entertained.

And yet, precisely because spirituality is not the possession of one religion only, much of what draws Jews to Hinduism is a domain that is common to both traditions. This is why some Orthodox Jewish teachers can travel to India without fear of religious compromise, because they are, after all, in quest of something that belongs to their tradition properly, even if it can be found more readily, by force of circumstances, in India. This is also what allows some Jews to transition from Hinduism to Judaism or to establish various modes of synergy between the religions. A common core remains across such transitions. It informs the quest, the exploration, the return, and, ultimately, the ability to construct firm bridges of meaning and sharing between the traditions. This is the bridge of spirituality.

F. The encounter features some major challenges and major opportunities. Complementing the theological and spiritual opportunities are some core challenges. The most formidable challenge is that of idolatry, and it has been dealt with in a separate volume. Second to it is the challenge to Jewish identity. As a religious community that is struggling with its continuity and identity for generations, the immediate instinct is to consider all instances of coming under the sphere of influence of another religion as a threat to Jewish identity and its long-term survival. Against this default perspective, it is worth noting that weakening of Jewish identity is not a necessary outcome of the encounter with Hinduism. This is noted in an analysis of types of identity construction, and how some find their way to Judaism following exposure to Hindu groups or spirituality. It is further noted in the significant percentage of observant Jews who make forays into Hindu spirituality, without thereby giving up their Jewish identity; on the contrary, in the framework of spirituality, "crossing the lines" has a beneficial impact on their overall Jewishness. Yet, it is clear that Hinduism is not simply a station along the road to Jewish observance. For many it has become spiritual home, occupying the place that Jewish leadership would wish for Judaism to occupy in the lives of these individuals.

There is no facile management of this challenge. It may comfort us to recall that we (leaders, thinkers, and teachers) are not really in control of the situation. Very few have asked our permission before exploring Hinduism. Jewish leadership follows its constituency in this matter, rather than leading on a path. The fact that much of the encounter happens "on the road," an encounter of travelers, certainly reduces a perceived threat. That it occurs in a world where freedom of choice is extensive and the choice of spiritual enrichment from another tradition is preferable to other potential influences are also factors worth bearing in mind. All in all, it seems there is room for a positive embrace of the spiritual encounter, especially as it relates to individuals with mature and well-formed religious identities. Ultimately, its benefits outweigh the associated risks. Jewish leadership has little to gain from opposing a process in which it understands little and which is largely beyond its control. Once again, one would wish there was greater reciprocity in the Jewish-Hindu spiritual encounter. Dangers to identity maintenance would be greatly reduced if Jewish tradition spoke as much to a Hindu audience as Hindu tradition speaks to a Jewish audience. Beyond natural psychological pride, it would allow an exchange that focuses on the common ground of spirituality on equal footing. Such is the desired spiritual exchange that we can look forward to.

A Personal Epilogue

I have been very personal in writing this book, bringing my own experiences and background to the table where possible. When Richard Marks, one of the few scholars working in this field, asked me what *I* had received from my own journey into Hinduism, I was surprised to realize I had a hard time formulating a response. The reason is that for all my fascination with and study of Hinduism, from an early age, I never traveled the imaginary path traced by this book. I was never an Israeli seeker traveling to India to enrich my spiritual quest. Nor was I a Jew who only discovered his religious identity following exposure to Hinduism. Rather, my engagement with Hinduism, as with other religions, grew from a mature and deeply committed sense of my Jewish identity and spiritual practice. However, this practice seemed to require openness to religious others, rather than self-containment within the bounds of the Jewish community of practice. Perhaps this was so because I realized something was missing at home, but could be brought back from the outside. Perhaps I grew up in the kind of home where my horizons were never limited in ways that would preclude recognizing spiritual value outside Judaism. And perhaps there is some inner direction and certitude that informs our core decisions that is beholden to but can never be fully comprehended by appeal to circumstances. Perhaps I just knew deep inside that for all the depth of my Jewish practice, there was still something to be gained by exposure to the spiritual worlds beyond Judaism.

I recall, in fact, the moment when I decided to study Transcendental Meditation. It was a Friday night, Sabbath eve. I was praying at the Western wall, as I had been every week for the past six years. I realized something was lacking in my prayers. I needed to go further, to make advances, and an inner knowledge directed me to study meditation. I must have heard of it enough to know it was an option. I may have also heard of other options. In any event, my choice to reach out to something Hindu came from what was in and of itself a purely Jewish moment, or rather a moment of pure quest for God. And studying TM was only made possible after consulting with my ultra-Orthodox rabbis and gaining their permission, including how to manage the initiatory puja.

One could see here a moment of pure spirituality—reaching out to another tradition in order to receive a technique that is supposed to enhance one's own spiritual practice. And so it was. So, one may say that in the first instance my draw was to spirituality, and especially to the power of a specific technique that I considered could be incorporated into my daily Jewish routine.

Reflecting upon this foundational moment I can legitimately say it was not *Hinduism* I was drawn to (even though its study did draw me and I was already immersed in its academic study). Rather, it was some dimension of the spiritual life associated with Hinduism. While my own situation is obviously quite particular, it may also be representative of one form of Jewish approach to Hinduism, one which is characteristic of many of the observant Israeli youth who explore the spiritual dimension of India.

My own spiritual training with a saffron-robed teacher did not so much take me into Hinduism, as into a spiritual understanding that allowed me to appreciate all religions in view of a certain spiritual perspective, which for lack of better term may be termed universal. Judaism and Hinduism, as well as other traditions, were appreciated against a common understanding of spiritual evolution. The upshot of such a training was the simultaneous deepening of my spiritual process within Judaism and the concomitant opening up to the spiritual reality of other traditions. But these were now experienced not so much as "other," running the risk of loss of identity, as much as further expressions of a common spiritual ground and therefore as sources of potential inspiration. Indeed, prior to a decade-long exploration of a certain kind of spiritual life in India, I was deeply immersed in a similar journey in the company of Christian teachers and communities.

I suppose this makes my own journey not one of seeking spirituality in India as much as of finding it. Blessed as I was with a rich spiritual life within and a good theoretical, as well as academic, foundation for engagements across religious traditions, I came to India where I found something that was in line with what I had already received, but in configurations of people, places, communities, and practices that had their own coloring, thereby enriching my own process. I therefore cannot say that I was changed by my encounter with Hinduism, though I was certainly enriched. Similarly, I cannot say I have multiple religious identities, even though I am certainly beholden to multiple voices of authority whom I take seriously and who have a command on my conscience.[5]

But perhaps the very framing of the question—what did I receive from Hinduism—is itself mistaken. Let me explain. As I reflect on my own process, visiting India more than a dozen times over the past decade and spending considerable time with specific religious leaders and communities, I note it is not really the *ism* of Hinduism, some alternative religious system, that speaks to me. What has enriched me are Hindus—specific, individual Hindus, some I have met in person, some I only know through books and disciples. These represent models for the spiritual life and provide a context for its practice. Hindus take God very seriously and so an entire life is constructed around the quest for God. Being in the company of such individuals, communities, teachings, and environments provides an alternative to the Jewish environment that often loses sight of the ultimate goal and certainly cannot provide a space for regeneration and refocusing around the goal. What draws me to India then are ashrams wherein to meditate, traditions that carry the memory of great masters, and communities that are formed around the sole purpose of reaching God. In this, there is little difference between these Hindu saints, individuals, and communities and their Christian counterparts. But the language, ambience, and coloring are different. This has allowed me to learn some different lessons in a Hindu context. The lessons learnt by being in the company of those who seek to realize the ideal that all is divine and all our actions should conform to this realization are different from lessons learnt from those who declare God is love and all should be loved in the divine love. The differences are of nuance, and so my spiritual journey has been one of gaining nuances, hearing the different music, and integrating it all in my own Jewish path. Thus, what I have received from Hinduism, much like what I have received from Christianity, is the lesson of how others live in God's presence and sharing the great presences that drive their tradition, their saints and teachers. And just as there is variety between the religions, so there has been variety within one religion, like Hinduism. How my vedantin friends live in God's presence and how my Vaishnava bhakta friends do so is quite different. For me, moving from one group to another, and spending time with members of one religion and then another, is a lesson in the great wealth of the spiritual life and the numerous ways in which God is reached and made real in our lives. I am forever touched by the sincerity, devotion, and totality of commitment of all the friends I have made in Hindu contexts. Each one of their lives is an example of dedication. Each one has multiple lessons to teach me. And each one's experiences can open up a window of experience that is relevant for me, often a new window that would have not opened were it not for my contact with them.

And thus, I must conclude that it is not Hinduism as a system that has drawn me year after year to India. It is the reality of the spiritual life, lived in intensity by communities of devotees, who provide for me a model, an example, a space, and an opportunity for sharing. Sharing and inspiration are the lot of those who have found. I consider myself to be blessed to be not only a seeker, but also to be a "finder." And such finding has allowed me to be enormously enriched by the reality of the spiritual life, supported as it is by the theoretical teachings, the stories of the great personalities, and the continuing presence of the great teachers of the spiritual traditions of Hinduism. To me, it is not about truth, with religious truth understood as a zero sum game, wherein only one religion can possess truth. Rather, the truth of religion is the power of lived reality and what it makes possible both in the life of a community and in the internal life as I myself experience it.

Perhaps a final thought is in order. As I have just described it, there is something about my travels into Hinduism that is at once deeply captivating and engaged with Hinduism, but also in some way detached from it. Much of what I have experienced in relation to Hinduism I may have also experienced in relation to Christianity or other religions. What, then, is so unique about Hinduism? Or differently put: perhaps that which is really unique about Hinduism lies outside the scope of my experience, which is in some ways confined to the very high end of refined schools of teaching and practice? I do not think so. At least on one occasion I could test my level of comfort with "All-Hinduness." I refer to a visit to the 2013 Kumbh Mela, a great supermarket of diverse religious communities practicing their diversity within one ritual space, time, and practice, all self-defined as Hindu. I note how at home I felt spiritually wandering from group to group. I visited multiple communities of all shades and practices, monks and householders, representing the huge array of Hindu groups. And throughout I felt at home, with a sense of deep fraternity, notwithstanding all outer forms of difference, theirs as well as mine. I do not think that 35 or 40 years ago, when I made my first intellectual, and then spiritual, foray into Hinduism, I could have felt this level of at-home-ness. Otherness is deeply ingrained in the Jewish psyche. There is plenty in the Hindu reality that feels different, strange, belonging to a religious other. It is with our hearts that we relate to others, making room for them. I do not think it would have been possible for me 30 years ago to fully make room in my heart for all that I saw or met. In fact, I do not think I needed to make room in my heart. The sense of union of ultimate quest, sharing in the spiritual life, and a deep sense of spiritual brotherhood was there without my needing to "make room" for it. Where did it come from? Certainly not from academic analyses of the religion. These do not have the power to touch the heart. It was the fruit of contact, of relationships, and of shared reality that had been built up over many years. The fruit of my many years of sharing within Hindu communities was not exclusively in the mind—in the form of a teaching, a synthesis, a recommendation. It was in the heart—in the capacity to recognize the deep unity and bonds that tie together spiritual seekers across religions. It takes many relationships, much time together, many hours of study, talk, and reflection to tackle the questions, issues, and challenges that uphold the invisible barriers that we carry in our heart. People with no or with lower religious conviction may not suffer from the same kinds of barriers that religiously educated Jews do. As I said, othering is fundamental to our religious formation. And to make the other one's own, to overcome the process whereby the strangeness and difference of the other create a distance in one's heart, is a long process. It need not be undertaken directly. In my case, it was the fruit of a long journey that focused on the spiritual riches of Hinduism. But one of its fruits, perhaps the most important one, is that I consider myself to be completely free of the subtle, all too subtle, boundaries of heart that keep the religious other at a distance. The kind of unity that has opened up is very different from a secular humanist unity. It is a unity that grows from deep common purpose, from shared concern. Because we have God as our common quest, we are deeply bonded, we can share, we can inspire each other. It is a very different bonding that occurs when that which is most precious stands at the heart of a relationship. To recognize that another religion or rather its practitioners share the same ultimate goal and are therefore partners and brothers on a common journey is not a trivial recognition. Much walking is required between formulating it as a thesis that is readily admitted and recognizing it as one's natural internal disposition toward the other. If you will, my entire journey to Hinduism may have been required, and is certainly justified, if I can look into my heart, and then look at others, and discover unity, where there was once subtle distancing and separation.[6]

My experience as described here in many ways resonates with the picture of the encounter as one that takes place in relation to saints, sages, and spirituality, putting aside (symbolically: to another volume) all concerns of those aspects of Hinduism that a Jew might find offensive. And indeed this picture is true. It represents one possible configuration of Hinduism itself and certainly one legitimate way of entering into it. I can see my own path reflected in that of some of the young seekers and thanks to my own experience I can recognize its potential benefits for their long-term development.

My spiritual life could have probably advanced even without the help and inspiration of friends from other religions. But it would have been less rich and it would have suffered from many of the maladies that are the result of a bad interiority, a self-imposed spiritual isolation. The greatest maladies are those of the heart. These we cannot correct on our own. For these we require the other. If we seek for our hearts to be truly open to all, we cannot get there without real relationships with others. If nothing else was achieved by years of befriending and sharing with Hindu spiritual teachers and communities than the cleansing of heart, so that traces of othering and isolation have given way to a sense of unity, the journey was certainly worthwhile.

Notes

Introduction

1. A good example for this kind of approach is Nathan Katz's approach, as it finds expression in various of his contributions. See, From Legend to History in the Ancient World, *Shofar* 17,3, 1999, pp. 7–22; The State of the Art of Hindu-Jewish Dialogue, *Indo-Judaic Studies in the Twenty-First Century*, ed. Nathan Katz et al., Palgrave Macmillan, New York, 2007, pp. 113–126.
2. See http://www.nytimes.com/2004/05/17/nyregion/orthodox-jews-in-brooklyn-burn-banned-wigs.html, dated May 17, 2004.
3. Avoda Zara is also considered as relevant to problems of Jewish identity, as discussed with reference to specific cases featured in the chapter on Jewish identity.

1 Situating the Project: Personal and Collective Dimensions

1. See Katz, From Legend to History in the Ancient World, *Shofar* 17,3, 1999, pp. 7–22.
2. See Meir Bar Ilan, India and the Land of Israel: Between Jews and Indians in Ancient Times, *Journal of Indo-Judaic Studies* 4, 2001, pp. 39–77.
3. The volume appeared as Alon Goshen-Gottstein and Eugene Korn (eds.), *Jewish Theology and World Religions*, Littman Library, Oxford, 2012. My paper on Hinduism in that volume is Encountering Hinduism: Thinking Through *Avodah Zarah*, pp. 263–298. This essay provides an overview of many of the theses in the present book and even more so of some of the key theses of *Same God, Other god*. The conference that ultimately led to that volume, as well as to the present volume, was hosted at Scranton University by Marc Shapiro. Without his support and partnership, the reader of the present volume might have been reading some other scholarly publication.
4. Nathan Katz made a contribution to the Scranton conference that expressed this awareness. However, his own contribution focused more upon the history of the Jews in India than upon the theological dimensions of the encounter and the broader challenges it presents.
5. Asymmetry of some kind is a feature of most relations between different religions. The asymmetry may stem from different levels of need or interest, as in the case of Judaism and Christianity, or from varying political and power relations that make the encounter more urgent or more problematic, for one side or the other. Hindu-Christian relations certainly suffer from asymmetry, marked as they are by colonial history and the hegemony of certain forms of discourse in theological and academic circles.

6. References for what follows may be found in Yulia Egorova, Describing the "Other," Describing the "Self": Jews, Hindu Reforms, and Indian Nationalists, *Indo-Judaic Studies in the Twenty-First Century: A View from the Margin*, ed. N. Katz et al., Palgrave Macmillan, New York, 2007, pp. 197–211. See also Alan Brill's post, http://kavvanah.wordpress.com/2013/11/11/some-modern-hindu-approaches-to-judaism/.

7. See also the comments by Radhakrishnan, brought by Brill. https://kavvanah.wordpress.com/2013/11/11/some-modern-hindu-approaches-to-judaism/.

8. 1824–1883, to be distinguished from his namesake, born in 1930, who has played an important role in Hindu-Jewish relations, as we shall see later in our study.

9. See Egorova, Describing the "Other," p. 202.

10. The comparative study of religion provides an academic venue for recognizing Judaism's distinctiveness. However, unless Judaism is studied on its own account and in relation to living Jewish communities, reference to Judaism, even in a comparative context, ends up either perpetuating Christian stereotypes or identifying Judaism with the Old Testament. See references to Dasgupta in Brill's post. That reading Judaism in terms of the Old Testament alone can nevertheless yield perceptive insights emerges from the discussion of Soderblom, in a later chapter of the present work.

11. See Margaret Chatterjee, *Gandhi and His Jewish Friends*, Macmillan Academic, Basingstoke, 1992, and more recently Shimon Lev, *Soulmates: The Story of Mahatma Gandhi and Hermann Kallenbach*, Orient BlackSwan, Hyderabad, 2012. Gandhi's friendship with Jews revolved around idealism, common battles, and the struggles of Jews and Indians for survival and independence. There is almost nothing of a specifically religious character that would allow his friendships, especially with Kallenbach, to be classified as an encounter between Judaism and Hinduism. See Chatterjee, p. 170, and compare p. 55. This is due to the persons with whom he formed friendships. The Jews he encountered were not particularly observant and hence most of the exchanges involving Gandhi and Jews relate to Zionism, rather than to Judaism. This also accounts for how Judaism at times is viewed by Gandhi through unflattering Christian stereotypes. Thus, in writing on Jewish responses to Nazism, Gandhi evokes the stereotypes of Jewish vengefulness and the "eye for eye" attitude, contrasted with Christian love. See Chatterjee, pp. 168–169 and Shimon Lev, Gandhi's Attitude to the Shoah, *Hayo Haya* 9, 2012, p. 20 [Hebrew], citing *Harijan*, 12.12.1939. See also Gandhi's spiritualizing the Land of Israel out of its concrete existence, Lev, *Soulmates*, p. 139.

12. Anna Guttman's *Writing Indians and Jews: Metaphorics of Jewishness in South Asian Literature*, Palgrave Macmillan, New York, 2013, leads us to the conclusion that in colonial and postcolonial Indian literature the figure of the Jew is quite present. But, as in the case of Gandhi, awareness of the Jew has little to do with awareness of Judaism.

13. To further complicate matters, much of the attention of Hindu intelligentsia in the earlier part of the twentieth century was focused on the Jewish problem and the Zionist movement, not leaving much room for a self-standing appreciation of Judaism. Rabindranath Tagore seems to be one figure who may have had a broader appreciation of Judaism, alongside his support for the Zionist movement. This is in part based on personal relationships, but also on the fact that he was a more cosmopolitan figure, and visited major Jewish communities in the United States. See Shimon Lev, Tagore, Jews and Zionism, *Mabu'a* 49, 2008, pp. 11–23 [Hebrew].

14. Still, the state of awareness of Judaism as a self-standing religion leaves much to be desired. The Satya Sai Baba movement is a case in point. This Hindu guru, who

passed away in 2011 and who was one of India's most popular gurus and who had thousands of Jewish followers, devised an interreligious symbol for his movement. Significantly, Judaism is not represented in this symbol. The underlying reasoning seems to, once again, appeal to Judaism's indistinguishability from Christianity. Later verbal communication attempts to correct this imbalance. See Charlene Leslie-Chaden, *A Compendium of the Teachings of S.S.S.B*, Sai Towers Publishing, Bangalore, 2004, p. 296. See further http://bdsteel.tripod.com/More/Relknow.htm. His American followers seem to have attempted to correct this imbalance, by providing a digest view of Judaism, culled from several introductory works, as part of their theory of the unity of all religions. See http://www.region7saicenters.org/saidocuments/Unity_of_Faiths_Judaism.pdf. Perhaps even more disgraceful is the absence of Judaism from the museum of world religions in Puttaparthi, part of the Satya Sai Baba complex, where even the smallest animistic religions are featured. Whatever this may say about this particular movement, populated as it is by thousands of Jewish members, it is also a testimony to the broader lack of awareness of Judaism as a distinct religion in the Indian subcontinent. I might add that a parallel museological exhibit, prepared by the Swaminarayan movement, in their Akshardham complex in Gandhinagar, Gujarat (and now in New Delhi, though I have not visited it), does present Judaism as a world religion. Both museological exhibits seek to portray their respective faith traditions (Satya Sai Baba and Swaminarayan Hinduisms) as a kind of culmination of all world religions. The difference in the presentation of Judaism can therefore not be ascribed to the purpose of the exhibit.

2   The Hindu-Jewish Encounter: The Present Context

1. I therefore find it difficult to accept Nathan Katz's broad generalization that "Hindu-Jewish dialogue is not some new fad; it is truly an ancient encounter that dates back more than two millennia" (see Nathan Katz, The State of the Art of Hindu-Jewish Dialogue, *Indo-Judaic Studies in the Twenty-First Century: A View from the Margin*, ed. Nathan Katz et al., Palgrave Macmillan, New York, 2007, p. 124). While it is true that some kind of encounter can be traced over millennia, this statement ignores the novelty of the present situation and its particular challenges. These challenges are new and can draw only minimal guidance or inspiration from the meager contact that has taken place over the centuries. I believe it is more helpful to the present enterprise if its radical novelty can be highlighted rather than the continuity of the encounter over the millennia.

2. There seems to be only one Jewish personality of any significance on the religious horizons of classical India, and his Jewishness is ethnic rather than specifically religious. See chapter 4.

3. Nathan Katz repeats the claim for a symmetrical encounter in three different places (which are essentially the same piece). See Nathan Katz, The State of the Art of Hindu-Jewish Dialogue, *Indo-Judaic Studies in the Twenty-First Century*, ed. Nathan Katz et al., Palgrave Macmillan, New York, 2007, pp. 113–126, which repeats claims made previously in How the Hindu-Jewish Encounter Reconfigures Interreligious Dialogue, *Shofar* 16,1, 1997, pp. 28–42. The thesis is repeated again in The Hindu-Jewish Encounter and the Future, *The Fifty Eighth Century: A Jewish Renewal Sourcebook*, ed. Shohama Wiener, Jason Aaronson, Northvale, NJ, 1996, pp. 331–343. Katz's description of a symmetrical dialogue grows out of his work on Indian Jews, but it is only appropriate, in terms of my own presentation, for the

meeting of Jews and Hindus in the diaspora. It does not describe what I consider to be the most important encounter, namely the encounter of Jews with Hinduism in India itself. The issue of symmetry, or lack thereof, would be one important point concerning which the present book takes issue with Katz's earlier work.

4. Indeed, these meetings were organized by the World Council of Religious Leaders, an organization whose stated goal is to bring together leadership of all world religions.

5. On Shmuel Hugo Bergman, see Miriam Dean-Otting, Hugo Bergman, Leo Baeck, and Martin Buber, Jewish Perspectives on Hinduism and Buddhism, *Journal of Indo Judaic Studies*, 1,2, 1999, pp. 7–26.

6. About half a dozen figures may be considered in this class. These include Mirra Alfassa, the Mother at Pondicherry's Aurobindo Ashram; Paul Brunton, who brought Ramana Maharshi to world attention, as did another Jewish disciple, S. S. Cohen; Maurice Frydman, known as Swami Bharatananda; and Swami Vijayananda, whom we shall study extensively later in this work.

7. It is interesting to note how this fact registers on the Jewish side. Arye Kaplan claims that 75 percent of members in some ashrams are Jewish. See Arye Kaplan, *Jewish Meditation: A Practical Guide*, Schoken, New York, 1985, p. vi. The sense that Jews are losing membership to Hindu movements thus looms large for Jewish educators who are aware of the Hindu movements. Tomer Persico suggests that Kaplan shapes his Jewish meditation along the lines of, and in response to, the kind of meditation that was most widely practiced in the 70s, namely mantra meditation. See Tomer Persico, *"Jewish Meditation": The Development of a Modern Form of Spiritual Practice in Contemporary Judaism*, PhD thesis, Tel Aviv University, 2012, pp. 385–389.

8. Daria Maoz, Every Age and Its Backpack, *From India Till Here*, ed. Elhanan Nir, Rubin Mass, Jerusalem, 2006, pp. 107–125 [Hebrew].

9. *From India Till Here*, ed. Elhanan Nir.

10. Dori Hanemman, What Does India Add to the Torah of the Land of Israel, *From India Till Here*, ed. Elhanan Nir, pp. 75–87.

11. See Jacob Katz, *Exclusiveness and Tolerance*, Oxford University Press, London, 1961.

12. These are listed in Alan Brill's presentation of Eastern Religions in his *Judaism and World Religions: Encountering Christianity, Islam and Eastern Traditions*, Palgrave Macmillan, New York, 2012, pp. 210–212. For a discussion of Benjamin of Tudela's possible travels to India, see Richard Marks, Hindus and Hinduism in Medieval Jewish Literature, *Indo-Judaic Studies in the Twenty-First Century: A View from the Margin*, ed. Nathan Katz et al., Palgrave Macmillan, New York, 2007, pp. 65–67.

13.. On the psychological dynamics of Israeli travel to India and on profiling parts of Indian culture, at the expense of others, see Laurie Patton and Shalom Goldman, Indian Love Call: Israelis, Orthodoxy and Indian Culture, *Judaism* 50,3, 2001, pp. 351–361. See also Daria Maoz, When Images Become "True": The Israeli Backpacking Experience in India, *Karmic Passages, Israeli Scholarship on India*, ed. David Shulman and Shalva Weil, Oxford University Press, New Delhi, 2008, pp. 214–231.

14. There is one kind of encounter that I do not engage in the present study, even though it also constitutes a site of encounter, in many ways the most challenging. I shall not enter the issue of mixed Jewish-Hindu marriages. The focus of the present work is encounters that take place from the starting position of committed religious identities, meeting across the boundaries of recognized religions. Interreligious marriage, more often than not, is only secondarily a religious encounter, with its primary

driving motivation coming from the social and affective dimensions of the individuals' lives. Consequently, it is nearly impossible to practice interreligious marriage while remaining fully faithful to one's tradition. On the phenomenon of Jewish-Hindu mixed marriages see Jeremy Caplan, Om Shalomers Come of Age, http://forward.com/articles/6137/om-shalomers-come-of-age/.

15. Margaret Chatterjee seems to be the only Indian author to have undertaken a serious study of some aspects of Jewish and Israeli reality. In any event, she is the only one who has written about the Israeli side of things. Significantly, she is the only Indian author to have contributed to Hananya Goodman's, *Between Jerusalem and Benares*, SUNY Press, Albany, NY, 1994. In conversation with friends she has resisted revealing her own religious background, and her Jewish identity cannot be discounted.

16. See David Shulman and Shalva Weil's prelude to *Karmic Passages, Israeli Scholarship on India*, pp. 1–7.

17. Introduction to *Karmic Passages*, p. vii.

18. In the context of the present work, it may not be superfluous to point out that despite the broad interest in India and Hinduism, little academic energy is actually invested in comparative, let alone theologically comparative, studies of Hinduism and Judaism. The only comparative study in *Karmic Passages*, that of Shlomo Biderman (himself a practicing Jew), compares Buddhist and Western notions of compassion, but not specifically Jewish ones. (Biderman's *Philosophical Journeys: India and the West*, Yediot Aharonot Press, Tel Aviv, 2003 [Hebrew] is more balanced in this respect, but does not focus specifically on Jewish-Hindu philosophical comparisons.) The service of Israeli academia to the concerns of the present book is thus less significant than one would hope. Comparative and theological studies, with dialogue in view, seem to be more characteristic of the American academic milieu than they are of the Israeli. This emerges from the various works edited by Nathan Katz, including the volumes of the *Journal of Indo-Judaic Studies* as well as *Indo-Judaic Studies in the Twenty-First Century*. Significantly, these give voice to predominantly North American scholarship. Katz's own biographical stake in the theological and comparative enterprise emerges from his biography, *Spiritual Journey Home: Eastern Mysticism to the Western Wall*, Ketav, Jersey City, 2009.

3   The Jews of India: What Can We Learn from Them?

1. For a history of ties between Jews and India, see Meir Bar Ilan, India and the Land of Israel: Between Jews and Indians in Ancient Times, *Journal of Indo Judaic Studies* 4, 2001, pp. 39–77.

2. See Henry Fischel, The Contribution of the Cochin Jews to South Indian and Jewish Civilizations, *Commemoration Volume: Cochin Synagogue Quatercentenary Celebrations*, ed. S. S.Koder, Cochin, 1971, pp. 15–64.

3. It is most interesting to examine bibliographies on Indian Jewry from this perspective. Several bibliographical lists have been published by Nathan Katz. See, An Annotated Bibliography about Indian Jewry, *Kol Binah* 8,1, 1991, pp. 6–33; Bibliography about Indian Jewry, *Journal of Indo-Judaic Studies* vol. 2, 1999, pp. 113–135, and vol. 3, 2000, pp. 126–132. It is striking how these bibliographies are arranged, and their arrangement accords well with the subject matter of the literature and its own concerns. Most of the materials are in the domain of ethnography and sociology. Materials are broken down according to categories such as Cochin Jews, Iraqi Jews, Bene Israel, etc. There is no halachic discussion, either as part of the

taxonomy or in the titles covered in the bibliographies. Philosophical and ideological analyses are also scarce. Whatever there is, in this respect, is the fruit of Western scholars of religion who engage in comparative studies, not of local Indian Jewry's own intellectual creativity.

4. For a reading of Yom Kippur celebration in these terms, see Shalva Weil, Yom Kippur: The Festival of Closing the Doors, *Between Jerusalem and Benares: Comparative Studies in Judaism and Hinduism,* ed. Hananya Goodman, SUNY Press, Albany, NY, 1994, pp. 85–100.

5. See, however, Meir Bar Ilan's attempt to read the caste system into standard rabbinic Judaism. Bar Ilan, India and the Land of Israel, pp. 49–51.

6. See Nathan Katz and Ellen Goldberg, *The Last Jews of Cochin: Jewish Identity in Hindu India,* University of South Carolina Press, Columbia, 1993, p. 249.

7. See Joan Roland, Religious Observances of Bene Israel: Persistence and Refashioning of Tradition, *Journal of Indo-Judaic Studies,* 3, 2000, p. 41.

8. It is worth noting that within a fairly limited sphere, some Jews could also engage in pilgrimage to sites venerated by Hindus and Muslims as well. See Roland, Religious Observances, p. 31.

9. S. D. Goitein and M. A. Friedman, *India Traders of the Middle Ages: Documents of the Cairo Genizah (India Book),* vols.1–3, Leiden, Boston, 2008, p. 25.

10. Much depends, of course, on the exact itinerary of Benjamin and on the identification of the places he visited and the religious communities he encountered. See Richard Marks, Hindus and Hinduism in Medieval Jewish Literature, *Indo-Judaic Studies in the Twenty-First Century: A View from the Margin,* ed. Nathan Katz et al., Palgrave Macmillan, New York, 2007, pp. 65–67. A later Jewish traveler to India does much the same, in describing what he sees in terms of biblical idolatry. On Jacob Sapir see Richard Marks, Hinduism, Torah and Travel: Jacob Sapir in India, *Shofar* 30,2, 2012, pp. 26–51. Contrast this with the positive application of biblical language by Azriel Carlebach, *India: A Road Journal,* Ayanot, Tel Aviv, 1956 [Hebrew].

11. See Alan Brill, *Judaism and World Religions: Encountering Christianity, Islam and Eastern Traditions,* Palgrave Macmillan, New York, 2012, pp. 210–212. See also Shirley Berry Isenberg, *India's Bene Israel, a Comprehensive Inquiry and Sourcebook,* Popular Prakashan, Bombay, 1988, p. 87.

4   Sarmad the Jew: A Precursor of the Encounter

1. The following discussion extracts a very detailed and textually oriented discussion by Alon Goshen-Gottstein, *Revisiting Sarmad the Jew,* forthcoming.

2. There is no standard edition of the Rubayats in English, and I have counted five different translations. These include Isaac A. Ezekiel, *Sarmad: Jewish Saint of India,* Punjab, Radha Soami Satsang Beas, 1966; M. G. Gupta, *Sarmad the Saint: Life and Works,* MG Publishers, Agra, 1991; Zahurul Hassan Sharib, *Sarmad and His Rubaiyat,* Sharib Press, Southampton, UK, 1994; and most recently Paul Smith, *Sarmad: Life and Poems,* Createspace Independent Pub, 2014. One edition is available on the internet. This is Fazl Mahmud Asiri's *Rubaiyat—i—Sarmad,* 1950, available at http://www.bahaistudies.net/asma/rubaiyat-i-Sarmad.pdf.

3. The Persian edition is Rahim Razazada Malik (ed.), *Dabistan-i Mazahib,* Teheran, Kitabkhanah-i Tahuri, 1983. English translation David Shea and Anthony Troyer, *Dabistan-i Mazahib or School of Manners,* Oriental Translation Fund of Great Britain and Ireland, Paris, 1843.

4. It is worth noting that Akbar's open interreligious court included Jews, who were part of spiritual discussions. See Fischel, below. From Akbar's edicts relating to synagogue building we also learn that they were not simply expatriated theologians from elsewhere, but that they could in theory belong to a Jewish community. Even so, it is striking that a tiny Jewish community would be featured alongside the other prominent religions of India. In terms of Indian knowledge of Judaism, this is very much at odds with the general situation, where Judaism is often not appreciated as a religious tradition in its own right.

5. This matter is treated at length in Katz's presentation, see below.

6. This matter comes up in his poetry. Sarmad writes: "I go to the mosque, but I am no Muslim." See Quatrain 218, p. 351 in the collection translated by Ezekiel.

7. Walter Fischel, The Bible in Persian Translation, *Harvard Theological Review* 45,1, 1952, pp. 22–24.

8. Beas, Radha Soami Satsang.

9. Ezekiel, *Sarmad*, pp. 40ff.

10. Ezekiel authored another work for the Radhasoami press on Saint Paltu, 1978. The saint fits even more closely with the Radhasoami worldview and there is no need to affirm his identity in any particular way. Sarmad figures in another Radhasoami publication on Judaism. This is Miriam Bokser Caravella's *The Holy Name: Mysticism in Judaism*, Radha Saomi Satsang Beas, New Delhi, 1989. Sarmad is cited there multiple times, and the author is obviously aware of Ezekiel's work. To her credit, while the author acknowledges he was Jewish and as a teacher unknown to "Western Judaism" (p. 17), she never features Sarmad as a specifically Jewish teacher. She cites him as a model for the spiritual life, not for the spiritual life as known and taught in Judaism. Bokser's work is critiqued in a later chapter of the present book.

11. Roger Kamenetz, *The Jew in the Lotus: A Poet's Rediscovery of Jewish Identity in Buddhist India*, HarperOne San Francisco, New York, 1994.

12. Kamenetz, *The Jew in the Lotus*, pp. 249–250.

13. The way Kamenetz presents Fischel's thesis takes it beyond Fischel. It is not simply that Sarmad wasn't really converted while contributing intellectually to the *Dabistan* and to the Torah's translation. With this formulation, these activities are *expressions* of his Judaism.

14. Kamenetz, *The Jew in the Lotus*, p. 250.

15. Quatrain 320 in Ezekiel's collection, p. 382. See further Quatrain 314, p. 380. It is interesting to note that a wikipedia article that lists Muslims who converted to Hinduism includes Sarmad. See http://en.wikipedia.org/wiki/List_of_converts_to_Hinduism_from_Islam. This list appears in various other places on the web.

16. Nathan Katz, The Identity of a Mystic: The Case of Sa'id Sarmad, a Jewish-Yogi-Sufi Courtier of the Mughals, *Numen* 47, 2000, pp. 142–160.

17. Translation based on Asiri, *Rubaiyat—i—Sarmad*, p. vii. Shea and Troyer, *Dabistan-i Mazahib*, p. 293: "I submit to Moses' law; I am of thy religion, and a guardian of the way. I am a Rabbi of the Yahuds, a Kafir, a Muselman." While Judaism is featured in both translations, it is privileged in Shea and Troyer's translation, making it the primary focus.

18. See Maulavi 'Abdu'l Wali, A Sketch of the Life of Sarmad, *Journal of the Asiatic Society of Bengal*, 20, 1924, p. 118.

19. The following text by the contemporary Jesuit Manucci, is brought by Fischel, Jews and Judaism at the Court of the Moghul Emperors, *Proceedings of the American Academy of Jewish Research*, 18, 1948–1949, pp. 137–177.

20. Extract from Alamgir Nama of Muhammad Kazim, written in 1688, translated in H. M. Elliot and J. Dowson, *The History of India as Told by Its Own Historians*, Trubner, London, 1877, vol. 7, p. 179.

21. Penned by a court historian, we can't really take this quote as instructive of Sarmad's own self-identity. It does teach us however that not only was Sarmad viewed as a Jew, and not simply a Muslim, but that his teachings were viewed in relation to Judaism. At the very least, there was nothing in Sarmad's teachings that would belie such an understanding.

22. See Katz's contextualization of such practices in seventeenth-century India, The Identity of a Mystic, pp. 158–160.

23. For a summary of this, see Katz, The Identity of a Mystic, pp. 153–157.

24. One should note that Sarmad's move from Judaism to Islam occurred in Iran, prior to arriving in India. His mystical breakthrough, finding expression in his practicing nudity, composing poetry, and also in expanding his religious identity to include Hinduism, all took place on Indian soil.

5   Judaism(s) and Hinduism(s)

1. See Jacob Neusner, William Scott Green, and Ernest S. Frerichs (eds.), *Judaisms and Their Messiahs at the Turn of the Christian Era*, Cambridge University Press, Cambridge, 1987.

2. See Jacob Neusner, Judaisms in Modern Times : Toward a General Theory, *Major Trends in Formative Judaism 5*, ed. Jacob Neusner, University of America, Lanham, 2002, pp. 209–237.

3. This is not to suggest that other streams of Judaism will take exception to the present work. The differences between various present-day Judaisms with reference to the subject matter of the present work is not significant. The only difference would be that some non-Orthodox groups may simply be less concerned with problems of idolatry and identity, as discussed in a later chapter in this volume and in *Same God, Other god*. Lesser concern for these issues does not amount to an alternative strategy for tackling them. Hence, confessing my Orthodox roots has little substantive implications, beyond establishing clarity within the playing field(s) of Judaism.

4. This statement of how to balance competing perspectives and definitions of "Judaism" is made primarily for purposes of theoretical discussion. My discussion of Judaism does not diverge from the common normative view of Judaism.

5. While we do not have an autonomous definition of "Hinduism," unless we resort to geographic definitions of the Middle Ages, recent research suggests that concern for establishing Hindu identity is not a purely modern preoccupation. See Andrew Nicholson, *Unifying Hinduism: Philosophy and Identity in Indian Intellectual History*, Columbia University Press, New York, 2010.

6. Thus, for the past decade or so, one forum in which the encounter between Judaism and Hinduism has been taking place is the annual meeting of the American Academy of Religion. Within that framework one of the program units is titled "Comparative Studies of Judaisms and Hinduisms." The plural, by means of which both religions are described, is noteworthy. It seeks to get around the problems of definition and to offer a broad perspective from which comparative studies may be carried out. Comparison is one of the historian's tools and the discussions within this group are always historical and descriptive, never theological and normative. This is one of the fora in which models of relations between these two religions can be explored,

but such explorations never carry the theological burden of the encounter between religious traditions and their practitioners. History and its descriptive work can live with the multiplicity of religious forms. It is interesting to contrast this with the name, and the work, of another group of scholars that meets in the margins of the American Academy of Religion. Significantly, that group is called "Society of Hindu-Christian Studies." There is an overlap in the membership of scholars participating in the work of both groups. It is therefore particularly noteworthy that the theological (Hindu-Christian) work is primarily done under a more unified rubric, while comparativist work (Hindu-Jewish), lives more comfortably with references to the religions in the plural.

7. While Nicholson's work makes us aware of earlier foundations, the full-fledged articulation of a unified Hindu identity is a modern project, indeed one that is still underway.

8. For a standard presentation of the etymological development of "Hindu," see http://en.wikipedia.org/wiki/Hinduism. The earliest uses of "Hindu" are geographic, not religious. It is only in the nineteenth century that "Hindu" and (its orientalist abstraction) "Hinduism" came to designate the religion presently known by that name. For an overview of differing constructions of the identity of Hindu communities, including the formation of contemporary Hindu identity, see Romila Thapar, Imagined Religious Communities? Ancient History and the Modern Search for a Hindu Identity, *Modern Asian Studies*, 23,2, 1989, pp. 209–231. See further, Deepak Sarma, Hinduism, *The Crisis of the Holy*, ed. Alon Goshen-Gottstein, Lexington Books, Lanham, 2014, pp. 111–113.

9. For some authors, Hindu tolerance is constitutive of Hindu identity. See Shakunthala Jagannathan, *Hinduism: An Introduction*, Vakils, Feffer and Simons, Bombay, 1991, p. 1. Hindu tolerance is an interesting point of intersection between the normative (as understood by these authors) and the descriptive, providing us with an important facet that cannot be ignored in an overall appreciation of Hinduism.

10. It should be noted that, unlike the Torah, recognition of the Vedas does not translate into an agreed-upon lifestyle or belief, as prescribed by the Vedas.

11. In the context of work at the United Nations, the Brahma Kumaris have obtained a status independent of Hinduism. An even more extreme expression of this dynamic is the financially motivated attempt by the Ramakrishna Mission to declare itself non-Hindu. Odd as this may seem, it is not equivalent to the hypothetical analogy of Lubavitch hassidim arguing they are not Jewish.

12. These are usually referred to as Sanskritic and non-Sanskritic traditions, owing to a distinction first introduced by M. N. Srinivas in his 1952, *Religion and Society among the Coorgs of South India*, Asia Publishing House, New York.

13. See Raymond Williams, *An Introduction to Swaminarayan Hinduism*, Cambridge University Press, Cambridge, 2001.

14. On media and migration and their effects on Hindu identity, see John Thatamanil, Managing Multiple Religious and Scholarly Identities: An Argument for a Theological Study of Hinduism, *Journal of the American Academy of Religion* 68,4, 2000, p. 793.

15. I owe much of my understanding of Hinduism in the diaspora to Vasudha Narayanan, who took part in programs I organized in Israel, and who has made diaspora Hinduism a focus of her studies.

16. See Vasudha Narayanan, Diglossic Hinduism: Liberation and Lentils, *Journal of the American Academy of Religion* 68,4, 2000, p. 767. Of the various essays in this issue of the journal, devoted to the topic of "Who Speaks for Hinduism?" Narayanan's

contribution is the one that points most strongly to the descriptive pole on the normative-descriptive axis.

17. The view is a philosophical one and could therefore not be inherently limited to a particular religion. For this reason, it is not surprising that the spiritual teachers who come out of this tradition, most of the Hindu teachers known in the West, are comfortable thinking of themselves and of their message as broader than Hinduism itself. Vedanta may be seen as a metareligious language that itself offers a vision of unity of all religions. Hence, the major Hindu contributions to interreligious dialogue and to the Hindu view of other religions draw on a vedantic understanding of religion, seeing it as identical to Hinduism itself. At the same time, the philosophical transreligious language of Vedanta allows religious teachers affiliated with it to present themselves, or their religious system, as being beyond the particularity of a specific religious tradition. One close friend, a swami, grudgingly agreed to my reference to him as my Hindu friend. He preferred to compromise by being labeled my "so-called Hindu friend." In ways that are hard to grasp for non-Hindus, various religious and spiritual systems could be exported to the West so that they could variously draw upon their Hindu (or Vedic) roots, or disenage themselves from it. To take some popular examples, both Transcendental Meditation and the Art of Living can be marketed as non-religions, while drawing heavily on Hindu resources, ideas, and even practices. It is not only a matter of commercialization and its attendant deceptions. This plays out a great complexity, inherent in the view of Vedanta as simultaneously the fundamental religious understanding within a specific religious tradition and a worldview that transcends the particularity of that religious tradition. Alan Brill, *Judaism and World Religions: Encountering Christianity, Islam and Eastern Traditions*, Palgrave Macmillan, New York, 2012, p. 233, raises the question of the implications this has for Judaism's dialogue with Hinduism. If Hinduism is equated with Vedanta, then rather than a dialogue between two religions, we end up with a dialogue between one religion and one metareligious mysticism or philosophy. On Maurice Fluegel, an Orthodox rabbi, and his suggestion of a common essence between Kabbalah and Vedanta, see Brill's discussion, *Judaism and World Religions*, pp. 212–3. Finally, it should be noted that in contrast to the ambiguity regarding whether or not *Advaita Vedanta* is a religion, the non-vedantic forms of Hinduism are unequivocally religious in character, as the case of ISKCON clearly indicates.

18. The possibility of an all-inclusive Jewish view of religions that would incorporate Hinduism as well has historical precedent. Eliyahu ben Amozegh, in late nineteenth century, developed a system of metaphysics wherein Kabbalah provides the synthesis of all religious systems, including other religions. Ben Amozegh was aware of Hinduism and of its pantheistic views. These were subsumed within his broader kabbalistic schemata. See Moshe Idel, Kabbalah in Elijah Benamozegh's Thought, appendix to *Elijah ben Amozegh: Israel and Humanity*, translated by Maxwell Luria, Mahwah, NJ, Paulist Press, 1994, pp. 363–377. See further Marc Gopin, An Orthodox Embrace of Gentiles: Interfaith Tolerance in the Thought of S. D. Luzzatto and E. Benamozegh, *Modern Judaism* 18, 1998, pp. 173–195.

19. I have been struck time and again by the appeal to vedantic teachings in the discourses of Mata Amritanandamayi (the hugging saint, commonly known as Amma or Ammachi). The teachings of this present-day Hindu guru, probably India's most popular present-day religious figure, are quite simple, coming as they do from the direct spiritual experience of a person with almost no formal, let alone theological or philosophical, formation. Nevertheless, the form of Hinduism to which she repeatedly appeals is that of Vedanta.

20. *Journal of the American Academy of Religion,*68, 4, 2000, pp. 705–835.
21. See Brian Smith, Who Does, Can and Should Speak for Hinduism? *Journal of the American Academy of Religion,* 68,4, 2000, pp. 741–749.
22. Daniel Sperber, in his forthcoming *The Halakhic Status of Hinduism* suggests that this scholarly and elitist perspective is also recognized by halachic authorities and cites Rabbi Menashe Klein's approach to the sheitel crisis as proof. See Klein's discussion in *Or Yisrael* 10,1, 2005, pp.33–35. The issue is clearly conceptualized in Joshua Flug, A Review of the Recent "Sheitel" Controversy, *Journal of Halacha and Contemporary Society* 49, 2005, 5–33. Flug devotes much attention to the question of who holds the key to interpretation and even accounts for the changed ruling of Rabbi Elyashiv by appealing to this consideration. See pp. 19–22.
23. An illustration from the life of Swami Vijayananda, whom we shall discuss in detail in a later chapter, is appropriate. Swami Vijayananda, a Jewish doctor who came to India in 1951, became a disciple of Anandamayi Ma and remained in India at her recommendation. While he became a swami, he never converted to Hinduism. In part, this was due to the fact that there is no classical conversion ceremony to Hinduism, but more pointedly, this goes back to Ma's own reticence, apparently influenced by her own conservative Bengali background, to accept non-Hindus as converts. For the Jewish Vijayananda this was most convenient, as he never sought to forego his Jewish identity. As we shall see below, in his own self-understanding, he had never become a Hindu, but only taken up Vedanta as his preferred spiritual path.
24. See Douglas Brooks, Taking Sides and Opening Doors: Authority and Integrity in the Academy's Hinduism, *Journal of the American Academy of Religion,* 68,4, 2000, p. 823. Brooks considers this part of what it means for Hinduism to have become a world religion. Needless to say, the term "world religions" is fraught with difficulties.

6   Judaism and Hinduism: Insights from the Comparative Study of Religion

1. Significantly, the traffic of ideas seems to be mainly a one-way street. As we shall note, this is also characteristic to a large extent of the modern encounter of Jews and Judaism with Hinduism. I am not familiar with any suggestions of specifically Jewish influences on Hindu religious thought. I am not referring to Judaism's indirect influence through Christianity, but to influences that are specifically Jewish and representative of postbiblical Judaism.
2. This field is much indebted to the ongoing efforts of Nathan Katz, who founded the *Journal of Indo-Judaic Studies* and who is also editor in chief of *Indo-Judaic Studies in the Twenty-First Century: A View from the Margin*, Palgrave Macmillan, New York, 2007. Participants in various initiatives organized by him show a strong awareness of the novelty of their academic enterprise and of their attempts to define a new field of studies.
3. Idel mentioned, on that occasion, the use of colors in prayer and meditation as an element that made its way into Judaism from Hindu sources. See, Moshe Idel, *Kabbalah: New Perspectives*, Yale University Press, New Haven, CT, 1988, pp. 107–108. For a recent presentation of Jewish mysticism that makes comparisons with Hinduism, see Idel's introduction to Jewish mysticism in Steven Katz (ed.), *Comparative Mysticism: An Anthology of Original Sources*, Oxford University Press, Oxford, 2013, p. 31.

4. For some theoretical statements of the meaning of the comparative enterprise see K. C. Patton and B. C.Ray, *A Magic Still Dwells: Comparative Religion in a Postmodern Age*, University of California Press, Berkeley, 2000.

5. Barbara Holdrege, *Veda and Torah: Transcending the Textuality of Scripture*, SUNY Press, Albany, New York, 1996. One notes that most of the book highlights fundamental differences between how the two scriptures are understood, owing largely to the difference between the oral (Hindu) and visual (Torah) expressions of the two scriptures. However, the fundamental understandings of scripture and language emerge as common structural ground, which in turn accounts for commonalities such as the theurgic and cosmic applications and expressions of scripture. Holdrege's work presents us with the challenge of considering to what degree the comparative enterprise relies on commonalities or differences in order to be really meaningful. Much of what makes the comparison meaningful is the embodiment of both scriptures in their respective, and similarly structured, communities; see below.

6. This trend may have been launched with the collection of essays *Between Jerusalem and Benares*, edited by Hananya Goodman, SUNY Press, Albany, NY, 1994. Goodman speaks of resonances between the traditions rather than of historical influences. Nathan Katz quotes Barbara Holdrege's recognition of Goodman's work as one of the fountainheads of the emerging field of Indo-Judaic Studies. See Katz's introduction, Indo-Judaic Studies in the Twenty First Century: A Perspective from the Margin, p. 4.

7. Similar exercises exist. Some interesting work has been done from this perspective on Jewish and Chinese religions. See Aharon Oppenheimer, *Sino-Judaica: Jews and Chinese in Historical Dialogue*, Tel Aviv University Press, Tel Aviv, 1999. While this work may be inspired by broader globalizing tendencies, reflecting international relations, and commercial interests, on the whole it carries little contemporary impact, in the absence of broad meaningful contact between the cultures and their representatives.

8. Actually, such comparativist exercises already serve the needs of nineteeth-century Jewish Reform theology in the works of David Einhorn and Samuel Hirsch. These authors do not engage Hinduism directly, but do so through treatments of contemporary historians and philosophers. Their purpose is apologetic, seeking to demonstrate Judaism's superiority to all ancient pagan religions, Hinduism included. Their treatment of Hinduism does not stem from a study of Hinduism or its texts. Rather, they view it in light of their a priori criteria for viewing religions. For present purposes, there is little value in their work, except maybe to demonstrate that knowledge of Hinduism as monotheism can be documented among nineteenth-century Jewish writers. See Gershon Greenberg, *Religionswissenschaft* and Early Reform Jewish Thought: Samuel Hirsch and David Einhorn, *Modern Judaism and Historical Consciousness: Identities, Encounters, Perspectives*, ed. Andreas Gotzmann and Christian Wiese, Brill, Leiden, 2007, pp. 110–144.

9. To a certain extent, the same may be said of the emergence of the academic field of Indo-Judaic Studies in the United States. While the direction may not be as linear as in the case of Israeli travelers to India, the work of Nathan Katz has close associations with his travels and spiritual experiences. See his autobiography, *Spiritual Journey Home: Eastern Mysticism to the Western Wall*, Ketav, Jersey City, 2009.

10. Charles Mopsik, Union and Unity in the Kabbla, *Between Jerusalem and Benares*, SUNY Press, New York, 1994, p. 242.

11. For an introduction to the field, see Francis Clooney, *Comparative Theology: Deep Learning across Religious Borders*, Wiley-Blackwell, Chichester, 2010.

12. In the context of a Jewish-Hindu comparative study, see the insightful comments of Braj Sinha, Divine Anthropos and Cosmic Tree: Hindu and Jewish Mysticism in Comparative Perspective, *Indo-Judaic Studies in the Twenty-First Century: A View from the Margin*, 2007, pp. 106–107. Having made various observations on the place of core common notions in both traditions, Sinha continues to explore the ways in which the two traditions could challenge each other's theological reflections. Such mutual challenging is already an expression of dialogue and encounter and goes beyond the purely descriptive work of the historian of religions. That a descriptive study should move toward reflection upon mutual challenges suggests how close these domains can be.

13. See John Thatamanil, Managing Multiple Religious and Scholarly Identities: An Argument for a Theological Study of Hinduism, *Journal of the American Academy of Religion* 68,4, 2000, pp. 791–803, especially p. 799ff.

14. Nathan Soderblom, *The Living God: Basal Forms of Personal Religion*. The Gifford lectures, delivered in the University of Edinburgh in the year 1931, London, H. Milford, Oxford University Press, 1933. Soderblom's discussion is Chapter 8 of his book, titled Religion as Revelation in History, pp. 264–317.

15. Soderblom, *The Living God*, p. 265. Already Swami Vivekananda observed that Judaism and Hinduism are religions that gave birth to other religions. See Yulia Egorova, Describing the "Other," Describing the "Self": Jews, Hindu Reforms, and Indian Nationalists, *Indo-Judaic Studies in the Twenty-First Century: A View from the Margin*, 2007, p. 200. Egorova references *The Complete Works of Swami Vivekananda*, vol. 1, p. 383. This understanding also made its way to the summits of Hindu-Jewish leadership. See http://www.millenniumpeacesummit.org/2nd-Hindu-Jewish_Summit_Report-Final.pdf, p. 10.

16. The historical overview of the respective importance of these religious cultures is a theme to which one returns repeatedly in encounters with individuals. I recall the issue coming up in the course of my exchanges with Swami Vijayananda, which I shall describe in a later chapter. Vijayananda shares Soderblom's perspective, though he probably never read him. The recognition that two religious cultures shaped the course of humanity's religious history means that equal respect needs to be accorded to both. The division between them is geographical. What Judaism did for the West, Hinduism has done for the East. For Vijayananda, the East is the domain of Hinduism and its daughter religions, and there is therefore no need for Judaism, and its daughter religions, to try to leave their religious imprint upon it. This insight may be related to another of Vijayananda's teachings that seekers from the West should not adopt Hindu forms of ritual practice. More on this in the discussion on Vijayananda in a later chapter.

17. The notion of complementarity of religious cultures may also allow us to revisit the problem of lack of symmetry in Jewish-Hindu relations. If we consider the encounter from the perspective of religious cultures, Judaism is being exposed for the first time on a mass scale to Indic religious culture. By contrast, Indic religious culture has been exposed for millennia to the religious cultures that sprang forth from Judaism—Christianity and Islam. This makes the singular contribution of Judaism to Hindu religious culture less easy to define and consequently makes the encounter less challenging, hence less potentially transformative, for Hindu interlocutors of Judaism.

18. Soderblom, *The Living God*, p. 300.

19. Soderblom, *The Living God*, p. 304.

20. On different senses of mitzvah, see Chapter 3 of my forthcoming Introduction to Judaism, *In God's Presence*.

21. Soderblom, *The Living God,* p. 307.
22. One typical example is R. C. Zaehner, *Hindu and Muslim Mysticism,* Athlone Press, London, 1960. Moshe Idel queries the originality of the typology of mystical/prophetic in Zaehner's work. See Kabbalah in Eliyahu ben Amozegh's Thought, appendix to *Elijah ben Amozegh: Israel and Humanity,* translated by Maxwell Luria, Paulist Press, Mahwa, 1994, p. 400, note 39. Idel points to Max Weber's brief contrast of the biblical prophet with the religious reality of India. See Max Weber, *Ancient Judaism,* translated H. Gerth and D. Martindale, Free Press, Glencoe, 1952, pp. 313–314. While it is possible that we have Weber to thank for this distinction, Weber does not develop a full-blown typology, and the common typology may have its roots in Solderblom's work. Weber's German original appeared in 1921 and Soderblom may have been aware of it.
23. Soderblom, *The Living God,* p. 317.
24. See Sinha, Divine Anthropos and Cosmic Tree, pp. 105–108.
25. Sinha, Divine Anthropos and Cosmic Tree, p. 106.
26. Sinha, Divine Anthropos and Cosmic Tree, p. 107.
27. For what follows, see Barbara Holdrege, What Have Brahmins to Do with Rabbis? Embodied Communities and Paradigms of Religious Traditions, *Shofar* 17,3, 1999, pp. 23–50.
28. Holdrege's methodological attempts to classify Judaism and Hinduism in relation to reigning Protestant paradigms provide, broadly speaking, the methodological and ideological background for those scholars involved in the emerging field of Indo-Judaic studies. This logic governs much of *Indo-Judaic Studies in the Twenty-First Century: A View from the Margin.* Because the editors of this volume took the trouble to ensure that participants in this volume, and in the conference from which it grew, responded to one another's work, Holdrege's earlier work ends up providing the rationale for a broader collective enterprise.
29. See further, Holdrege, What Have Brahmins to Do with Rabbis?, p. 25, note 2.
30. I refer to the forms that have crystallized mainly during the twentieth century, through the encounter with Hindu spiritual teachers, almost all of whom taught under the vedantic umbrella. An important exception is provided by the ISKCON movement. Despite philosophical differences, it too is missionary and transcends traditional ethnic and geographic boundaries. However, it does so while carrying over the orthopraxic dimensions of its form of Hinduism into new social settings, rather than downplaying the orthopraxic dimension of Hinduism in favor of more philosophical and metaphysical emphases.
31. Against this backdrop, it is worth noting the recent work of Elan Divon, *Reaching Beyond the Religious: Seven Universal Wisdom Themes from Seven Thousand Years of Human Experience,* Iuniverse, Bloomington IN, 2010. This book does not fit neatly into one of the categories of the present book. It is best described as a comparative reading of Judaism and Hinduism that highlights ideas, but even more so narratives, in search of common depth structures. These depth structures are then presented as universal wisdom that can speak to anyone, beyond the particularity of the two traditions. The work stakes its own ground and devises its own methodology in what is a crossover between comparative literary and conceptual analysis, and the quest for meaning, wisdom, and spirituality in daily life. One notes that Divon relies exclusively on biblical materials in his presentation of Judaism, hence the heavy reliance on depth narrative structures. His depiction of Hinduism resorts to a broader range of materials. I had initially thought this reflected a particular religious affiliation, such as do the works studied in the Appendix to Chapter 10.

In personal communication with him I learned this is mainly due to what he has studied and mastered and does not reflect an ideological or religious choice.

32. I exclude from this summary statement the analyses of individual philosophical motifs in both traditions. There is, in theory, no end to the possibilities of contrasting individual themes and motives in two bodies of religious literature. Several studies explore such comparisons between a Jewish and a Hindu author. However, the significance of such comparisons seems to me limited to the interest they evoke in a particular theme. As they do not appeal to larger issues and broader structures, they contribute more to the understanding of the thought of two individuals than to the understanding of two religious traditions and their relations. An example of such studies is Lyone Fein, Limit and Its Discontents: The Arising of Desire as Discussed by Patanjali and Isaac Luria, *Journal of Indo-Judaic Studies* 3, 2000, pp. 72–85. One area that holds great promise for comparative purposes is hermeneutics and the approach to scripture. See, recently, Daniel Klein, Rabbi Ishmael, Meet Jaimini: The Thirteen Midot of Interpretation in Light of Comparative Law, *Hakirah* 16, 2013, pp. 91–111. Holdrege's study of Veda and Torah does not explore this dimension.

33. See Kathryn McClymond, Differing Intentions in Vedic and Jewish Sacrifices, *Journal of Indo-Judaic Studies* 4, 2001, pp. 23–38. McClymond is aware of Holdrege's methodological work and follows it.

34. See R. Dennis Hudson, A Hindu Response to the Written Torah, *Between Jerusalem and Benares*, ed. Hananya. Goodman, SUNY Press, Albany, NY, 1994, pp. 55–84. The result is the opposite of those polemical efforts that identified Judaism and Christianity, to the former's detriment, discussed earlier.

35. Melila Hellner-Eshed, In India Even the Tourists Believe in God, *From India Till Here*, ed. Elhanan Nir, Rubin Mass, Jerusalem, 2006, pp. 53–60 [Hebrew]. An earlier Jewish visitor to India had a different reaction. See Peretz Hirschbein, *India*, translated by U. Z. Greenberg, Mitzpa, Tel Aviv, 1931, p. 41 [Hebrew]. For him, the high ideals of Tagore and Gandhi cannot be reconciled with the reality of worship and sacrifice.

36. Hellner plays on the rabbinic epithet of God as place, *Hamakom*.

37. Selections from Hellner, In India Even the Tourists Believe in God, pp. 55–58.

38. This is equally true of spiritual seekers who approach Kabbalah and Indian-based spiritualities as related commodities in today's spiritual supermarket. See Véronique Altglas, *From Yoga to Kabbalah: Religious Exoticism and the Logics of Bricolage*, Oxford University Press, Oxford 2014.

39. It is even more striking if one sees in the vedantic tradition as much, and possibly more, of a tradition of scriptural interpretation and philosophical reflection as a tradition that is based upon mystical experience. See John Thatamanil, *The Immanent Divine: God, Creation and the Human Predicament, an East-West Conversation*, Fortress Press, Minneapolis, 2006, pp. 60–66.

40. Such work may be ideologically motivated, as are the works by Rosen and Boxer, discussed in an appendix to a later chapter. Or it may be scientifically motivated, as is E. M. Abrahams's work, *A Comparative Survey of Hindu, Christian and Jewish Mysticism*, Sri Satguru Publications, Delhi, 1995. This reworking of a PhD thesis is based entirely on secondary material and advances discussion little, beyond suggesting basic parallels to the mystical life, seen mainly from the perspective of the Hindu tradition, with which the author seems to have greater familiarity. Some points that are worthy of note are the parallels between sefirot and chakras (pp. 196–197), and the suggested parallels between brahman and ein-sof, considered in terms of their functionality in the philosophical/mystical system.

41. See note 26.

42. See Diane Sharon, Mystic Autobiography: A Case Study in Comparative Literary Analysis, *Journal of Indo-Judaic Studies* 1,2, 1999, pp. 27–52. A shorter version appeared as The Mystic's Experience of God: A Comparison of the Mystical Techniques and Experiences of a 13th Century Jewish Mystic and a 20th Century Indic Yogi, *The Fifty-Eighth Century, a Jewish Renewal Sourcebook*, ed. Shohama Wiener, Jason Aaronson, Northvale, NJ, 1996, pp. 315–330. The author is a biblical scholar, not a scholar of Kabbalah, and her knowledge, as that of so many of those who refer to Kabbalah in the comparative context, is second hand. Do these early articles grow out of her own personal spiritual experiences with the twentieth-century figure Swami Muktananda, whom she compares to Abulafya (the most readily available Jewish mystic for purposes of comparison with mystic phenomena of other religions)? Other scholars, affiliated with Muktananda, can be found in the Academy. See the work by Douglas Brooks, Taking Sides and Opening Doors: Authority and Integrity in the Academy's Hinduism, *JAAR* 68,4, 2000, pp. 817–829.

43. See Appendix to chapter 10.

44. Ibid.

45. The author Miriam Bokser Caravella is the daughter of Rabbi Ben Zion Bokser, who was a translator of kabbalistic and mystical materials and who published several important anthologies. His daughter would thus come honestly by her own predisposition to present Judaism in kabbalistic terms. Curiously, as the author seeks to present the Jewish mystical tradition, she draws more heavily on the Hebrew Bible than on any other text. Still, it is significant that in seeking to portray Judaism in light of another religion, she so naturally assumes Jewish mysticism as her address within Judaism.

46. Charles Mopsik's insightful words were already quoted above.

47. See Arthur Green, Shekhinah, the Virgin Mary and the Song of Songs: Reflections on a Kabbalistic Symbol in Its Historical Context, *AJS Review* 26,1, 2002, pp. 1–52.

48. From an autobiographical perspective, I find it very significant that Nathan Katz, in *Spiritual Journey Home*, Ktav, Jersey City, 2009, p. xv, considers this parallel to be the heart of his own spiritual journey. Note, however, that even though Katz is exposed to Hinduism, most of his significant experiences, including initiation, actually take place within a Buddhist context. Thus, it is India that impacts him, more than Hinduism. See p. xii of his introduction. The title of Chapter 6, "Becoming a Hindu in Benares" is therefore really a misnomer.

49. Braj Sinha, Feminizations of the Divine: *Sakti* and *Shekhinah* in Tantra and Kabbalah, *Journal of Indo-Judaic Studies* 10, 2009, pp. 25–45; Neela Bhattacharya Saxena, Shekhina on the "Plane of Immanence": An intimation of the Indic Great Mother in the Hebraic Wholly Other, *Journal of Indo-Judaic Studies* 12, 2012, pp. 27–44.

50. Nathan Katz, in the framework of a theoretical statement, with regard to the future of the Jewish-Hindu encounter, suggests that Jewish esotericism has a crucial role in this dialogue. See Katz, The Hindu-Jewish Encounter and the Future, *The Fifty Eighth Century: A Jewish Renewal Sourcebook*, ed. Shohama Wiener, p. 337.

7   The Passage to India: The Quest for Spirituality

1. See Hugh Urban, *Tantra: Sex, Secrecy, Politics, and Power in the Study of Religion*, Motilal Banarsidass, Delhi, 2007, pp. 155–156. See further, Abhik Roy and Michele Hammers, Swami Vivekananda's Rhetoric of Spiritual Masculinity, *Western Journal of Communication* 78,4, 2014, pp. 545–562.

2. See Barbara Holdrege, What Have Brahmins to Do with Rabbis? Embodied Communities and Paradigms of Religious Traditions, *Shofar* 17,3, 1999.

3. See *Minding the Spirit: The Study of Christian Spirituality,* ed. Elizabeth Dreyer and Mark Burrows, Johns Hopkins, Baltimore, MD, 2005; *Exploring Christian Spirituality: Essays in Honor of Sandra M Schneiders,* ed. Bruce Lescher and Elizabeth Liebert, Paulist Press, Mahwa, 2006.

4. Amma speaks Malayalam only. The comment is therefore relevant to how she is being translated and to the regular use of "Spirituality" in English translations of her discourses.

5. See Moshe Idel, *Hasidism: Between Ecstacy and Magic,* SUNY Press, Albany, New York, pp. 65–81. Yehuda Halevy's presentation of Hinduism in *Kuzari* 1, 60–62, relates negatively to Indian religion in precisely these terms, considering the inefficacy of Hindu spirituality. It is rather ironic that today's Jewish seekers turn to India with a sense of the efficacy of Hindu practice in terms of spirituality, though we must recognize that they refer to the third sense of spirituality in the present discussion.

6. Sandra Schneiders, A Hermeneutical Approach to the Study of Christian Spirituality, *Minding the Spirit: The Study of Christian Spirituality,* ed. Elizabeth Dreyer and Mark Burrows, p. 51.

7. Elhanan Nir, Where Is the Time of No Movement, *From India Till Here,* ed. Elhanan Nir, Rubin Mass, Jerusalem, 2006, p. 12 [Hebrew], my translation.

8. Nir, Where Is the Time of No Movement, pp. 22–23. Judaism represents the return to the world and the spiritual life practiced in the world.

9. I have recently learned of a Safed-based organization that seeks to provide Jewish meditation techniques to alumni of the passage to India, working with meditation techniques derived from the tradition of the Ari. Rabbi Meir Sendor has been instrumental in facilitating the work of the Hashra'a Center of Safed.

10. Shalva Weil, The Influence of Indo-Judaic Studies in Israel, or the Salience of Spirituality, *Journal of Indo-Judaic Studies* 7–8, 2004–5, pp. 5–11. The piece was originally intended to serve as Weil's introduction to the volume *Indo-Judaic Studies in the Twenty-First Century,* hence the first part of its title.

11. Some of these ideas were articulated in my paper "When Will I See the Face of God? On the Experience of God's Presence in Our Religious World, *Akdamot* 9, 2000, pp. 119–130 [Hebrew].

12. The maxim is often ascribed to the Zohar; however, as Isaiah Tishby has shown, it does not exist in this form in the Zohar. While the idea has precedents and analogues, the maxim itself seems to have been created by Moses Hayim Luzatto (1707–1746). See Isaiah Tishby, "God, the Torah and Israel Are One": The Source of the Saying in Ramhal's Commentary on the *Idra Rabba, Kiryat Sefer* 50, 1975, pp. 480–492 [Hebrew]; Bracha Sack, More on the Saying "Kudsha-beik-hu Orayta ve-Yisrael Kola Had," *Kiryat Sefer* 57, 1982, pp. 179–184 [Hebrew].

13. The practice is shared by Sufism. My impression is that, in quantative terms, the practice of *japa* is more pervasive than the Sufi practice of *dhikr*. It is more common, takes up more time, is practiced in a broader range of circumstances, and for longer.

14. Maharishi Mahesh Yogi is the prime example, teaching meditation as a technique, while divesting it of its religious meaning. While Maharishi did not make a personal God the focus or goal of the system, the Divine, as understood in classical Vedanta, maintains its place of importance in his various writings.

15. My admiring thoughts were, I must admit, somewhat tempered by concern for how realistic were Vinod's goals. To what extent had he been told too many stories that

lacked spiritual realism, leading him to a false expectation of achieving something that could not be all that readily achieved, even if it does exist?

16. Lakh, in Indian english, is 100,000; crore is 10,000,000.

17. Rivka Miriam, On Two Conflicting Visits to India, *From India Till Here*, ed. Elhanan Nir, Rubin Mass, Jerusalem, 2006, p. 41–42, 45.

18. Not only the earth, as in Isaiah. Christian liturgy achieves the same by adding the heaven to the earth, filled by God's glory.

19. *Tikunei Zohar*, Tikun 57 (91b) and Tikun 70 (122b). This statement is often juxtaposed with the previous paraphrase of Isaiah in hassidic literature. See *Noam Elimelech* on Terumah, *Degel Machane Ephraim* on Beshalach and Re'eh.

20. Bavli *Yoma* 69b.

21. Yoel Glick, *Living the Life of Jewish Meditation: A Comprehensive Guide to Practice and Experience* Jewish Lights Publishing, Woodstock Vermont, 2014.

22. Full disclosure: Yoel and I are close friends and fellow travelers on the spiritual path, drawing from the same sources. I can only state my hope that this closeness does not prejudice my view of his work.

23. This is how Glick's overall teaching method may be characterized. Prior to the publication of this book, Glick has put together a significant body of teachings that follows this pattern. See daatelyon.org.

24. Glick, *Living the Life of Jewish Meditation*, p. viii.

25. Though his training with his teacher was not exclusively in Hinduism.

26. Ramakrishna occupies a place of honor, based on the frequency of citations in his name. The only figure who is mentioned more frequently than Ramakrishna is the Ba'al Shem Tov.

27. Glick, *Living the Life of Jewish Meditation*, p. ix.

28. Glick, *Living the Life of Jewish Meditation*, p. xx.

29. This touches on the question of Glick's intended audience. Whereas at face value, Glick's project is most suitable for Jewish seekers who have had exposure to Hinduism, the above discussion suggests Glick is seeking to correct something more fundamental within Judaism, as presently practiced. Accordingly, his project is relevant also, and perhaps especially, for the spiritually devout who may be missing something in their spiritual life. The problems attendant upon addressing a traditional audience emerge in the review of his work by hassidic author Dovid Sears. See https://kavvanah.wordpress.com/2014/10/27/dovid-searsreview-of-yoel-glick-part-i/and https://kavvanah.wordpress.com/2014/10/19/interview-with-yoel-glickpart-2/.

30. For a summary statement of this possibility, see Moshe Idel, Reifications of Language in Jewish Mysticism, *Mysticism and Language*, ed. Steven Katz, Oxford University Press, New York and Oxford, 1992, pp. 42–79. I am much struck by the absence of the term "silence" from the index of a work like Idel's *Kabbalh: New Perspectives*, Yale University Press, New Haven, 1988, as well as from all other monographs by him I consulted. Elliot Wolfson's theoretically dense discussion in *Language, Eros, Being: Kabbalistic Hermeneutics and Poetic Imagination*, Fordham University Press, New York, 2005, ends up pointing in the same direction, with some important nuance. It is noteworthy that all theoretical discussion of silence is taken from twentieth-century philosophers and not from the kabbalists themselves.

31. For one case study of the respective place of speech and silence in the teachings of a Jewish mystic, see Alon Goshen-Gottstein, Speech, Silence, Song: Epistemology and Theodicy in a Teaching of R. Nahman of Breslav, *Philosophia* 30, 2003, pp. 143–187.

32. At the same time, I know from exchanges with Yoel that his method is not simply eclectic but informed by certain positions that are either historical reconstructions of

Judaism or broader approaches to issues of comparative religion. These relate to his spiritual perspective both as theoretical preconditions and as theoretical constructs that grow from it. The work before us does not reveal the full extent of Glick's theoretical engagement with some of the issues that are pointed out in my discussion. Glick has made a strategic decision to create a user's manual and to not include in it his theological, historical, or comparative reasoning, at least not in a systematic way. As a matter of fact, I know that he has removed some of those theoretical discussions from his work, given his understanding of the purpose of the present book.

33. This is why I think it is a mistake to read Glick as offering an Advaita Vedanta reading of Judaism, as Alan Brill suggests. See https://kavvanah.wordpress.com/2014/10/19/interview-with-yoel-glick-part-2/. Glick's project is the spiritual life as such and not a particular philosophical system.

34. Glick, *Living the Life of Jewish Meditation*, p. xv.

35. We noted it above with reference to E. M.Abrahams, *A Comparative Survey of Hindu, Christian and Jewish Mysticism*, Sri Satguru Publications, Delhi, 1995. Rene Guenon, *Studies in Hinduism*, Sophia Perennis, Hillsdale, 2001, pp. 26–28, offers a detailed parallelism between chakras and sefirot. Guenon presents this as an original observation that had not been previously made. Guenon first published this study in 1933 in Voile d'Isis Oct/Nov. 1933. I am grateful to Paul Fenton for drawing my attention to Guenon's work.

36. See further on this Alan Brill, Hindu Tantra and Kabbalistic Judaism, https://kavvanah.wordpress.com/2014/10/21/hindu-tantra-and-kabbalistic-judaism/.

37. The pattern of relationship between the religions varies from chapter to chapter. To take the extreme cases, the chapter on steadiness of mind is all Hindu, while the discussion of contemplation is devoid of Hindu sources. Glick is served by both traditions as resources, upon which he draws at will. Despite his opening statement, he is not bound to a predefined formula for the interaction of both traditions.

38. Chapter 8 of his work, with earlier references on p. 51ff. The phenomenon of spiritual borrowing of Hindu practice and converting it to a Jewish spiritual language can be found also in the adaptation of Hindu liturgical musical practices to Jewish worship. Rabbi Andrew Hahn is known as Kirtan Rabbi. His practice is in fact a Jewish musical adaptation of a Hindu form of worship that uses mantric repetition set to music. See kirtanrabbi.com. Whereas Glick offers meditation techniques that complement standard liturgical practices, Hahn imports Hindu devotional methods into the heart of Jewish liturgy.

39. See the discussion of Persico Tomer, *"Jewish Meditation": The Development of a Modern Form of Spiritual Practice in Contemporary Judaism*, PhD thesis, Tel Aviv University, 2012.

40. Glick, *Living the Life of Jewish Meditation*, p. 93.

41. There are precedents for this and I believe Amritanandamayi is one such precedent.

42. Glick never engages the fundamental difference of attitude to the divine name in both traditions, where one tradition makes it the focal point of devotion, while the other avoids reference to the name, as a sign of reverence.

43. The problem of theological propriety is encountered in several important junctures, where theological formulations proper to Hinduism are deemed, with no argument, not only appropriate to Judaism but as its spiritual quest and the very quest of the spiritual life. This applies to the facility of declaration of the possibility of union with God and to the affirmation of one's own identity with the Divine. See pp. 18 and 48. From this perspective, the first part of Chapter 11, describing union, is particularly

problematic and, not surprisingly, lacks convincing Jewish sources. The same holds true for Chapter 12, where we find a discussion of personal and impersonal meditation, devoid of Jewish sources. I am not sure I would even know how to say in Jewish terms what Glick is saying here.

44. Glick provides a Hebrew version of chanting *kiriye eleison*, claiming this simple prayer is used to evoke the All Merciful's infinite compassion by all of the Abrahamic faiths (p. 103). If so, this would be a common Jewish-Christian-Muslim prayer and a great common ground for interreligious prayer. In fact, it is being introduced from Christianity into Judaism by Glick.

45. Glick, *Living the Life of Jewish Meditation*, p. 114ff.

46. Glick informs me that these practices were devised with theory in view and an attempt to remain faithful to it. In my view, they can be considered independently of their theoretical grounding.

47. Glick, *Living the Life of Jewish Meditation*, p. 59 ff.

48. The theme of loss appears repeatedly, as Glick either projects or recovers biblical motifs that illustrate the spiritual life, as he presents it. See, for example, Glick, *Living the Life of Jewish Meditation*, p. 91.

49. https://kavvanah.wordpress.com/2014/10/14/interview-with-yoel-glick-part-one/, question 9. This statement illicits strong reactions in Sears's review, part 2. Glick seems to have got himself into unnecessary controversy, first, by agreeing to speak in terms that are not common to both traditions and have not been adequately defined (realized, enlightened) and, second, by suggesting there are today enlightened individuals on the Hindu side, and not on the Jewish side. As it is, his project is one of introducing spiritual giants of the two traditions to his audience through their written legacy. Nowhere does Glick refer to a living teacher of either tradition.

50. See N. Wieder, *Islamic Influences on the Jewish Worship*, East-West Library, Oxford, 1947 [Hebrew]; Mordechai Friedman, Abraham Maimuni's Prayer Reforms: Continuation or Revision of His Father's Teachings? *Traditions of Maimonideism*, ed. Carlos Fraenkel, Brill, Leiden, 2009, pp. 139–154; Paul Fenton, Abraham Maimonides (1186–1237): Founding a Mystical Dynasty, *Jewish Mystical Leaders and Leadership in the 13th Century*, ed. M.Idel and M.Ostow, Aronson, Northvale, NJ, 1998, pp. 127–154.

8   Saints: Encountering the Divine in Humanity

1. This touches upon the choice of category by means of which we speak of such individuals. I am presently engaged in a project of developing the category of "Religious Genius" as a means of describing exemplary individuals in different religious traditions, with the support of the John Templeton Foundation. Unlike "saints" and other categories, this category is not charged through its use by any particular religious tradition.

2. See Bavli *Hullin* 92a. The text has a very limited echo in later Jewish literature.

3. The matter deserves more detailed investigation. It seems to me that on the whole even in those contexts where non-Jews are seen in a positive light, they are singled our for moral excellence, sometimes even for faithfulness to ritual and the religious life. They are certainly recognized for wisdom. But reference to them as saints, as people of outstanding holiness, enjoying special and close relationships with God, is something one rarely, if ever, comes across. My impression is that this is the case both in relation to Christianity and in relation to Islam, though further study could

reveal greater recognition of Muslim spiritual excellence, especially in the context of Jewish Sufism.

4. Wisdom is the paradigmatic exception and it provides a framework within which to appreciate members of other religions. A good example of this may be found in R. Yaakov Emden's *Resen Mat'eh*, a revolutionary tractate, in which he assesses Christianity and its founder. Despite saying some of the most positive things ever said about Jesus and Christianity, even Emden does not portray Christians in terms of saintliness. He speaks of them in terms of morality, historical purpose, and wisdom. The vocabulary of *zadikim* is reserved for Jews. One assumes that a person as widely read as Emden could have been exposed not only to the New Testament, which he analyzes in detail in this tract ate, but also to the lives of Christians and their moral and spiritual examples. This kind of literature seems to not have made any impression upon even one of the most open-minded of rabbinic authors.

5. Hindus often translate the native Hindu term *sadhu*, meaning holy man or renunciant as "saint." This intuitive translation, using a term that is heavily charged in light of Christian history and convention, corresponds to our ability to convey the Jewish notion of *zadikim* by the same term. On the challenges associated with "saints," see my concept paper titled "Religious Genius," authored for the above-mentioned project.

6. This is reflected in Elhanan Nir, Where Is the Time of Non-Movement, *From India Till Here*, ed. E.Nir, Rubin Mass, Jerusalem, 2006, pp. 7–31.

7. Recognition of this will be expressed in how we dub these individuals. Nir uses classical rabbinic terminology, referring to them as *zadikim*, thereby expressing the recognition that they are of a kind with Jewish saints, can be compared, and that one can learn from the Hindu species of the same genum. It has been noted that one of the characteritics of Azriel Carlebach's *India: A Road Journal*, Ayanot, Tel Aviv, 1956 [Hebrew] is its choice of positive biblical language to describe Hindu religious reality, rather than the potentially more derogatory rabbinic terminology.

8. As a matter of fact, during the first Hindu-Jewish summit, Israeli Chief Rabbi, Yonah Metzger, visited the Delhi Akshardham complex. It thus made its impact on the margins of the first official encounter between Judaism and Hinduism. The interface between museological, spiritual, and ritual dimensions of this establishment poses interesting challenges, as far as Avoda Zara is concerned, but I imagine that circumstances did not permit the Chief Rabbi a thorough study of the problem.

9. See Gilbert Rosenthal, "As-If" Theology and Liberal Judaism, *Conservative Judaism* 39,1, 1986, pp. 34–45

10. On Moses, see my discussion in chapter 8 of *Israel in God's Presence*, forthcoming.

11. See Rudolf Mach, *Der Zaddik in Talmud und Midrasch*, Brill, Leiden, 1957; E. E. Urbach, *The Sages: Their Concepts and Beliefs*, Magness Press, Jerusalem, 1975, pp. 487–511; Arthur Green, The Zaddik as *Axis Mundi* in Later Judaism, *Journal of American Academy of Religion* 45,3, 1977, pp. 327–347; Gershom Scholem, *On the Mystical Shape of the Godhead*, Schoken, New York, 1991, Chapter 3; Moshe Idel, *Hasidism: Between Ecstasy and Magic*, SUNY Press, Albany, NY, 1995, Chapter 6.

12. See the discussion of Maimonides' definition of Avoda Zara in *Same God, Other god*.

13. The most pronounced case in recent memory are charges leveled by contemporary *mitnagedim* against Rabbi Menachem Schneerson, the Lubavitcher Rebbe. See also David Berger, *The Rebbe, the Messiah and the Scandal of Orthodox Indifference*, Littman Library, London, 2001.

14. This is one of the central issues discussed in *Same God, Other god.*

15. See Susan Palmer, Rajneesh Women: Lovers and Leaders in a Utopian Commune, *The Rajneesh Papers: Studies in a New Religious Movement,* ed. Susan Palmer and Arvind Sharma, Motilal Banarsidass, Delhi, 1993, pp. 103–136. The author's introduction references additional relevant sources.

16. As one example of many, see http://www.rickross.com/reference/saibaba/saibaba7.html.

17. Another famous swami whose name has been associated with sexual scandals is Swami Muktananda. However, to the best of my knowledge his disciples did not refer to him as bhagwan. Coming to terms with their founder's problematic sexual behavior and transformation of the movement and its orientation are conscious foci of the movements leaders and thinkers. Their response seems to be the opposite of the denial that characterizes other instances. See Gene Thursby, Swami Muktananda and the Seat of Power, *When Prophets Die: The Postcharismatic Fate of New Religious Movements,* ed. Timothy Miller, SUNY Press, Albany, NY, 1991, pp. 165–182. See also Douglas Brooks, Taking Sides and Opening Doors: Authority and Integrity in the Academy's Hinduism, *Journal of American Academy of Religion* 68,4, 2000, pp. 817–829. News of such problems associated with one leading contemporary religious figure have reached my ear, but as they are not public I shall not go beyond this basic statement.

9   The Wisdom of India: Ancient Images and Contemporary Challenges

1. See Meir Bar Ilan, India and the Land of Israel: Between Jews and Indians in Ancient Times, *Journal of Indo Judaic Studies* 4, 2001.

2. War of the Jews, 7, pp. 323–388 See Frances Schmidt, Between Jews and Greeks: The Indian Model, *Between Jerusalem and Benares,* ed. Hananya. Goodman, SUNY Press, Albany, NY, 1994, pp. 48–53.

3. War of the Jews, 7, pp. 351–356.

4. See Schmidt's entire discussion, Between Jews and Greeks, pp. 41–53.

5. There are very few studies on this issue. I am indebted in what follows to two articles by Richard Marks. The first is Abraham, the Easterners and India: Jewish Interpretation of Genesis 25,6, *Journal of Indo-Judaic Studies* 3, 2000, pp. 49–71; the second is Chapter 3 in *Indo-Judaic Studies in the Twenty-First Century,* pp. 57–73, titled Hindus and Hinduism in Medieval Jewish Literature, as well as to Abraham Melamed, The Image of India in Medieval Jewish Culture: Between Adoration and Rejection, *Jewish History* 20, 2006, pp. 299–314 [Hebrew]. My own presentation reworks some of the materials brought by Marks and Melamed, according to my specific thematic focus.

6. Melamed demonstrates how this Muslim view is itself a continuation of older hellenistic views.

7. Or in some cases leads to casting wisdom as a kind of prophecy. See Shem Tov Falaquera, Ethical Epistle, ed. A. M. Haberman, *Kovetz al Yad* 1, Jerusalem, 1936, pp. 76–78, translated by Melamed, p. 21: "I am from the land of India, from the seed of ancient sages. All my ancestors had ancient beliefs, but only I am left, a prophet of wisdom, an old man of cunning."

8. I would suggest this is a more appropriate way of summarizing the data and its nuances, than the repeated emphasis on the ambivalence and tension between

adoration and rejection that Melamed argues for. I do not find his presentation of such sustained ambivalence justified by the texts.

9. See Marks, Abraham, the Easterners and India, p. 62ff.

10. The Book of Beliefs and Opinions 3,9.

11. I find this to be a more compelling reading of Saadiah, than the reading of Marks, according to whom Saadiah views them as a religious sect that accepts only the prophetic authority of Adam. See Richard Marks, Hindus and Hinduism in Medieval Jewish Literature, p. 59. What we have here is a theoretical construct, and not a view of the historical India, as understood in medieval times. This is no doubt of interest, in and of itself. Hinduism serves as a meaningful theoretical alternative to Christianity and Islam.

12. Quoted in Richard Marks, Hindus and Hinduism, p. 63.

13. Kuzari 1,61.

14. Richard Marks provides a thorough exposition of Halevy's discussion in a chapter of his forthcoming *The Jewish Interest in Hinduism: A History of Ideas from Judah Halevi to Jacob Sapir*. It is worth noting that even though Halevy speaks of images, he is not, as Marks points out, referring to Hindu image worship, but offers a view of talismanic magic, relying on images, which he, and other medieval authors, ascribes to the Indians. There is no suggestion in Halevy that Hindus worship other gods. The wisdom paradigm may therefore assume a monotheistic view of God. The same cannot be said of Saadiah, who shares the view of Indian idol worship and even recognizes Hindu theory, but nevertheless refers to Indians as worshippers of idols. See his commentary to Ex. 32, 1–6, where he speaks of Indians, rather than Brahmins. Marks reconstructs Halevy's views, based on various Muslim authorities, revealing thereby how extensive Halevy's knowledge of contemporary Muslim literature is. The charge of magic is a second strand in Halevy's thinking, which may be conceptually indebted to the lack of true revelation, but at the end of the day functions as a self-standing critique of Hindu practice. The critique is based on the inefficacy of astral magic rather than on issues of appropriate worship and is in line with Halevy's overall reasoning that judges religions by the degree of their efficacy in drawing forth the Divine.

15. Indeed, as Marks shows, what draws forth Halevy's ire is where Hindu claims for their tradition go beyond the historical boundaries established by biblical revelation. It is thus the undermining of revelation that leads to what is in fact the longest treatment of Hinduism in medieval Jewish literature (though still a fairly short one at that). This point is particularly interesting, given contemporary self-understanding of Hindus as belonging to an ancient, possibly the most ancient religion.

16. Halevy is representative of a broader trend among Jewish philosophers in the Middle Ages. Wisdom and magic are conflated, and the wise men of India, or the East in general, are presented as magicians. See Dov Schwartz, *Astrology and Magic in Jewish Thought in the Middle Ages*, Bar Ilan University Press, Ramat Gan, 1999, pp. 170, 214. I am grateful to Alan Brill for referencing these sources. On the wisdom of the East, see Zohar I, 99b–100a, and see Richard Marks, Abraham, the Easterners and India, pp. 49–71.

17. Menashe ben Israel, *Nishmat Hayim* 4,21, Jerusalem, 1998.

18. As noted, Marks devotes a special study to this verse's interpretation.

19. Alan Brill, *Judaism and World Religions: Encountering Christianity, Islam and Eastern Traditions*, Palgrave Macmillan, New York, 2012, p. 208, refers to Menashe's knowledge of the Portugese Pedro Teixiera, and his writings of 1610.

20. It is quite curious that Abraham should serve as a figure through whom other religions are legitimated, even if partially. We see here that such legitimation extends

beyond the realm of what are considered today "Abrahamic" faiths, and includes the religion of India, as well. For other associations of Abraham and Hindu tradition, see David Flusser, Abraham and the Upanishads, *Between Jerusalem and Benares*, pp. 33–40. It is interesting to note that Muslim authors also associated Abraham and brahaman and Hinduism in general with Abraham. See Seyyed Hossein Nasr, *Sufi Essays*, G. Allen and Unwin, London, 1972, p. 139. On the problematic nature of the designation of certain religions as "Abrahamic," see my own Abraham and Abrahamic Religions in Contemporary Interreligious Discourse: Reflections of an Implicated Jewish Bystander, *Studies in Interreligious Dialogue* 12,2, 2002, pp. 165–183 and more recently Aaron Hughes, *Abrahamic Religions: On the Uses and Abuses of History*, Oxford University Press, New York, 2012.

21. Rabbi Matityahu Glazerson, *From Hinduism to Judaism*, Himelsein Glazerson Publishers, Jerusalem, 1984.

22. Yitzchak Ginsburgh, http://torahscience.org/Chanuka,%20India%20and%20the%20 Structure%20of%20the%20Soul.pdf. This teaching is discussed in http://kavvanah. wordpress.com/2013/11/27/rabbi-yitzchak-ginsburgh-on-chanukah-and-israelis-in- india/.

23. Ginsburgh, p. 1.

24. It is noteworthy that Ginsubrgh's teaching plays on the word צלם, which describes both the image of God that has to be reconstituted through the spiritual search in India and the false images associated with image worship. He uses the term exclusively in the former context, avoiding, like Glazerson, any discussion of image worship.

25. See Melamed. Note in particular how India and Africa were confused in the common imagination, as described by Melamed Abraham, The Image of India in Medieval Jewish Culture: Between Adoration and Rejection, *Jewish History* 20, 2006, p. 310ff.

26. This is the subject of a forthcoming study by Richard Mark's, who studies the various medieval Jewish authority from this angle.

27. See his commentary on Gen. 24,2; 46, 3; Ex. 8,22; 19,9; Psalms 2,12 and Daniel 1,15. These examples and more are discussed by Marks in a chapter on Ibn Ezra in his forthcoming work.

28. So for Ibn Ezra. Other authors, as demonstrated by Marks, use the same data to opposite conclusions.

29. Scholars seem to differ on whether Benjamin ever made it to India in person or not. According to Melamed, p. 311, Benjamin's description is influenced by Muslim texts and does not constitute an eyewitness report. Furthermore, as in many cases in the Middle Ages, India and Ethiopia or Africa have been confused and identified, thereby detracting further from the reliability of this witness. Marks, Hindus and Hinduism, pp. 65–67, on the other hand, reads Benjamin as a faithful report of his own travels, even if it was reworked by reference to biblical materials.

30. This is also true of Maimonides' reference to the people of India, in the Guide of the Perplexed 3,29 and 3,46. However, Maimonides is not really helpful to our discussion. India is related to in the framework of his broader treatment of the Sabians. As such, it has little to do not only with the Indian religion per se, but even with the broader cultural image of India in the Middle Ages. Situating Indian religion within a discussion that focuses on idolatry may or may not indicate awareness of the actual religious practices of Hinduism. In any event, it is worth noting that Maimonides approaches Hinduism with sensibilities similar to the contemporary ones, and very much at odds with the common approach to Hinduism as wisdom, current in the Middle Ages.

31. Indian teachers tend to emphasize the experiential aspect that informs the philosophical and mystical insights that contribute to contemporary Hinduism's teachings. This is particularly true in relation to the Upanishads and the teachings of Vedanta. While the Vedas do come under the category of texts that have been heard, and therefore form a parallel of sorts to revealed scripture, there are meaningful differences in understanding the nature of such revelation. For a description of the Hindu understanding of scripture, see Wilfred Cantwell Smith, *What Is Scripture? A Comparative Approach*, Fortress Press, Minneapolis, 1993, Chapter 6.
32. A. J. Heschel, *God in Search of Man*, Farrar Straus, New York, 1955, p. 15.
33. Notably Gutman Locks, *There Is One*, Jerusalem, self published, 1989. Some modern Hindu figures provide the basis against which a Jewish thinker could articulate his own unique positions. Sri Aurobindo is one such figure. See Miriam Dean-Otting, Hugo Bergman, Leo Baeck, and Martin Buber, Jewish Perspectives on Hinduism and Buddhism, *Journal of Indo Judaic Studies*, 1,2, 1999, pp. 7–26. See also Chapter 5 of Margaret Chatterjee, *Studies in Modern Jewish and Hindu Thought*, Macmillan, London, 1997, devoted to a comparison of Sri Aurobindo and Rav Kook.
34. As indicated above in relation to the volume *Karmic Passages*, travelers to India have provided feeders for the academic study of Hinduism. A similar process may be envisaged in terms of theological reflection, in dialogue with Hinduism and other Eastern religions.
35. The essays collected in *From India Till Here* provide a first taste of such encounters, as do various posts and publications on the Internet by Rabbi Yakov Nagen. The movement can be recognized also in the autobiographical reports of Nathan Katz and David Zeller. See Nathan Katz, *Spiritual Journey Home: Eastern Mysticism to the Western Home*, Ktav, Jersey City, 2009 and David Zeller, *The Soul of the Story: Meetings with Remarkable People*, Jewish Lights, Woodstock, 2006. Reflections on the spiritual significance of the encounter with Indian religion as an instrument for Jewish spiritual regeneration can also be found in Odeya Zuriely's *Transitions*, Rubin Mass, Jerusalem, 2009 [Hebrew], see in particular pp. 33–38.
36. Rabbi Yoel Glick has developed a small body of teachings, captured in a genre and style particular to him, where wisdom teachings of Jewish and Hindu masters blend into a composite spiritual vision. It is noteworthy that his website is named *da'at elyon*, higher wisdom or the wisdom or consciousness of the highest. See www.daatelyon.org. On Glick's major contribution to the field, see Appendix to Chapter 7.
37. Francis Clooney, *Hindu God, Christian God*, Oxford University Press, Oxford, 2001.
38. In a Jewish context, combining it with classical Jewish learning, notably by Ohad Ezrahi. I consider these attempts flaky and not on par with parallel Christian attempts. The drive may, in the future, yield more mature fruits.
39. I found particularly helpful the work of Brockington, even though it is more comparativist and descriptive than constructive. See John Brockington, *Hinduism and Christianity*, Macmillan, London, 1992.
40. This doesn't mean that God-talk has ceased completely. It has continued through some of the existing genres, such as hassidic teaching, as exemplified in works of the late Rabbis Schneerson of Lubavitch and Berezovsky of Slonim and others. The point I am making is that Jewish religious thought and how it perceives God and the world has not been significantly challenged in quite a while.
41. One of the theological challenges of the encounter consists of exploring the very tension and distinction between monotheism and monism. The distinction is indebted as much to the question of God and creation, discussed here, as to the question of the relationship between the personal and impersonal God, to be discussed

presently. The challenge is to reflect upon whether monism might be the higher goal that monotheism points to, and therefore a metaphysical fulfillment of monotheism, or whether the metaphysical view of creation and the theological understanding of God should be kept distinct. Of course, this is not only a discussion to be had between religions, but also a discussion within Judaism. Jewish proponents of a pantheistic, or panentheistic, view would intuitively recognize monism, or panentheism, as the higher meaning of the recognition of the one God.

42. One author who would respond positively to these questions is Gutman Locks, mentioned in note 33.

43. See Lynn White Jr., The Historical Roots of Our Ecological Crisis, *Science* 155, 1967, pp. 1203–1207.

44. Exclusive focus upon the creation story ignores the covenantal-revelational framework that offsets the perspective that is suggested through this reading of the creation story. See the various responses to White in *Judaism and Environmental Ethics*, ed. Martin D. Yaffe, Lexington Books, Lanham, MD, 2001, listed in the index. It is worth noting that in the context of the new beginning of creation, following the flood, most of Gen. 1,28 is repeated, with the exception of reference to conquering. See Gen. 9,1–2.

45. See Norbert Samuelson, *Jewish Faith and Modern Science: On the Death and Rebirth of Jewish Philosophy*, Rowman and Littlefield, Plymouth, 2009.

46. Maimonides, Laws of the Foundation of the Torah, Chapter 1, 1–6, my translation.

47. This in contradistinction to what seems to be the plain sense of the introduction to the ten commandments, linking the Sinai revelation with the particularity of Israel's tale, the Exodus from Egypt, as the preamble to the particular covenantal relationship God is about to conclude with Israel. Rabbinic interpretation, while losing sight of the overall covenantal structures, remains true to the biblical understanding, in reading the opening statement of the decalogue as "accepting the yoke of the kingdom of heaven," which, as Kimelman has demonstrated, provides continuity with the biblical covenant. See Reuven Kimelman, The *Shema* Liturgy: From Covenant Ceremony to Coronation, *Kenishta: Studies of the Synagogue World*, ed. Joseph Tabory, Bar Ilan University Press, Ramat Gan, 2001, pp. 9–105. Thus, this reading of Maimonides is original and it is only on common philosophical soil that it can grow.

48. The third attribute that goes along with these two, based on the teaching of the Upanishads, is bliss.

49. The question of "truth" and which view is metaphysically "correct" is therefore not simply a difference between religions, but also a difference between different voices within the same religion.

50. This formulation accords with the tenets of Advaita Vedanta. Other schools understand worship differently. Accordingly, rather than worship everything *as* God, ultimately making worship an impossibility, God is worshipped *in* everything, without ultimately being identified with everything. This also has consequences for what objects are worshipped. Non-monist schools tend to focus their worship on the person of God (usually of Vishnu), rather than on various manifestations in nature.

51. The "same God" issue provides a core axis for analysis in *Same God, Other god*. I reference this subject here only briefly, inasmuch as it has implications for wisdom and for the possibility of inspiration across traditions.

52. A dialogue with philosophy or Kabbalah is of obvious interest and will in some way impact an encounter based on more conventional understandings of God.

53. This raises the interesting question of the relationship between Christian and Hindu reference to incarnation. I would propose that while in many respects similar claims

may be made on both sides, the fundamental metaphysical background is different. In the Christian context one is not dealing with a metaphysic that is dualistic in this sense and that requires bridging. Hence the difficulty in accounting for incarnation, against the background of traditional Judaism, and hence the uniqueness of the incarnation in Jesus, seen as a one-time event. For a Jewish appreciation of the Christian incarnation, see my Judaisms and Incarnational Theologies: Mapping Out the Parameters of Dialogue, *Journal of Ecumenical Studies*, 39,3–4, 2002, pp. 219–247. For a comparative presentation of Hindu and Christian incarnation, see Clooney, *Hindu God, Christian God*, Chapter 4.

54. It is enough to read randomly through Mahendra Gupta, *The Gospel of Sri Ramakrishna*, Ramakrishna-Vivekananda Center, Calcutta, 1942, and multiple editions since, if one wishes to gain an appreciation for how deeply this question runs at the heart of Hindu religious thought.

55. See Arthur Marmorstein, *The Old Rabbinic Doctrine of God*, Oxford University Press, London, 1927; David Stern, Imitatio Hominis: Anthropomorphism and the Character(s) of God in Rabbinic Literature, *Prooftexts* 12, 1992, pp. 151–174.

56. In a reflective moment, David Shulman puts forward the hypothesis that Jews worship a *saguna* God with no visible form, while Hindus worship a *nirguna* God, who can take on form. If things are seen in this light, is it even possible to place a value judgement, let alone to consider one form of religion superior to the other, or is one moved to simply recognize fundamental systemic differences? See Shulman's Preface to Hananya Goodman (ed)., *Between Jerusalem and Benares*, p. xii.

57. Much would depend, of course, on what kabbalistic teaching and what school of Hindu thought are compared. If we compare an Advaita Vedanta position to certain schools, or certain understandings, of early Kabbalah, where ein-sof is distinct from God possessing attributes, the comparison may be made. But the theistic Hindu schools refer to the great deities as *saguna brahman*, thereby complicating the identification of the absolute and being beyond form. Similarly, ein-sof is also personalized over time. Kabbalistic traditions that speak of aspects within the ein-sof suggest it is a higher realm and is not necessarily a formless absolute. Indeed, it may be that from the outset, or close to the outset, ein-sof expresses not philosophical speculation of a negative theology, but rather some kind of positive understanding of the absolute. See Sandra Valabregue-Perry, *Concealed and Revealed "Ein Sof" in Theosophic Kabbalah*, Cherub Press, Los Angeles, 2010. Later reference to *Ein Sof Baruch Hu*, may He be blessed, as the focus of devotion, would thus accord with fundamental understandings of ein-sof. In light of Valabregue-Perry's study, it may be that rather than contrast ein-sof and brahman as philosophical concepts, we do better to recognize both of them as means of dealing with the same basic dynamic—that of the relationship between unity and plurality.

58. This in turn also reflects the broader asymmetry of the present encounter, to which I refer repeatedly.

59. The sole exception is Ananda, *Hindu View of Judaism*, APC Publications, New Delhi, 1996. The book draws heavily on the theology of Ramakrishna and is of little value to the present discussion.

60. For a somewhat entertaining illustration of how this plays out in a Hindu academic context, see Alan Brill's post, http://kavvanah.wordpress.com/2013/11/27/ramana-maharshi-on-judaism/. This teacher knows his Judaism through Ramana Maharshi. Ramana, in turn, cites some stock verses that are popular in vedantic readings of the Bible, but without reference to Judaism as a specific religion.

61. For reflections on crisis in Hinduism, see Deepak Sharma, Hinduism, *The Crisis of the Holy: Challenges and Transformations in World Religions,* Lexington Books, Lanham, MD, 2014, pp. 111–123.

62. It is worth noting that the book titled *Om Shalom,* which will be discussed in greater detail in the following chapter, focuses, inter alia, on questions concerning God's nature, absolute and relative, and how God can be approached. In this sense, the book is true to the kind of agenda that can emerge when dialogue is real, opening paths to new self-understanding.

10   The Encounter within: Hinduism and Configurations of Jewish Identity

1. India and its sages figure early on in discussions that are concerned with Jewish identity. However, these discussions are not based on the actual encounter with India, but they use India as a foil for another identity struggle, with Hellenism. See Francis Schmidt, Between Jews and Greeks: The Indian model, *Between Benares and Jerusalem,* ed. Hananya. Goodman, SUNY Press, Albany, NY, 1994, p. 43.

2. Identity is rich and textured. It is articulated not only through the expression of core faith tenets and fundamental observances, but through myriad details that define how one goes about doing some of the most basic things. Identity informs all aspects of one's life. Therefore, in theory everything about how one lives can become an identity marker. The present discussion focuses on identity construction in a narrower sense, as governed by immediate relations with other religions. For a presentation of a broad range of identity-forming strategies see Sacha Stern, *Jewish Identity in Early Rabbinic Writings,* Leiden, Brill, 1994. While Stern's work is focused on the rabbinic period, much of what Stern records remains true for millennia, considering the formative status of rabbinical literature for later Judaism.

3. It is acknowledged that some forms of contact with Hinduism in the diaspora, especially exposure to Hindu religious groups with outreach mechanisms, do not comply with the description of a travel-based encounter, though they too have only become possible thanks to contemporary ease of travel.

4. See my A Jewish View of Islam, *Islam and Interfaith Relations,* ed. L. Ridgeon and P. Schmidt-Leukel, SCM Press, Norwich, 2006, pp. 84–108.

5. It is worth reflecting on the context of the dialogue of the Chief Rabbinate with Hindu religious leaders, in light of this claim. This dialogue, which will occupy our attention later, is driven by the foreign policy needs of Israel, and Israel's foreign ministry played an important role in driving the process. It will therefore be interesting to see what degree of continuity or discontinuity this dialogue has with the experience of Israeli and Jewish travelers to India, who carry most of the present-day encounter.

6. I was recently approached by an institute of Jewish learning with a request to organize a travel to India for Jewish students in search of a spiritual process. Apparently, there is already precedent for such visits within the Hillel campus ministries. The organizers of such initiatives obviously assume that some answer to a problem that they face as Jewish educators will be found through the encounter with India or with Hinduism. While they may not be able to articulate how the process would work, nor to provide assurances that would assuage the fears typically associated with encounters with other religions, they seem to consider that the visit to India holds such promise, that they are willing to risk the experiment, regardless of these

considerations. The process, in their minds, is likely informed by the notion of spirituality.

7. See, for example, Chapter 11 in *Judaic-Hindu Studies in the Twenty-First Century*, pp. 197–211. Julia Egerova's chapter is titled: Describing the "Other": Describing the "Self." See also Daria Maoz, When Images Become "True": The Israeli Backpacking Experience in India, Chapter 11 of *Karmic Passages: Israeli Scholarship on India*, ed. David Shulman and Shalva Weil, Oxford University Press, New Delhi, 2008, pp. 214–231. Maoz explores the role of India in processes of identity construction. Her discussion, however, focuses on the formation of personal and psychological identity, rather than the collective or religious identity that is the focus of the present discussion.

8. See Ronie Parciack, West Asia, South Asia, Travels to the Other Side of the Self, Chapter 10 in *Karmic Passages*, pp. 191–213.

9. Parciack, West Asia, South Asia, p. 192.

10. Laurie Patton and Shalom Goldman, Indian Love Call: Israelis, Orthodoxy and Indian Culture, *Judaism* 50,3, 2001, pp. 351–361.

11. Compare the views of Rabbi Itzchak Ginsburgh, chapter 9.

12. A less charged perspective is offered by Pinchas Giller, who sees Indian reality as an alternative to the Israeli reality and in particular to the reality of military occupation. Giller offered this insight in a paper presented in response to Daniel Sperber's book-in-progress at a panel of the American Academy of Religion, 2013.

13. There are, of course, various practical factors that account for this. Israelis travel to India because it is cheap and because they can function in English. The availability of vegetarian food is also a great advantage. These reasons precede the various theoretical reasons for why India is a preferred destination, but do not replace them. India's role in the Israeli psyche, as documented in the just cited studies, is far more comprehensive than the practical considerations related to travel to India. Because Hinduism is primarily centered in India, the travel to India is also an encounter with Hinduism. Buddhism, by contrast, lacks one primary geographic location with which it is identified.

14. While the preceding discussion focused on the reality of Israeli travellers, the concern for spirituality is characteristic of Jewish society as a whole. The following discussion therefore explores the relationship between Hinduism and Judaism, rather than simply Israeli identity. Hinduism is also relevant for Jewish practitioners in the diaspora, notwithstanding Hellner-Eshed's observation concerning the preference of American Jews for Buddhism.

15. The spirituality-identity axis emerges as the primary axis for discussions of present-day crises in all religions. See Alon Goshen-Gottstein (ed.), *The Crisis of the Holy: Challenges and Transformations in World Religions*, Lexington Books, Lanham, MD, 2014.

16. That is, in sum, what discussions of Avoda Zara concern themselves with.

17. February 9, 2009.

18. Swamiji observes silence. Consequently, his answers are given in writing and are often terse, lacking the ability to fully tease out a subject, in ways that a verbal exchange might enable.

19. Nathan Katz, *Spiritual Journey Home: Eastern Mysticism to the Western Wall*, Ketav, Jersey City, 2009, tells of several Tibetan teachers who adopt this stance. See pp. 107ff. Significantly, the Dalai Lama himself takes another position, in response to a question posed by Katz. Katz's concern of Jewish brain drain to Buddhism is addressed by the Dalai Lama who responds by saying: "if you want to keep your

people in your religion, you must open your doors to spirituality" (p. 111). Rodger Kamenetz's description of the same dialogue session in *The Jew in the Lotus: A Poet's Rediscovery of Jewish Identity in Buddhist India*, HarperSanFrancisco, NY, 1994, pp. 226–231 is more complex. The Dalai Lama indeed quotes his public teachings, in which he encourages people to follow their own traditional religion. Nevertheless, his response to Katz's concerns underlines the need for openness, both in sharing the esoteric tradition and in terms of willingness to accept the spiritual choices made by seekers, and for an experience-based means of adopting religion.

20. On a more recent visit, in January 2013, swami pushed one Israeli disciple to follow the ways of Torah. Due to the method of communication, the ensuing attempt to balance the two perspectives did not meet with great success. This tell us, however, that the exchange of February 2009 may not contain the entire picture.

21. This is the heart of the debate in the Middle Ages with the followers of Maimonides, who sought to understand observance of the Jewish commandments in precisely such terms, leading to their abandonment. In terms of both historical and present-day Judaism, such an approach remains episodic. There is no school that considers mitzvot obsolete as a consequence of attaining a spiritual state. Movements in Judaism, such as Reform, that have over the past 150 years argued for the obsolescence of mitzvot have done so using historical, rather than spiritual, arguments. One interesting source, in the context of the present discussion, is Mordechai Yosef Leiner's *Mey Hashiloach* on Gen. 22,12. However, even for this maverick author, who certainly had antinomian tendencies, at the end of the day, ritual is upheld, even if for social reasons.

22. For a classical spiritual statement of the enduring efficacy and purposefulness of mitzvot, regardless of one's spiritual achievements, see R. Nathan of Breslov, *Likutey Halachot, Hilchot Shiluach Haken*, 4.

23. See W. D. Davies, *Torah in the Messianic Age*, SBL, Philadelphia, PA,1952; Moshe Idel, "Torah Hadashah": Messiah and the New Torah in Jewish Mysticism and Modern Scholarship, *Kabbalah* 21, 2010, pp. 57–109. See also in this context David Berger, Torah and the Messianic Age: The Polemical and Exegetical History of a Rabbinic Text, *Studies in Medieval Jewish Intellectual and Social History: Festschrift in Honor of Robert Chazan*, ed. D. Engel et al., Brill, Leiden, 2010, pp. 169–187.

24. The same is true of contemporary Jewish converts to Christianity (at least to Catholicism). I have yet to encounter one who repudiates or is ashamed of his Jewish roots or birth.

25. Some religions may actively conceptualize such affiliation, as in the case of Judaism, that conceptualizes the significance of community through notions of covenant, election, and the centrality it affords to the Jewish people within its religious world-view. Others may approach community in a less conceptually formulated way. Indeed, one could argue that Hinduism may have a weaker sense of community, and that this may have ramifications on its social thinking and action. Nevertheless, there is no religion devoid of a sense of community, even if it is theorized in different ways, or given a weaker expression within the religion's overall economy.

26. See Shemot Rabba 1,1.

27. If anything, Israelis may rediscover their Judaism as a consequence of the encounter with *India*. This could include encounter with aspects of Hinduism, but is broader in scope.

28. In terms of numbers, TM, in its heyday, boasted tens of thousands of meditators in Israel. ISKCON, by contrast, with all the markers of an alternative religious identity, including ritual, clothes, names, etc., was never able to draw more than several dozen

enthusiasts, with only a handful of dedicated members at its core. To continue the comparison, in the United States, ISKCON was able to draw so many Jewish members that its leadership, following the death of its founder, Acharya Bhaktivedanta, was, as already mentioned, nearly half Jewish.

29. See p. 97.

30. See p. 98.

31. http://www.hakolhayehudi.co.il

32. Judith Linzer, *Torah and Dhrama, Jewish Seekers in Eastern Religions*, Jason Aaronson, Northvale, NJ, 1996.

33. A large number of her case studies involve Zen. Indeed, the book's title reveals specific interest in Buddhism, as does the final section, devoted to Jewish-Buddhist dialogue. There is no parallel section devoted to Hinduism. Linzer herself practices Zen and the book draws heavily on her own experiences as a practitioner. Of those involved with Hinduism, about half were involved with TM (Transcendental Meditation). While clearly having its origins in Hinduism, it is hard to speak meaningfully of TM as Hinduism, in terms of the present discussion. All in all, there are no more than three to four cases of meaningful contact with Hinduism, and even those do not always represent full-fledged Hindu practice or belonging. The most impressive and suggestive case is that of Rabbi Dovid Zeller, who is greatly inspired by India and receives much by sharing its practices, but is never described as properly belonging, during a certain phase of his life, to a Hindu group.

34. The statement by Maurice Friedman, p. 204, is particularly clear, and in my view typical.

35. This seems to be in contrast to the experiences of Jews engaged in Buddhism, particularly Zen. These seem to continue upholding both practices. This impression is substantiated by Linzer's case studies and finds further support in other works. See *Besides Still Waters: Jews, Christians and the Way of the Buddha*, ed. H. Kasimow and J. Keenan, Wisdom Publications, Sommerville, 2003. A likely explanation is that Buddhism is practiced as a technique, while Hinduism is closer to a religion. A technique can be more readily integrated into a broader religious framework than a parallel religious system. This would require accounting for why we lack similar integration in relation to TM and other movements that have distilled Hindu teachings into a technique that is almost free of religious trappings. The answer is most likely related to the rise and fall of those movements and may not reflect on the capacity of integration of such practices within Jewish observance.

36. See in particular statements quoted on p. 123ff. and 186ff.

37. This is the impression one also comes away with from reading Sara Yocheved Rigler's *God Winked: Tales and Lessons from my Spiritual Adventures*, Mekor Press, New York, 2012.

38. Nathan Katz, in *Spiritual Journey Home*, is an important exception to this characterization.

39. The concern for Avoda Zara obviously plays further into this dynamic. But in the context of the present discussion, this is only a secondary consideration.

40. Linzer's study focuses heavily on issues of Jewish identity. See in particular pp. 88–118. However, this entire discussion focuses on the identitarian dimensions of these returnees' attitudes to their Jewish identity. Consequently, anti-Semitism, whether external or internalized, plays an important role in her analysis. In her entire book there is not a single case that explores the possibility of multiple religious identities, in terms of Hinduism and Judaism (as opposed to Buddhism). Her discussion of identity is therefore of little help to the present discussion of the impact of the encounter with Hinduism upon Jewish identity.

41. Scholem's letter was shared by Boaz Huss at a conference on Jewish-Indian Encounters, held at the University of Haifa, November 27, 2012.

42. See Kumari Yayawardena, *The White Woman's Other Burden: Western Women and South Asia during British Rule*, Routledge, New York, 1995, Chapter 15: The "Jewish Mother" of Pondicherry, Mira Alfaasa Joins Aurobindo, pp. 207–217.

43. http://en.wikipedia.org/wiki/Max_Th%C3%A9on.

44. The critical perspective of a distant family member can be found at http://www.alfassa.com/momma.html.

45. http://www.madrasi.info/the-mother.php.

46. See Yayawardena, *White Woman's Other Burden,* p. 214.

47. http://en.wikipedia.org/wiki/Maurice_Frydman; http://www.among-friends.ca/spiritual-writings/maurice-frydman.htm.

48. Radhanath Swami, *The Journey Home: Autobiography of an American Swami,* Mandala, San Rafael, 2010.

49. If we add the teaching and writing activities of Paul Brunton and Suleyman Cohen, we are pushed to the conclusion that an extremely high percentage of Jewish disciples end up making a meaningful contribution to Indian culture and society. Of course, the statistic may be misleading, inasmuch as we only know of those individuals who have made a mark on society. Other individuals may have come and gone, without leaving a (Jewish) stamp on Indian society.

50. At the Kumbh Mela of 2013, I encountered an Israeli who plays a leadership role in the organization of a Western female guru, ordained by Sai Baba, called Sai Ma. While not part of a Hindu organization, one must also recall the Jewish Richard Alpert, known as Ram Dass. On his Jewishness, and his own sense of being a "lousy Jew," see Rodger Kamenetz, *The Jew in the Lotus,* pp. 264–269. And if artistic contribution counts, it is worth recaling his spiritual brother, Krishna Das, a devotee of the same guru. Krishna Das is the foremost proponent of Kirtan singing and thus a visible Hindu presence. Other than parentage, Judaism seems to play no role in his spiritual life. Except for a passing joke about Jewish women, there is no reference to his Jewish roots in his biography, *Chants of a Lifetime: Searching for a Heart of Gold,* Hay House, New Delhi, 2010. Even his visit to Auschwitz was deeply appreciated, but not on account of his Jewish roots. See http://www.elephantjournal.com/2013/03/an-interview-with-krishna-das-melissa-codispoti/.

51. See Swami Chidanand Saraswati, *Drops of Nectar,* Ganga Press, Rishikesh, 2004 Note this is a different figure than the Swami Chidananda, Swami Sivananda's disciple, mentioned in the book's dedication.

52. Another Jewish Hindu Swami is Radhanath Swami, author of *The Journey Home: Autobiography of an American Swami,* Mandala Publishing, San Rafael, 2008. Significantly, the subtitle refers to him as an American, not a Jewish, swami. Indeed, while his Jewish roots are mentioned several times in the book, they seem to play a very minor role in his spiritual formation. Even though he mentions having prayed in synagogues in his youth (p. 302), there is no indication of Jewish formation or teaching in the book. In fact, my reading of the book is of a retrojection of a mature religious identity back onto the 19-year-old boy, whose story the book tells. Accordingly, the scope of knowledge of the boy Richard reflects his later training. Hence the predominance of Christianity and the absence of Judaism. The general kind of openness to Judaism, expressed in his "letter" to his father (p. 180), would also be typical of this later identity. Note that even his concerns about idolatry are not ascribed exclusively to a Jewish formation, but to a broader awareness of the teachings of Christianity and Islam (p. 134). While Israel figures in the background,

in the choice of a traveling partner who chose to go there, the author chooses India instead. All in all, the book reflects a dismally low level of Jewish affiliation and knowledge, beyond parental roots. Against this written testimony, it is interesting to consider some oral testimonies concerning ISKCON swamis in general, whose interest in their Jewish roots is piqued, when visiting Israel. A story of the same Radhanath Swami (true or apocryphal, I do not know) tells of a moving encounter at the Western Wall, which for a moment raised the question of whether he was to return to Judaism, despite his many accomplishments in Hinduism. A vision of Krishna at the Western Wall provided his answer and reassurance. Such an image (even if only a literary figure) could provide an emblem for a certain kind of dual religious belonging. I am grateful to Rukmini Walker for sharing Radhanath Swami's work with me.

53. Another work, scheduled to appear more or less at the same time as the present volume, illustrates this process in an interesting way. Jayadvaita Swami's *Vanity Karma: Ecclesiastes, the Bhagavad Gita, and the Meaning of Life,* The Bhaktivedanta Book Trust, Los Angeles, 2015, is an attempt to read the biblical book of Ecclesiastes in light of the author's Vaishnava spiritual tradition, and in particular the Bhagavad Gita. The work's logic is biographical. As a young teen the author was struck by the book of Ecclesisates and the emptiness of life it describes, which echoed the author's own existential sense. The author's particular biography took him into Krishna Consciousness, where he found a meaning beyond Ecclesiastes and an answer to his existential quest. This is not a study of Judaism and Hinduism or strands of those traditions. Rather, it is the story of a Jewish boy who identifies questions in a biblical book and finds answers to them in Hindu tradition. One imagines the story could have equally unfolded into a discovery of hassidic Judaism under other circumstances. Structurally, this is the just the reverse of the procedure described by Nir, Chapter 7. While the work may not reveal much beyond the biographical, concerning the relationship between the two traditions, it is an important exercise in reading across traditions. Because its scope is limited—one biblical work, rather than an entire religion—it provides us with the only example of a comparative theological exegetical reading, of a Jewish (biblical) book and a part of Hindu scripture. This exercise is valuable and much more mature than the supposed dialogue presented below in Steven Rosen's *Om Shalom: Judaism and Krishna Consciousness,* Folk Books, New York, 1990.

54. Both Ram Das and Krishna Das, just mentioned, are disciples of the same saint.

55. Ma Jaya Sati Bhagawati, The Light of Every Candle, *The Fifty Eighth Century: A Jewish Renewal Sourcebook*, ed. Shohama Wiener, Jason Aaronson, New York, 1996, pp. 265–272, available also at http://www.kashi.org/wp-content/themes/kashi/docs/The%20Fifty-Eigth%20Century.pdf.

56. Contrast this with the story of Sarah Rigler, note 37 in this chapter

57. A collection of essays that explores this issue from within Jewish-Buddhist relations is *Beside Still Waters*, cited earlier.

58. While the immediate historical context within which these instances of multiple religious identities occur may be considered one of crisis, the crisis may itself be an expression of the systemic contours that provide Judaism and Hinduism (or certain forms of it) with their unique religious profile. We recall Soderblom's portrayal of Judaism, in contrast with Hinduism. While his presentation was selective, hence slanted, in how each of these religions was portrayed, the basic contrasts and dynamics that emerge from his description do describe remarkably well the tensions, challenges, and opportunities that inform the cases of multiple religious identity that we shall be studying. Thus, the crisis may be more systemic than simply the product of

certain historical factors. If so, Judaism's encounter with Hinduism touches upon spiritual concerns and dynamics that are fundamental to Judaism.

59. Hananya Goodman, thanks to whom I am in possession of some of the following biographical information, suggests this is Rabbi Nathan Netter, Rabbi of Metz.

60. I owe much to Aurelie Simonet, who spent a number of years with him and who graciously communicated much of what she knew to either Hananya Goodman or myself.

61. http://www.anandamayi.org/devotees/inthesteps.htm.

62. I possess recordings of these exchanges that future students of his life may find interesting.

63. For a Buddhist analogue, see Nathan Katz's *Spiritual Journey Home*, pp. 54–55, where Katz tells us of an eminent Buddhist monk who is a Jew, and of Aya Khema, an important Buddhist nun, who like Vijayananda affirms: "Of course I am still Jewish. Jewish is something you *are*, and I am proud of our heritage." Vijayananda's Judaism, however, seems to have had more substance than simply ethnic heritage.

64. A discussion of the inappropriateness of entry into Hindu temples can be found in his *Some Aspects of Ma Anandamayi's Teachings*, http://www.anandamayi.org/devotees/Jvv2.htm. Chapter 13 of this work is titled "Hindu Temple and Worship." Interestingly, he juxtaposes the Hindu mind with the Western mind and suggests the incompatibility of the two when it comes to temple worship, even to entry into Hindu temples. It seems impossible to divorce this attitude, including the avoidance of entry into Hindu temples, from his Orthodox Jewish upbringing. A quote in a later note, showing his conflicts as he passes by the Sinai and considers the demands of biblical faith in relation to Hindu worship, proves the point. Yet, the discussion is never framed in specifically Jewish terms. These have been replaced by broader reference to "Western." See also his relativizing statement in relation to mythology: "It is impossible to adopt the mythology of a religion when one has not been born and brought up in it, which one has not absorbed into the marrow of one's bones" (Part 2, Chapter 3 of his autobiography).

65. His position echoes the classical views on permissibility of *shituf*, that is, the worship of another being alongside God, for non-Jews. What is appropriate for non-Jews is considered as inappropriate for Jews. Growing up in Ashkenaz (Mainz), he is likely to have imbibed such an attitude from his rabbinic stepfather. However, whether consciously or not, this position has undergone modification from a legal formulation to a cultural formulation. Its focus is, accordingly, not the permissibility of a given form of worship for non-Jews, but the fact that it is considered superfluous or out of context for Jews.

66. I recall one time I visited him during Hannuka. His Jewish disciples had brought Hannuka lights and I was asked to light them. Swamiji delighted in the ceremony and spoke of it with great feeling and approval. Tellingly, the initiative came from others, with his clear approval, rather than from himself.

67. Sadhvi Bhagawati recently shared with me her own frustration at the narrow-mindedness of one of these emissaries, while expressing profound appreciation for their continuing efforts and sacrifices. She highlighted the positive contribution she is able to make through her chosen path as preferable to narrow role models and expectations placed upon her by Chabad emissaries. There is no doubt that gender perspectives and opportunities should be taken seriously when discussing opportunities for spiritual growth in Judaism and Hinduism.

68. One moment is telling. On his way to India he passes the Suez Canal, and reflects on the meaning of his own travels to India, in light of the great event of Sinai: "This

son of the Mediterranean, what is he setting out to look for among the descendants of the Rishis? Is this worshipper of the "jealous God," going to bow down before the images and idols of Ind? Is it not written in the tablets that Moses borne down from the mountains, 'Thou shalt have no other god before me. Thou shalt not bow down thyself to them nor serve them?' And the philosophy of India is so different from that of the Mediterranean! Between the Hindu mind and that of Mediterranean man lies an entire world! Their archetypes, the impressions and attitudes buried deep in their unconscious, are surely fundamentally different?" The one word that is lacking in this description is "Jewish." It is replaced by Mediterranean man, as though what was under discussion were a matter of culture and geography, rather than of fundamentals of religious faith.

69. Significantly, the only Jewish tradition that he does bring is not attributed to Jewish tradition but to a Cabbalistic legend. In Chapter 3 of his autobiography he tells the story of the existence of 36 masters who have achieved perfect wisdom, and on whose count God preserves the world. His reading of this Jewish tradition is telling: "No doubt they include Hindus and Christians, Jews, Moslems and Buddhists but they never discuss dogma." Jews are but one of many religions.

70. http://www.anandamayi.org/devotees/Jvv2.htm.

71. The fact that Vijayananda authored his earlier works, while someone else edited materials from later years could of course account for the different emphases, making the suggestion of an evolution in his Jewish identification superfluous. If so, his earlier writings were penned for a Hindu publication, where he did not feel it appropriate to be open about his Jewish roots. Still, it seems to me that the politics of concealment exceed what is necessary in such a context, especially given theoretical Hindu openness to all religions. This makes the suggestion of evolution in his position in relation to Judaism more probable.

72. He maintained good relations with his family throughout his stay in India. In this he did not follow the stricter observances that recommend renunciants break family ties.

73. While the explanation he offered for his lack of observance of the mitzvot is formulated in terms of the worldview to which he subscribed for nearly 60 years, we must also recall that his ceasing to observe the commandments antedates his becoming a renunciant, and for that matter his coming to India. As far as I can tell, by his 20s he was no longer practicing Judaism publicly and visibly. His autobiography presents him as engaged in a quest for Oriental wisdom, while his public profile in conquered France was anything but Jewish. It seems he thus encountered India as a self-identified Jew, who had nevertheless ceased to practice Judaism as a spiritual path, maintaining strong identity and affiliation with the Jewish people.

74. His case is thus much closer to those of post-Maimonidean philosophers in medieval Europe, who were led to view the mitzvot as no longer necessary, once proper philosophical knowledge was attained. While Vijayananda's philosophical perspective was not attained through association with a neutral philosophical system, but through one associated with another religious worldview, at the end of the day his lack of observance was more philosophical than it was religious, to the degree that "religious" signals buying into the totality of a particular alternative religious worldview.

75. http://www.nrg.co.il/online/15/ART1/551/718.html.

76. My translation.

77. Katz, *Spiritual Journey Home*, pp. 74–75.

78. See Lawrence Fine, Tikkun: A Lurianic Motif in Contemporary Jewish Thought, *From Ancient Israel to Modern Judaism: Essays in Honor of Marvin Fox*, ed. J.Neusner

et al., Scholars Press, Atlanta, GA, 1989, vol. 4, pp. 35–53. See further the essays in *Jewish Political Studies Review* 25, 2013.

79. Classical opposition to other religions would even consider a life lived nominally as a Jew, though devoid of any spiritual content or practice, as preferable to a life of spiritual fulfillment in another religion.

80. See previous chapter.

81. There are different dimensions to how one might be *wrong*, as suggested in *Same God, Other god*. For present purposes it does not matter whether we are dealing with moral error, metaphysical error, or with energetic "bonding" with forces that should be avoided, thereby making it wrong.

82. Extending this logic could lead to the position that everything that is within the realm of the other is ipso facto Avoda Zara. While such a clear articulation of the relationship of Avoda Zara and otherness is rarely encountered in theoretical reflections on Avoda Zara, it does inform certain halachic positions. See Shut Ziz Eliezer, Part 14,91; See also Part 10,1. For present purposes I wish to raise the concern for Avoda Zara as compromising or threatening identity, without going to the extreme that identity protection requires avoidance of all forms of interreligious contact or influence.

83. One could suggest that in relation to non-Jews Avoda Zara expresses a concern for truth. It takes on an additional dimension when applied within—the concern for preserving identity.

84. Primarily Swami Premswaroopananda, a female swami who presently runs the center and concerning whom much of what has been related here applies equally.

85. Biography would seem to make all the difference. Vijayananda was observant, then dropped his observance, and moved to India. The move to India never provided an incentive to return to active Jewish practice. The Israeli group, by contrast, was originally nonobservant, and their journey into Hinduism took place within a broader spiritual search that had its effects also upon their active Jewish practice.

86. I intentionally avoid use of the term "syncretistic." Some might choose to describe their practices thus. I myself do not find the term helpful. On the contrary, it functions more as a derogatory term that judges practices unfavorably. The entire phenomenon of multiple religious identities is a broad phenomenon that nowadays touches all world religions. It is a pastoral as well as theological challenge, and a knee-jerk application of a category that has not been fully thought through is not helpful to the present discussion.

87. The problem of forced participation arose also in relation to the relaying of the meditation technique of TM. Teachers on that occasion perform a puja, with clear trappings of Hindu worship, directed to the photo of Maharishi Mahesh Yogi's own guru. Many rabbinic authorities forbade practicing TM for this reason. See Yisrael Hess, *Emunot*, Jerusalem, Techiyat Yisrael, 1989, p. 249. However, this one time ceremony can be more readily overlooked, and its role in the experience of the future meditator is so minor as to almost be ignored.

88. More on this in *Same God, Other god*.

89. I am not able to state to what degree Jewish practice is viewed as equally nonessential and how both sets of practice are relativized in terms of vedantic philosophy. If one practice emerges as more essential than the other, in either theoretical or psychological terms, this might provide us a key to which identity is considered primary. However, the challenges of a multiple religious identity do not change much if one identity is primary and the other secondary.

90. Of the various opinions discussed in *Same God, Other god,* that of the Meiri would provide the best ammunition for such a view. While he might not endorse the

specifically Hindu approach, considering it an error in and of itself, the error is not so grave as to lead to charges of Avoda Zara. For Meiri, ritual does not define Avoda Zara. The practices would therefore be tolerable, even if practiced by Jews. It is worth noting that Meiri is willing to recognize Jewish converts to other religions in terms of their new identity, because the validity proffered by an authentic religious system takes one beyond the charges of Avoda Zara and even beyond the bounds of the community. But this is precisely where the rubber of identitarian concerns hits the road. Do we really wish to accommodate practices that will ultimately have identitarian consequences? See further David Berger's struggles, Jews, Gentiles and the Modern Egalitarian Ethos: Some Tentative Thoughts, *Formulating Responses in an Egalitarian Age*, ed. Marc Stern, Rowman and Littlefield, Lanham, MD, 2005, pp. 83–108, especially pp. 93ff.

91. See in particular the contributions by Elhanan Nir, Melila Hellner, and Rivka Miriam.

92. It would be interesting to reflect upon the following typology of Indian gurus and their means of reaching out to the West. It seems to me that we can think of a threefold typology. Some gurus offer a teaching. The pioneer of all gurus, Swami Vivekananda, seems to have been above all a teacher. Some offer an entire way of life, attempting to export Hinduism to a large extent to the West. Acharya Bhaktivedanta, founder of ISKCON, is a prime example of that. The third group consists of gurus who offer a technique or a distillation of Hinduism. While Maharishi Mahesh Yogi, founder of Transcendental Meditation, may provide the salient example, this is true in fact of all those teachers who import yoga, in its various forms, to the West.

93. See the excellent comments of John Thatamanil concerning the impact of encounter with Vedanta upon him, as a Christian. As Thatamanil suggests, of necessity a creative tension ensues between one's proper religion and the perspectives gained by serious engagement with another. Moreover, relations that have been formed with teachers and members of another tradition have their own power of conviction and authorty, and they force the individual to redefine and continually engage his own tradition in light of those relations, what they have taught him, and their moral and spiritual command. See John Thatamanil, Managing Multiple Religious and Scholarly Identities: An Argument for a Theological Study of Hinduism, *Journal of the American Academy of Religion* 68,4, 2000, p. 799ff.

94. It is rare to have living teachers in both traditions. Nevertheless, quite often the cultivation of a relationship with a living guru leads to renewed appreciation of Jewish masters and their writings.

95. Here, however, we must distinguish philosophy from religion. Adopting the philosophical worldview of Hinduism while maintaining Jewish practice may not justify viewing Hinduism as the primary religion.

96. Apparently, Rosen has a somewhat complex relationship with the movement itself. See http://www.vnn.org/editorials/ET9908/ET20-4549.html. Nevertheless, he is clearly an important voice in presenting this form of Vaishnavism to the broader public and to the academic world, regardless of internal Vaishnava politics and personalities.

97. See one of several instances, p. 132.

98. The description of Rabbi Shimmel's experiences with the different Jewish communities, p. 65, is clearly an imaginary projection of a text book reading of the different communities of Jews in India.

99. I am not the only one to have noticed this. Rahul Peter Das, *Essays on Vaisnavism in Bengal,* Firma Klm Private Limited, Calcutta, 1997, p. 61, notes that while the conversations in these two books "are very informative and interesting," they sometimes give

the impression "that someone who though learned, possesses an ultimately only inferior knowledge, is being instructed by Rosen" and wonders whether "this represents the true tenor of the conversations or is rather based on editorial changes." He cites his own personal experience in having his own work manipulated by Rosen. His thinking did not go far enough to imagine that the entire dialogue is a fabrication by Rosen.

100. Rosen is well aware of this, as his discussion on pp. 143–148 indicates. He seems to have failed to grasp the import of this theory for actual Jewish practice and how it extends beyond the Tetragram to other divine names.

101. In Rosen's introduction, p. i, he draws an analogy between his own work and the *Kuzari* of Rabbi Yehuda Halevy. The analogy might be a giveaway to his acknowledgment of the fictitious nature of his work. However, if Halevy brought together an anonymous philosopher, Christian, Muslim, and Jew, Rosen names and fills in the biography of his rabbinic interlocutor so as to suggest a real personality, and not a literary creation. Indeed, he has succeeded in deceiving the few readers who have noticed his work and have taken the book to be a genuine example of Hindu-Jewish dialogue. See Cynthia Ann Humes, Om Shalom: Judaism and Krishna Consciousness, *Shofar* 17,3, 1999, pp. 111–113.

102. Steven Rosen and Alvin van Pelt Hart, *East-West Dialogues: Krsna Consciousness and Christianity*, Folk Books, New York, 1989.

103. Twenty years later, Rosen would seek to achieve the same goals by consciously and explicitly constructing a fictitious literary setting, rather than hiding behind a purported true dialogue. See Steven Rosen, *Christ and Krishna: Where the Jordan Meets the Ganges*, Folk Books, New York, 2011. One reviewer of this latter work is aware of the possibility that our Rabbi Shimmel is no more than a literary character. See http://harmonist.us/2011/11/review-christ-and-krishna-where-the-jordan-meets-the-ganges/.

104. I will not refer to the numerous mistakes in the presentation of Judaism. They begin with the first page of the dialogues, p. 7, where Shamai is presented as Hillel's "assistant," and continue throughout. No real-life rabbi would commit errors as gross as those of Rabbi Shimmel. They conclude with the presentation, on p. 200, of the Satmar Rebbe as a source for contemporary practice of Jewish meditation. All in all, the multiple mistakes in the presentation of Judaism can be ascribed to the basic fact of Rosen's having learned Judaism from books, thereby missing out on all that one would learn through life experience and real relationships, both by way of spiritual experience and by way of getting the fine points in focus.

105. I have seen time and again how missionaries, whether Hindu or Christian, distort scriptures and teachings as part of their missionary thrust. Rosen's work feels to me of a different type. While on some level his interests obviously remain missionary, I read this book more as a working out of fundamental issues than as a means of winning souls.

106. Given the fictitious nature of the entire enterprise, I take this introduction too to be Steven Rosen's own literary creation.

107. Compare the strategies offered by Nir in *From India Till Here,* chapters 9 and 8.

108. See Rosen, *Om Shalom*, pp. 22–23, 55–56, 61, 170, 179, 185.

109. Pushing providence to its limits, pp. 55–56, or reflecting on the relative merits of spiritual achievement versus value of particular birth, p. 23.

110. See Rosen, *Om Shalom* p. 170.

111. The larger part of the third dialogue is devoted to vegetarianism, a topic that is close to Rosen's heart and on which he has authored several books.

112. Obviously Shimmel never quotes from books that would have been beyond Rosen's reach and some of the books he is said to have read are quite incongruous considering the rabbinic library.

113. It should be noted that Shimmel and Rosen spend an inordinate and disproportionate amount of time discussing Christianity. Shimmel is unusually well-versed in *both* Hinduism and Christianity.

114. Another work that covers the same religious bases is *The Rabbi and I*, by William Glick a.k.a. Isa Das, published on the internet at http://www.equalsouls.org/. Glick too is a member of ISKCON. Glick's work is far cleaner than Rosen's, inasmuch as it rarely goes beyond his own attempts at comparative religious studies. He has read a limited number of presentations of Kabbalah and other Jewish sources and has searched out parallels with his own version of Hinduism. The result, as Nathan Katz acknowledges, can be thoughtful and provocative. Obviously, an agenda is served by identifying these comparisons. However, the method is cleaner and comes closer to academic conventions of comparison. Consequently, explicit issues of identity and ideology are put aside and the work must be judged by how convincing, or unconvincing, suggested parallels seem to the reader.

115. Quotes from the second edition, 2003.

116. http://www.bookrags.com/tandf/radhasoami-movements-tf/. For academic discussions of the Radhasoami movement, see M. Juergensmeyer, *Radhasoami Reality: The Logic of a Modern Faith*, Princeton University Press, Princeton, NJ, 1991; D. C. Lane, *The Radhasoami Tradition: A Critical History of Guru Successorship*, Garland, New York and London, 1992.

117. In this respect, the problem of definition and the appropriateness of application of the label "Hindu" to a religious movement is similar to issues raised in relation to the Brahma Kumari movement.

118. What makes Radha Soami heterdox from a Sikh perspective, namely the continuing reliance on a living guru rather than on the cessation of guruhood and its supplantation by scripture, is precisely what brings it back to the broader Hindu fold, thereby making it appropriate for the present discussion of Judaism and Hinduism.

119. In some ways this work follows the example of an earlier work, *Yoga and the Bible* by Joseph Leeming, RSSB, Amritsar 1963. "Bible" here is exclusively New Testament. By the very structure of this work, however, the two bodies of knowledge are brought into dialogue or rather the one is read against the other. This is less deceptive than the pretense to a presentation of Judaism only.

120. I would like to clarify that it is legitimate for the faithful to share their faith and to seek to spread it. The problem with missionary work is when it uses tactics deemed unacceptable, either by the target group or by what should be considered proper practice in the spreading of faith. Twisting Judaism to make it look like Radha Soami theology should be considered unacceptable.

121. Miriam Caravella Bokser, *The Holy Name: Mysticism in Judaism*, Radhasoami Satsang Beas, New Delhi, 1989, p. xvi.

122. Bokser, *The Holy Name*, pp. xiv–xv. More on struggles with particularity, see p. 118.

123. "My purpose is not to compare Judaism with Sant Mat. I am not attempting to give a definitive interpretation or history of Judaism, nor am I implying that there is a coherent system of Jewish mysticism which is analogous to Sant Mat. Rather, I hope to present a mosaic of elements that are found in common in both systems, and which reveal the universal thread that can be found in all religions and spiritual paths" (p. xviii).

124. The message—"find a guru," as opposed to—"our guru is the only worthy guru," is a sophisticated technique of religious public relations, even if in theoretical terms it is sincere. In real-life terms it addresses effectively the market of seekers of spirituality, most of whom, it is assumed, do not in fact find a worthy teacher. It seems to me this marketing strategy is not unique to Caravella, and various Indian religious

groups seem to use it. As noted in the chapter 8, this is the main message of the Akshardham complex of the Swaminarayan BAPS movement.

125. See Bokser, *The Holy Name,* pp. 21–26, for example.

126. Ibid., p. 52.

127. Compare the discussion above of Yoel Glick's work, in appendix to chapter 7.

128. Bokser, *The Holy Name,* pp. 80–88.

129. Ibid.,, pp. 90–91.

130. Ibid., p. 100.

131. Ibid., pp. 105–109.

132. Ibid., p. 118.

133. A disproportionate number of references are provided to the Bible, with almost no references to the major works of the hassidic movement. Like Rosen, Caravella lacks the tools necessary for better execution of her project. Hers is not a project that can be carried out simply based on second-hand knowledge of the sources.

134. Once again, she ends up rejecting the Jewish sources in favor of what seems to her the correct method, derived from her master's teachings. Relying on the Bible is handy in this context. The Bible is far more pliable and lends itself more readily to her readings than do the kabbalistic sources. Consequently, when describing Jewish meditation practices, she argues that the biblical testimonies are preferable to the later kabbalistic ones, in that they involve a practice more similar to her own. See Bokser, *The Holy Name,* p. 146.

135. Bokser, *The Holy Name,* p. 166.

136. Ibid., p. 201. See, however, my Judaism and incarnational theologies.

137. See Yitzhak Baer, *A History of the Jews in Spain,* Jewish Publication Society, Philadelphia, PA, 1961, vol. 1, p. 243ff.

138. Bokser, *The Holy Name,* pp. 219–224.

139. The collection *From India Till Here* is a model case.

140. See note 95. See also his "mother's" introduction, Rosen, *Om Shalom,* p. 4.

141. Rosen, *Om Shalom,* pp. 3–4.

142. For a comparative presentation of Jewish and Hindu (among other) models of leadership see *The Future of Religious Leadership,* ed. Alon Goshen-Gottstein, Lexington Books, Lanham, MD, 2016.

143. This is the overall impression one gets from reading some of the essays in *From India Till Here.*

144. In the framework of the Elijah Interfaith Institute, we have been convening conversations within specific religious traditions in order to work on their respective issues in the field of theology of religions. As noted earlier on, the present monograph grows out of such deliberations. A follow-up project convened scholars to think through the question of particularity as a key component of a Jewish view of other religions. The resources and syllabi that emerged out of the project are featured in a dedicated website of the Elijah Institute, funded by the Henry Luce Foundation.

11   The Encounter Becomes Official: Hindu-Jewish Summits

1. See http://www.hinduwisdom.info/Glimpses_XIII6.htm. The Chief Rabbi's office has not retained a copy of a statement made on that occasion, and I rely on media reports.

2. A follow-up meeting was held in the United States in 2009, but it will not be discussed here, as it left no written record that could serve as a basis for analysis. See http://www.ajc.org/site/c.ijITI2PHKoG/b.6396951/k.68E4/HinduJewish_Relations.htm.

3. See http://www.acharyasabha.org/.

4. The situation with India-Israel relations is quite different and much more reciprocal, on many fronts. In fact, it may be that the ethnic dimension of Jewishness is so prominent as to eclipse its religious particularity. Anna Guttman's *Writing Indians and Jews: Metaphorics of Jewishness in South Asian Literature*, Palgrave Macmillan, New York, 2013, shows us multiple literary expressions of awareness of Jewishness by Indian authors. As her analysis suggests, in a postcolonial perspective, issues of identity loom large and the Jew is a rich site for exploring issues of identity. The framework of her discussion, however, relates Jewishness to Indianness, suggesting interesting intersections with the figure of the Muslim. Nowhere does this lead to engagement with Jewish identity in religious terms, and nowhere does it broach upon the encounter of Hinduism and Judaism.

5. The sole exception has been Ananda, *Hindu View of Judaism,* APC Publications, New Delhi, 1996.

6. As of May 2011, all these documents were featured on the Council's home page, suggesting their importance as recent accomplishments of the Council. See http://www. millenniumpeacesummit.com/index.html. Copies of the various documents have been loaded to other websites, and I have kept copies of all documents, which I shall post to my own website, in the event that the links are, at any point, no longer functional.

7. The talk was published in a volume of conference proceedings. See Arvind Sarma (ed.), *Part of the Problem, Part of the Solution: Religion Today and Tomorrow,* Greenwood Publishing, Westport, CT, 2008, pp. 80–84.

8. For a scholarly portrayal of the two religions in precisely these terms, see Barbara Holdrege, What Have Brahmins to Do with Rabbis? Embodied Communities and Paradigms of Religious Traditions, *Shofar* 17,3, 1999, pp. 23–50.

9. This sums up the situation from the perspective of the purpose and intent that lay behind the summits. As Swami Agamananda, a disciple of Swami Dayananda, who helped organize the summits and who commented on my manuscript, points out to me, once discussions got underway, there was keen interest in engaging theological issues, and to a certain extent this discussion occupied center stage.

10. See, for example Swami Vishveshvarananda, 1,27.

11. Three fundamental attributes of the absolute: truth, existence, bliss.

12. Part of message of Swami Vishveshvarananda, 1,27.

13. Swami Vishveshvaratirthaji Ashtamatha, 1,9.

14. Sri Swami Balagangadharanathaji, 1,9.

15. I explore the significance of this distinction in great detail in *Same God, Other god.*

16. Swami Chidanand, 1,10.

17. Both statements on 1,9.

18. Swami Dayananda's opening address does speak of agreeing to differ, but he does not single out the notion of God as an important site for such differences. See 1,15.

19. Rabbi Metzger is struck by similarity of metaphors, but not of the basic concept of God. See 1,28. The first summit features a presentation by a Hindu on "similarities between our traditions" (1,32–33), but no equivalent Jewish presentation. In his report on the first summit, Meylekh Viswanath reports that in response to the expressions of basic similarity between Judaism and Hinduism, claimed by Hindu leaders, Rabbi David Rosen felt obliged to clarify the limits to religious relativism and that Judaism did not recognize the equality of all religions. This clarification does not seem to have made it to the transcripts of the meeting published by its organizers. See Meylekh Viswanath, The Hindu-Jewish Encounter, New Delhi, February 2007, *The Journal of Indo-Judaic Studies* 9, 2007, p. 109.

20. Reviewing, on behalf of Swami Dayananda, an earlier version of the present manuscript, Swami Agamananda notes that this lack of reciprocity was a great disappointment to the Hindu side, which sought to learn more of the Jewish view of God but was unable to. In fact, a special meeting of the scholars' group devoted to "The Concept of God" was convened in New Delhi in May 2011 in order to help fill this gap.
21. Rabbi Ratzon Arusi, 2,31.
22. Rabbi David Brodman, 2,37.
23. Soloveitchik's piece "Confrontation" and a series of reflections that engage it from a contemporary perspective can be found on Boston College's website.
24. The import of this reference does not emerge from the transcript. At face value, Rabbi Kook upholds a Hindu worldview. Was he cited to offer a theological counterpart? The obvious errors in wording in this transcript, which I did not correct, suggest that whoever edited this text did not grasp its full import, and therefore the meaning of this reference remains unclear. Judging by the overall quality of the transcript, it seems that the lack of a Jewish proof of the proceedings, prior to their publication, may be one more instance of asymmetry. The response of Swami Parmatmananda, 2,34, suggests that it was understood as offering the correct balance—transcendent *and* immanent—as opposed to Spinoza who is purely immanent, pantheistic. Accordingly, Swami Parmatmananda affirms Hinduism's belief in the transcendent. While helpful, this response would not lead to a revision of Rabbi Cohen's views, given the comparison he draws between Christianity and Hinduism.
25. 2,32 and 2,40.
26. Of course, as Swami Agamananda points out to me, this may not satisfy or conform with Hindu self-understanding, but it is nevertheless an important means of bridging a theological gap.
27. See 2,34 and 2,36.
28. This does remain an option on the Jewish side as well. In *Same God, Other god*, I discuss the positions of Rabbis Steinsaltz and Sperber. Sperber's *The Halakhic Status of Hinduism* is largely constructed on this reasoning. Sperber, by his own testimony, is largely indebted to Dayananda in his view of Hinduism, and it would seem also in the emphasis placed on proper philosophical understanding as the key to resolving charges of Avoda Zara.
29. This is already a paraphrase of Brodman's words, in view of what might be a Hindu view. I thank Swami Agamananda for pointing out to me the gap between Brodman's words and my own paraphrase.
30. Bawa Jain concludes his report on the second meeting with a full-page juxtaposition of the *Shema* with a verse from the Gita. The juxtaposition would have been one further instance of missing the point, from a Jewish perspective, were it not for Rabbi Brodman's intervention.
31. The alternative, which would be more appropriate for Sugunendra Theerta Swami, would be the full identification of Lord Krishna with the Absolute. But that would reopen the conversation with the Jewish interlocutor raising the question of the same God from another angle.
32. Brodman's application of the criterion of intentionality may be the wrong way of going about developing a Jewish or halachic view of Hinduism. It certainly has played an insignificant role in prior assessments of other religions as Avoda Zara. But that he should seek to do so is itself suggestive of Jewish sensibilities.
33. One participant, though not one of the main voices in the dialogue, voiced to me his skepticism regarding the entire project. He portrayed the Hindus as trying to prove

they believe in one God, but "who really believes them?" This participant, who is one of the less theologically inclined among the participants, obviously failed to draw the distincton between the philosophical achievements of the summit and the halachic issue of Avoda Zara.

34. See 1,37. Meiri's views are elaborated in great detail in *Same God, Other god*. Briefly, Meiri considers Avoda Zara to be no longer applicable, applying the criterion of moral living to distinguish proper from false religion. Accordingly, the religions known to him are considered free of Avoda Zara. How this might relate to Hinduism is explored in *Same God, Other god*.

35. I myself adopt this strategy in *Same God, Other god*.

36. Obviously, an out-and-out discussion of Avoda Zara as an internal Jewish category and its halachic ramifications would have been impossible in terms of tact and diplomacy, certainly at this early stage of the relationship.

37. There is a significant gap between the statement that all gods are one or even that God is one and the classical monotheistic formulation that there is no god but God. The distinction between philosophy and worship is certainly a context in which this distinction may be meaningful. On this distinction as the mosaic distinction, according to Jan Assman, see *Same God, Other god*.

38. Rosen's appeal to Meiri might be the simplest way of dealing with the problem. Alternatives are discussed in *Same God, Other god*.

39. I have numbered the clauses, not numbered in the original, and omitted the eighth clause that is related to the group's process, rather than to its common recognition.

40. Rabbi Jonathan Sacks, *Dignity of Difference*, London, Continuum, 2002. See http://www.telegraph.co.uk/news/uknews/1412530/Dr-Sacks-rewrites-book-after-criticism.html. For echoes within the Orthodox Jewish world, see http://www.chabadtalk.com/forum/showthread.php3?t=3674.

41. These expectations precede the meeting and do not flow from its discussions. Swami Agamananda points out that in fact these concerns are not covered in the substance of the dialogues and therefore reflect the prior agendas of the organizing communities.

42. See https://www.youtube.com/watch?v=KB3eMbItvrk.

43. When I first raised these objections with David Rosen, who was responsible for drafting the statement on the Jewish side, he completely concurred with them. Swami Agamananda suggests to me that Clause 5 of the second declaration, referring to spirituality, was meant to address Jewish concern about the exodus of Jewish youth to Hindu spirituality. But, as she notes, this was not addressed in the actual discussions, which means it was never brought to the attention of Hindu leaders. Moreover, the clause does not deliver the message clearly enough.

44. Contrast this with the ongoing concern for Jewish identity, voiced throughout Nathan Katz's biography, *Spiritual Journey Home: Eastern Mysticism to the Western Wall*, Ketav, Jersey City, 2009 See especially pp. 107–112.

45. I omit the 9th Clause as it refers to structures and procedures of the dialogue and not its substance.

46. Swami Agamananda clarifies: the Vatican and the World Council of Churches. If so, the appeal is not meant to neutral parties that could serve as referees, but to the parties supposedly engaged in missionary activity. Thus, Jews are brought on board to aid in the Hindu appeal directed at bodies carrying out missionary activity.

47. As reported above by Swami Agamananda, its purpose seems to be to address Jewish concerns over the draw of Jewish youth to Hindu spirituality.

48. Presentation by Rajiv Malhotra, who also funded the summit. Inclusion of this clause in the statement may have therefore been necessary due to his financial involvement. See 1, 40–41.
49. See 1,16.
50. March 9, 2008, cited in 3,9–12.
51. http://www.hinduismtoday.com/modules/smartsection/item.php?itemid= 1587/%20april-june%202008%20issue. Katz's statement refers to the first summit, and would be even stronger, in view of the second. Katz seems to consider this statement such a highlight that he presents it as the culmination of the introduction to his autobiography, *Spiritual Journey Home*, p. xvii.
52. How these two statements could be related to one another is explored from various angles in *Same God, Other god*.
53. Rabbi Sperber, who is a signatory of the first declaration and who published a piece on the sheitel crisis, only points to the declaration to indicate how complex the issue is, following this first declaration. See http://www.jewishideas.org/articles/how-not-make-halakhic-rulings.
54. To the Jewish voices who see in the summit's declaration a breakthrough also in terms of Avoda Zara I must add that of Rabbi David Rosen, who played an important role in drafting the statement. When I shared with him my article Encountering Hinduism from *Jewish Theology and World Religions*, ed. Alon Goshen-Gottstein and Korn Eugene, Littman Library, Oxford, 2012, pp. 263–298, where I discuss Steinsalz's position at great length, he felt I had overrated Steinsaltz's importance, especially in light of the just published statement, cosigned by the Chief Rabbinate. A statement coming out of such a body had weight and representativity that in his view exceeded those of Steinsalz. I take exception to his evaluation. The Chief Rabbis never affirmed in terms of internal Jewish categories that Hinduism was not Avoda Zara. They acknowledged, and if need be affirmed, Hindu self-understanding. By contrast, Steinsalz applied this understanding to traditional halachic and attitudinal approaches to other religions, thereby bringing it more within the realm of halacha. Clearly, neither the Chief Rabbinate nor Steinsaltz issued a *pesak*, but Steinsalz at least used halachic thinking and engaged the halachic process.
55. The Israeli branch of the organization is run by Rabbi David Rosen's wife, Sharon, and thus it may be less a sign of general interest in the statement than of the natural flow of information within a family and the organizations it serves.

12   Hinduism and a Jewish Theology of Religions

1. Alan Race, *Christians and Religious Pluralism: Patterns in the Christian Theology of Religions*, Orbis Books, Maryknoll, NY, 1983.
2. See Alan Brill, *Judaism and Other Religions: Models of Understanding*, Palgrave Macmillan, New York, 2010.
3. See p. 96.
4. See *Same God, Other god*, Chapter 10.
5. I am not aware that Meiri claims anywhere that all religions he considers valid are grounded in authentic revelation. Unlike a major trend in Jewish philosophy that approaches religion through the criterion of revelation (and we have seen this also with reference to Jewish evaluations of the imagined wisdom of India), Meiri seems to base his evaluation on the actual workings of religion and their effectiveness. This is likely due to the broader philosophical context that informs his thinking.

6. Were the religion to conform with the mandates of the halacha, it would come under the noachide commandments and therefore be part of our own revelation. Exclusivism, in this reading, can never be absolute such that it invalidates all religions outside Judaism. My use of exclusivism is therefore slightly imprecise, seeking to capture an attitude, not only a philosophical position.

7. The most notable instance of an inclusivist perspective leading to major spiritual transformation within Judaism is probably Abraham Maimonides's indebtedness to Islam, justified as bringing home the lost spiritual treasures of Judaism.

8. Note: the only person in both Jewish-Hindu summits to evoke Meiri was Rabbi David Rosen. None of the Rabbinate officials appealed to him.

9. Note, however: For Meiri the ability to validate other religions was based on his ability to ignore certain aspects of those religions and their theology, in favor of what he deemed most important, the moral and spiritual life. Thus, a theological dialogue and philosophical enrichment are not necessary outcomes of the pluralist option.

10. An early proponent of the idea of multiple revelations was Rabbi Nethanel Al-Fayumi. See Alan Brill, *Judaism and Other Religions*, pp. 111–112. His pioneering work, as well as that of other pluralists, has not been extended to the kind of dialogue envisioned here. But this is more a function of contemporary sociological circumstances than an outcome of the philosophical position itself.

13   Summary and a Personal Epilogue

1. Indeed, when I think of someone like Swami Atmapriyananda, with whom I have had just as many hours of spiritual and personal exchanges, his attitude of genuine interest in the particularity and uniqueness of each tradition is the opposite. Much depends therefore on personality, orientation, and formation. But perhaps the difference might be ascribed not simply to personality, but to the greater importance attached to interreligious harmony in the Ramakrishna order, following the personal experiences of its founder. Still, one might have equally argued that Ramakrishna's experiential discovery of the unity of all religions would have led to dismissal of all differences between religions as trivial. In this context, it is worth recalling that the only Hindu-based examination of Judaism was undertaken from a Ramakrishna perspective. See Ananda, *Hindu View of Judaism*, APC Publications, New Delhi, 1996. See also the recent publication by Srinivas Bharadwaj, *The H-Source of the Bible: Enhancing the Documentary Hypothesis to Include a New Source to the Bible*, self-published on Amazon, 2015, though it focuses on the Bible and not on Judaism.

2. See Ashok Vohra, Metaphysical Unity, Phenomenological Diversity and the Approach to the Other: An Advaita Vedanta Position, *The Religious Other: Hostility, Hospitality and the Hope of Human Flourishing*, ed. Alon Goshen-Gottstein, Lexington Books, Lanham, MD, 2014, pp. 99–115.

3. Herein lies a great paradox of the Hindu objection to missionary work. If all is one, and if there is no real otherness, all otherness being only part of metaphysical illusion, why worry about the particularity of religious identity, let alone fight to protect the particularity of one identity over another? Hindus are well aware of this tension. It is clear they operate on multiple levels, and that metaphysical truths do not always translate one on one to social policies. In fact, it is argued that such deep attitudes were the basis for conversion and its acceptance in earlier generations. This requires a statement of why this point in time calls for a different approach, and most often the response is couched in terms of an identity now threatened in ways it was not previously.

4. This is the intention behind clause 5 of the declaration of the second Jewish-Hindu summit.

5. Compare the remarks of John Thatamanil, Managing Multiple Religious and Scholarly Identities: An Argument for a Theological Study of Hinduism, *Journal of the American Academy of Religion* 68,4, 2000.

6. Perhaps we can take the language of journey and consider it not only in light of one person's personal experiences, but in terms of the encounter itself. As we have seen, travel and journey play an important part in the present-day Jewish encounter with Hinduism. Perhaps the fullest vision of the import of the encounter may be obtained if we consider that we are all on a journey, if you will—on a pilgrimage. The journey and its encounters, for both parties, are part of a greater process of pilgrimage, whose full significance we do not yet grasp. I find the notion that religions are themselves on a pilgrimage a fruitful notion. I noted the ease with which Christians can apply this notion. Thus, when Pope Benedict invited members of other faiths to a gathering in Assisi in 2011, the invitation spoke of "the Pilgrim Church," as a means of framing the meeting, conceived as common pilgrimage. Our history of exile may shape our religious concept of movement in space in different terms. While I wouldn't know how to frame the present insight in Jewish terms, I remain challenged by it.

Bibliography

Abhik Roy and Hammers Michele, Swami Vivekananda's Rhetoric of Spiritual Masculinity, *Western Journal of Communication* 78,4, 2014, pp. 545–562.

Abrahams E. M., *A Comparative Survey of Hindu, Christian and Jewish Mysticism*, Sri Satguru Publications, Delhi, 1995.

Altglas Véronique, *From Yoga to Kabbalah: Religious Exoticism and the Logics of Bricolage*, Oxford University Press, Oxford 2014.

Ananda, *Hindu View of Judaism*, APC Publications, New Delhi, 1996.

Baer Yitzhak, *A History of the Jews in Spain*, Jewish Publication Society, Philadelphia, PA, 1961.

Bar Ilan Meir, India and the Land of Israel: Between Jews and Indians in Ancient Times, *Journal of Indo Judaic Studies* 4, 2001, pp. 39–77.

Ben Israel Menashe, *Nishmat Hayim*, Jerusalem, 1998.

Berger David, Jews, Gentiles and the Modern Egalitarian Ethos: Some Tentative Thoughts, *Formulating Responses in an Egalitarian Age*, ed. Marc Stern, Rowman and Littlefield, Lanham, MD, 2005, pp. 83–108.

———, Torah and the Messianic Age: The Polemical and Exegetical History of a Rabbinic Text, *Studies in Medieval Jewish Intellectual and Social History: Festschrift in Honor of Robert Chazan*, ed. D. Engel et al., Brill, Leiden, 2010, pp. 169–187.

Bokser Caravella Miriam, *The Holy Name: Mysticism in Judaism*, Radha Saomi Satsang Beas, New Delhi, 1989.

Brill Alan, *Judaism and Other Religions: Models of Understanding*, Palgrave Macmillan, New York, 2010.

———, *Judaism and World Religions: Encountering Christianity, Islam and Eastern Traditions*, Palgrave Macmillan, New York, 2012.

Brockington John, *Hinduism and Christianity*, Macmillan, London, 1992.

Brooks Douglas, Taking Sides and Opening Doors: Authority and Integrity in the Academy's Hinduism, *Journal of the American Academy of Religion* 68,4, 2000, pp. 817–829.

Cantwell Smith Wilfred, *What Is Scripture? A Comparative Approach*, Fortress Press, Minneapolis, MN, 1993.

Caplan Jeremy, Om Shalomers Come of Age, http://forward.com/articles/6137/om-shalomers-come-of-age/.

Carlebach Azriel, *India: A Road Journal*, Ayanot, Tel Aviv, 1956 [Hebrew].

Chatterjee Margaret, *Gandhi and His Jewish Friends*, Macmillan Academic, Basingstoke, 1992.

———, *Studies in Modern Jewish and Hindu Thought*, Macmillan, London, 1997.

Chidanand Swami Saraswati, *Drops of Nectar*, Wisdom Tree, New Delhi, 1999.

Clooney Francis, *Comparative Theology: Deep Learning across Religious Borders*, Wiley-Blackwell, Chichester, 2010.

———, *Hindu God, Christian God*, Oxford University Press, Oxford, 2001.

Davies W. D., *Torah in the Messianic Age*, SBL, Philadelphia, PA, 1952.

Dayananda Swami, Proselytization and Religious Freedom, *Part of the Problem, Part of the Solution: Religion Today and Tomorrow*, ed. Sarma Arvind, Greenwood Publishing, Westport, CT, 2008, pp. 80–84.

Dean-Otting Miriam, Hugo Bergman, Leo Baeck and Martin Buber: Jewish Perspectives on Hinduism and Buddhism, *Journal of Indo Judaic Studies* 1,2, 1999, pp. 7–26.

Divon Elan, Reaching beyond the Religious: Seven Universal Wisdom Themes from Seven Thousand Years of Human Experience, Iuniverse, Bloomington IN, 2010.

Dreyer Elizabeth and Burrows S. Mark (eds.), *Minding the Spirit: The Study of Christian Spirituality*, Johns Hopkins, Baltimore, MD, 2005.

Egerova Yulia, Describing the "Other," Describing the "Self": Jews, Hindu Reforms, and Indian Nationalists, *Indo-Judaic Studies in the Twenty-First Century: A View from the Margin*, ed. N. Katz et al., Palgrave Macmillan, New York, 2007, pp. 197–211.

Elliot H. M. and Dowson J., *The History of India as Told by Its Own Historians*, Trubner, London, 1877.

Ezekiel Isaac A., *Sarmad: Jewish Saint of India*, Radha Soami Satsang Beas, Punjab, 1966.

Fazl Asiri Mahmud, *Rubaiyat-i-Sarmad*, 1950, http://www.bahaistudies.net/asma/rubaiyat-i-Sarmad.pdf.

Fenton Paul, Abraham Maimonides (1186–1237): Founding a Mystical Dynasty, *Jewish Mystical Leaders and Leadership in the 13th Century*, ed. M. Idel and M.Ostow, Jacob Aronson, Northvale, NJ, 1998, pp. 127–154.

Fine Lawrence, Tikkun: A Lurianic Motif in Contemporary Jewish Thought, *From Ancient Israel to Modern Judaism: Essays in Honor of Marvin Fox*, ed. J. Neusner et al., Scholars Press, Atlanta, GA, 1989, vol. 4, pp. 35–53.

Fischel Walter, The Bible in Persian Translation, *Harvard Theological Review* 45,1, 1952, pp. 22–24.

——, The Contribution of the Cochin Jews to South Indian and Jewish Civilizations, *Commemoration Volume: Cochin Synagogue Quartercentenary Celebrations*, ed. S. S. Koder, Cochin, 1971, pp. 15–64.

Flug Joshua, A Review of the Recent "Sheitel" Controversy, *Journal of Halacha and Contemporary Society* 49, 2005, pp. 5–33.

Flusser David, Abraham and the Upanishads, *Between Jerusalem and Benares*, ed. Hananya Goodman, SUNY Press, Albany, NY, 1994, pp. 33–40.

Friedman Mordechai, Abraham Maimuni's Prayer Reforms: Continuation or Revision of His Father's Teachings? *Traditions of Maimonideism*, ed. Carlos Fraenkel, Brill, Leiden, 2009, pp. 139–154.

Glick William, *The Rabbi and I*, by a.k.a. Isa Das, http://www.equalsouls.org/.

Goitein S. D. and Friedman M. A., *Indian Traders of the Middle Ages: Documents of the Cairo Genizah (India Book)*, vols.1–3, Brill, Leiden Boston, 2008.

Goodman Hananya, *Between Jerusalem and Benares*, SUNY Press, Albany, NY, 1994.

Gopin Marc, An Orthodox Embrace of Gentiles: Interfaith Tolerance in the Thought of S. D. Luzzatto and E. Benamozegh, *Modern Judaism* 18, 1998, pp. 173–195.

Goshen-Gottstein Alon, Abraham and Abrahamic Religions in Contemporary Interreligious Discourse: Reflections of an Implicated Jewish Bystander, *Studies in Interreligious Dialogue* 12,2, 2002, pp. 165–183.

—— (ed.), *The Crisis of the Holy: Challenges and Transformations in World Religions*, Lexington Books, Lanham, MD, 2014.

——, Encountering Hinduism: Thinking Through *Avodah Zarah*, *Jewish Theology and World Religions*, ed. Alon Goshen-Gottstein and Korn Eugene, Littman Library, Oxford, 2012, pp. 263–298.

—— (ed.), *The Future of Religious Leadership*, Lexington Books, Lanham, MD, 2016.

——, Jewish View of Islam, *Islam and Interfaith Relations*, ed. L. Ridgeon and P. Schmidt, SCM Press, Leukel, 2006, pp. 84–108.

——, Judaisms and Incarnational Theologies: Mapping Out the Parameters of Dialogue, *Journal of Ecumenical Studies*, 39,3–4, 2002, pp. 219–247.

——, Speech, Silence, Song: Epistemology and Theodicy in a Teaching of R. Nahman of Breslav, *Philosophia* 30, 2003, pp. 143–187.

——, "When Will I See the Face of God?" On the Experience of God's Presence in Our Religious World, *Akdamot* 9, 2000, pp. 119–130 [Hebrew].

Goshen-Gottstein Alon and Korn Eugene (eds.), *Jewish Theology and World Religions*, Littman Library, Oxford, 2012.

Green Arthur, Shekhinah, the Virgin Mary and the Song of Songs: Reflections on a Kabbalistic Symbol in its Historical Context, *Association for Jewish Studies Review* 26,1, 2002, pp. 1–52.

——, The Zaddik as *Axis Mundi* in Later Judaism, *Journal of the American Academy of Religion* 45,3, 1977, pp. 327–347.

Green William Scott, Frerichs Ernest S. (eds.), *Judaisms and Their Messiahs at the Turn of the Christian Era*, Cambridge University Press, Cambridge, 1987.

Greenberg Gershon, *Religionswissenschaft* and Early Reform Jewish Thought: Samuel Hirsch and David Einhorn, *Modern Judaism and Historical Consciousness: Identities, Encounters, Perspectives*, ed. Andreas Gotzmann and Christian Wiese, Brill, Leiden, 2007, pp. 110–144.

Guenon Rene, *Studies in Hinduism*, Sophia Perennis, Hillsdale, NJ, 2001.

Gupta M. G., *Sarmad the Saint: Life and Works*, MG Publishers, Agra, 1991.

Gupta Mahendra, *The Gospel of Sri Ramakrishna*, Ramakrishna-Vivekananda Center, Calcutta, 1942.

Guttman Anna, *Writing Indians and Jews: Metaphorics of Jewishness in South Asian Literature*, Palgrave Macmillan, New York, 2013.

Hanemman Dori, What Does India Add to the Torah of the Land of Israel, *From India Till Here*, ed. Elhanan Nir, Rubin Mass, Jerusalem, 2006, pp. 75–87 [Hebrew].

Hellner-Eshed Melila, In India Even the Tourists Believe in God, *From India Till Here*, Rubin Mass, Jerusalem, 2006, pp. 53–60 [Hebrew].

Hess Yisrael, *Emunot*, Jerusalem, Techiyat Yisrael, 1989 [Hebrew].

Hirschbein Peretz, *India*, trans. U. Z. Greenberg, Mitzpa, Tel Aviv, 1931, [Hebrew].

Holdrege Barbara, *Veda and Torah: Transcending the Textuality of Scripture*, SUNY Press, Albany, NY, 1996.

——, What Have Brahmins to Do with Rabbis? Embodied Communities and Paradigms of Religious Traditions, *Shofar* 17,3, 1999, pp. 23–50.

Hudson Dennis R., A Hindu Response to the Written Torah, *Between Jerusalem and Benares*, ed. Hananya Goodman, SUNY Press, Albany, NY, 1994, pp. 55–84.

Hughes Aaron, *Abrahamic Religions: On the Uses and Abuses of History*, Oxford University Press, New York, 2012.

Humes Cynthia Ann, Om Shalom: Judaism and Krishna Consciousness, *Shofar* 17,3, 1999, pp. 111–113.

Idel Moshe, *Hasidism: Between Ecstasy and Magic*, SUNY Press, Albany, NY, 1995.

——, Jewish Mysticism: An Introduction, *Comparative Mysticism: An Anthology of Original Sources*, ed. S. Katz, Oxford University Press, Oxford, 2013, pp. 25–36.

——, Kabbalah in Elijah Benamozegh's Thought, appendix to *Elijah ben Amozegh: Israel and Humanity*, trans. Maxwell Luria, Paulist Press, Mahwa, 1994, pp. 363–377.

——, Kabbalah: New Perspectives, Yale University Press, New Haven, CT, 1988.

Idel Moshe, Reifications of Language in Jewish Mysticism, *Mysticism and Language*, ed. Steven Katz, Oxford University Press, New York and Oxford, 1992, pp. 42–79.

———, "Torah Hadashah": Messiah and the New Torah in Jewish Mysticism and Modern Scholarship, *Kabbalah* 21, 2010, pp. 57–109.

Isenberg Shirley Berry, *India's Bene Israel, a Comprehensive Inquiry and Sourcebook*, Popular Prakashan, Bombay, 1988.

Jagannathan Shakunthala, *Hinduism: An Introduction*, Vakils, Feffer and Simons, Bombay, 1991.

Jayadvaita Swami, *Vanity Karma: Ecclesiastes, the Bhagavad Gita, and the Meaning of Life*, The Bhaktivedanta Book Trust, Los Angeles, 2015.

Juergensmeyer M., *Radhasoami Reality: The Logic of a Modern Faith*, Princeton University Press, Princeton, NJ, 1991.

Kamenetz Rodger, *The Jew in the Lotus: A Poet's Rediscovery of Jewish Identity in Buddhist India*, HarperSanFrancisco, New York, 1994.

Kaplan Arye, *Jewish Meditation: A Practical Guide*, Schoken, New York, 1985.

Kasimow H. and Keenan J. (eds.), *Besides Still Waters: Jews, Christians and the Way of the Buddha*, Wisdom Publications, Sommerville, 2003.

Katz Jacob, *Exclusiveness and Tolerance: Studies in Jewish-Gentile Relations in Medieval and Modern Times*, Oxford University Press, Oxford, 1961.

Katz Nathan, An Annotated Bibliography about Indian Jewry, *Kol Binah* 8,1, 1991, pp. 6–33.

———, Bibliography about Indian Jewry, *Journal of Indo-Judaic Studies* 2, 1999, pp. 113–135, and 3, 2000, pp. 126–132.

———, The Hindu-Jewish Encounter and the Future, *The Fifty Eighth Century: A Jewish Renewal Sourcebook*, ed. Shohama Wiener, Jason Aaronson, Northvale, NJ, 1996, pp. 331–343.

———, How the Hindu-Jewish Encounter Reconfigures Interreligious Dialogue, *Shofar* 16,1, 1997, pp. 28–42.

———, The Identity of a Mystic: The Case of Sa'id Sarmad, a Jewish-Yogi-Sufi Courtier of the Mughals, *Numen* 47, 2000, pp. 142–160.

———, Indo-Judaic Studies in the Twenty First Century: A Perspective from the Margin, *Indo-Judaic Studies in the Twenty-First Century*, ed. Nathan Katz et al., Palgrave-Macmillan, New York, 2007, pp. 1–15.

———, From Legend to History in the Ancient World, *Shofar* 17,3, 1999, pp. 7–22.

———, *Spiritual Journey Home: Eastern Mysticism to the Western Wall*, Ketav, Jersey City, 2009.

———, The State of the Art of Hindu-Jewish Dialogue, *Indo-Judaic Studies in the Twenty-First Century*, ed. Nathan Katz et al., Palgrave Macmillan, New York, 2007, pp. 113–126.

Katz Nathan and Goldberg Ellen, *The Last Jews of Cochin: Jewish Identity in Hindu India*, University of South Carolina Press, Columbia, 1993.

Kimelman Reuven, The *Shema* Liturgy: From Covenant Ceremony to Coronation, *Kenishta: Studies of the Synagogue World*, ed. Joseph Tabory, Bar Ilan University Press, Ramat Gan, 2001, pp. 9–105.

Klein Daniel, Rabbi Ishmael, Meet Jaimini: The Thirteen Midot of Interpretation in Light of Comparative Law, *Hakirah* 16, 2013, pp. 91–111.

Klein Menashe, Concerning Wigs Coming from India, *Or Yisroel* 37, 2004, pp. 31–45 [Hebrew].

Krishna Das, *Chants of a Lifetime: Searching for a Heart of Gold*, Hayhouse, New Delhi, 2010.

Lane D. C., *The Radhasoami Tradition: A Critical History of Guru Successorship*, Garland, New York and London, 1992.

Lescher Bruce and Liebert Elizabeth (eds.), *Exploring Christian Spirituality, Essays in Honor of Sandra M Schneiders*, Paulist Press, New York, 2006.

Leslie-Chaden Charlene, *A Compendium of the Teachings of S.S.S.B*, Sai Towers Publishing, Bangalore, 2004.

Lev Shimon, Gandhi's Attitude to the Shoah, *Hayo Haya* 9, 2012, p. 20 [Hebrew].

———, *Soulmates: The Story of Mahatma Gandhi and Hermann Kallenbach*, Orient BlackSwan, Hyderabad, 2012.

———, Tagore, Jews and Zionism, *Mabu'a* 49, 2008, pp. 11–23 [Hebrew].

Linzer Judith, *Torah and Dharma, Jewish Seekers in Eastern Religions*, Jason Aaronson, Northvale, NJ, 1996.

Locks Gutman, *There Is One*, self published, Jerusalem, 1989.

Lyone Fein, Patanjali and Luria Isaac, *Journal of Indo-Judaic Studies* 3, 2000, pp. 72–85.

Ma Jaya Bhagawati Sati, The Light of Every Candle, *The Fifty Eighth Century: A Jewish Renewal Sourcebook*, ed. Shohama Wiener, Jason Aaronson, Northvale, NJ, 1996, pp. 265–272.

Mach Rudolf, *Der Zaddik in Talmud und Midrasch*, Brill, Leiden, 1957.

Maoz Daria, Every Age and Its Backpack, *From India Till Here*, ed. Elhanan Nir, Rubin Mass, Jerusalem, 2006, pp. 107–125 [Hebrew].

———, When Images Become "True," The Israeli Backpacking Experience in India, *Karmic Passages, Israeli Scholarship on India*, ed. David Shulman and Shalva Weil, Oxford University Press, New Delhi, 2008, pp. 214–231.

Marks Richard, Abraham, the Easterners and India: Jewish Interpretation of Genesis 25,6, *Journal of Indo-Judaic Studies* 3, 2000, pp. 49–71.

———, Hinduism, Torah and Travel: Jacob Sapir in India, *Shofar* 30,2, 2012, pp. 26–51.

———, Hindus and Hinduism in Medieval Jewish Literature, *Indo-Judaic Studies in the Twenty-First Century: A View from the Margin*, ed. Nathan Katz et al., Palgrave Macmillan, New York, 2007, pp. 65–67.

Marmorstein Arthur, *The Old Rabbinic Doctrine of God*, Oxford University Press, London, 1927.

Maulavi Wali Abdu'l, A Sketch of the Life of Sarmad, *Journal of the Asiatic Society of Bengal* 20, 1924, pp. 111–122.

McClymond Kathryn, Differing Intentions in Vedic and Jewish Sacrifices, *Journal of Indo-Judaic Studies* 4, 2001, pp. 23–38.

Melamed Abraham, The Image of India in Medieval Jewish Culture: Between Adoration and Rejection, *Jewish History* 20, 2006, pp. 299–314 [Hebrew].

Miriam Rivka, On Two Conflicting Visits to India, *From India Till Here*, Rubin Mass, Jerusalem, 2006, pp. 33–52 [Hebrew].

Mopsik Charles, Union and Unity in the Kabbalah, *Between Jerusalem and Benares*, SUNY Press, New York, 1994, pp. 223–242.

Narayanan Vasudha, Diglossic Hinduism: Liberation and Lentils, *Journal of the American Academy of Religion* 68,4, 2000, pp. 761–779.

Nasr Seyyed Hossein, *Sufi Essays*, G. Allen and Unwin, London, 1972.

Neusner Jacob, Judaisms in Modern Times : Toward a General Theory, in Jacob Neusner, *Major Trends in Formative Judaism 5*, University of America, Lanham, MD, 2002, pp. 209–237.

Nicholson Andrew, *Unifying Hinduism: Philosophy and Identity in Indian Intellectual History*, Columbia University Press, New York, 2010.

Nir Elhanan (ed.), *From India Till Here*, Rubin Mass, Jerusalem, 2006 [Hebrew].

———, Where Is the Time of Non-Movement, *From India till Here*, ed. E. Nir, Rubin Mass, Jerusalem, 2006, pp. 7–31.

Oppenheimer Aharon, *Sino-Judaica: Jews and Chinese in Historical Dialogue*, Tel Aviv University Press, Tel Aviv, 1999.

Palmer Susan, Rajneesh Women: Lovers and Leaders in a Utopian Commune, *The Rajneesh Papers: Studies in a New Religious Movement*, ed. Susan Palmer and Arvind Sharma, Motilal Banarsidass, Delhi, 1993, pp. 103–136.

Parciack Ronie, West Asia, South Asia: Travels to the Other Side of the Self, *Karmic Passages, Israeli Scholarship on India*, ed. David Shulman and Shalva Weil, Oxford University Press, New Delhi, 2008, pp.191–213.

Patton K. C. and Ray B. C., *A Magic Still Dwells: Comparative Religion in a Postmodern Age*, University of California, Berkeley, 2000.

Patton Laurie and Goldman Shalom, Indian Love Call: Israelis, Orthodoxy and Indian Culture, *Judaism* 50,3, 2001, pp. 351–361.

Persico Tomer, "*Jewish Meditation*": *The Development of a Modern Form of Spiritual Practice in Contemporary Judaism*, PhD thesis, Tel Aviv University, 2012.

Race Alan, *Christians and Religious Pluralism: Patterns in the Christian Theology of Religions*, Orbis Books, Maryknoll, NY, 1983.

Radhanath Swami, *The Journey Home: Autobiography of an American Swami*, Mandala Publishing, San Rafael, 2008.

Rahul Das Peter, *Essays on Vaisnavism in Bengal*, Firma Klm Private Limited, Calcutta, 1997.

Razazada Rahim Malik (ed.), *Dabistan-i Mazahib*, Teheran, Kitabkhanah-i Tahuri, 1983. English translation David Shea and Anthony Troyer, *Dabistan-i Mazahib or School of Manners*, Oriental Translation Fund of Great Britain and Ireland, Paris, 1843.

Rigler Sara Yocheved, *God Winked: Tales and Lessons from my Spiritual Adventures*, Mekor Press, New York, 2012.

Roland Joan, Religious Observances of the Bene Israel: Persistence and Refashioning of Tradition, *Journal of Indo-Judaic Studies*, 3, 2000, pp. 22–47.

Rosen Steven, *Christ and Krishna: Where the Jordan Meets the Ganges*, Folk Books, New York, 2011.

———, *Om Shalom: Judaism and Krishna Consciousness*, Folk Books, New York, 1990.

Rosen Steven and van Pelt Hart Alvin, *East-West Dialogues: Krsna Consciousness and Christianity*, Folk Books, New York, 1989.

Rosenthal Gilbert, "As-If" Theology and Liberal Judaism, *Conservative Judaism* 39,1, 1986, pp. 34–45.

Sack Bracha, More on the Saying "Kudsha-beik-hu Orayta ve-Yisrael Kola Had," *Kiryat Sefer* 57, 1982, pp. 179–184 [Hebrew].

Samuelson Norbert, *Jewish Faith and Modern Science: On the Death and Rebirth of Jewish Philosophy*, Rowman and Littlefield, Plymouth, 2009.

Saxena Neela Bhattacharya, Shekhina on the "Plane of Immanence": An Intimation of the Indic Great Mother in the Hebraic Wholly Other, *Journal of Indo-Judaic Studies* 12, 2012, pp. 27–44.

Schmidt Francis, Between Jews and Greeks: The Indian Model, *Between Benares and Jerusalem*, ed. Hananya. Goodman, SUNY Press, Albany, NY, 1994, pp. 41–53.

Schneiders Sandra, A Hermeneutical Approach to the Study of Christian Spirituality, *Minding the Spirit: The Study of Christian Spirituality*, ed. Elizabeth Dreyer and Mark Burrows, Johns Hopkins, 2005, pp. 49–60.

Scholem Gershom, *On the Mystical Shape of the Godhead*, Schoken, New York, 1991.

Schwartz Dov, *Astrology and Magic in Jewish Thought in the Middle Ages*, Bar Ilan University Press, Ramat Gan, 1999.

Sharma Deepak, Hinduism, *The Crisis of the Holy: Challenges and Transformations in World Religions,* ed. Alon Goshen Gottstein Lexington Books, Lanham, MD, 2014, pp. 111–123.

Sharon Diane, Mystic Autobiography: A Case Study in Comparative Literary Analysis, *Journal of Indo-Judaic Studies* 1,2, 1999, pp. 27–52.

———, The Mystic's Experience of God : A Comparison of the Mystical Techniques and Experiences of a 13th Century Jewish Mystic and a 20th Century Indic Yogi, *The Fifty-Eighth Century: A Renewal Sourcebook,* ed. Shohama Wiener, Jason Aaronson, Northvale, NJ, 1996, pp. 315–330.

Shulman David and Weil Shalva, prelude to *Karmic Passages, Israeli Scholarship on India,* Oxford University Press, New Delhi, 2008, pp. 1–7.

Shulman David, Preface to Hananya Goodman (ed.), *Between Jerusalem and Benares,* SUNY Press, Albany, NY, 1994, pp. xi–xiii.

Sinha Braj, Divine Anthropos and Cosmic Tree: Hindu and Jewish Mysticism in Comparative Perspective, *Indo-Judaic Studies in the Twenty-First Century: A View from the Margin,* pp. 93–112.

———, Feminizations of the Divine: *Sakti and Shekhinah* in Tantra and Kabbalah, *Journal of Indo-Judaic Studies* 10, 2009, pp. 25–45.

Smith Brian, Who Does, Can and Should Speak for Hinduism? *Journal of the American Academy of Religion* 68, 4, 2000, pp. 741–749.

Smith Paul, *Sarmad: Life and Poems,* CreateSpace Independent Pub., 2014.

Soderblom Nathan, *The Living God: Basal Forms of Personal Religion,* H. Milford, Oxford University Press, London, 1933

Srinivas T. M. N., *Religion and Society among the Coorgs of South India,* Asia Publishing House, 1952.

Stern David, Imitatio Hominis: Anthropomorphism and the Character(s) of God in Rabbinic Literature, *Prooftexts* 12, 1992, pp. 151–174.

Stern Sacha, *Jewish Identity in Early Rabbinic Writings,* Brill, Leiden, 1994.

Thapar Romila, Imagined Religious Communities? Ancient History and the Modern Search for a Hindu Identity, *Modern Asian Studies,* 23,2, 1989, pp. 209–231.

Thatamanil John, Managing Multiple Religious and Scholarly Identities: An Argument for a Theological Study of Hinduism, *Journal of the American Academy of Religion* 68,4, 2000, pp. 791–803.

———, *The Immanent Divine: God, Creation and the Human Predicament: An East-West Conversation,* Fortress Press, Minneapolis, MN, 2006.

Thursby Gene, Swami Muktananda and the Seat of Power, *When Prophets Die: The Postcharismatic Fate of New Religious Movements,* ed. Timothy Miller, SUNY Press, Albany, NY, 1991, pp. 165–182.

Tishby Isaiah, "God, the Torah and Israel Are One": The Source of the Saying in Ramhal's Commentary on the *Idra Rabba, Kiryat Sefer* 50, 1975, pp. 480–492 [Hebrew].

Urbach E. E., *The Sages: Their Concepts and Beliefs,* Magness Press, Jerusalem, 1975.

Urban Hugh, *Tantra: Sex, Secrecy, Politics, and Power in the Study of Religion,* Motilal Banarsidass, Delhi, 2007.

Vijayananda Swami, *Some Aspects of Ma Anandamayi's Teachings,* http://www.anandamayi.org/devotees/Jvv2.htm.

———, *The Conversations of Kankhal,* 1999, http://www.anandamayi.org/devotees/Jvv2.htm.

Viswanath Meylekh, The Hindu-Jewish Encounter, New Delhi, February 2007, *The Journal of Indo-Judaic Studies* 9, 2007, pp. 108–112.

Vohra Ashok, Metaphysical Unity, Phenomenological Diversity and the Approach to the Other: An Advaita Vedanta Position, *The Religious Other: Hostility, Hospitality and the Hope of Human Flourishing*, ed. Alon Goshen-Gottstein, Lexington Books, Lanham, MD, 2014, pp. 99–115.

Weber Max, *Ancient Judaism*, trans. H.Gerth and D. Martindale, Free Press, Glencoe, 1952.

Weil Shalva, The Influence of Indo-Judaic Studies in Israel, or the Salience of Spirituality, *Journal of Indo-Judaic Studies* 7–8, 2004–5, pp. 5–11.

——,Yom Kippur: The Festival of Closing the Doors, *Between Jerusalem and Benares: Comparative Studies in Judaism and Hinduism*, ed. Hananya Goodman, SUNY Press, Albany, NY, 1994, pp. 85–100.

Wieder N., *Islamic Influences on the Jewish Worship*, Oxford, 1947 [Hebrew].

White Lynn Jr., The Historical Roots of Our Ecological Crisis, *Science* 155, 1967, pp. 1203–1207.

Williams Raymond, *An Introduction to Swaminarayan Hinduism*, Cambridge University Press, Cambridge, 2001.

Wolfson Elliot, *Language, Eros, Being: Kabbalistic Hermeneutics and Poetic Imagination*, Fordham University Press, New York, 2005.

Yayawardena Kumari, *The White Woman's Other Burden: Western Women and South Asia during British Rule*, Routledge, New York, 1995, Chapter 15: The "Jewish Mother" of Pondicherry, Mira Alfaasa Joins Aurobindo, pp. 207–217.

Zaehner R. C., *Hindu and Muslim Mysticism*, Athlone Press, London, 1960.

Zahurul Sharib Hassan, *Sarmad and His Rubaiyat*, Sharib Press, Southampton, 1994.

Zeller David, *The Soul of the Story: Meetings with Remarkable People*, Jewish Lights, Woodstock, 2006.

Zuriely Odeya, *Transitions*, Rubin Mass, Jerusalem, 2009 [Hebrew].

Index

Printed in the USA
CPSIA information can be obtained
at www.ICGtesting.com
LVHW011934271123
764946LV00005B/465